CONTENTS

BARCELONA

It's tempting to say that there's nowhere quite like Barcelona – there's certainly no other city in Spain to touch it for sheer style, looks or energy. The glossy mags and travel press dwell enthusiastically on its outrageous architecture, designer shopping, cool bars and vibrant cultural scene, but Barcelona is more than just this year's fad. It's a confident, progressive city, one that is tirelessly self-renewing while preserving all that's best about its past. As old neighbourhoods bloom, and landmark museums and sights are restored with panache, there's still an enduring embrace of the good things in life, from the daily market to the late-night café.

Casa Milà

Fundació Antoni Tàpies

The province of Catalunya (Catalonia in English), of which Barcelona is the capital, has a historical identity going back as far as the ninth century, and through the long period of domination by outside powers, as well as during the Franco dictatorship, it proved impossible to stifle the Catalan spirit. The city reflects this independence, being at the forefront of Spanish political activism, radical design and architecture, and commercial dynamism.

This is seen most perfectly in the glorious *modernista* (Art Nouveau) buildings that stud the city's streets and avenues. Antoni Gaudí is the most famous of those who have left their mark on Barcelona in this way: his Sagrada Família church is rightly revered, but just as fascinating are the (literally) fantastic houses, public buildings and parks that he and his contemporaries designed.

The city also boasts an extensive medieval Old Town – full of pivotal buildings from an earlier age of expansion – and a stupendous artistic legacy, from national (ie, Catalan) collections of Romanesque, Gothic and contemporary art to major galleries containing the life's work of the Catalan artists Joan Miró and Antoni Tàpies (not to mention a celebrated showcase of the work of Pablo Picasso).

Barcelona is equally proud of its cutting-edge restaurants – featuring some of the best chefs in Europe – its late-night bars, even its football

Best places for a Barcelona picnic

Parc de la Ciutadella is the city centre's favourite green space, while the gardens of Montjuïc offer some fantastic views. Any time the sun shines, the beach between Barceloneta and Port Olímpic makes for a great alfresco lunch, though for a real in-the-know experience stock up at the market and head for the Collserola hills.

Despite its size, Spain's second city is a surprisingly easy place to find your way around. In effect, it's a series of self-contained neighbourhoods stretching out from the harbour, flanked by parks, hills and woodland. Much of what there is to see in the centre – Gothic cathedral, Picasso museum, markets, Gaudí buildings and art galleries – can be reached on foot, while a fast, cheap, integrated public transport system takes you directly to the peripheral attractions and suburbs. Meanwhile, bike tours, sightseeing buses and cruise boats all offer a different way of seeing the city.

True, for all its go-ahead feel, Barcelona has its problems, not least a petty crime rate that occasionally makes the international news. But there's no need to be unduly paranoid, and it would be a shame to stick solely to the main tourist sights as you'll miss out on so much. Tapas bars hidden down decrepit alleys, designer boutiques in gentrified Old Town quarters, street opera singers belting out an aria, bargain lunches in workers' taverns, neighbourhood funicular rides, unmarked gourmet restaurants, craft workshops, restored medieval palaces and specialist galleries all exemplify Barcelona just as much as the Ramblas or Gaudí's Sagrada Família.

Milk

team, the mercurial, incomparable FC Barcelona. Add a spruced-up waterfront, five kilometres of resort-standard sandy beach, and Olympic-rated sports and leisure facilities, and you have a city that entertains and cossets locals and visitors alike.

When to visit

Barcelona is an established city-break destination with a year-round tourist, business and convention trade. Different seasons have different attractions, from spring dance festivals to Christmas markets, but there's always something going on. As far as the weather is concerned, the best times to go are spring and autumn, when the temperatures are comfortably warm and walking the streets isn't a chore. In summer, the city can be very hot and humid while August sees many shops, bars and restaurants close as the locals head out of the city in droves. It's worth considering a winter break, as long as you don't mind the prospect of occasional rain. It's generally still warm enough to sit out at a café, for example, even in December or January.

Where to...

Shop

Designer and high-street fashion can be found in the Eixample along **Passeig de Gràcia** and **Rambla de Catalunya**, though for new names and boutiques the best hunting ground is in the Old Town streets around **Passeig del Born** (La Ribera). Second-hand and vintage clothing stores line **Carrer de la Riera Baixa** (El Raval), there's music and streetwear along nearby **Carrer dels Tallers**, and for antiques and curios it's best in the streets near **Carrer Banys Nous** (Barri Gòtic). The markets, meanwhile, are king, from the heavyweight **Boqueria** to lesser-known gems like the **Mercat Santa Caterina** in trendy Sant Pere or Gràcia's **Mercat de la Llibertat**.
OUR FAVOURITES: Artesania Catalunya, see page 40. Bulevard dels Antiquaris, see page 101. El Corte Inglés, see page 30.

Eat

In popular Old Town areas food and service can be indifferent and expensive. There are some great bars and restaurants in tourist-heavy **La Ribera** and the **Barri Gòtic**, but you should explore the up-and-coming neighbourhoods of **Sant Pere**, **El Raval** and **Poble Sec** for the best local finds. Michelin stars and big bills are mostly found in the **Eixample**, while for the best fish and seafood head for harbourside **Barceloneta** or the **Port Olímpic**. The suburb of **Gràcia** is also a nice, village-like place to spend the evening, with plenty of good mid-range restaurants.
OUR FAVOURITES: Ca l'Estevet, see page 59. Bodega la Plata, see page 42. Gresca, see page 117.

Drink

Whatever you're looking for, you'll find it here, from bohemian boozer to cocktail bar. **Passeig del Born** (La Ribera) is one of the hottest destinations, with Sant Pere hard on its heels, while there's an edgier scene in **El Raval** and around **Carrer de Blai** (Poble Sec). The main concentration of designer bars (and the city's gay scene) is in the **Esquerra de l'Eixample**, while the theme bars of **Port Olímpic** are mainstream playgrounds for locals and visitors. Bars usually stay open till any time between 11pm and 2 or 3am.
OUR FAVOURITES: Boada's Cocktails, see page 31. Can Paixano, see page 51. Milk, see page 44.

Go out

Clubs in Barcelona start late and go on until 5 or 6am, and while Thursday to Sunday sees the most action, there are **DJs** on the decks every night. The big-name venues tend to be in the old industrial zones like **Poble Nou**; downtown clubs are often jazz-orientated, though local rock, pop, indie and even flamenco get regular airings in venues across the **Barri Gòtic** and **El Raval**. For typically Catalan surroundings, a concert at Sant Pere's **Palau de la Música Catalana** can't be beaten, while the principal venue in the Eixample is **L'Auditori**.
OUR FAVOURITES: Arena Madre, see page 119. Bikini, see page 135. Sala Apolo, see page 89.

Barcelona at a glance

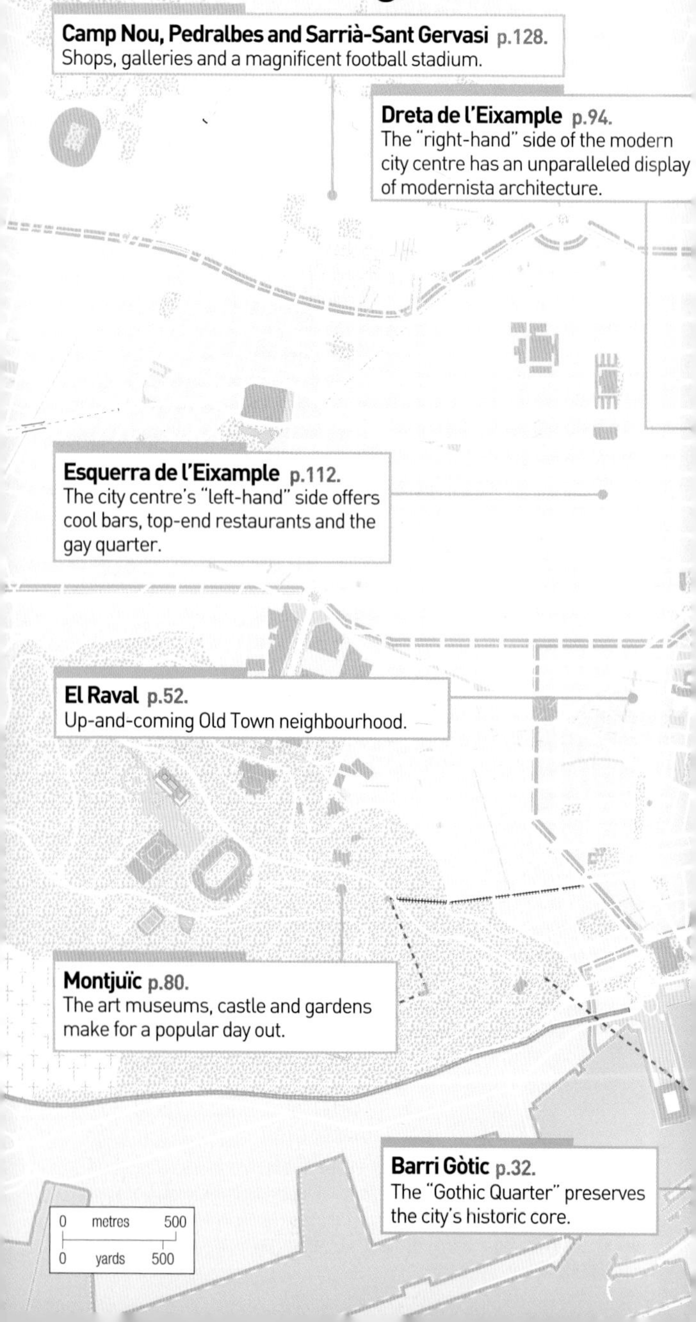

Camp Nou, Pedralbes and Sarrià-Sant Gervasi p.128.
Shops, galleries and a magnificent football stadium.

Dreta de l'Eixample p.94.
The "right-hand" side of the modern city centre has an unparalleled display of modernista architecture.

Esquerra de l'Eixample p.112.
The city centre's "left-hand" side offers cool bars, top-end restaurants and the gay quarter.

El Raval p.52.
Up-and-coming Old Town neighbourhood.

Montjuïc p.80.
The art museums, castle and gardens make for a popular day out.

Barri Gòtic p.32.
The "Gothic Quarter" preserves the city's historic core.

0 metres 500
0 yards 500

Along the Ramblas p.24.
Barcelona's most famous avenue.

Gràcia and Parc Güell p.120.
Visit Gràcia to see Gaudí's inspiring urban park.

Sagrada Família and Glòries p.104.
Barcelona's most amazing building is Gaudí's unfinished masterwork of a church.

Sant Pere p.64
A great market plus fashionable bars, boutiques and restaurants.

La Ribera p.68.
The medieval artisans' quarter is home to the Picasso Museum.

Parc de la Ciutadella p.76.
A favourite park on the edge of the Old Town.

Port Olímpic and Poble Nou p.90.
Beaches, bars and urban recreation along the city's revitalized waterfront.

Port Vell and Barceloneta p.46.
Top beaches and seafood restaurants.

15 Things not to miss

It's not possible to see everything that Barcelona has to offer in one trip - and we don't suggest you try. What follows is a selective taste of the city's highlights, from museums and galleries to restaurants and clubs. All highlights are colour-coded by chapter and have a page reference to take you to the Guide, where you can find out more.

> The Ramblas

See page 24

The city's iconic central thoroughfare, where hawkers, stallholders, eccentrics and tourists collide to gleeful effect.

< Sagrada Família

See page 104

The most famous unfinished church in the world – a pilgrimage to the "Sacred Family" temple is a must for Gaudí fans.

∨ Parc Güell

See page 121

A public park without compare, where contorted stone pavilions, gingerbread buildings and surreal ceramics combine unforgettably.

< **Caixa Forum**

See page 81

There's always an exhibition worth seeing in the city's best arts and cultural centre – as well as all sorts of events.

∨ **El Xampanyet**

See page 75

Step into this La Ribera institution for a glass of Catalan fizz and a bite or two before dinner.

< La Seu

See page 32

Pride of the Gothic era, the city's majestic medieval cathedral anchors the Old Town.

∨ Tickets

See page 88

A chance to taste some of Albert and Ferran Adrià's famous dishes at the former *El Bulli* chefs' (relatively) affordable tapas joint.

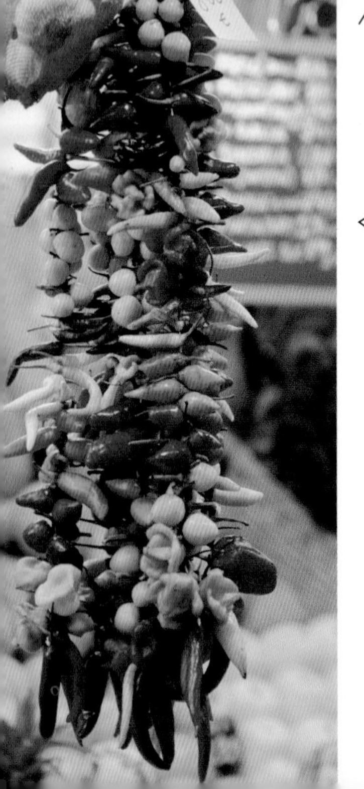

^ **Camp Nou and FC Barcelona**

See page 128

Tour one of Europe's most magnificent stadiums, home to the local football heroes.

< **Mercat de la Boqueria**

See page 27

The city's finest food market is a show in its own right, busy with locals and tourists from dawn to dusk.

∧ **Gran Teatre del Liceu**

See page 28

Book ahead for opera tickets at this renowned city landmark, though the guided tours are open to all.

∨ **Parc de Collserola**

See page 136

Barcelona is enclosed by a ring of hills that form an impressive natural park.

∧ City beaches

See page 91

The great urban escape is to the city's four kilometres of sand-fringed sea, dotted with parks and playgrounds.

< Jardí Botànic de Barcelona

See page 87

These impressive botanical gardens spread across a hillside above the Olympic Stadium.

< Parc de la Ciutadella

See page 76

Whatever the season, the city's nicest park always springs a surprise.

∨ Port Olímpic

See page 90

Twin towers and the landmark Frank Gehry fish dominate Barcelona's liveliest resort area.

Day One in Barcelona

The Ramblas. See page 24. Everyone starts with a stroll down Barcelona's most emblematic street.

Mercat de la Boqueria. See page 27. Wander through the stalls of one of Europe's best markets and soak up the vibrant atmosphere.

La Seu. See page 32. The calm cloister of Barcelona's cathedral is a haven amid the bustle of the Gothic Quarter.

Museu d'Història de Barcelona. See page 36. This place holds the archaeological history of Roman Barcelona – right under your feet.

Lunch. See page 43. Stop near the church of Santa María del Pi for alfresco drinks and a market-fresh meal at *Taller de≈Tapas.*

Museu Picasso. See page 68. Walk through the tight-knit medieval streets of La Ribera to this must-see museum, housed in the city where Picasso developed his inimitable style.

Parc de la Ciutadella. See page 76. Take time out in the museums, palmhouses and gardens of the city's favourite park.

Port Olímpic. See page 90. The beach, boardwalk and seafront promenade set the scene for a blissful sundowner.

Dinner. See page 61. Some of the city's hottest restaurants are in the resurgent Raval. Try *Suculent* for bistro classics from up-and-coming star chef Toni Romero.

Mercat de La Boqueria

Museu Picasso

Port Olímpic

Day Two in Barcelona

Sagrada Família. See page 102. To avoid the worst of the bustling crowds, arrive at Gaudí's masterpiece at opening time.

Passeig de Gràcia. See page 94. Europe's most extraordinary urban architecture decorates the modern city's main avenue.

Museu Egipci de Barcelona. See page 97. A captivating collection including mummies, amulets and sarcophagi transports you back to ancient Egypt.

Lunch. See page 103. Join the queue for a spot at *Tapas 24*, where Michelin-starred chef Carles Abellán gets back to basics with simple comfort food.

Museu Nacional d'Art de Catalunya. See page 83. The triumphant landscaped approach to Montjuïc culminates in the extraordinary Catalan National Art Gallery.

Fundació Joan Miró. See page 86. The modernist building on Montjuïc houses the life's work of Catalan artist Joan Miró.

Ride the Telefèric de Montjuïc. See page 87. A thrilling cable car swoops you across the inner harbour from Montjuïc to Port Vell.

Barceloneta. See page 48. For marina or beach views, grab a table at an outdoor café in the old fishermen's quarter.

Dinner. See page 74. After cold beer and tapas in up-and-coming Sant Pere, dine in Catalan style at La Ribera's *Senyor Parellada*.

Sagrada Família

Telefèric del Port

Senyor Parellada

Modernista Barcelona

Visionary modernista architects, like Antoni Gaudí, changed the way people looked at buildings. Their style, a sort of Catalan Art Nouveau, left Barcelona with an extraordinary architectural legacy that goes far beyond the famous sights of the Sagrada Família church and Parc Güell.

Hospital de la Santa Creu i de Sant Pau. See page 105. Don't miss Lluís Domènech i Montaner's innovative public hospital, near the Sagrada Família.

La Pedrera. See page 99 Inventive design permeates every aspect of Gaudí's fantastical "stone quarry" apartment building.

Casa Amatller. See page 95. Catch a guided tour of this stunning house belonging to a nineteenth-century chocolate manufacturer.

Lunch. See page **102**. Take a lunch stop at Cafè del Centre, a 19th century *modernista* cafè.

Palau de la Música Catalana. See page 64. Book in advance for a tour of this dramatic concert hall, or buy a ticket for an evening performance.

Arc de Triomf. See page 76. Gateway to the Ciutadella park is this giant red-brick arch.

Castell dels Tres Dragons. See page 78. The park's eye-catching "castle" is a *modernista* showcase for the city's natural science museum.

Dinner. See page 124. In summer, Parc Güell is open until well into the evening – and the bars and restaurants of fashionable Gràcia are close at hand.

Palau de la Música Catalana

Casa Amatller

Arc de Triomf

Budget Barcelona

Barcelona may be one of Europe's most fashionable cities, but it remains remarkably good value as far as most visitors are concerned. Here's how to eat well, see the major sights and enjoy yourself, without breaking the bank.

The Ramblas. See page 24. Barcelona's greatest show – a stroll down the Ramblas – is a free spectacle around the clock.

MNAC. See page 83. The ticket for the showpiece National Art Gallery is valid for two full days, and there's free entry on the first Sunday of every month.

Lunch. See page 41. Virtually every restaurant offers a weekday *menú del dia*, so lunch is a bargain at places like *Cafè de l'Acadèmia* where dinner might cost three times as much.

Relax at the beach. See page 91. Enjoy four kilometres of sand, boardwalks and promenades.

Font Màgica. See page 81. There's no charge to watch this magnificent display of water and light.

Caixa Forum. See page 81. Entry to this dazzling arts and cultural centre costs less than a cocktail.

Parc de la Ciutadella. See page 76. Unfurl a picnic blanket in the city's green lung.

Dinner. See page 67. Many of Barcelona's markets also have stylish restaurants attached – like *Cuines Santa Caterina* in Sant Pere's dramatic Mercat Santa Caterina.

Museu Nacional d'Art de Catalunya

Caixa Forum

Cuines Santa Caterina

Kas

PLACES

Bar Marsella

Along the Ramblas

No day in the city seems complete without a stroll along the Ramblas, Spain's most famous thoroughfare. Cutting through Barcelona's Old Town areas, and connecting Plaça de Catalunya with the harbour, it's at the heart of the city's self-image – lined with cafés, restaurants, souvenir shops, flower stalls and newspaper kiosks. The name (from the Arabic *ramla* or "sand") refers to a seasonal streambed that was paved over in medieval times. Since the nineteenth century it's been a fashionable promenade, and today the show goes on, as human statues, portrait painters, buskers and card sharps add to the vibrancy of Barcelona's most enthralling street. There are metro stops at Catalunya (top of the Ramblas), Liceu (middle) and Drassanes (bottom), or you can walk the entire length in about twenty minutes.

Plaça de Catalunya

MAP P.26, POCKET MAP D10
Ⓜ Catalunya.

The huge formal square at the top of the Ramblas stands right at the heart of the city. It's not only the focal point of events and demonstrations – notably a mass party on New Year's Eve – but also the site of prominent landmarks like the main city tourist office, the white-faced El Corte Inglés department store and El Triangle shopping centre.

Plaça de Catalunya

The Ramblas itself actually comprises five separate named sections, starting with the northern stretch, Rambla Canaletes, nearest Plaça de Catalunya, which is marked by an iron fountain – a drink from this supposedly means you'll never leave Barcelona. Further down is the sudden profusion of flower stalls on Rambla Sant Josep, near the Boqueria market. The bird market which used to be on Rambla Estudis closed down due to stricter animal protection legislation.

Església de Betlem

MAP P.26, POCKET MAP C11.
Ramblas 107 Ⓜ Liceu.
Daily 8am–1.30pm & 6–9pm.

It seems hard to believe, but the Ramblas was a war zone during

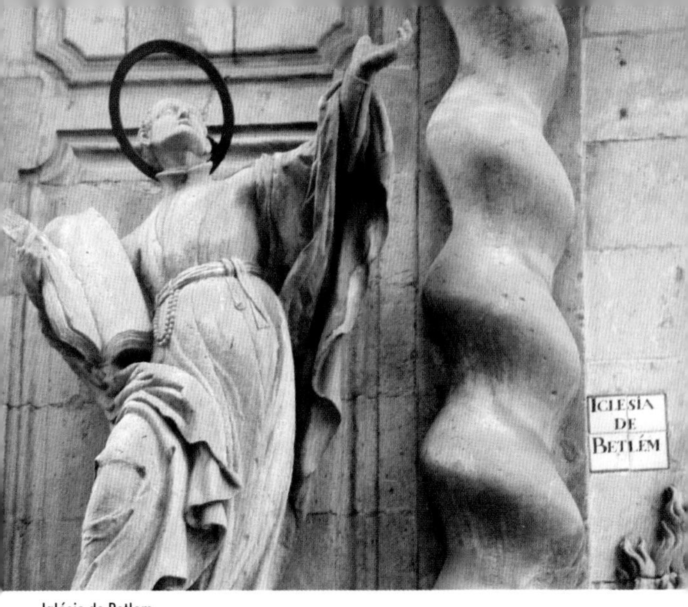

Iglésia de Betlem

the Spanish Civil War as the city erupted into factionalism in 1937. George Orwell was caught in the crossfire (an episode recorded in his *Homage to Catalonia*) and, with anarchists sacking the city's churches at will, the rich interior of the Baroque Església de Betlem was completely destroyed. However, the main facade on C/del Carme still sports a fine sculpted portal.

Palau Moja

MAP P.26, POCKET MAP D11. Ramblas 188 Ⓜ Liceu Ⓣ 669 792 894. Ⓦ palaumoja.com. Ticket office daily 10am–9pm. Restaurant daily 9.30am–midnight.

The arcaded Palau Moja dates from the late eighteenth century and still retains an exterior staircase and elegant great hall. The palace's gallery (entrance is around the corner in C/Portaferrissa) is occasionally open for exhibitions relating to all things Catalan. Take a look at the illustrated tiles above the fountain at the start of C/de la Portaferrissa, showing the medieval gate (the Porta Ferriça) and market once sited here.

Palau de la Virreina

MAP P.26, POCKET MAP C12. Ramblas 99 Ⓜ Liceu Ⓣ 933 161 000, Ⓦ bcn.cat/cultura. Galleries Tue–Sun noon–8pm; for current exhibitions see Ⓦ http://ajuntament.barcelona.cat/lavirreina/ca/; information office daily 10am–8.30pm.

Graceful eighteenth-century Palau de la Virreina is the HQ of the cultural department of the Ajuntament (city council), and there's a ground-floor information centre where you can find out about upcoming events and buy tickets. Various galleries and studios house changing exhibitions of contemporary art and photography, while at the back of the palace courtyard you can usually see the city's enormous Carnival giants (*gegants*), representing the thirteenth-century Catalan king Jaume I and his wife Violant. The origin of these ornate, five-metre-high figures is unclear, though they probably first enlivened medieval travelling fairs and are now an integral part of Barcelona's festival parades.

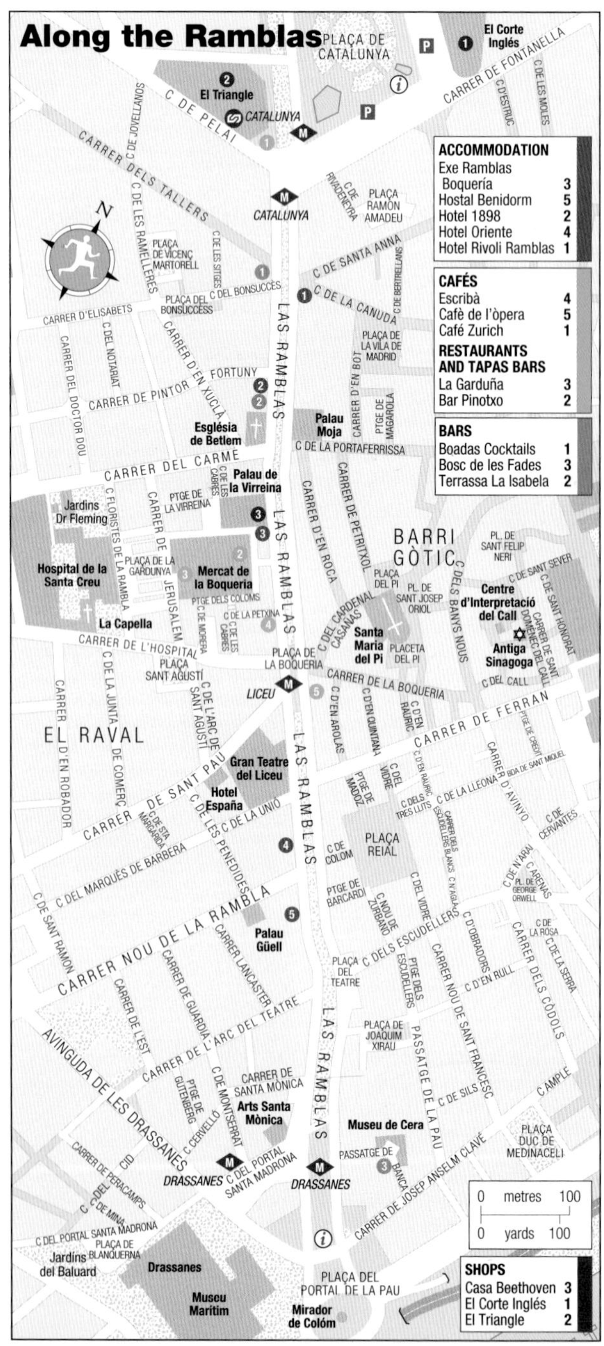
Along the Ramblas
PLAÇA DE CATALUNYA
El Corte Inglés
El Triangle
CATALUNYA
C DE PELAI
CARRER DE FONTANELLA
C D'ESTRUC
C DE LES MOLES
C DE JOVELLANOS
CARRER DELS TALLERS
C DE LES RAMELLERES
C DE RIVADENEYRA
PLAÇA RAMON AMADEU
PLAÇA DE VICENÇ MARTORELL
C DE LES SITGES
C DEL BONSUCCÉS
PLAÇA DEL BONSUCCÉS
C DE SANTA ANNA
C DE LA CANUDA
C DE BERTRELLANS
CARRER D'ELISABETS
C DEL NOTARIAT
CARRER DEL DOCTOR DOU
CARRER D'EN XUCLÀ
CARRER DE PINTOR FORTUNY
LAS RAMBLAS
PLAÇA DE LA VILA DE MADRID
CARRER D'EN BOT
PTGE DE MAGAROLA
Església de Betlem
Palau Moja
C DE LA PORTAFERRISSA
CARRER DEL CARME
C DE LES CABRES
Palau de la Virreina
PTGE DE LA VIRREINA
Jardins Dr Fleming
C FLORISTES DE LA RAMBLA
CARRER DE JERUSALEM
CARRER D'EN ROCA
CARRER DE PETRITXOL
BARRI GÒTIC
PL. DE SANT FELIP NERI
PLAÇA DE LA GARDUNYA
Hospital de la Santa Creu
Mercat de la Boqueria
PTGE DELS COLOMS
C DE MORERA
C DE LA PETXINA
PLAÇA DEL PI
PL. DE SANT JOSEP ORIOL
C DELS BANYS NOUS
C DE SANT SEVER
C DE SANT HONORAT
Centre d'Interpretació del Call
La Capella
C DEL CARDENAL CASAÑAS
Santa Maria del Pi
PLACETA DEL PI
Antiga Sinagoga
CARRER DE SANT DOMÈNEC DEL CALL
CARRER DE L'HOSPITAL
PLAÇA SANT AGUSTÍ
PLAÇA DE LA BOQUERIA
CARRER DE LA BOQUERIA
C DEL CALL
LICEU
C DE L'ARC DE SANT AGUSTÍ
C DE LA JUNTA DE COMERÇ
CARRER D'EN ROBADOR
EL RAVAL
C D'EN AROLAS
C D'EN QUINTANA
C D'EN RAURIC
CARRER DE FERRAN
PTGE DE CREDIT
Gran Teatre del Liceu
Hotel España
CARRER DE SANT PAU
C DE STA MARGARIDA
C DE LES PENEDIDES
C DE LA UNIÓ
PTGE DE MADOZ
C DEL VIDRE
C DELS TRES LLITS
C DE LA LLEONA
CARRER D'AVINYÓ
BDA DE SANT MIQUEL
C DE CERVANTES
PLAÇA REIAL
C DE COLOM
CARRER DELS ESCUDELLERS BLANCS
C N'AGLA
C DE N'ARAI
C ARENAS
PL. DE GEORGE ORWELL
C DEL MARQUÈS DE BARBERÀ
C DE SANT RAMON
CARRER NOU DE LA RAMBLA
PTGE DE BARCARDI
C NOU DE ZURBANO
Palau Güell
CARRER LANCASTER
C DE LA ROSA
C DE LA SERRA
PLAÇA DEL TEATRE
C DELS ESCUDELLERS
PTGE DELS ESCUDELLERS
CARRER NOU DE SANT FRANCESC
C D'OBRADORS
C D'EN RULL
CARRER DELS CÒDOLS
CARRER DE GUARDIA
CARRER DE L'EST
CARRER DE L'ARC DEL TEATRE
PLAÇA DE JOAQUIM XIRAU
PASSATGE DE LA PAU
AVINGUDA DE LES DRASSANES
PTGE DE GUTENBERG
C DE MONTSERRAT
CARRER DE SANTA MÒNICA
Arts Santa Mònica
C DE SILS
C AMPLE
Museu de Cera
PASSATGE DE BANCA
PLAÇA DUC DE MEDINACELI
C CERVELLÓ
DRASSANES
C DEL PORTAL SANTA MADRONA
CARRER DE JOSEP ANSELM CLAVÉ
CARRER DE PERACAMPS
C DEL CID
C DE MINA
C DEL PORTAL SANTA MADRONA
PLAÇA DE BLANQUERNA
Jardins del Baluard
Drassanes
Museu Marítim
Mirador de Colóm
PLAÇA DEL PORTAL DE LA PAU
0 metres 100
0 yards 100
ACCOMMODATION
Exe Ramblas Boquería 3
Hostal Benidorm 5
Hotel 1898 2
Hotel Oriente 4
Hotel Rivoli Ramblas 1
CAFÉS
Escribà 4
Cafè de l'òpera 5
Café Zurich 1
RESTAURANTS AND TAPAS BARS
La Garduña 3
Bar Pinotxo 2
BARS
Boadas Cocktails 1
Bosc de les Fades 3
Terrassa La Isabela 2
SHOPS
Casa Beethoven 3
El Corte Inglés 1
El Triangle 2

An insider's guide to the Ramblas

There are pavement cafés and restaurants all the way down the Ramblas, but the food can be indifferent and the prices high, so be warned. (For better value, go into the Boqueria market, where the traders eat.) The strolling crowds, too, provide perfect cover for pickpockets – keep a wary eye on your possessions at all times, especially when watching the buskers or shopping at the kiosks. And – however easy it looks to win – if you're going to play cards or dice with a man on a street, you've only yourself to blame if you get ripped off.

Mercat de la Boqueria

MAP P.26, POCKET MAP C12.
Ramblas 91 Ⓜ Liceu ⓣ 933 182 584, Ⓦ boqueria.info. Mon–Sat 8am–8pm.

Other markets might protest, but the city's glorious main food market really can claim to be the best in Spain. It's officially called the Mercat Sant Josep, though everyone knows it as La Boqueria. A riot of noise and colour, it's as popular with locals who come here to shop daily as with snap-happy tourists. Everything radiates out from the central fish and seafood stalls – bunches of herbs, pots of spices, baskets of wild mushrooms, mounds of cheese and sausage, racks of bread, hanging hams and overloaded meat counters. It's easy to get waylaid at the entrance by the fruit cartons and squeezed juices, but the flagship fruit and veg stalls here are pricey. It's better value further in, in particular in the small outdoor square just beyond the north side of the market where the local allotment holders and market-gardeners gather. Everyone has a favourite market stall, but don't miss Petras and its array of wild mushrooms (it's at the back, by the market restaurant, *La Garduña*) or Frutas y Verduras Jesús y Carmen, which is framed with colourful bundles of exotic chillies. And of course, there are some excellent stand-up tapas bars in the market as well, open from dawn onward for the traders.

Plaça de la Boqueria

MAP P.26, POCKET MAP C12.
Ⓜ Liceu.

The halfway point of the Ramblas is marked by Plaça de la Boqueria, with its large round pavement **mosaic by Joan Miró**. It's become something of a symbol for the city and is one of a number of public works in Barcelona by the artist, who was born just a couple of minutes away in the Barri Gòtic. Over at Ramblas 82, **Casa Bruno Quadros** – the lower floor is now the Caixa Sabadell – was built in the 1890s to house an umbrella store, which explains its delightful facade, decorated with Oriental designs, dragons and parasols.

Mercat de la Boqueria

Gran Teatre del Liceu

Gran Teatre del Liceu

MAP P.26, POCKET MAP C13. Ramblas 51–59 Ⓜ Liceu Ⓦ liceubarcelona.cat. Box office ⓣ 934 859 913; tours ⓣ 934 859 914. Mon–Fri (except Aug) 9.30 am, 10.30am, 11.30am & 12.30pm. Guided tour €16, audio guided tours €9 & €6.

Barcelona's celebrated opera house was first founded in 1847 and rebuilt after a fire in 1861 to become Spain's grandest theatre. Regarded as a bastion of the city's late nineteenth-century commercial and intellectual classes, the Liceu was devastated again in 1893 when an anarchist threw two bombs into the stalls during a production of *William Tell* – twenty people died. It then burned down for the third time in 1994, when a workman's blowtorch set fire to the scenery of an opera set. The latest restoration of the lavishly decorated interior took five years, and the opera house opened again in 1999, complete with a modern extension, the Espai Liceu, which also houses a music and gift shop and a café. You'll see and learn most on the more expensive, hour-long 10am guided tour (the other, shorter, cheaper tours are self-guided). Highlights include the Salon of Mirrors and the impressive gilded auditorium containing almost 2300 seats, making it one of the world's largest opera houses. Some tours also include the option of visiting the glorious *modernista*-styled rooms of the Cercle del Liceu, the opera house's private members' club.

For Liceu performances, check the website for details and make bookings well in advance. The traditional meeting place for audience and performers alike, meanwhile, is the famous *Cafè de l'òpera*, just across the Ramblas.

The Ramblas statues

Time stands still for no man – not even for the famed human statues of the Ramblas, who make a living out of doing just that. A motley crew of figures once flanked the length of the street, but change is inevitable, and in 2012 – in an effort to keep pedestrian traffic moving, and prevent pickpockets from preying on the gathering crowds – the city moved the human statues to the wide stretch of Rambla de Santa Mònica. The number of statues was then capped to thirty a year, with performers being required to audition for the permit-only slots. Despite the cutback in territory and number, the remaining human statues are still an attraction. Be it Galileo or a horned demon, these stalwarts of the Ramblas continue to climb upon their plinths and strike a pose. What else is a statue going to do?

Arts Santa Mònica

MAP P.26, POCKET MAP C14.
Ramblas 7 Ⓜ Drassanes Ⓣ 923 162 810, Ⓦ artssantamonica.gencat.cat. Tue–Sat 11am–9pm, Sun & hols 11am–5pm. Free.
Down from the Liceu, the bottom part of the Ramblas (Rambla de Santa Mònica) was historically a theatre and red-light district, and it still has a rough edge or two. Flagship building is the Augustinian convent of Santa Mònica, which dates originally from 1626, making it the oldest building on the Ramblas. It was remodelled in the 1980s as a contemporary arts centre, and hosts regularly changing exhibitions – it's an unusual gallery space dedicated to "artistic creation, science, thought and communication" so there's usually something worth seeing, from an offbeat art installation to a show of archive photographs. Meanwhile, pavement artists and palm readers set up stalls outside on the Ramblas, augmented on weekend afternoons by a street market selling jewellery, beads, bags and ornaments.

Museu de Cera

MAP P.26, POCKET MAP C14.
Ramblas 4–6, entrance on Ptge. de Banca Ⓜ Drassanes Ⓣ 933 172 649, Ⓦ museocerabcn.com. July–Sept daily 10am–10pm; Oct–June Mon–Fri 10am–1.30pm & 4–7.30pm, Sat & Sun 11am–2pm & 4.30–8.30pm. €15.
You'd have to be hard-hearted indeed not to derive some pleasure from the city's wax museum. Located in a nineteenth-century bank building, it presents an ever more ludicrous series of tableaux in cavernous salons and gloomy corridors, depicting recitals, meetings and parlour gatherings attended by an anachronistic – not to say perverse – collection of characters, from Hitler to Princess Diana. Needless to say, it's enormously amusing, culminating in cheesy underwater tunnels and space capsules and an unpleasant "Terror Room". Even if this doesn't appeal, it is definitely worth poking your head into the museum's extraordinary grotto bar, the *Bosc de les Fades*.

Arts Santa Mònica

Shops

Casa Beethoven

MAP P.26, POCKET MAP C12.
Ramblas 97 Ⓜ Liceu. Mon, Tue, Thu & Fri 9am–8pm, Wed 9.30am–2pm & 4–8pm, Sat 9am–2pm & 5–8pm; closed Aug.

Wonderful old shop selling sheet music from wooden library stacks, plus CDs and music reference books – not just classical, but also rock, jazz and flamenco.

El Corte Inglés

MAP P.26, POCKET MAP E10.
Pl. de Catalunya 14 Ⓜ Catalunya Ⓦ elcorteingles.es. Mon–Sat 9.30am–10pm (on certain days to 9pm).

The city's biggest department store has nine retail floors (fashion, cosmetics, household goods, toys), a good basement supermarket and – best of all – a top-floor café with terrific views. For music, books, computers and sports gear, head for the nearby branch at Av. Portal de l'Àngel 19.

Escribà

El Triangle

MAP P.26, POCKET MAP D10.
Pl. de Catalunya 4 Ⓜ Catalunya Ⓦ eltriangle.es. June–Sept Mon–Sat 9.30am–10pm, Oct–May Mon–Sat 9.30am–9pm.

Shopping centre dominated by the flagship FNAC store, which specializes in books (good English-language selection), music, film and computer stuff. Also a Camper (for shoes), Massimo Dutti (fashion) and Sephora (cosmetics), plus lots of boutiques, and a café on the ground floor next to the extensive newspaper and magazine section.

Cafés

Escribà

MAP P.26, POCKET MAP C12.
Ramblas 83 Ⓜ Liceu Ⓣ 933 016 027, Ⓦ escriba.es. Daily 9am–9pm.

Wonderful pastries and cakes from the renowned Escribà family business in a classy Art Nouveau shop. Many rate this as the best bakery in Barcelona.

Cafè de l'òpera

MAP P.26, POCKET MAP C12.
Ramblas 74 Ⓜ Liceu Ⓣ 933 177 585, Ⓦ cafeoperabcn.com. Daily 8.30am–2.30am.

If you're going to pay through the nose for a seat on the Ramblas, it may as well be at this famous old café-bar opposite the opera house, which retains a *fin-de-siècle* feel. Surprisingly, it's not a complete tourist-fest and locals pop in day and night for drinks, cakes and tapas.

Café Zurich

MAP P.26, POCKET MAP D10.
Pl. Catalunya 1 Ⓜ Catalunya Ⓣ 933 179 153. Mon–Fri 8am–11pm, Sat 9am–midnight, Sun 9am–11pm.

The most famous meet-and-greet café in town, right at the top of the Ramblas and underneath El Triangle shopping centre. It's good for drinks, less so for food.

There's a huge pavement terrace, but sit inside if you don't want to be bothered by endless rounds of buskers and beggars.

Restaurants and tapas bars

La Garduña

MAP P.26, POCKET MAP C12.
Mercat de la Boqueria, C/Jerusalem 18 Ⓜ Liceu ⓣ 647 223 776. Mon–Sat 7am–noon.

Tucked away at the back of the frenetic Boqueria market, this is an especially enticing place for lunch when there's a good-value *menú del dia* – basically, you'll be offered the best of the day's produce at pretty reasonable prices, and if you're lucky you'll get an outdoor seat with market views. At dinner, most mains are €9–20.

Bar Pinotxo

MAP P.26, POCKET MAP C12.
Mercat de la Boqueria, Ramblas 91 Ⓜ Liceu ⓣ 933 171 731. Closed Aug.

The market's most renowned refuelling stop – which is located just inside the main entrance on the right – attracts traders, chefs, tourists and celebs, who stand three deep at busy times. A coffee, a grilled sandwich and a glass of cava is the local breakfast of choice, or let the cheery staff steer you towards the tapas and daily specials (€5–15), with anything from a slice of tortilla to fried baby squid on offer.

Bars

Boadas Cocktails

MAP P.26, POCKET MAP D11.
C/dels Tallers 1 Ⓜ Catalunya ⓣ 933 189 592, ⓦ boadascocktails.com. Mon–Sat noon–2am (Fri & Sat until 3am); closed 3 weeks in Aug.

Inside Barcelona's oldest cocktail bar, tuxedoed bartenders shake,

Boadas Cocktails

stir and pour classic drinks for a well-dressed crowd against an Art Deco background. It's a timeless place that's a perfect start for a sophisticated night on the town.

Bosc de les Fades

MAP P.26, POCKET MAP C14.
Ptge. de Banca 5 Ⓜ Drassanes ⓣ 933 172 649. Mon–Fri 10am–1am, Sat & Sun 11am–1.30am.

Down an alley by the wax museum, the "Forest of the Fairies" is festooned with gnarled plaster tree trunks, hanging branches, fountains and stalactites. It's a bit cheesy, which is perhaps why it's a huge hit with the twenty-something crowd who huddle in the grottoes with a cocktail or two.

Terrassa La Isabela

MAP P.26, POCKET MAP C5.
Ramblas 109 Ⓜ Liceu ⓣ 935 529 552, ⓦ terraza-laisabela.com. Daily noon–0.30am.

Get a bird's-eye look at the Ramblas from *Hotel 1898*'s stylish rooftop terrace bar. The food and cocktails aren't cheap but the views are priceless.

Barri Gòtic

The Barri Gòtic, or Gothic Quarter, on the east side of the Ramblas, forms the heart of Barcelona's Old Town. Its buildings date principally from the fourteenth and fifteenth centuries, and culminate in the extraordinary Gothic cathedral known as La Seu. Around here are hidden squares, some fascinating museums, the city's old Jewish quarter and the remains of the Roman walls. It takes the best part of a day to see everything – longer if you factor in the abundant cafés, antique shops, boutiques and galleries. Note that the southern area, en route to the harbour, is rather less gentrified than the cathedral district – take care at night in the poorly lit streets. Metros Liceu (west), Jaume I (east) and Drassanes (south) provide access to the neighbourhood.

La Seu

MAP P.34, POCKET MAP E12.
Pl. de la Seu Ⓜ Jaume I. Mon–Fri 8.30am–12.30pm & 5.45–7.30pm, Sat 8.30am–12.30pm and 5.15–8pm, Sun 8.30am–1.45pm & 5.15–8pm. Free during general admission times, otherwise tourist admission charge obligatory (Mon–Fri 12.30–7.45pm, Sat 12.30-5.30pm, Sun 2–5.30pm), €7, includes entrance to all sections.

Barcelona's cathedral is one of the great Gothic buildings of Spain, dedicated to Santa Eulàlia, who was martyred by the Romans for daring to prefer Christianity – her ornate tomb rests in a crypt beneath the high altar. A magnificent fourteenth-century **cloister** looks over a lush tropical garden complete with soaring palm trees

La Seu

and honking white geese. There's also glittering church treasure on show in the cathedral museum.

Performances of the Catalan national dance, the *sardana*, take place in front of the cathedral (usually Sun at noon, plus Easter–Nov Sat at 6pm), while the pedestrianized Avinguda de la Catedral hosts an antiques market every Thuday, and a Christmas craft fair in December.

Museu Diocesà

MAP P.34, POCKET MAP E12.
Av. Catedral 4 Ⓜ Jaume I ☎ 932 687 582. Daily: March–Oct 10am–8pm; Nov–Feb 10am–6pm. €15.

Stand back to look at the cathedral buildings and it's easy to see the line of Roman towers that originally stood on this spot incorporated into the later medieval structures. One such tower formed part of the cathedral almshouse, now the Museu Diocesà, whose soaring spaces have been beautifully adapted to show an impressive collection of religious art and church treasures. The ticket also includes entrance into the temporary art and architecture exhibitions held here.

Reial Cercle Artístic

MAP P.34, POCKET MAP D12.
C/Arcs 5 Ⓜ Jaume I ☎ 933 181 774, Ⓦ reialcercleartistic.cat. Daily 10am–10pm. €10.

The handsome Gothic palace housing the Royal Art Circle hosts various free exhibitions and concerts, though the big draw is the collection of 44 original sculptures by Salvador Dalí, completed in the 1970s. A lovely terrace restaurant above the Gothic streets also offers a pricey lunch, while on your way to or from the cathedral spare a glance for the graffiti-like frieze surmounting the nearby **Collegi d'Arquitectes** on Plaça Nova – designed by that other inimitable master, Pablo Picasso.

Plaça del Reial

Plaça del Rei

MAP P.34, POCKET MAP E12
Ⓜ Jaume I.

The harmonious enclosed square of Plaça del Rei was once the palace courtyard of the Counts of Barcelona. Stairs climb from here to the palace's main hall, the fourteenth-century **Saló del Tinell**. It was here that Ferdinand and Isabella received Christopher Columbus on his triumphant return from his famous voyage of 1492. At one time the Spanish Inquisition met in the hall, taking full advantage of the popular belief that the walls would move if a lie was spoken. Nowadays it hosts temporary exhibitions, while concerts are occasionally held in the hall or outside in the square. The palace buildings include the beautiful fourteenth-century **Capella de Santa Agata**, and the romantic Renaissance **Torre del Rei Martí**. There's no public access to the tower, but the interiors of the hall and chapel can usually be seen during a visit to the adjacent Museu d'Història de Barcelona.

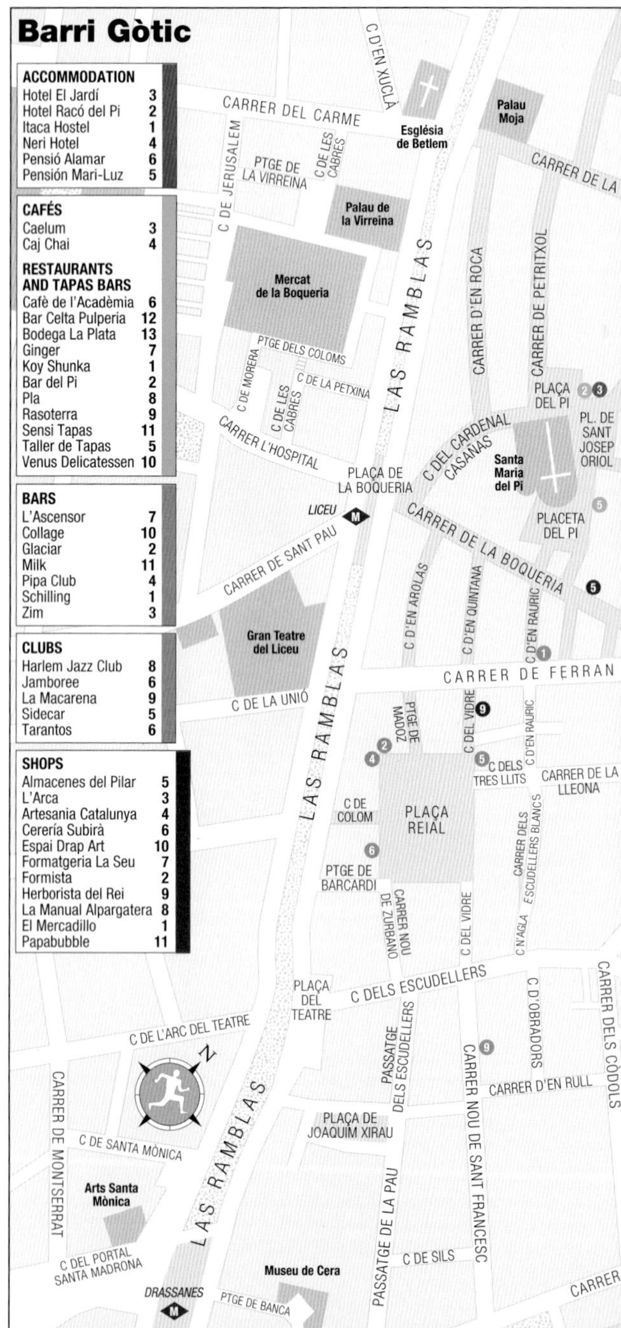

Barri Gòtic
ACCOMMODATION
Hotel El Jardí 3
Hotel Racó del Pi 2
Itaca Hostel 1
Neri Hotel 4
Pensió Alamar 6
Pensión Mari-Luz 5
CAFÉS
Caelum 3
Caj Chai 4
RESTAURANTS AND TAPAS BARS
Cafè de l'Acadèmia 6
Bar Celta Pulperia 12
Bodega La Plata 13
Ginger 7
Koy Shunka 1
Bar del Pi 2
Pla 8
Rasoterra 9
Sensi Tapas 11
Taller de Tapas 5
Venus Delicatessen 10
BARS
L'Ascensor 7
Collage 10
Glaciar 2
Milk 11
Pipa Club 4
Schilling 1
Zim 3
CLUBS
Harlem Jazz Club 8
Jamboree 6
La Macarena 9
Sidecar 5
Tarantos 6
SHOPS
Almacenes del Pilar 5
L'Arca 3
Artesania Catalunya 4
Cerería Subirà 6
Espai Drap Art 10
Formatgeria La Seu 7
Formista 2
Herborista del Rei 9
La Manual Alpargatera 8
El Mercadillo 1
Papabubble 11
C D'EN XUCLÀ
CARRER DEL CARME
Església de Betlem
Palau Moja
CARRER DE LA
C DE JERUSALEM
PTGE DE LA VIRREINA
C DE LES CABRES
Palau de la Virreina
Mercat de la Boqueria
LAS RAMBLAS
CARRER D'EN ROCA
CARRER DE PETRITXOL
PTGE DELS COLOMS
C DE MORERA
C DE LA PETXINA
C DE LES CABRES
PLAÇA DEL PI
PL. DE SANT JOSEP ORIOL
CARRER L'HOSPITAL
C DEL CARDENAL CASAÑAS
Santa Maria del Pi
PLAÇA DE LA BOQUERIA
LICEU
PLACETA DEL PI
CARRER DE SANT PAU
CARRER DE LA BOQUERIA
C D'EN AROLAS
C D'EN QUINTANA
C D'EN RAURIC
Gran Teatre del Liceu
CARRER DE FERRAN
C DE LA UNIÓ
PTGE DE MADOZ
C DEL VIDRE
C D'EN RAURIC
C DELS TRES LLITS
CARRER DE LA LLEONA
C DE COLOM
PLAÇA REIAL
CARRER DELS ESCUDELLERS BLANCS
PTGE DE BARCARDI
CARRER NOU DE ZURBANO
C DEL VIDRE
C N'AGLA
PLAÇA DEL TEATRE
C DELS ESCUDELLERS
C D'OBRADORS
CARRER DELS CÒDOLS
C DE L'ARC DEL TEATRE
PASSATGE DELS ESCUDELLERS
CARRER NOU DE SANT FRANCESC
CARRER D'EN RULL
CARRER DE MONTSERRAT
PLAÇA DE JOAQUIM XIRAU
C DE SANTA MÒNICA
Arts Santa Mònica
PASSATGE DE LA PAU
C DE SILS
C DEL PORTAL SANTA MADRONA
Museu de Cera
DRASSANES
PTGE DE BANCA
CARRER

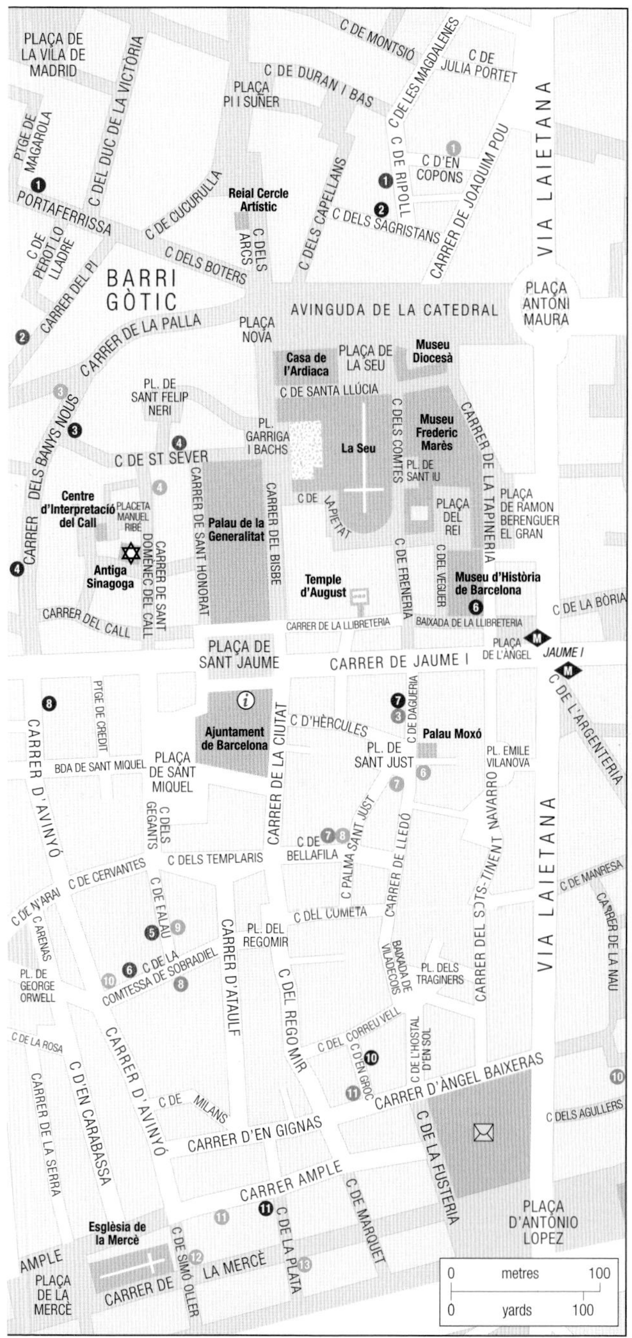

BARRI GÒTIC
PLAÇA DE LA VILA DE MADRID
C DE MONTSIÓ
C DE DURAN I BAS
PLAÇA PI I SUÑER
C DE LES MAGDALENES
C DE JULIA PORTET
VIA LAIETANA
C DEL DUC DE LA VICTÒRIA
PTGE DE MAGAROLA
PORTAFERRISSA
C DE CUCURULLA
Reial Cercle Artístic
C DELS ARCS
C DELS CAPELLANS
C DE RIPOLL
C D'EN COPONS
C DELS SAGRISTANS
CARRER DE JOAQUIM POU
C DE PEROT LO LLADRE
CARRER DEL PI
C DELS BOTERS
PLAÇA ANTONI MAURA
AVINGUDA DE LA CATEDRAL
CARRER DE LA PALLA
PLAÇA NOVA
Casa de l'Ardiaca
PLAÇA DE LA SEU
Museu Diocesà
PL. DE SANT FELIP NERI
C DE SANTA LLÚCIA
CARRER DELS BANYS NOUS
PL. GARRIGA I BACHS
La Seu
C DELS COMTES
Museu Frederic Marès
CARRER DE LA TAPINERIA
C DE ST SEVER
PL. DE SANT IU
Centre d'Interpretació del Call
PLACETA MANUEL RIBÉ
CARRER DE SANT HONORAT
Palau de la Generalitat
CARRER DEL BISBE
C DE LA PIETAT
PLAÇA DEL REI
PLAÇA DE RAMON BERENGUER EL GRAN
Antiga Sinagoga
CARRER DE SANT DOMÈNEC DEL CALL
Temple d'August
C DE FRENERIA
C DEL VEGUER
Museu d'Història de Barcelona
CARRER DEL CALL
CARRER DE LA LLIBRETERIA
BAIXADA DE LA LLIBRETERIA
C DE LA BÒRIA
PLAÇA DE SANT JAUME
CARRER DE JAUME I
PLAÇA DE L'ÀNGEL
JAUME I
C DE L'ARGENTERIA
PTGE DE CREDIT
Ajuntament de Barcelona
C DE LA CIUTAT
C D'HÈRCULES
C DE DAGUERIA
Palau Moxó
PL. DE SANT JUST
PL. EMILE VILANOVA
CARRER D'AVINYÓ
BDA DE SANT MIQUEL
PLAÇA DE SANT MIQUEL
C DELS GEGANTS
C DE BELLAFILA
C PALMA SANT JUST
CARRER DE LLEDÓ
CARRER DEL SOTS-TINENT NAVARRO
C DELS TEMPLARIS
C DE CERVANTES
C DE MANRESA
CARRER DE LA NAU
C D'EN ARAI
C ARENAS
C DE FALAU
C DEL CUMETA
CARRER D'ATAULF
PL. DEL REGOMIR
C DE LA COMTESSA DE SOBRADIEL
BAIXADA DE VILADECOLS
PL. DELS TRAGINERS
PL. DE GEORGE ORWELL
C DEL REGOMIR
C DE LA ROSA
C DEL CORREU VELL
C D'EN GROC
C DE L'HOSTAL D'EN SOL
C D'EN CARABASSA
CARRER DE LA SERRA
C DE MILANS
CARRER D'ÀNGEL BAIXERAS
C DELS AGULLERS
CARRER D'EN GIGNAS
C DE LA FUSTERIA
CARRER AMPLE
C DE MARQUET
PLAÇA D'ANTÒNIO LOPEZ
C DE LA PLATA
Església de la Mercè
C DE SIMÓ OLLER
CARRER DE LA MERCÈ
AMPLE
PLAÇA DE LA MERCÈ
0 metres 100
0 yards 100

Museu Frederic Marès

MAP P.34, POCKET MAP E12.
Pl. de Sant Iu 5–6 Ⓜ Jaume I ⓣ 932 563 500, ⓦ www.museumares.bcn.cat. Tue–Sat 10am–7pm, Sun & hols 11am–8pm. €4.20, free Sun after 3pm & first Sun of the month.

Don't miss a visit to one of the Old Town's most fascinating museums, which occupies a wing of the old royal palace. It celebrates the diverse passions of sculptor, painter and restorer Frederic Marès (1893–1991), whose beautifully presented collection of ancient and medieval sculpture does little to prepare visitors for Marès' true obsession, namely a kaleidoscopic array of curios and collectibles. Entire rooms are devoted to keys and locks, cigarette cards and snuffboxes, fans, gloves and brooches, walking sticks, dolls' houses, old gramophones and archaic bicycles – to list just a sample of what's in the collection.

Museu d'Història de Barcelona (MUHBA)

MAP P.34, POCKET MAP E12.
Pl. del Rei, entrance on C/del Veguer Ⓜ Jaume I ⓣ 932 562 100, ⓦ www.museuhistoria.bcn.cat. Tue–Sat 10am–7pm, Sun 10am–8pm. €7.

The Barcelona History Museum comprises half a dozen sites across the city, though its principal hub is what's known as the "Conjunt Monumental" (or monumental ensemble) of Plaça del Rei, whose crucial draw is an amazing underground archeological section – nothing less than the remains of the Roman city of Barcino (first century BC to the sixth century AD), which stretch under the surrounding streets as far as the cathedral. Excavations and explanatory diagrams show the full extent of the streets and buildings – from lookout towers to laundries – while models, mosaics, murals and finds help flesh out the reality of daily life in Barcino.

There's a well-stocked book and gift shop on site (entrance on C/ Llibreteria), while the museum ticket also allows entry to the other MUHBA sites, notably the Poble Sec air-raid shelter and Pedralbes monastery.

Església de Santa María del Pi

MAP P.34, POCKET MAP D12.

Temple d'August de Barcelona

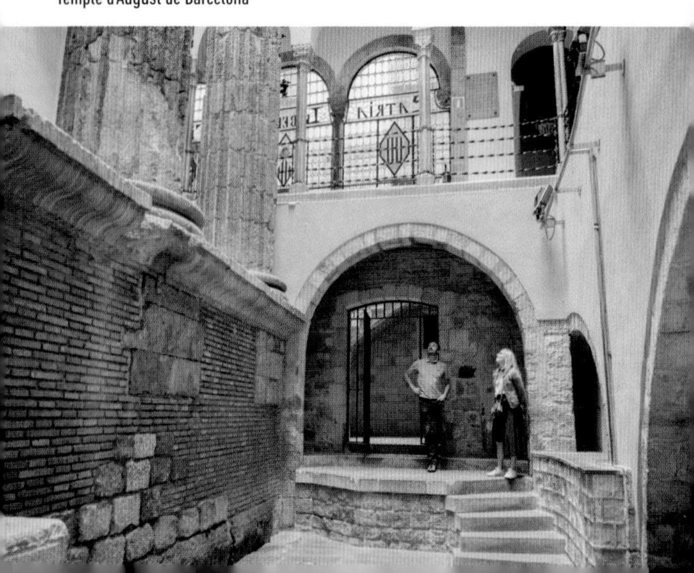

Palau de la Generalitat

Pl. Sant Josep Oriol Ⓜ Liceu, Ⓦ www.basilicadelpi.cat. Daily 10am–6pm. €4.
The fourteenth-century church of Santa María is known for its marvellous stained glass, particularly a 10m-wide rose window (often claimed, rather boldly, to be the largest in the world). The church flanks Plaça Sant Josep Oriol, the prettiest of three delightful adjacent squares and an ideal place for an outdoor coffee and a browse around the weekend **artists' market** (Sat 11am–8pm, Sun 11am–2pm).

The church is named after the pine tree that once stood here. A **farmers' market** spills across Plaça del Pi on the first and third Friday, Saturday and Sunday of the month, while the characteristic cafés of narrow **Carrer de Petritxol** (off Plaça del Pi) are the places to head to for a cup of hot chocolate – *Dulcinea* at no. 2 is the traditional choice – and a browse around the street's commercial art galleries. The most famous is **Sala Pares** at C/Petritxol 5, known as the site of Picasso's first solo exhibition.

Temple d'August de Barcelona

MAP P.34, POCKET MAP D1. Centre Excursionista de Catalunya, C/Paradis 10 Ⓜ Jaume I. Mon 10am–2pm, Tue–Sat 10am–7pm, Sun 10am–8pm. Free.
Four impressive Roman columns and the architrave of a temple dedicated to the Emperor Augustus make an incongruous spectacle, tucked away in the green-painted interior courtyard of the Centre Excursionista de Catalunya (Catalan Hiking Club). Some of the oldest constructions in Barcelona, they managed to remain intact despite medieval buildings rising up around.

Antiga Sinagoga

MAP P.34, POCKET MAP D12, C/Marlet 5, corner with C/Sant Domènec del Call Ⓜ Liceu Ⓣ 933 170 790, Ⓦ sinagogamayor.com. Mon–Fri 10.30am–6.30pm, Sun 10.30am–3pm, Sat closed. €2.50.
Barcelona's medieval Jewish quarter was centred on C/Sant Domènec del Call, where a synagogue existed from as early as the third century AD until the pogrom of 1391, but even after that date the building survived

in various guises and has since been sympathetically restored. The city authorities have signposted a few other points of interest in what's known as "El Call Major", including the **Centre d'Interpretació del Call** in nearby Plaçeta Manuel Ribé (Tue–Fri 11am–2pm, Sat & Sun 11am–7pm; free), whose informative storyboards (in English) shed more light on Barcelona's fascinating Jewish heritage.

Casa de L'Ardiaca

MAP P.34, POCKET MAP E12.
C/Santa Llúcia 3 Ⓜ Jaume I. Aug–Sept Mon–Fri 10am–7pm, Sat 10am–8pm, Oct–July Mon–Fri 9am–8.45pm, Sat 10am–8pm.

Originally the residence of the archdeacon of La Seu cathedral, this fourteenth-century house encloses a tiny cloistered and tiled courtyard, renovated by *modernista* architect Lluís Domènech i Montaner. It's now used for changing temporary exhibitions and the city's historical archives.

Palau de la Generalitat

MAP P.34, POCKET MAP D12/13.
Pl. de Sant Jaume Ⓜ Jaume I Ⓣ 934 024 600. Tours on 2nd and 4th Sun of the month (not Aug), every hour, 10am–noon; also on April 23 and Sept 11 & 24. Passport or ID required. Free.

The home of the Catalan government presents its oldest aspect around the side, where the fifteenth-century C/del Bisbe facade contains a medallion portraying Sant Jordi (St George, patron saint of Catalunya). Inside, there's a beautiful first-floor cloister, the intricately worked chapel and salon of Sant Jordi as well as an upper courtyard planted with orange trees. You can visit the interior on a one-hour guided tour on alternate Sundays (only one or two tours each day are in English), while the Generalitat is also open on public holidays, particularly April 23 – the **Dia de Sant Jordi** (St George's Day). A nationalist holiday in Catalunya, this is also a local Valentine's Day, when it's traditional to exchange books and roses.

Plaça de Sant Jaume

MAP P.34, POCKET MAP D13.
Ⓜ Jaume I.

The spacious square at the end of the main C/de Ferran is at the heart of city and regional government business, and the traditional place for demonstrations and local festivals. Whistle-happy local police try to keep things moving, while taxis and bike-tour groups weave among the pedestrians.

Ajuntament de Barcelona

MAP P.34, POCKET MAP D13.
Pl. de Sant Jaume Ⓜ Jaume I Ⓣ 934 027 000. Public admitted Sun 10am–1.30pm, entrance on C/Font de Sant Miquel. Free.

On the south side of Plaça de Sant Jaume stands Barcelona's city hall. On Sundays you're allowed into the building for a self-guided tour around the splendid marble galleries and staircases. The highlights are the magnificent fourteenth-century council chamber, known as the **Saló de Cent**, and the dramatic historical murals in the **Saló de les Cròniques** (Hall of Chronicles).

Palau Moxó

MAP P.34, POCKET MAP E13.
Pl. de Sant Just 4 Ⓜ Jaume I Ⓣ 933 152 238, Ⓦ palaumoxobcn.blogspot.com. Guided tours for groups by reservation only. €13.

The Palau Moxó has been in the hands of the same family since 1770, which makes it unique in Barcelona – especially since most other palatial Baroque residences were destroyed during the Civil War. You'll see grand salons and intimate chambers on the weekly guided tours, while regular concerts provide another taste of the noble life.

Plaça Reial

MAP P.34, POCKET MAP C13.
Ⓜ Liceu.

The elegant Plaça Reial – hidden behind an archway off the Ramblas

Basílica de La Mercè

– is studded with palm trees and decorated iron lamps (designed by the young Antoni Gaudí), and bordered by pastel-coloured arcaded buildings. Sitting in the square certainly puts you in mixed company – buskers, eccentrics, tramps and bemused visitors – though most of the really unsavoury characters have been driven off over the years and predatory waiters are usually the biggest nuisance these days. Don't expect to see too many locals until night falls, when the surrounding bars come into their own. Passing through on a Sunday morning, look in on the **coin and stamp market** (10am–2pm).

Carrer d'Avinyó

MAP P.34, POCKET MAP D13/14.
Ⓜ Liceu.

Carrer d'Avinyó, running south from C/de Ferran towards the harbour, cuts through the most atmospheric part of the southern Barri Gòtic. Formerly a red-light district, it still looks the part – lined with dark overhanging buildings – but the funky cafés, streetwear shops and boutiques tell the story of its creeping gentrification. A few rough edges still show, particularly around **Plaça George Orwell**, a favoured hangout for locals with its cheap cafés, restaurants and bars, some of which offer seating on the lively square.

La Mercè

MAP P.34, POCKET MAP D14.
Ⓜ Drassanes.

In the eighteenth century, the harbourside neighbourhood known as La Mercè was home to the nobles and merchants enriched by Barcelona's maritime trade. Most moved north to the more fashionable Eixample later in the nineteenth century, and since then Carrer de la Mercè and surrounding streets (particularly Ample, d'en Gignàs and Regomir) have been home to a series of old-style taverns known as *tascas* or *bodegas* – a glass of wine from the barrel and a plate of tapas here is one of the Old Town's more authentic experiences.

At Plaça de la Mercè, the **Església de la Mercè** is the focus of the city's biggest annual bash, the Festes de la Mercè every September, dedicated to the co-patroness of Barcelona, whose image is paraded from the church. It's an excuse for a week of partying, parades, special events and concerts, culminating in spectacular pyrotechnics along the seafront.

Shops

Almacenes del Pilar

MAP P.34, POCKET MAP D13.
C/Boqueria 43 Ⓜ Liceu Ⓦ almacenesdelpilar.com. Mon–Sat 9am–2pm & 4–8pm; closed Aug.

A world of frills, lace, cloth and material used in the making of Spain's traditional regional costumes. You can pick up a decorated fan for just a few euros, though quality items go for a lot more.

L'Arca

MAP P.34, POCKET MAP D12.
C/Banys Nous 20 Ⓜ Liceu Ⓦ larca.es. Mon–Sat 11am–2pm & 4.30–8.30pm; closed Aug.

Catalan brides used to fill up their nuptial trunk (*l'arca*) with embroidered linen and lace, and this shop is a treasure-trove of vintage and antique textiles. Period costumes can be hired or purchased as well – one of Kate Winslet's *Titanic* costumes came from here.

Artesania Catalunya

MAP P.34, POCKET MAP D12.

L'Arca

C/Banys Nous 11 Ⓜ Liceu Ⓦ artesania-catalunya.com. Mon–Sat 10am–8pm, Sun & hols 10am–2pm.

It's always worth a look in the showroom of the arts and crafts promotion board. Exhibitions change but most of the work is contemporary in style, from basketwork to glassware, though traditional methods are still very much encouraged.

Cerería Subirà

MAP P.34, POCKET MAP E13.
Bxda. Llibreteria 7 Ⓜ Jaume I. Mon–Thu 9.30am–1.30pm & 4–8pm, Fri 9.30am–8pm, Sat 10am–8pm.

Barcelona's oldest shop (it's been here since 1760) boasts a beautiful interior, selling unique handcrafted candles.

Espai Drap Art

MAP P.34, POCKET MAP E14.
C/Groc 1 Ⓜ Jaume I Ⓦ drapart.org. Tue–Fri 11am–2pm & 5–8pm, Sat 6–9pm.

The Drap Art creative recycling organization has a shop and exhibition space for artists to show their wildly inventive wares, from trash bangles to tin bags.

Formatgeria La Seu

MAP P.34, POCKET MAP E13.
C/Daguería 16 Ⓜ Jaume I Ⓦ www.formatgerialaseu.com. Tue–Sat 10am–2pm & 5–8pm; closed Aug.

Sells the best farmhouse cheeses from independent producers all over Spain. Chatty Scottish owner Katherine is usually on hand to advise, and you can try before you buy with a €3 tasting plate – ask about the "formatgelat", a cheese–ice cream fusion that's unique to the shop.

Formista

MAP P.34, POCKET MAP E12.
C/Sagristans 9 Ⓜ Jaume I Ⓦ formista.wordpress.com. Mon–Sat 11am–9pm, Sun noon –3pm.

Gallery–shop hybrid selling unique handmade objects by international designers and artists. There are sleek leather handbags alongside porcelain jewellery, hand-printed textiles and more.

Herborista del Rei

MAP P.34, POCKET MAP D13.
C/del Vidre 1 Ⓜ Liceu Ⓣ 933 180 512, Ⓦ herboristadelrei.com. Mon 2.30–8.30pm, Tue–Sat 10.30am–8.30pm.

A renowned, early nineteenth-century herbalist's shop, tucked off Plaça Reial, which stocks more than 250 medicinal herbs designed to combat all complaints.

La Manual Alpargatera

MAP P.34, POCKET MAP D13.
C/d'Avinyó 7 Ⓜ Liceu Ⓦ lamanualalpargatera.com. Mon–Fri 9.30am–8pm, Sat 10am–8pm.

In this traditional workshop they make and sell *alpargatas* (espadrilles) to order, as well as producing other straw, rope and basket work.

El Mercadillo

MAP P.34, POCKET MAP D12.
C/Portaferrissa 17 Ⓜ Liceu. Mon–Sat 11am–9pm.

The camel at the entrance marks this hippy-dippy indoor street market of shops and stalls selling skate-wear, vintage gear and jewellery.

Papabubble

MAP P.34, POCKET MAP D14.
C/Ample 28 Ⓜ Jaume I Ⓦ papabubble.com. Mon–Fri 10am–2pm & 4–8.30pm, Sat 10am–8.30pm, Sun 11am–7.30pm; closed Aug.

Groovy young things roll out home-made candy to a chill-out soundtrack. Come and watch them at work, sample a sweet, and take home a gorgeously wrapped gift.

Cafés

Caelum

MAP P.34, POCKET MAP D12.
C/Palla 8 Ⓜ Liceu Ⓣ 933 026 993, Ⓦ caelumbarcelona.com. Mon–Thu 10.30am–8.30pm, Fri & Sat 10.30am–11pm, Sun 10.30am–9pm; open afternoons in Aug.

Caelum

The lovingly packaged confections in this upscale café-deli (the name is Latin for "heaven") are made in convents and monasteries across Spain. Choose from marzipan sweets from Seville, Benedictine preserves or Cistercian cookies.

Caj Chai

MAP P.34, POCKET MAP D12.
C/Sant Domènec del Call 12 Ⓜ Liceu Ⓣ 933 019 592, Ⓦ cajchai.com. Daily 10.30am–10pm.

This refined backstreet boudoir offers a menu of painstakingly prepared teas, from Moroccan mint to organic Nepalese oolong, plus brownies, baklava and sandwiches.

Restaurants and tapas bars

Cafè de l'Acadèmia

MAP P.34, POCKET MAP E13.
C/Lledó 1 Ⓜ Jaume I Ⓣ 933 198 253. Mon–Fri 1.30–4pm & 8.30–11.30pm; closed 2 weeks in Aug.

Bar Celta Pulperia

Great for a date or a lazy lunch, with creative Catalan dishes served in a romantic stone-flagged restaurant or outside in the medieval square. Expect classy grills, fresh fish, rice dishes, seasonal game and a taste of local favourites like salt cod, wild mushrooms or grilled veg. Prices are pretty reasonable (mains €11–18) and it's always busy, so dinner reservations are essential. A no-choice *menú del dia* is a bargain for the quality (and it's even cheaper eaten at the bar).

Bar Celta Pulperia

MAP P.34, POCKET MAP D14.
C/de la Mercè 16 Ⓜ Drassanes Ⓣ 933 150 006, Ⓦ barcelta.com. Tue–Sun noon–midnight.
This brightly lit, no-nonsense Galician tapas bar specializes in dishes like *pop gallego* (octopus) and fried green *pimientos* (peppers), washed down with heady regional wine (dishes €3–16). Eat at the U-shaped bar or at tables in the back room, and while it's not one for a long, lazy meal, it's just right to kick off a bout of bar-hopping. There is a spinoff on C/Princesa 50.

Bodega La Plata

MAP P.34, POCKET MAP E14.
C/de la Mercè 28 Ⓜ Drassanes Ⓣ 933 151 009. Mon–Sat 10am–3.15pm & 6.15–11pm.
A classic taste of the Old Town, with a marble tapas counter open to the street (anchovies are the speciality) and dirt-cheap wine straight from the barrel.

Ginger

MAP P.34, POCKET MAP E13.
C/Palma Sant Just 1 Ⓜ Jaume I Ⓣ 933 105 309, Ⓦ ginger.cat. Tue–Thu 6.30pm–2.30am, Fri & Sat 6.30pm–3am; closed 2 weeks in Aug.
Cocktails and fancy tapas in a slickly updated 1970s-style setting. It's a world away from *patatas bravas* and battered squid – think roast duck vinaigrette, stuffed aubergine rolls, tuna tartare and vegetarian satay for around €6.50–9 a pop.

Koy Shunka

MAP P.34, POCKET MAP E12.
C/Copons 7 Ⓜ Jaume I Ⓣ 934 127 939, Ⓦ koyshunka.com. Tue–Sun 1.30–3pm & 8.30–10.30pm.
The city's hottest Japanese chef, Hideki Matsuhisa, has branched out from his original *Shunka* restaurant with a rather more hip, nearby sister joint, where peerless sushi and dishes like grilled Wagyu beef and roast black cod await. With pricey rice rolls, mains around €20, and €82 and €118 tasting menus, it's a more rarefied experience all round, and you'll definitely need to book.

Bar del Pi

MAP P.34, POCKET MAP D12.
Pl. Sant Josep Oriol 1 Ⓜ Liceu Ⓣ 933 022 123. Tue–Fri 9am–11pm, Sat 10.30am–11pm, Sun 10am–10pm.
Best known for its terrace tables on one of Barcelona's prettiest squares. Linger over drinks and sandwiches as the Old Town reveals its charms, especially during the weekend artists' market.

Pla

MAP P.34, POCKET MAP E13.
C/Bellafilla 5 Ⓜ Jaume I ☎ 934 126 552, Ⓦ restaurantpla.cat. Mon–Fri 6–11.30pm, Sat & Sun 1.30–4pm, 6–11.30pm, Fri & Sat 7pm–midnight.

Cosy, candlelit and romantic, *Pla* is usually filled with twinkle-eyed couples. Expect to spend around €40 per person in return for creative international dishes. Sister restaurant *Bar del Pla* (C/Montcada 2) is a top choice for traditional tapas with subtle creative twists.

Rasoterra

MAP P.34, POCKET MAP D13.
C/Palau 5 Ⓜ Jaume I ☎ 933 186 926, Ⓦ rasoterra.cat. Wed–Sun 1–4pm & 7–11pm,

Plant based diet is definitely not boring and this lovely bistro has some ingenious recipes to prove it. The menu is intriguing and the vegan and vegetarian options are far from routine. Rasoterra also supports the slow food movement, so if you're looking for a place to just chill and take a break while enjoying some exciting and new tastes - this is where you need to go.

Sensi Tapas

MAP P.34, POCKET MAP D14.
C/Ample 26 Ⓜ Jaume I ☎ 932 956 588, Ⓦ sensi.es. Daily 6.30–11.45pm.

Best to make reservations as this intimate space in stone and dark wood and splashes of red quickly fills with diners looking for tapas with an exotic spin. There are impeccably executed classics like buttery *patatas bravas*, but the stars of the show, such as the tender Iberian pork *tataki*, take their cues from further afield (€5–12).

Taller de Tapas

MAP P.34, POCKET MAP D12.
Pl. Sant Josep Oriol 9 Ⓜ Liceu ☎ 933 018 020, Ⓦ tallerdetapas.com. Sun–Thu 9pm–midnight, Fri & Sat 9pm–1am.

The fashionable "tapas workshop" sucks in tourists with its pretty location by the church of Santa María del Pi. There's a year-round outdoor terrace, while the open kitchen turns out reliable, market-fresh dishes, with fish a speciality at dinner, from grilled langoustine to seared tuna (most tapas €4–12). There are other branches around town (including one at C/Argenteria 51 in the Born), though this was the first.

Venus Delicatessen

MAP P.34, POCKET MAP D13.
C/d'Avinyó 25 Ⓜ Liceu ☎ 936 760 315. Mon–Fri 8.30am–1pm, Sat & Sun 9.30am–1pm

Not a deli, despite the name, but it's a handy place serving Mediterranean bistro cuisine throughout the day and night. It's also good for vegetarians – dishes like lasagne, couscous, moussaka and salads are mostly meat-free and cost around €7–10.

Bar del Pi

Bars

L'Ascensor

MAP P.34, POCKET MAP E13.
C/Bellafila 3 Ⓜ Jaume I Ⓣ 933 185 347. Sun–Thu 6pm–2.30am, Fri–Sat 6pm–3am.
Sliding antique wooden elevator doors signal the entrance to "The Lift", but it's no theme bar – just an easy-going local hangout, great for a late-night drink.

Collage

MAP P.34, POCKET MAP E14.
C/Consellers 4 Ⓜ Jaume I Ⓣ 931 793 785, Ⓦ collagecocktailbar.com. Daily 7pm–2.30am.
A stylish vintage place with a relaxed, pleasant atmosphere. The knowledgeable bartenders will mix you a creative drink and offer insightful advice on mixing. If that piques your interest you can even go to their cocktail making class for a well spent afternoon.

Glaciar

MAP P.34, POCKET MAP C13.
Pl. Reial 3 Ⓜ Liceu Ⓣ 933 021 163. Sun–Thu 8.30pm–2.30am, Fri & Sat 8.30pm–3am.
At this traditional Barcelona meeting point the terrace seating is packed most sunny evenings and at weekends, and the comings and goings in the Old Town's funkiest square are half the entertainment.

Milk

Milk

MAP P.34, POCKET MAP E14.
C/d'en Gignàs 21 Ⓜ Jaume I Ⓣ 932 680 922, Ⓦ milkbarcelona.com. Sun–Thu 9am–2am, Fri & Sat 9–2.30am.
Irish-owned bar and bistro that's carved a real niche as a welcoming neighbourhood hangout. Decor, they say, is that of a "millionaire's drawing room", with its sofas, cushions and antique chandeliers. Get there early for the famously relaxed brunch (daily 9am–4.30pm), or there's dinner and cocktails every night to a funky soundtrack.

Pipa Club

MAP P.34, POCKET MAP C13.
Pl. Reial 3 Ⓜ Liceu Ⓣ 933 024 732, Ⓦ bpipaclub.com. Daily 10pm–2am.
Historically a pipe-smoker's haunt, it's a wood-panelled, jazzy, late-night kind of place – ring the bell to be let in and make your way up the stairs.

Schilling

MAP P.34, POCKET MAP D13.
C/de Ferran 23 Ⓜ Liceu Ⓣ 933 176 787, Ⓦ cafeschilling.com. Daily 10am–2.30am.
Something of a haven on this heavily touristed drag, *Schilling* has a certain European "grand-café" style, with its high ceilings, big windows and upmarket feel. It has a loyal gay following, but it's a mixed, chilled place to meet friends, grab a *copa* and move on.

Zim

MAP P.34, POCKET MAP E13.
C/Daguería 20 Ⓜ Jaume I. Mon–Sat 6–11pm; closed Aug.
The owner of the adjacent Formatgeria La Seu (cheese shop) offers up this tiny, hole-in-the-wall

tasting bar for selected wines from boutique producers. It can be a real squeeze, and hours are somewhat flexible, but for a reviving glass or two accompanied by farmhouse cheese, cured meat and artisan-made bread, you can't beat it.

Clubs

Harlem Jazz Club

MAP P.34, POCKET MAP D13. C/Comtessa de Sobradiel 8 Ⓜ Jaume I Ⓣ 933 100 755, Ⓦ harlemjazzclub.es. Closed Aug.

For many years *the* hot place for jazz, where every style gets an airing, from African and Gypsy to flamenco and fusion. Live music Tue–Sun at 10.30pm and midnight (weekends 11.30pm & 2am). Entry €5–10, depending on the night and the act.

Jamboree

MAP P.34, POCKET MAP C13. Pl. Reial 17 Ⓜ Liceu Ⓣ 933 191 789, Ⓦ masimas.com.

They don't get the big jazz names here that they used to, but the nightly gigs (at 8pm & 10pm; from €12) still pull in the crowds, while the wild Monday-night WTF jazz, funk and hip-hop jam session (from 8pm; €5) is a city fixture. Stay on for the club, which kicks in after midnight (entry €10) and you get funky sounds and retro pop, rock and disco until 5am.

La Macarena

MAP P.34, POCKET MAP D14. C/Nou de Sant Francesc 5 Ⓜ Drassanes Ⓦ macarenaclub.com. Mon–Thu & Sun midnight–5am, Fri & Sat midnight–6am.

Once a place where flamenco tunes were offered up to La Macarena, the Virgin of Seville – now, a heaving temple to all things electro. Entry free until around 1am, then from €5.

Sidecar

MAP P.34, POCKET MAP D13. Pl. Reial 7 Ⓜ Liceu Ⓣ 933 177 666,

Tarantos

Ⓦ sidecar.es. Thu 7pm–5am, Fri & Sat 7pm–6am.

Hip music club – pronounced "See-day-car" – with gigs (usually at 10.30pm) and DJs (from 12.30am) that champion rock, indie, roots and fusion acts, so a good place to check out the latest Catalan hip-hop, rumba and flamenco sounds. Entry €7–10, though some gigs up to €20.

Tarantos

MAP P.34, POCKET MAP C13. PL. REIAL 17 Ⓜ LICEU Ⓣ 933 191 789, Ⓦ masimas.com.

Jamboree's sister club is the place for short, exuberant flamenco tasters, where young singers, dancers and guitarists perform nightly at 8.30pm, 9.30pm & 10.30pm (with extra sessions in July and August). Purists are a bit sniffy, but it's a great introduction to the scene. Entry €10.

Port Vell and Barceloneta

Barcelona has an urban waterfront that merges seamlessly with the Old Town, providing an easy escape from the claustrophobic medieval streets. The harbour at the bottom of the Ramblas has been thoroughly overhauled in recent years and Port Vell (Old Port), as it's now known, presents a series of heavyweight tourist attractions, from sightseeing boats and maritime museum to the aquarium. By way of contrast, Barceloneta – the wedge of land to the east, backing the marina – retains its eighteenth-century character, and the former fishing quarter is still the most popular place to come and eat paella, fish and seafood. Metro Drassanes, at the bottom of the Ramblas, is the best starting point for Port Vell; Barceloneta has its own metro station.

Mirador de Colóm

MAP P.46, POCKET MAP C15.
Pl. Portal de la Pau Ⓜ Drassanes ⓣ 933 025 224. Daily: March–Sept 8.30am–8.30pm; Oct–Feb 8.30am–7.30pm. €4.

The monument at the foot of the Ramblas commemorates the visit made by Christopher Columbus in June 1493, when the navigator received a royal welcome in Barcelona. Columbus tops a grandiose iron column, 52m high, guarded by lions, and you can ride the lift up to the panoramic viewing platform at Columbus's feet. Meanwhile, from the quayside in front of the Columbus monument, Las Golondrinas sightseeing boats depart on regular trips throughout the year around the inner harbour.

Mirador de Colóm

Museu Marítim

MAP P.46, POCKET MAP B14/15.
Av. de les Drassanes Ⓜ Drassanes ⓣ 933 429 920, Ⓦ mmb.cat. Daily 10am–8pm. €10, free Sun after 3pm.

Barcelona's medieval shipyards, or Drassanes, were in continuous use – fitting and arming Catalunya's war fleet or trading vessels – until well into the eighteenth century. Once waterside, they now lie 100m back from the Mediterranean thanks to the city's ever-expanding concrete sprawl. The stone-vaulted buildings make a fitting home for the excellent Maritime Museum, which has brand-new facilities throughout thanks to a recent large-scale renovation project. The courtyard café is a particularly pleasant spot to pass a quiet hour or two. There's a regularly

Museu Marítim

changing schedule of up to eleven temporary exhibitions, plus a range of activities, such as navigation and stargazing, that can be booked through the website. The museum entry ticket also includes a short tour of the *Santa Eulàlia*, a vintage three-masted schooner moored down on the Moll de la Fusta harbourside (closed Mon, check hours at the museum).

L'Aquàrium

MAP P.46, POCKET MAP G8–H8.
Moll d'Espanya Ⓜ Drassanes ⓣ 932 217 474, ⓦ aquariumbcn.com. Daily: July & Aug 10am–9.30pm; June & Sept 10am–9pm; Jan–March & Nov, Dec 10am–7.30pm (8pm weekends), Apr–May & Oct 10am–8pm (8.30 weekends). €20.
Port Vell's high-profile aquarium drags in families and school parties throughout the year to see "a magical world, full of mystery". Or, to be more precise, to see 11,000 fish and sea creatures in 35 themed tanks representing underwater caves, tropical reefs and other maritime habitats. It's vastly overpriced, and despite the claims of excellence it offers few new experiences, save perhaps the 80-metre-long walk-through underwater tunnel, which brings you face to face with gliding rays and cruising sharks.

Maremàgnum

MAP P.46, POCKET MAP G8.
Moll d'Espanya Ⓜ Drassanes. Daily 10am–10pm.
From near the Columbus statue, the wooden Rambla de Mar swing-bridge strides across the harbour to the Maremàgnum mall and leisure centre on Moll d'Espanya. It's a typically bold piece of Catalan design, its soaring glass lines tempered by the undulating wooden walkways that provide scintillating views back across the harbour to the city. Inside there are two floors of gift shops and boutiques, plus a range of cafés and fast-food outlets.

Stroll further along the Moll d'Espanya and you'll find a huge wooden scale model of *Ictineo II*, the world's first real functioning submarine. It was built in 1862 by luckless local inventor Narcis Monturiol I Estarriol, whose company went bankrupt before he could benefit from his work of engineering genius.

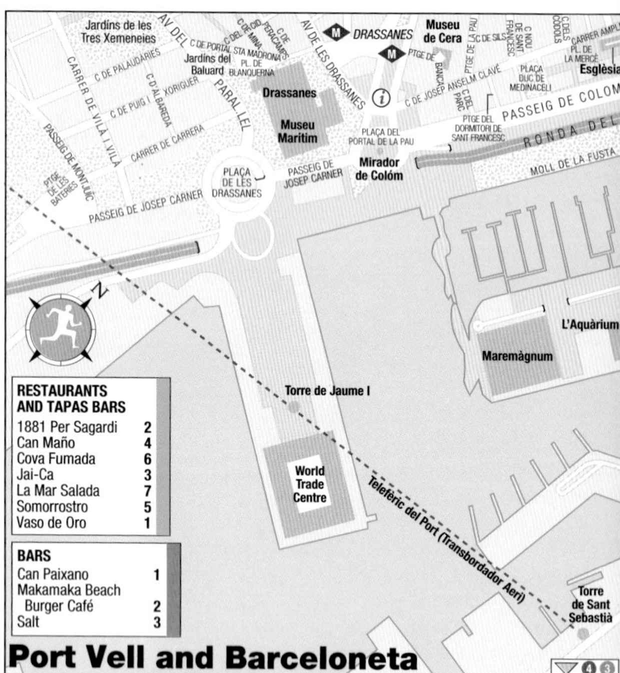

Museu d'Història de Catalunya

MAP P.46, POCKET MAP F15.
Palau de Mar, Pl. de Pau Vila 3
Ⓜ Barceloneta Ⓣ 932 254 700, Ⓦ mhcat.net. Tue–Sat 10am–7pm (Wed until 8pm), Sun and hols 10am–2.30pm. €4.50; last Tue of month free.

A dramatic harbourside warehouse conversion contains a museum tracing the history of Catalunya from the Stone Age to the present day. Poke around the interior of a Roman grain ship or compare the rival nineteenth-century architectural plans for the Eixample. The *1881 Per Sagardi* Basque restaurant on the top floor – no museum ticket needed – boasts glorious views over the port from its terrace, a top spot for sunset cocktails.

Barceloneta

MAP P.46, POCKET MAP H8–J7.
Ⓜ Barceloneta.

There's no finer place for lunch on a sunny day than Barceloneta, an

The cross-harbour cable car

The most thrilling ride in the city is across the harbour on the Telefèric del Port (Transbordador Aeri), or cable car, which sweeps from the Sant Sebastià tower at the foot of Barceloneta to Montjuïc. Departures are every 15min (daily: March–May, Sept & Oct 10.30am–7pm; June–Aug 10.30am–8pm; Nov–Feb 11am–5.30pm; €11 one way, €16.50 return), but expect queues in summer and at weekends as the cars only carry about twenty people at a time.

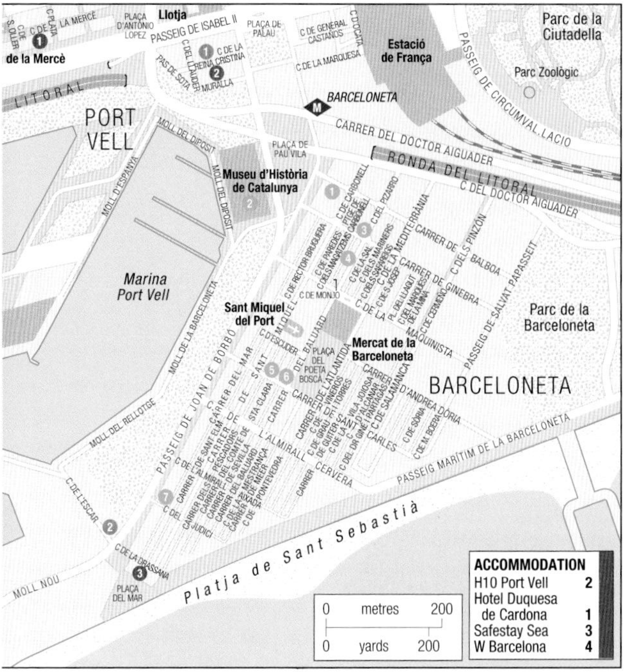

ACCOMMODATION

H10 Port Vell	2
Hotel Duquesa de Cardona	1
Safestay Sea	3
W Barcelona	4

eighteenth-century neighbourhood of tightly packed, gridded streets with bustling harbour on one side and sandy beach on the other. There's a local market, the **Mercat de la Barceloneta** (Mon–Thu & Sat 7am–3pm, Fri 7am–8pm), with a couple of excellent bars and restaurants, while Barceloneta's famous seafood restaurants are found across the neighbourhood, but most characteristically lined along the harbourside Passeig Joan de Borbó.

Platja de Sant Sebastià

MAP P.46, POCKET MAP G9–K8.

Ⓜ Barceloneta.

Barceloneta's beach – the first in a series of sandy city beaches – curves from the flanks of the neighbourhood, past the swimming pools of the Club Natació and out to the landmark sail-shaped *W Barcelona* hotel. Closer to the Barceloneta end there are beach bars, outdoor cafés and sculptures, while a double row of palms backs the esplanade that runs above the sands as far as the Port Olímpic (a 15min walk). Bladers, skaters, joggers and cyclists have one of the Med's best views for company.

Cross-harbour cable car

Restaurants and tapas bars

1881 Per Sagardi

MAP P.46, POCKET MAP F15.
Pl. de Pau Vila 3 Ⓜ Barceloneta Ⓣ 932 210 050, Ⓦ sagardi.com. Daily 1–midnight; terrace daily 10am–midnight (summer 2am).

Head to the roof of the waterfront Museu d'Història de Catalunya and you'll be met with the smell of wood smoke. Main courses at this grill-led restaurant are about €22–30 each but it's worth paying just to sit on the terrace with a Martini and watch the yachts sailing in and out of the harbour.

Can Maño

MAP P.46, POCKET MAP F15.
C/Baluard 12 Ⓜ Barceloneta Ⓣ 933 193 082. Mon 8–11pm, Tue–Fri 8.30am–4pm & 8–11pm, Sat 8.30am–4pm; closed Aug.

There's rarely a tourist in sight in this classic old-fashioned diner. Your choice is fried or grilled fish, supplemented by a few daily seafood specials and basic meat dishes. It's an authentic, no-frills experience that's likely to cost you less than €15 a head.

Cova Fumada

Cova Fumada

MAP P.46, POCKET MAP H8.
C/Baluard 56 Ⓜ Barceloneta Ⓣ 932 214 061. Mon–Wed 9am–3.30pm, Thu & Fri 9am–3.30pm & 6–8.20pm, Sat 9am–1.30pm; closed Aug.

Behind brown wooden doors on the market square (there's no sign) is this rough-and-ready tavern with battered marble tables and antique barrels. That it's always packed is a testament to the quality of the market-fresh tapas (€2–10), from the griddled prawns to the *bomba* (spicy potato meatball).

Jai-Ca

MAP P.46, POCKET MAP F15.
C/Ginebra 9 & 13 Ⓜ Barceloneta Ⓣ 932 683 265. No.9 & No.13 Mon–Thu & Sun 9am–midnight, Fri & Sat 9am–0.30am.

A great choice for tapas (dishes up to €10), with bundles of razor clams, stuffed mussels, crisp baby squid and other seafood platters.

La Mar Salada

MAP P.46, POCKET MAP H8.
Pg. de Joan de Borbó 58 Ⓜ Barceloneta Ⓣ 932 212 127, Ⓦ lamarsalada.cat. Mon–Fri 1–4pm & 8–11pm, Sat & Sun 1–11pm.

While many of the restaurants in Barceloneta have let standards slip, *La Mar Salada* has instead raised the bar. Buying freshly-landed fish straight from the dock directly opposite, the chefs offer creative seafood dishes at bargain prices. The €17.50 lunchtime set menu is superb value, and there's even a sunny terrace to eat it on.

Somorrostro

MAP P.46, POCKET MAP H8.
C/Sant Carles 11 Ⓜ Barceloneta Ⓣ 932 250 010, Ⓦ restaurantesomorrostro.com. Daily 1pm–midnight.

Creative "boat-to-table" Mediterranean cuisine with a mission: preserving and promoting the livelihood and traditions of this fishing community. The three-course evening menu (€17; available to the first 15 customers) is great value, and it's good fun watching the open kitchen in action.

Vaso de Oro

MAP P.46, POCKET MAP F15.
C/Balboa 6 Ⓜ Barceloneta Ⓣ 933 193 098. Ⓦ www.vasodeoro.com. Daily 11am–midnight; closed 3 weeks in Aug.

An old favourite for stand-up tapas (€4–15) – there's no menu, but order the *patatas bravas*, some thick slices of fried sausage, grilled shellfish and a dollop of tuna salad and you've touched all the bases. Unusually, you'll find that they also brew their own beer; light and dark.

Bars

Can Paixano

MAP P.46, POCKET MAP E14.
C/de la Reina Cristina 7 Ⓜ Barceloneta Ⓣ 933 100 839, Ⓦ canpaixano.com. Mon–Sat 9am–10.30pm; closed 2 weeks in Aug.

A must on everyone's itinerary is this counter-only joint where the drink of choice – all right, the only drink – is cava by the glass or bottle. It's popular, so you may have to fight your way in.

Makamaka Beach Burger Café

MAP P.46, POCKET MAP H8.
Pg. de Joan de Borbó 76 Ⓜ Barceloneta Ⓣ 932 213 520. Ⓦ makamaka.es. Mon–Thu & Sun 11–2.30am, Fri & Sat 11–3am.

Can Paixano

You really can't ask for more: creative cocktails and some of the city's finest burgers served on a large, beachside *terrassa*. Laidback, late night and lots of fun; it's Hawaii-meets-Barcelona.

Salt Beach Club

MAP P.46.
Pg. del Mare Nostrum 19-21 Ⓜ Barceloneta Ⓣ 932 952 819. Ⓦ saltbeachclub.com. Apr Sun-Thu 1pm–5pm, Fri & Sat 1pm–midnight, May Mon–Sun 1pm–1am.

More famous for their - slightly pricey - drinks than their food. The beachfront bar with a beautiful ocean view and seats right in the sand make for a pleasant place to have a drink on a cloudless evening.

It takes two

You want a seafood paella or an *arròs negre* (black rice with squid ink), or maybe a garlicky *fideuà* (noodles with seafood) – of course you do. Problem is, you're on your own and virtually every restaurant that offers these classic Barcelona dishes does so for a minimum of two people (often you don't find out until you examine the menu's small print). Solution? Ask the waiter upfront, as sometimes the kitchen will oblige single diners, or look for the dishes on a *menú del dia* (especially on Thu, traditionally rice day), when there should be no minimum. Probably best not to grab a stranger off the street to share a paella, however desperate you are.

El Raval

The Old Town area west of the Ramblas is known as El Raval (from the Arabic word for suburb), and has always formed a world apart from the nobler Gothic quarter. Traditionally a red-light area, and once notorious for its sleazy Barri Xinès (China Town), it still has some very seedy corners (particularly south of Carrer de Sant Pau), though it's changing rapidly, notably in the "upper Raval" around Barcelona's contemporary art museum, MACBA. Cutting-edge galleries, designer restaurants and fashionable bars are all part of the scene these days, while an arty, affluent crowd rubs shoulders with the area's Asian and North African immigrants and the older, traditional residents. Metros Catalunya, Liceu, Drassanes and Paral.lel serve the neighbourhood.

Museu d'Art Contemporani de Barcelona (MACBA)

MAP P.54, POCKET MAP B10/11–C10/11. Pl. dels Àngels 1 Ⓜ Catalunya Ⓣ 934 120 810, Ⓦ macba.cat. Mon & Wed–Fri 11am–8pm, Sat 10am–8pm, Sun & hols 10am–3pm, September 10am–8pm; €10.

The iconic contemporary art museum – with a stark main facade constructed entirely of glass – anchors the regenerated upper Raval. The collection represents the main movements in art since 1945, mainly (but not exclusively) in Catalunya and Spain, and depending on the changing exhibitions you may catch works by major names such as Joan Miró, Antoni Tàpies or Eduardo Chillida. Joan Brossa, leading light

Museu d'Art Contemporani de Barcelona

of the Catalan Dau al Set group of the 1950s, also has work here. There are free guided tours of the permanent collection (tour times vary; check website for details), and a good museum shop.

Filmoteca de Catalunya

MAP P.54, POCKET MAP B13. Pl. Salvador Seguí 1–9 Ⓜ Liceu Ⓦ filmoteca.cat. Cinema Tue–Fri 5–10pm, Sat & Sun 4.30–10pm. Exhibition Hall Tue–Sun 4–9pm. €4.

The Josep Lluís Mateo-designed Filmoteca de Catalunya marks yet another step in the government's push to revitalize El Raval. Opened in early 2012, the building has two below-ground cinemas, as well as a film library, a bookshop and spaces for permanent and temporary cinema-related exhibitions. All the films are shown in their original language with Spanish or Catalan subtitles.

Centre de Cultura Contemporània de Barcelona (CCCB)

MAP P.54, POCKET MAP B10–C10. C/Montalegre 5 Ⓜ Catalunya Ⓣ 933 064 100, Ⓦ cccb.org. Tue–Sun 11am–8pm. €6, free Sun after 3pm.

There's a wide range of city-related exhibitions on show at the contemporary culture centre (ranging from photography to architecture), as well as a varied cinema, concert and festival programme. The imaginatively restored building was once an infamous workhouse and asylum, and the main courtyard still retains its old tile panels and presiding statue of patron saint, Sant Jordi. At the back, the *C3* café-bar makes the most of its *terrassa* overlooking the modern square joining the CCCB to MACBA.

CCCB

Plaça de Vicenç Martorell

MAP P.54, POCKET MAP C11. Ⓜ Catalunya.

The Raval's nicest traffic-free square lies just a few minutes' walk from MACBA. The small playground here is well used by local families, and the arcaded square features a first-rate café, the *Kasparo* – a real find if you're looking for a break from sightseeing. Meanwhile, around the corner are several other cafés, while the narrow **Carrer del Bonsuccés**, **Carrer Sitges** and **Carrer dels Tallers** house a concentrated selection of the city's best independent music stores, and urban- and streetwear shops.

The beat from the street

The Barcelona sound – *mestiza* – is a cross-cultural musical fusion whose heartland is the immigrant melting-pot of the Raval. Parisian-born Barcelona resident Manu Chao kick-started the whole genre, but check out the Carrer dels Tallers music stores for the other flag-bearers – Cheb Balowski (Algerian–Catalan fusion), Ojos de Brujo (Catalan flamenco and rumba), GoLem System (dub/reggae) and Macaco (rumba, raga, hip-hop).

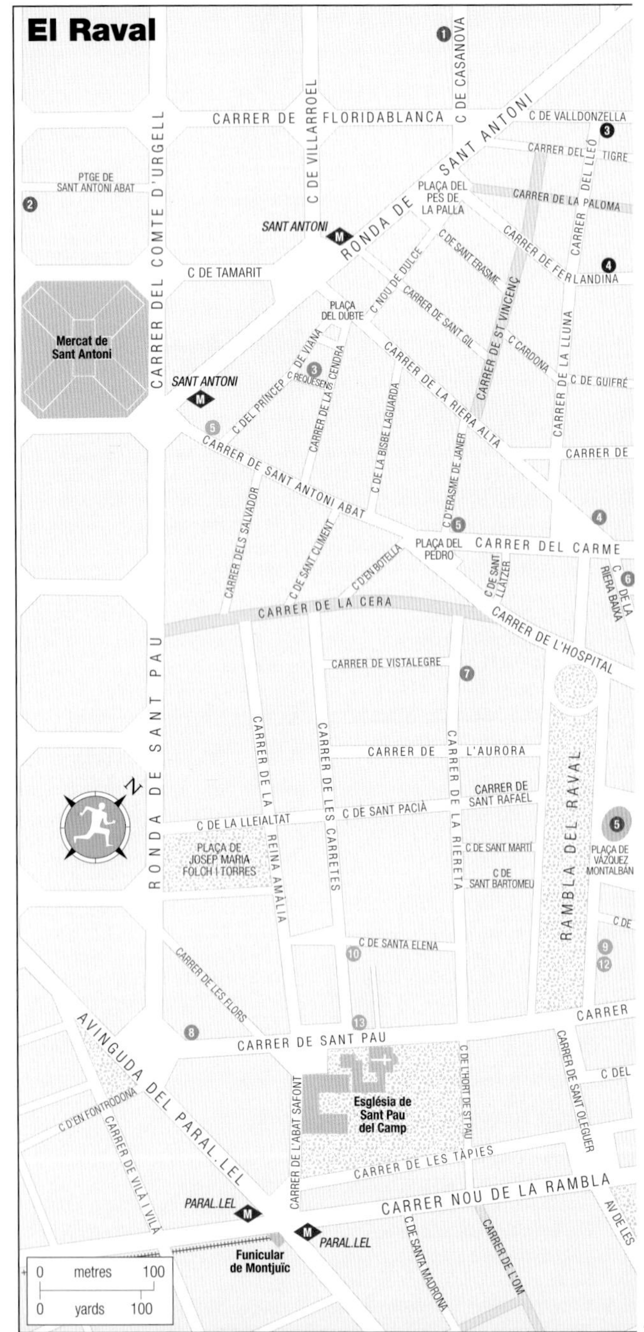

El Raval
CARRER DE FLORIDABLANCA
C DE CASANOVA
C DE VILLARROEL
CARRER DEL COMTE D'URGELL
PTGE DE SANT ANTONI ABAT
RONDA DE SANT ANTONI
C DE VALLDONZELLA
CARRER DEL TIGRE
CARRER DEL LLEÓ
PLAÇA DEL PES DE LA PALLA
CARRER DE LA PALOMA
SANT ANTONI
C DE TAMARIT
CARRER DE FERLANDINA
C DE SANT ERASME
C NOU DE DULCE
CARRER DE SANT GIL
CARRER DE ST VINCENÇ
PLAÇA DEL DUBTE
Mercat de Sant Antoni
C DE VIANA
C REQUESENS
C DEL PRÍNCEP
CARRER DE LA CENDRA
C CARDONA
CARRER DE LA LLUNA
CARRER DE LA RIERA ALTA
C DE GUIFRÉ
C DE LA BISBE LAGUARDA
CARRER DE SANT ANTONI ABAT
CARRER DE
C D'ERASME DE JANER
CARRER DELS SALVADOR
C DE SANT CLIMENT
C D'EN BOTELLA
PLAÇA DEL PEDRO
CARRER DEL CARME
C DE SANT LLÀTZER
C DE LA RIERA BAIXA
CARRER DE LA CERA
CARRER DE L'HOSPITAL
CARRER DE VISTALEGRE
RONDA DE SANT PAU
CARRER DE LA REINA AMÀLIA
CARRER DE LES CARRETES
CARRER DE LA RIERETA
CARRER DE L'AURORA
CARRER DE SANT RAFAEL
C DE SANT PACIÀ
C DE LA LLEIALTAT
RAMBLA DEL RAVAL
PLAÇA DE JOSEP MARIA FOLCH I TORRES
C DE SANT MARTÍ
C DE SANT BARTOMEU
PLAÇA DE VÁZQUEZ MONTALBÁN
C DE
C DE SANTA ELENA
CARRER DE LES FLORS
CARRER
CARRER DE SANT PAU
AVINGUDA DEL PARAL.LEL
C DE L'HORT DE ST PAU
CARRER DE SANT OLEGUER
C DEL
C D'EN FONTRODONA
CARRER DE VILÀ I VILÀ
CARRER DE L'ABAT SAFONT
Església de Sant Pau del Camp
CARRER DE LES TÀPIES
CARRER NOU DE LA RAMBLA
AV DE LES
PARAL.LEL
C DE SANTA MADRONA
CARRER DE L'OM
Funicular de Montjuïc
0 metres 100
0 yards 100

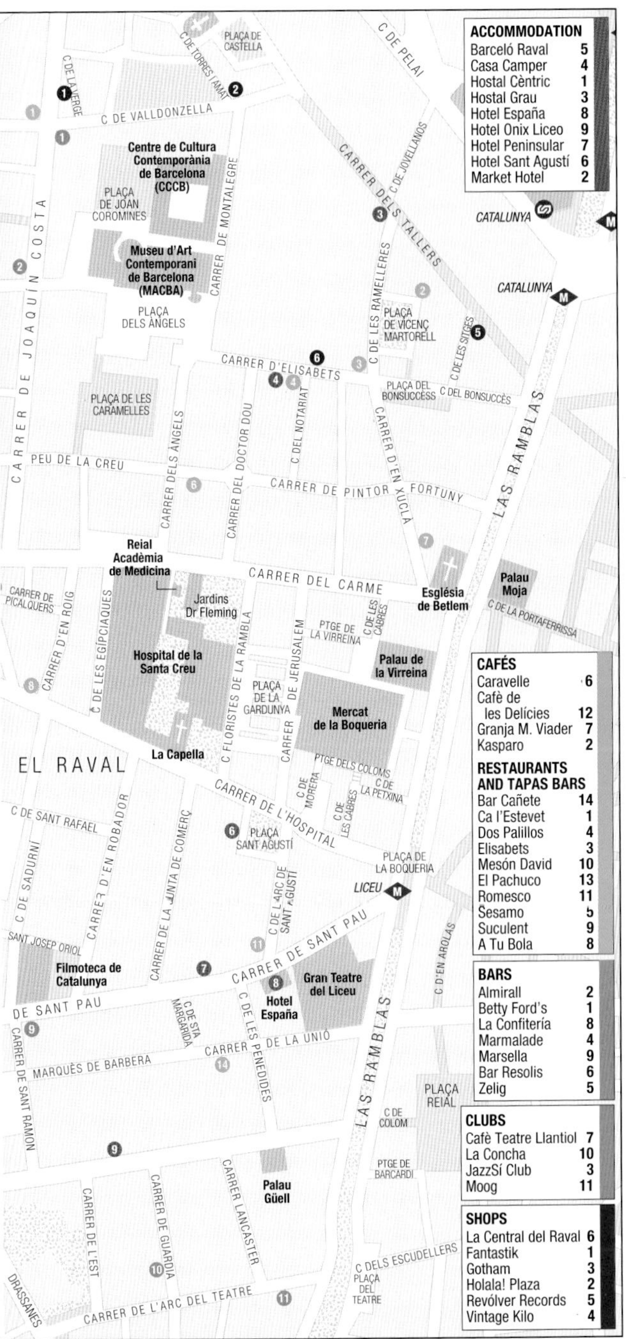

ACCOMMODATION
Barceló Raval 5
Casa Camper 4
Hostal Cèntric 1
Hostal Grau 3
Hotel España 8
Hotel Onix Liceo 9
Hotel Peninsular 7
Hotel Sant Agustí 6
Market Hotel 2
CAFÉS
Caravelle 6
Cafè de les Delícies 12
Granja M. Viader 7
Kasparo 2
RESTAURANTS AND TAPAS BARS
Bar Cañete 14
Ca l'Estevet 1
Dos Palillos 4
Elisabets 3
Mesón David 10
El Pachuco 13
Romesco 11
Sésamo 5
Suculent 9
A Tu Bola 8
BARS
Almirall 2
Betty Ford's 1
La Confitería 8
Marmalade 4
Marsella 9
Bar Resolis 6
Zelig 5
CLUBS
Cafè Teatre Llantiol 7
La Concha 10
JazzSí Club 3
Moog 11
SHOPS
La Central del Raval 6
Fantastik 1
Gotham 3
Holala! Plaza 2
Revólver Records 5
Vintage Kilo 4
Centre de Cultura Contemporània de Barcelona (CCCB)
Museu d'Art Contemporani de Barcelona (MACBA)
Reial Acadèmia de Medicina
Jardins Dr Fleming
Hospital de la Santa Creu
La Capella
Església de Betlem
Palau Moja
Palau de la Virreina
Mercat de la Boqueria
Filmoteca de Catalunya
Gran Teatre del Liceu
Hotel España
Palau Güell
EL RAVAL
PLAÇA DE CASTELLA
PLAÇA DE JOAN COROMINES
PLAÇA DELS ÀNGELS
PLAÇA DE LES CARAMELLES
PLAÇA DE VICENÇ MARTORELL
PLAÇA DEL BONSUCCÉS
PLAÇA DE LA GARDUNYA
PLAÇA SANT AGUSTÍ
PLAÇA DE LA BOQUERIA
PLAÇA REIAL
PLAÇA DEL TEATRE
C DE PELAI
C DE VALLDONZELLA
C DE TORRES I AMAT
C DE LA VERGE
CARRER DE JOAQUÍN COSTA
CARRER DE MONTALEGRE
CARRER DELS TALLERS
C DE JOVELLANOS
C DE LES RAMELLERES
C DE LES SITGES
CARRER D'ELISABETS
C DEL BONSUCCÉS
C DEL NOTARIAT
CARRER D'EN XUCLÀ
PEU DE LA CREU
CARRER DELS ÀNGELS
CARRER DEL DOCTOR DOU
CARRER DE PINTOR FORTUNY
LAS RAMBLAS
CARRER DEL CARME
CARRER DE PICALQUERS
CARRER D'EN ROIG
C DE LES EGÍPCIAQUES
C FLORISTES DE LA RAMBLA
CARRER DE JERUSALEM
PTGE DE LA VIRREINA
C DE LES CABRES
C DE LA PORTAFERRISSA
PTGE DELS COLOMS
C DE MORERA
C DE LA PETXINA
CARRER DE L'HOSPITAL
C DE SANT RAFAEL
C DE SADURNÍ
CARRER D'EN ROBADOR
CARRER DE LA JUNTA DE COMERÇ
C DE L'ARC DE SANT AGUSTÍ
CARRER DE SANT PAU
SANT JOSEP ORIOL
C DE STA MARGARIDA
C DE LES PENEDIDES
CARRER DE LA UNIÓ
MARQUÈS DE BARBERA
CARRER DE SANT RAMON
C D'EN AROLAS
C DE COLOM
PTGE DE BARCARDI
CARRER DE L'EST
CARRER DE GUARDIA
CARRER LANCASTER
C DELS ESCUDELLERS
CARRER DE L'ARC DEL TEATRE
DRASSANES
CATALUNYA
LICEU

El Gato del Raval

Hospital de la Santa Creu

MAP P.54, POCKET MAP B12–C12. Entrances on C/del Carme and C/ de l'Hospital Ⓜ Liceu ⓣ 935 537 801, Ⓦ santpaubarcelona.org. Mon–Sat 9.30am–6.30pm, Sun 9.30am–2.30pm (Nov–March Mon–Sat 9.30am–4.30pm, Sun 9.30am–2.30pm). €14, guided tour daily 10.30am. €19, first Sun of the month free.

The neighbourhood's most historic relic is the Gothic hospital complex founded in 1402. After the hospital shifted location in 1930, the buildings were subsequently converted to cultural and educational use (including the Catalan national library), and visitors and students now wander freely through the charming medieval cloistered garden. Inside the C/del Carme entrance (on the right) you can see some superb seventeenth-century decorative tiles, while opposite is a remarkable eighteenth-century anatomical theatre inside the **Reial Acadèmia de Medicina** (open Wed only 10am–noon; free; ring the bell). The hospital's former chapel, **La Capella** (entered separately from C/de l'Hospital), is an exhibition space for new contemporary artists.

Rambla del Raval

MAP P.54, POCKET MAP B12–13. Ⓜ Liceu.

The most obvious manifestation of the changing character of El Raval is the palm-lined boulevard that was gouged through former tenements and alleys, providing a huge pedestrianized space between C/de l'Hospital and C/de Sant Pau. The *rambla* has a distinct character all of its own, mixing kebab joints, phone shops and grocery stores with an increasing number of fashionable cafés and bars. Signature building, halfway down, is the glow-in-the-dark, designer *Barceló Raval* hotel, while kids find it hard to resist a clamber on the bulbous cat sculpture. A weekend street market (selling everything from samosas to hammocks) adds a bit more character.

Just off the top of the *rambla*, **Carrer de la Riera Baixa** is at the centre of the city's second-hand and

High-society hotel

Some of the most influential names in Catalan *modernista* design came together to transform the dowdy nineteenth-century **Hotel España** (MAP P.54, POCKET MAP C13; C/de Sant Pau 9–11; Ⓦ www.hotelespanya.com) into one of the city's most lavish addresses. With a gloriously tiled dining room, an amazing marble fireplace and a mural-clad ballroom, the hotel was the fashionable sensation of its day. A contemporary restoration has done a wonderful job of showing off the classy interior – there are guided tours (€5) on Tuedays (12.15pm) and Fridays (4.30pm). In the summer no tours are available.

Palau Güell

vintage clothing scene. A dozen funky little independent clothes shops provide the scope for an hour's browsing.

Palau Güell

MAP P.54, POCKET MAP C13. C/Nou de la Rambla 3–5 Ⓜ Liceu ⓣ 934 725 775, ⓦ palauguell.cat. Tue–Sun & hols 10am–8pm (Nov–March until 5.30pm), last admission 1hr before closing. €12, first Sun of the month free.

El Raval's outstanding building is the extraordinary townhouse designed (1886–90) by the young Antoni Gaudí for a wealthy industrialist. At a time when other architects sought to conceal the iron supports within buildings, Gaudí displayed them instead as decorative features. Columns, arches and ceilings are all shaped and twisted in an elaborate style that was to become the hallmark of Gaudí's later works, while the roof terrace culminates in a fantastical series of tiled chimneys. Visitor numbers are limited – expect to queue or to receive a time-specific ticket.

Església de Sant Pau del Camp

MAP P.54, POCKET MAP A13. C/de Sant Pau 101 Ⓜ Paral.lel ⓣ 934 410 001. Mon–Sat 10am–1.30pm & 4–7.30pm. Admission to cloister €3.

The unusual name of the church of Sant Pau del Camp (St Paul of the Field) is a graphic reminder that it once stood in open countryside beyond the city walls. Sant Pau was a Benedictine foundation of the tenth century, and above the main entrance are primitive thirteenth-century carvings of fish, birds and faces, while others adorn the charming cloister.

Mercat de Sant Antoni

MAP P.54, POCKET MAP E5. C/del Comte d'Urgell 1 Ⓜ Sant Antoni ⓦ mercatdesantantoni.com. Mon–Sat 8am–8pm.

The neighbourhood's impressive nineteenth-century produce market is another that's been entirely remodelled and reopened. The new central foyer is designed to accentuate the remaining medieval structure. There are stalls with fresh produce and a flea market and, on Sundays, a book market outside the building. The traditional bolt hole is *Els Tres Tombs*, the restaurant-bar on the corner of Ronda de Sant Antoni, open from 6am until late for a good-natured mix of locals, market traders and tourists.

Shops

La Central del Raval

MAP P.54, POCKET MAP C11.
C/d'Elisabets 6 Ⓜ Catalunya Ⓦ lacentral.com. Mon–Fri 10am–9pm, Sat 10.30am–9pm.

Occupying a unique space in the former Misericordia chapel, this is a fantastically stocked arts and humanities treasure-trove, with books piled high in every nook and cranny and a big English-language section. There are further outlets in MACBA (contemporary art museum) and MUHBA (Barcelona History Museum).

Fantastik

MAP P.54, POCKET MAP B10.
C/Joaquin Costa 62 Ⓜ Universitat Ⓦ fantastik.es. Mon–Fri 11am–2pm & 4–8.30pm, Sat 11am–3pm & 4–9pm.

Beguiling gifts, crafts and covetable objects from four continents. You'll never know how you lived without them, whether it's Chinese robots, African baskets, Russian domino sets or Vietnamese kitchen scales.

Gotham

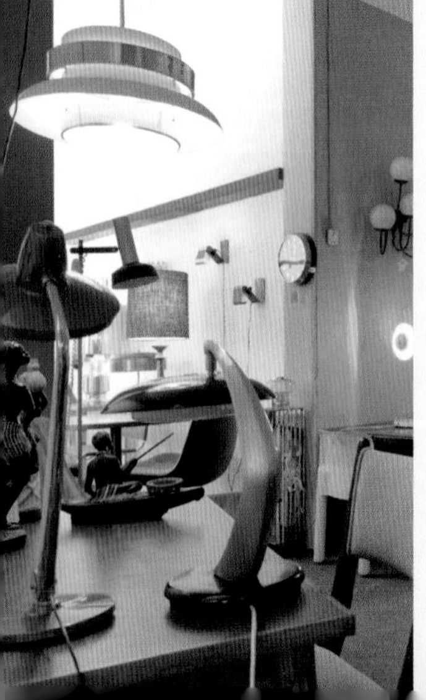

Gotham

MAP P.54, POCKET MAP B10.
C/Lleó 28 Ⓜ Universitat Ⓣ 934 124 647, Ⓦ gotham-bcn.com. Mon–Fri 5–8pm, other times by appointment only.

This stylish shop is the place to come for retro (1950s to 1980s) furniture, lighting, homeware, accessories and original designs.

Holala! Plaza

MAP P.54, POCKET MAP C10.
Pl. Castella 2 Ⓜ Universitat Ⓦ holala-ibiza.com. Mon–Sat 11am–9pm.

Vintage heaven in a warehouse setting (up past CCCB), for denim, flying jackets, Hawaiian shirts, baseball gear and much, much more. Also check out the other Raval stores at C/Riera Baixa 11 and C/dels Tallers 73.

Revólver Records

MAP P.54, POCKET MAP C11.
C/dels Tallers 11 Ⓜ Catalunya Ⓣ 934 126 248, Ⓦ revolverrecords.es. Mon–Sat 10am–9pm.

Revólver Records sells the city's best selection of vinyl and CDs at the lowest prices. It's defiantly old school: a record shop like they used to make them.

Vintage Kilo

MAP P.54, POCKET MAP B11.
C/dels Tallers 35 Ⓜ Catalunya Ⓣ 653 641 546, Ⓦ vintagekilo.com. Mon–Sat 11am–9pm.

Trendy second-hand vintage clothing from the 70s and 80s sold by the kilo, ranging from biker jackets to Hawaiian shirts. The stock is varied, stylish and carefully selected with a lot of North American gems.

Cafés

Caravelle

MAP P.54, POCKET MAP B13.
C/Pintor Fortuny 31 Ⓜ Catalunya Ⓣ 933 178 892. Mon 9.30am–5.30pm, Tue–Fri 9.30am–1am, Sat 10am–1am, Sun 10am–5.30pm

A place with a slightly hipster vibe and sparse but elegant decor. Offers delicious breakfasts and brunches you can wash down with great coffee. If you're looking for a drink with your breakfast, you won't be disappointed either.

Cafè de les Delícies

MAP P.54, POCKET MAP B13.
Rambla de Raval 47 Ⓜ Liceu Ⓣ 934 415 714. Mon 8am–2pm & 6–9pm, Tue 10am–2pm & 5–6pm, Wed 8am–2pm & 5–9pm, Thu 8am–noon & 2–10pm, Fri 7am–1am, Sat midnight–1am & 11am–midnight, Sun 1pm–9pm.
One of the first off the blocks in this revamped neighbourhood, and still perhaps the best, plonking thrift-shop chairs and tables beneath exposed pipes and girders and coming up with something cute, cosy, mellow and arty. Locals meet for breakfast, sandwiches and tapas.

Granja M. Viader

MAP P.54, POCKET MAP C11.
C/Xuclà 4–6 Ⓜ Catalunya Ⓣ 933 183 486, Ⓦ granjaviader.cat. Mon–Sat 9am–1.15pm & 5–9.15pm.
The oldest traditional *granja* (milk bar) in town is a real historical survivor – it has a plaque outside for services to the city. The original owner was the inventor of "Cacaolat", but you could also try *mel i mató* (curd cheese and honey).

Kasparo

MAP P.54, POCKET MAP C11.
Pl. Vicenç Martorell 4 Ⓜ Catalunya Ⓣ 933 022 072, Ⓦ kasparo.es. Summer: Tue–Sat 9am–midnight, winter: Tue–Sat 9am–10.30pm closed 4 weeks over Dec & Jan.
A place to relax, in the arcaded corner of a quiet square, with outdoor seating year-round. There's muesli, Greek yoghurt and toast and jam for early birds. Later, sandwiches, tapas and assorted *platos del dia* (dishes of the day) are on offer – things like hummus and bread, vegetable quiche or couscous.

Granja M. Viader

Restaurants and tapas bars

Bar Cañete

MAP P.54, POCKET MAP C13.
C/de la Unió 17 Ⓜ Liceu Ⓣ 932 703 458, Ⓦ barcanete.com. Mon–Sat 1pm–midnight.
Gleaming mirrors, dark wood furnishings and white-clad waiters set the scene for some of the city's classiest tapas, featuring premium ingredients (and pricetags to match if you don't choose carefully). Take your pick from classic seafood and meat dishes sourced fresh from the local market.

Ca L'Estevet

MAP P.54, POCKET MAP B10.
C/Valldonzella 46 Ⓜ Universitat Ⓣ 933012 939, Ⓦ restaurantestevet.com. Mon–Sat 1–3.30pm & 7.30–10.45pm.
Ca l'Estevet, an unshifting rock in the fickle seas of foodie fashions, has been serving up old-school Catalan cuisine since 1940 (and, under a different name, for 50 years before that). The practice has made perfect; try the €18 lunch menu or tuck into grilled *botifarra* sausages,

roasted kid or *escudella i carn d'olla* (meat stew).

Dos Palillos

MAP P.54, POCKET MAP C11.
C/d'Elisabets 9 Ⓜ Catalunya Ⓣ 933 040 513, Ⓦ dospalillos.com. Tue & Wed 7.30–11.30pm, Thu–Sat 1.30–3.30pm & 7.30–11.30pm; closed 2 weeks in Dec/Jan & 3 weeks in Aug.

Albert Raurich, former *chef de cuisine* at "world's best restaurant" *El Bulli*, swapped Catalan food for Asian fusion after falling in love with Japan. Try his à la carte dim sum in the front galley bar (from steamed dumplings to grilled oysters and stir-fried prawns, average spend €30) or book for the back room where tasting menus (€75 and €90) wade their way through the highlights.

Elisabets

MAP P.54, POCKET MAP C11.
C/d'Elisabets 2 Ⓜ Catalunya Ⓣ 933 175 826, Ⓦ elisabets1962.com. Mon–Thu 7.30am–midnight, Fri 7.30am–1am, Sat 9am–midnight; closed Aug.

Reliable Catalan home cooking served at cramped tables in a jovial brick-walled dining room. Everyone piles in early for breakfast, the hearty lunch (1–4pm) is hard to beat for price, or you can just have tapas, sandwiches and drinks at the bar.

Mesón David

MAP P.54, POCKET MAP A13.
C/de les Carretes 63 Ⓜ Paral.lel Ⓣ 934 415 934. Daily 1pm–11.45pm.

This down-to-earth Galician bar-restaurant is a firm favourite with neighbourhood families, who bring their kids before they can even walk. The weekday *menú del dia* is a steal – maybe lentil broth followed by grilled trout – while traditional Galician dishes like octopus or the *combinado Gallego* ("ham, salami, ear") go down well with the regulars. Lunch is around €12, otherwise most dishes €7–15, and there's a good-natured bang on the clog gong for anyone who leaves a tip.

Dos Palillos

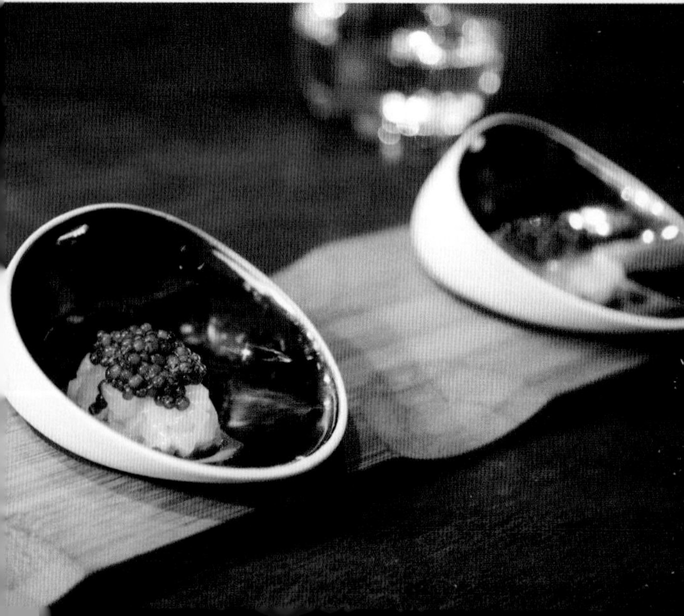

El Pachuco

MAP P.54, POCKET MAP A13.
C/de Sant Pau 110 Ⓜ Liceu ⓣ 931 796 805. Daily 1.30pm–1.30am, Fri & Sat till 3am.

A tiny place with authentic Mexican cuisine. Great tacos and amazing quesadillas attract crowds, so be ready for a long (up to 1.5hrs) wait at its most crowded - but be patient, it's definitely worth it. The experience will be complete if you order a margarita cocktail, too. Cash only.

Romesco

MAP P.54, POCKET MAP C13.
C/Sant Pau 28 Ⓜ Liceu ⓣ 933 189 381, ⓦ restaurante-romesco.blogspot.com. Mon–Fri 1–11.30pm, Sat 1–4pm & 8–11.30pm; closed Aug.

As long as you accept *Romesco*'s limitations (dining under strip lights, gruff waiters) you can hardly go wrong, as the most expensive thing on the menu is a €10 grilled steak and most dishes go for €6 or less. It's basic but good, with big salads, country broths and grilled veg to start, followed by tuna steak, lamb chops or grilled prawns from the market.

Sesamo

MAP P.54, POCKET MAP A11.
C/Sant Antoni Abat 52 Ⓜ Sant Antoni ⓣ 934 416 411. Tue–Sun 7pm–midnight.

A classy fusion tapas place offering up a vegetarian-orientated chalkboard menu of innovative dishes that roll out of an open kitchen. Try veggie-stuffed courgette rolls (a sort of Catalan sushi), slow-roast tomato tart or a daily risotto and pasta dish, all in the €7–15 range. The Catalan wines and cheeses are a high point too.

Suculent

MAP P.54, POCKET MAP B13.
Rambla de Raval 43 Ⓜ Liceu ⓣ 934 436 579, ⓦ suculent.com. Wed–Sun 1pm–4pm & 8–11.30pm; closed for two weeks in August.

A Tu Bola

As well as meaning "succulent", the name of this bistro is a play on the Catalan words *sucar lent* – to dip slowly – and you'll do just that, using fresh, warm bread to mop up sauces from dish after lip-smacking dish. The steak tartare on grilled marrowbone (€15) will put hairs on your chest and bring tears of joy to your eyes. The same team of chefs also serves tapas a few doors down at *Taverna del Suculent*.

A Tu Bola

MAP P.54, POCKET MAP B12.
C/de Hospital 78 Ⓜ Liceu ⓣ 933 153 244, ⓦ atubolarest.com. Mon–Fri 1pm–midnight (Wed 11pm), Sat & Sun 1pm–1am.

Falafel-like balls of fresh ingredients come in unexpected but delightful flavour combinations here. Home-made harissa and soft drinks bear hallmarks of the attention to detail that lifts this far above typical street-food standard. There aren't many seats and prices are low (about €12 a head) so expect a wait at busy times.

La Confitería

the late-night munchies by getting to grips with their famed burger menu.

La Confitería

MAP P.54, POCKET MAP A13.
C/de Sant Pau 128 Ⓜ Paral.lel. Mon–Thu 7pm–2am, Fri and Sat 6pm–3am, Sun 5pm–2am.

This old bakery and confectioner's – carved wood bar, faded tile floor, murals, antique chandeliers and mirrored cabinets – is now a popular bar and meeting point. It's out on a limb in the Raval, but the glorious interior is certainly worth a detour, and it's a handy stop-off in any case on the way to a night out in Poble Sec.

Marmalade

MAP P.54, POCKET MAP B11.
C/de Riera Alta 4–6 Ⓜ Sant Antoni Ⓣ 934 423 966, Ⓦ marmaladebarcelona.com. Mon–Thu 7pm–2am, Fri and Sat 10am–2.30am, Sun 10am–2am.

A hugely glam facelift for the old Muebles Navarro furniture store goes for big, church-like spaces and a backlit Art Deco bar that resembles a high altar. Cocktails, bistro meals and gourmet burgers pull in a relaxed dine-and-lounge crowd, and there's a popular weekend brunch too. If you like the style, give the more informal Barri Gòtic sister bar, *Milk*, a whirl.

Bars

Almirall

MAP P.54, POCKET MAP B11.
C/de Joaquin Costa 33 Ⓜ Universitat Ⓣ 933 189 917, Ⓦ casaalmirall.com. Mon 4.30pm–1.30am, Tue & Wed 4pm–2.30am, Thur noon–2.30am, Fri & Sat noon–3am, Sun noon–00.30am.

Dating from 1860, Barcelona's oldest bar is a *modernista* classic – make sure you check out the ornate doors, marble counter, vintage furniture and stupendous, glittering bar. It's long been a venerated leftist hangout and because it's not too young and not too loud, it's always good for a late-night drink away from the party crowd.

Betty Ford's

MAP P.54, POCKET MAP B10.
C/de Joaquín Costa 56 Ⓜ Universitat Ⓣ 933 041 368. Daily 7pm–2.30am.

With a friendly, welcoming atmosphere and a vibe somewhere between a student lounge and a beach bar, *Betty Ford's* is a bouncy place full of bouncy young things sipping colourful cocktails and cold Australian beer. You can deal with

Marsella

MAP P.54, POCKET MAP B13.
C/de Sant Pau 65 Ⓜ Liceu Ⓣ 934 427 263. Daily 10pm–2.30am.

Authentic, atmospheric, sleaze-period bar – named after the French port of Marseilles – where absinthe is the drink of choice. It's frequented by a spirited mix of oddball locals and young trendies, all looking for a slice of the old Barri Xines.

Bar Resolis

MAP P.54, POCKET MAP B11.
C/Riera Baixa 22 Ⓜ Sant Antoni Ⓣ 934 412 948. Mon–Thu 6pm–1am, Fri 6pm–2am, Sat 1pm–2am.

A decayed, century-old bar turned into a cool hangout with decent tapas, from veggie *bruschette* to steamed mussels. They didn't do much – a lick of paint, polish the panelling, patch up the brickwork – but now punters spill out of the door onto "secondhand clothes street" and a good time is had by all.

Zelig

MAP P.54, POCKET MAP A11.
C/del Carme 116 Ⓜ Sant Antoni Ⓦ zelig-barcelona.com. Tue–Thu & Sun 11am–2am, Fri & Sat 11am–3am.

The photo-frieze on granite walls and a fully stocked cocktail bar make it very much of its *barri*, but *Zelig* stands out from the crowd. It offers a chatty welcome, a tendency towards 1980s sounds and a slight whiff of camp.

Clubs

Cafè Teatre Llantiol

MAP P.54, POCKET MAP A12.
C/Riereta 7 Ⓜ Sant Antoni Ⓣ 933 299 009, Ⓦ llantiol.com. Shows daily 8.30pm–midnight.

Local-language theatre isn't accessible to nonspeakers, but you might want to give this idiosyncratic café-cabaret a try. As well as Catalan-language plays, there are shows featuring a mix of mime, song, clowning, magic and dance, and sometimes there's English-language standup comedy too.Tickets €10–15.

La Concha

MAP P.54, POCKET MAP B13.
C/Guardia 14 Ⓜ Drassanes Ⓣ 933 024 118, Ⓦ laconchadelraval.com.Sun–Thu 5pm–2.30am, Fri–Sat 5pm–3.30am.

The Arab-flamenco fusion here creates a great atmosphere, worth braving the slightly dodgy area for. It's a kitsch, gay-friendly joint, dedicated to the "incandescent presence" of Sara Montiel, Queen of Song and Cinema (and LGBT icon), with uninhibited dancing by tourists and locals alike. Admission free.

JazzSí Club

MAP P.54, POCKET MAP A11.
C/Requesens 2 Ⓜ Sant Antoni Ⓣ 933 290 020, Ⓦ tallerdemusics.com.

This is a great place for inexpensive (€6–8) gigs in a tiny sweatbox of a club associated with the Taller de Musics (music school). Every night from around 7.45 or 8pm there's something different, from exuberant rock, blues, jazz and jam sessions to the popular weekly Cuban (Thuday) and flamenco (Friday) nights. There are usually a couple of sessions a night, with an interval in between – your first drink is included in the price, and the bar is as cheap as chips.

Moog

MAP P.54, POCKET MAP C14.
C/Arc del Teatre 3 Ⓜ Drassanes Ⓣ 933 191 789, Ⓦ masimas.com. Mon–Thu 9pm–4am, Fri 9pm–2am.

Influential club with a minimalist look, playing techno, electro, drum 'n' bass and trance to a cool but up-for-it crowd. There's a second, less manic dancefloor as well. Admission €10.

Moog

Sant Pere

Perhaps the least visited part of the Old Town is the medieval *barri* of Sant Pere, the area that lies immediately north of the Barri Gòtic and across Carrer de la Princesa from La Ribera. It has two remarkable buildings – the *modernista* concert hall, known as the Palau de la Música Catalana, and the stylishly designed neighbourhood market, Mercat Santa Caterina. There's been much regeneration in the *barri* over recent years, and it's well worth an afternoon's stroll or a night out, with new boulevards and community projects alongside DJ bars and designer shops. To walk through the neighbourhood, you can start at Metro Urquinaona, close to the Palau de la Música Catalana, with Metro Jaume I marking the southern end of Sant Pere.

Palau de la Música Catalana

MAP P.64, POCKET MAP E11.
C/Sant Pere Més Alt Ⓜ Urquinaona

Ⓣ 902 442 882, Ⓦ palaumusica.org. Guided tours daily 10am–3.30pm, plus Easter week & July 10am–6pm, August 9am–6pm, in English every 30min. €20.

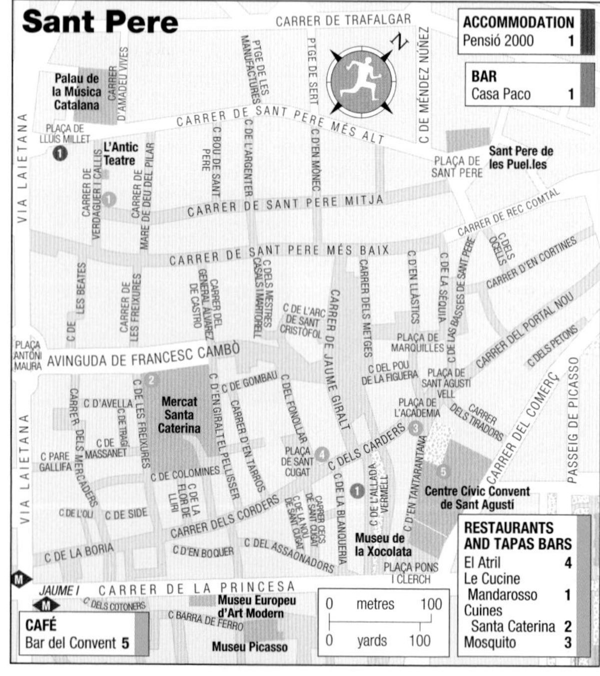

Palau de la Música Catalana

Barcelona's most extraordinary concert hall was built in 1908, to a design by visionary *modernista* architect Lluís Domènech i Montaner. The elaborate exterior is simply smothered in tiles and mosaics, while a mighty bulbous stained-glass skylight caps the second-storey auditorium (which contemporary critics claimed to be an engineering impossibility). The more recent Petit Palau offers a smaller auditorium space, while to the side a contemporary glass facade and courtyard provide the main public access. Concerts here (throughout the year) include performances by the Orfeo Català choral group and the Barcelona city orchestra, though you can also catch anything from flamenco to world music. Numbers are limited on the very popular fifty-minute guided tours, so it's best to buy a ticket a day or two in advance (by phone, online or at the box office).

L'Antic Teatre

MAP P.64, POCKET MAP E11.
C/Verdaguer i Callis 12 Ⓜ Urquinaona
Ⓣ 933 152 354, Ⓦ www.anticteatre.com.

An independent theatre with a wildly original programme, from video shows and offbeat cabaret to modern dance and left-field music. The best bit may just be the magical, light-strung garden-bar (daily 4pm–midnight), a real insiders' place but open to all.

Plaça de Sant Pere

MAP P.64, POCKET MAP G11.
Ⓜ Arc de Triomf.

The neighbourhood extends around three parallel medieval streets, carrers de Sant Pere Més Alt (upper), Mitja (middle) and Baix (lower), which contain the bulk of the finest buildings and shops – a mixture of boutiques, textile shops, groceries and old family businesses. The streets all converge on the original neighbourhood square, Plaça de Sant Pere, whose foursquare church flanks one side, overlooking a flamboyant iron drinking fountain. Originally built in the shape of a Greek cross, the church, **Sant Pere de les Puel.les**, dates back to 945 AD and was the city's first convent of Benedictine nuns. It occasionally hosts concerts.

Mercat Santa Caterina

MAP P.64, POCKET MAP F12.
Av. Francesc Cambò 16 Ⓜ Jaume I Ⓣ 933 195 740, Ⓦ mercatsantacaterina.com. Mon, Wed & Sat 7.30am–3.30pm, Tue, Thu & Fri 7.30am–8.30pm.

An eye-catching renovation of the neighbourhood market retained its original walls but added slatted wooden doors and windows and a dramatic multicoloured wave roof. It's one of the best places in the city to shop for food, and its market restaurant and bar are definitely worth a visit in any case. During renovation work, the foundations of a medieval convent were discovered here and the excavations are visible in the **Espai Santa Caterina** (Mon–Sat 10am–7pm; free) at the rear of the market.

Plaça de Sant Agusti Vell

MAP P.64, POCKET MAP G12.
Ⓜ Jaume I.

The pretty, tree-shaded Plaça de Sant Agusti Vell sits in the middle of an ambitious urban regeneration project, which has transformed previously crowded alleys. To the north, locals tend organic allotments in the middle of the landscaped Pou de la Figuera *rambla*, while south down **Carrer d'Allada Vermell** are overarching trees, a children's playground and a series of outdoor cafés and bars. Meanwhile, running down from Plaça de Sant Agusti Vell**, Carrer dels Carders** – once "ropemakers' street" – is now a funky retail quarter mixing grocery stores, cafés, boutiques and craft shops.

Mercat Santa Caterina

Centre Cívic Convent de Sant Agusti

MAP P.64, POCKET MAP F12–G12.
C/del Comerç 36 Ⓜ Jaume I Ⓣ 932 565 000, Ⓦ conventagusti.com. Mon–Fri 9am–10pm, Sat 10am–2pm & 4–9pm. Admission charges vary, some events free.

Driving many of the neighbourhood improvements is the community centre installed inside the revamped Convent de Sant Agusti, whose thirteenth-century cloister provides a unique performance space. There's a full cultural programme here, from workshops to concerts, with a particular emphasis on electronic and experimental music and art, and don't miss the excellent convent café.

Museu de la Xocolata

MAP P.64, POCKET MAP F12–G13.
C/del Comerç 36 Ⓜ Jaume I Ⓣ 932 687 878, Ⓦ museuxocolata.cat. Mon–Sat 10am–7pm, Sun 10am–3pm. €5.

Part of the Convent de Sant Agusti contains Barcelona's chocolate museum, which is a rather uninspiring plod through the history of the stuff. Whether you go in or not depends on how keen you are to see models of Gaudí buildings or religious icons sculpted in chocolate. There are some very nice chocs to buy in the shop though (free to enter), while at the adjacent Escola de Pastisseria, glass windows look onto the students learning their craft in the kitchens.

Cafés

Bar del Convent

MAP P.64, POCKET MAP G12.
Pl. de l'Acadèmia, C/del Comerç 36 Ⓜ Jaume I ⓣ 932 565 017, ⓦ bardelconvent.com. Tue–Sat 10am–9pm, closed in August.
The cloister café-bar is a bargain for lunch and light meals, with soups, stir-fries, lasagne and couscous for €4–7. At night it's more of a bar, with a range of live shows, DJs and concerts.

Restaurants and tapas bars

El Atril

MAP P.64, POCKET MAP F12.
C/dels Carders 23 Ⓜ Jaume I ⓣ 933 101 220, ⓦ elatrilbarcelona.es. Sun–Thu 12.30pm–11.30pm, Fri & Sat 12.30pm–midnight.
The "Music Stand" is a cosy bar-restaurant complete with summer *terrassa* and an international menu, from Thai red curry to *moules frites* (mains €10–15). There's a good-value lunch, and dinner from 7pm, otherwise it's modern tapas, drinks and a decent Sunday brunch.

Le Cucine Mandarosso

MAP P.64, POCKET MAP E11.
C/de Verdaguer i Callís 4 Ⓜ Verdaguer ⓣ 932 690 780, ⓦ lecucinemandarosso.com. Tue–Sat 1.30pm–4pm & 9pm–midnight, Sun 1.30–4.30pm & 9pm–midnight.
This little piece of Napoli in Barcelona imports the southern Italian city's characteristics: crowded, friendly, cheap, charming and single-minded about delicious, simple food. No reservations at lunchtimes turns getting a table into a lottery but the €11 set menu makes it worth trying.

Cuines Santa Caterina

MAP P.64, POCKET MAP F12.
Mercat Santa Caterina, Av. Francesc Cambó 16 Ⓜ Jaume I ⓣ 932 689 918, ⓦ grupotragaluz.com. Bar Sun–Thu 9am–11pm, Fri & Sat until 11.30pm; restaurant lunch Mon–Fri 1pm–4pm, Sat & Sun 1pm–4.30pm, dinner Sun–Thu 7.30pm–11pm, Fri & Sat until 11.30pm.
A ravishing open-plan tapas bar and market restaurant with tables under soaring rafters. Food touches all bases – pasta to sushi, Catalan rice to Thai curry – with most things costing €9–12.

Mosquito

MAP P.64, POCKET MAP F12.
C/dels Carders 46 Ⓜ Jaume I ⓣ 932 687 569, ⓦ mosquitotapas.com. Mon 7.30pm–1am, Tue–Sun 1pm–1am.
Asian tapas bar with paper lanterns, artisan beers and an authentic, made-to-order dim sum menu (dishes €3–5), from shrimp dumplings to tofu rolls.

Bar

Casa Paco

MAP P.64, POCKET MAP F12.
C/d'Allada Vermell 10 Ⓜ Jaume I ⓣ 933 149 320. Mon–Thu 9am–2am, Fri until 3am, Sat 1pm–3am, Oct–March opens 6pm.
This cool music joint is a hit on the weekend DJ scene. There's a great terrace under the trees.

Casa Paco

La Ribera

The traditional highlights of the old artisans' quarter of La Ribera are the Museu Picasso (Barcelona's single biggest tourist attraction) and the graceful church of Santa María del Mar. The cramped streets between the two were at the heart of medieval industry and commerce, and it's still the neighbourhood of choice for local designers, craftspeople and artists, whose boutiques and workshops lend La Ribera an air of creativity. Galleries and applied art museums occupy the medieval mansions of Carrer de Montcada – the neighbourhood's most handsome street – while the *barri* is at its most hip in the area around the Passeig del Born, whose cafés, restaurants and bars make it one of the city's premier nightlife centres. The most direct access point for La Ribera is Metro Jaume I.

Museu Picasso

MAP P.70, POCKET MAP F13.
C/de Montcada 15–23 Ⓜ Jaume I Ⓣ 932 563 000, Ⓦ museupicasso.bcn.cat. Mon 10am–5pm, Thu 9am–9.30pm, Tue–Sun 9am–8.30pm, €11, first Sun of the month & Thu 6pm–9.30pm free.

The celebrated Museu Picasso is one of the most important collections of Picasso's work in the world, but even so some visitors are disappointed, since the museum contains none of his best-known pictures and few in the

Museu Picasso

Cubist style. But there are almost 4000 works in the permanent collection – housed in five adjoining medieval palaces – which provide a fascinating opportunity to trace Picasso's development from his drawings as a young boy to the mature works of later years. Paintings from his art-school days in Barcelona (1895–97) show tantalizing glimpses of the city that the young Picasso was beginning to explore, while works in the style of Toulouse-Lautrec reflect his interest in Parisian art. Other selected works are from the famous Blue Period (1901–04) and Pink Period (1904–06), and from his Cubist (1907–20) and Neoclassical (1920–25) stages. The large gaps in the main collection only underline Picasso's extraordinary changes of style and mood, best illustrated by the jump to 1957, a year represented by his interpretations of Velázquez's masterpiece *Las Meninas*.

As well as showing changing selections of sketches, prints and drawings, the museum addresses Picasso's work as a ceramicist, highlighting the vibrantly decorated dishes and jugs donated by his wife Jacqueline.

Museu Europeu d'Art Modern

A free guided tour is the best way to get to grips with the collection – in English currently on Sundays at 11am (book in advance by phone or via the website). There's a courtyard café, and, of course, a shop full of Picasso-related gifts.

Museu Europeu d'Art Modern

MAP P.70, POCKET MAP F13.

Picasso in Barcelona

Although born in Málaga, **Pablo Picasso** (1881–1973) spent much of his youth – from the age of 14 to 23 – in Barcelona. This time encompassed the whole of his Blue Period (1901–04) and provided many of the formative influences on his art. Not far from the Museu Picasso you can see many of the buildings in which Picasso lived and worked, notably the Escola de Belles Arts de Llotja (C/Consolat del Mar, near Estació de França), where his father taught drawing and where Picasso himself absorbed an academic training. The apartments where the family lived when they first arrived in Barcelona were at Pg. d'Isabel II 4 and C/Reina Cristina 3, both near the Escola, while Picasso's first real studio (in 1896) was located over on C/de la Plata at no. 4. A few years later, many of his Blue Period works were finished at a studio at C/del Comerç 28. His first public exhibition was in 1901 at the extravagantly decorated *Els Quatre Gats* tavern (C/Montsió 3, Barri Gòtic; ⓦ 4gats.com); you can still have a meal there today.

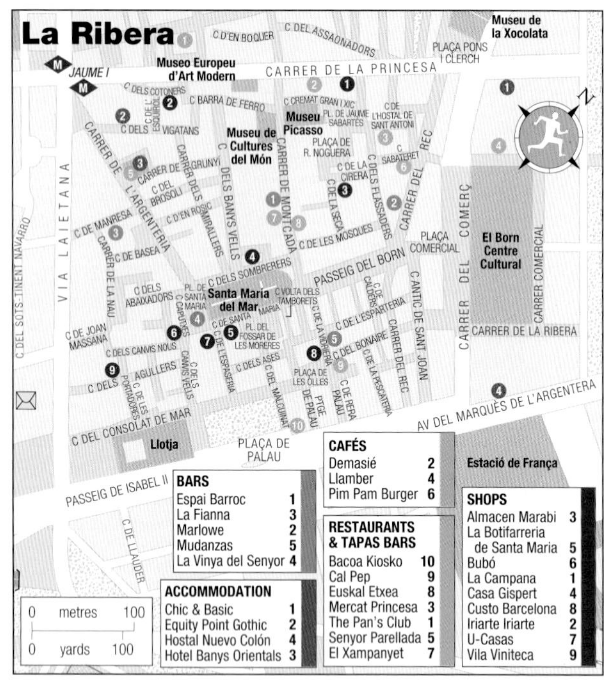

C/Barra de Ferro 5 Ⓜ Jaume I ☎ 933 195 693, 🌐 meam.es. Tue–Sun 11am–7pm. €9, guided tour €11 (Sat & Sun noon).

There is not one photograph on display at the Museu Europeu d'Art Modern, a fact you may find hard to believe considering how photorealistic many of the paintings are. Located in a renovated eighteenth-century palace – and just metres from the Museu Picasso – the museum focuses primarily on modern and contemporary figurative art. Its three floors brim with haunting, humorous and sometimes disturbing works by the likes of Eduardo Naranjo, Paul Beel and Carlos Saura Riaza. It's also home to modern, Art Deco and Catalan sculptures.

Església de Santa María del Mar

MAP P.70, POCKET MAP F13.
Pl. de Santa Maria Ⓜ Jaume I ☎ 933 102 390. Mon–Sat 9am–1pm & 5–8.30pm, Sun 10am–2pm & 5–8pm; guided tours Mon–Sat 1–5pm, Sun 2–5pm. Entrance free; tours €10.

The Ribera's flagship church is perhaps the most beautiful in all Barcelona. It was begun on the order of King Jaume II in 1324, and finished in only five years. Built on what was the seashore in the fourteenth century, Santa María was at the centre of the medieval city's trading district (nearby C/ Argentería, for example, is named after the silversmiths who once worked there), and it came to embody the commercial supremacy of the Crown of Aragon, of which Barcelona was capital. It's an exquisite example of Catalan-Gothic architecture – as all the later Baroque trappings were destroyed during the Civil War, eyes instead are concentrated on the simple spaces of the interior, especially the stained glass. Check local listings magazines for choral concerts here

– the acoustics are as stunning as the architecture.

Passeig del Born

MAP P.70, POCKET MAP F13.
Ⓜ Jaume I.

Fronting the church of Santa María del Mar is the fashionable Passeig del Born, once the site of medieval fairs and entertainments ("born" means tournament) and now an avenue lined with a parade of plane trees shading a host of classy bars, delis and shops. At night the Born becomes one of Barcelona's biggest bar zones, as spirited locals frequent a panoply of drinking haunts – from old-style cocktail lounges to thumping music bars. Shoppers and browsers, meanwhile, scour the narrow medieval alleys on either side of the *passeig* for boutiques and craft workshops – carrers Flassaders, Vidreria and Rec, in particular, are noted for clothes, shoes, jewellery and design galleries.

El Born Centre Cultural

MAP P.70, POCKET MAP G13.
Pl. Comercial 12 Ⓜ Jaume I/Barceloneta Ⓣ 932 564 190, Ⓦ elborncentrecultural.cat. Tue–Sun 10am–8pm. Free access to the centre, €5.50 guided tours.

The Antic Mercat del Born (1873–76) was the biggest of Barcelona's nineteenth-century market halls. It was the city's main wholesale fruit and veg market in 1971, and was then due to be demolished, but was saved thanks to local protests. It lay empty for decades, but in 2013 reopened as El Born Centre Cultural; the extensive archeological remains of eighteenth-century shops, factories, houses and taverns are showcased inside the building's restored glass-and-cast-iron frame.

Museu de Cultures del Món

MAP P.70, POCKET MAP E13.
C/Montcada 12–14 Ⓜ Jaume I
Ⓦ museuculturesmon.bcn.cat. Tue–Sat 10am–7pm, Sun 10am–8pm. €5.

The newly opened Museum of World Cultures in the Palau Nadal and Palau Marqués de Llió brings together archaeological collections from around the world that show the diversity of global art throughout history.

Passeig del Born

Shops

Almacen Marabi

MAP P.70, POCKET MAP F13.
C/Cirera 6 Ⓜ Jaume I Ⓦ almacenmarabi.blogspot.com. Mon–Sat noon–2.30pm & 5–8.30pm.

Mariela Marabi, originally from Argentina, makes handmade felt finger dolls, mobiles, puppets and animals of extraordinary invention. She's often at work at the back, while her eye-popping showroom also has limited-edition pieces by other selected artists and designers.

La Botifarreria de Santa Maria

MAP P.70, POCKET MAP F14.
C/Santa Maria 4 Ⓜ Jaume I Ⓦ labotifarreria.com. Mon–Sat 8.30am–2.30pm & 5–8.30pm.

If you ever doubted the power of the humble Catalan pork sausage, drop by this designer temple-deli where otherwise beautifully behaved locals jostle at the counter for the day's home-made *botifarra*, plus rigorously sourced hams, cheese, pâtés and salamis. True disciples can even buy the T-shirt.

Casa Gispert

Bubó

MAP P.70, POCKET MAP E14.
C/Caputxes 10 Ⓜ Jaume I Ⓦ bubo.es. Daily 10am–9pm (Fri & Sat until 11pm, Sun until 10pm).

There are chocolates and then there are Bubó chocolates – jewel-like creations and playful desserts by pastry maestro Carles Mampel. This very classy shop is complemented by their minimalist new-wave tapas place, *Bubóbar*, a couple of doors down at no. 6.

La Campana

MAP P.70, POCKET MAP F13.
C/Princesa 36 Ⓜ Jaume I Ⓦ lacampanadesde1890.com. Daily 10am–9pm; closed Feb.

This lovely old shop from 1890 presents handmade pralines and truffles, but is best known for its beautifully packaged squares and slabs of *turrón*, traditional Catalan nougat.

Casa Gispert

MAP P.70, POCKET MAP F13.
C/Sombrerers 23 Ⓜ Jaume I Ⓦ casagispert.com. Mon–Sat 10am–2pm & 4–8pm (Nov & Dec 10am–8pm).

Roasters of nuts, coffee and spices for over 150 years. It's a truly delectable store of wooden boxes, baskets, stacked shelves and tantalizing smells, and there are organic nuts and dried fruit, teas and gourmet deli items available too.

Custo Barcelona

MAP P.70, POCKET MAP F14.
Pl. de les Olles 7 Ⓜ Barceloneta Ⓦ custo.com. Mon–Sat 10am–9pm, Sun noon–8pm.

Where the stars get their T-shirts – hugely colourful (highly priced) designer tops and sweaters for men and women. There are other branches around town (at Ramblas 109, C/de Ferran 36, and at L'Illa shopping), while last season's gear gets another whirl at Pl. del Pi in the Barri Gòtic.

Iriarte Iriarte

MAP P.70, POCKET MAP E13.
C/Cotoners 12 Ⓜ Jaume I Ⓦ iriarteiriarte.com. Tue–Sat 4.30–8.30pm.

Atelier-showroom for sumptuous handmade leather bags and belts. The alley (off C/Cotoners) has several other interesting craft workshops and galleries to browse.

U-Casas

MAP P.70, POCKET MAP F14.
C/Espaseria 4 Ⓜ Jaume I Ⓦ casasclub.com. Mon–Sat 10.30am–8.30pm (Fri & Sat until 9pm).

Casas has four lines of shoe stores across Spain, with the U-Casas brand at the young and funky end of the market. Never mind the shoes, the stores are pretty spectacular, especially here in the Born where an enormous shoe-shaped bench-cum-sofa takes centre-stage. Other branches are at C/dels Tallers 2 (Raval), C/Portaferrissa 25 (Barri Gòtic) and L'Illa and Maremàgnum shopping centres.

Vila Viniteca

MAP P.70, POCKET MAP E14.
C/Agullers 7 & 9 Ⓜ Jaume I Ⓦ vilaviniteca.es. Mon–Sat 8.30am–8.30pm (closes Sat at 2.30pm in July & Aug).

A very knowledgeable specialist in Catalan and Spanish wines. Pick your vintage and then nip over the road for the gourmet deli part of the operation.

Cafés

Demasié

MAP P.70, POCKET MAP G13.
C/de la Princessa 28 Ⓜ Jaume I Ⓣ 932 691 180. Daily 8.30am–9.30pm.

For those with a sweet tooth, this is the perfect place to begin your day or have a snack in between sightseeing. A cosy café offering mouth-watering cinnamon rolls and various types of cookies, cupcakes and cakes.

Custo Barcelona

Llamber

MAP P.70, POCKET MAP G13.
C/de la Fusina 5 Ⓜ Jaume I Ⓣ 933 196 250.Sun–Wed 9am–midnight, Thu–Sat 9am–00.30am.

A modern factory of first-rate Asturian tapas in a former industrial warehouse facing the Mercat del Born cultural centre. There are full dishes at around €10–€14 each, but the emphasis is very much on eating and drinking in groups. The wine list is full of bargains and the €15.50 lunch menu is one of the best in the area. Open 365 days a year.

Pim Pam Burger

MAP P.70, POCKET MAP F13.
C/Sabateret 4 Ⓜ Jaume I Ⓣ 933 152 093, Ⓦ pimpamburger.com. Daily noon–midnight.

An acceptable choice for a quick burger, hot dog or sandwich (€2.50–6). There are a few stools and tables if you'd rather not eat on the hoof, while *Pim Pam Plats*, around the corner on C/del Rec, is their outlet for budget-beating take-home meals.

Restaurants and tapas bars

Bacoa Kiosko

MAP P.70, POCKET MAP F14.
Av. del Marquès de l'Argentera 1 Ⓜ Barceloneta Ⓣ 933 107 313, Ⓦ bacoaburger.com. Daily 12.30pm–midnight.

In one of Barcelona's best gourmet burger outlets, great-tasting artisan bread rolls and home-made sauces set the tone, while a dozen superb types of burger (€6–9) come any way you like, from Catalan (with a roast garlic aioli) to Japanese (with teriyaki sauce).

Cal Pep

MAP P.70, POCKET MAP F14.
Pl. de les Olles 8 Ⓜ Barceloneta Ⓣ 933 107 961, Ⓦ www.calpep.com. Mon 7.30–11.30pm, Tue–Fri 1pm–3.45pm & 7.30–11.30pm, Sat 1.15–3.45pm & 7.30–11.30pm; closed Easter week & Aug.

There's no equal in town for off-the-boat and out-of-the-market tapas. You may have to queue, and prices are high for what's effectively a bar meal (up to €60), but it's definitely worth it for the likes of impeccably fried shrimp, grilled sea bass, Catalan sausage, or squid and chickpeas – all overseen by Pep himself, bustling up and down the counter.

Cal Pep

Euskal Etxea

MAP P.70, POCKET MAP F13.
Pl. de Montcada 1–3 Ⓜ Jaume I Ⓣ 933 102 185, Ⓦ gruposagardi.com. Daily 10am–12.30am (Fri & Sat until 1am).

The bar at the front of the local Basque community centre is great for sampling *pintxos* – elaborately fashioned pint-sized tapas, held together by a stick. Just point to what you want (and keep the sticks so the bill can be tallied).

Mercat Princesa

MAP P.68 POCKET MAP F13.
C/Flassaders Ⓜ Jaume I Ⓣ 932 681 518. Mon-Fri 1pm-midnight, Sat & Sun 12.30pm-midnight.

Enjoy food from more than a dozen gourmet stalls (think plump Chinese dumplings, grilled artisan sausafes and artfully mounded *montaditos*) at communal tables. A great option for the sheer variety.

The Pan's Club

MAP P.70, POCKET MAP F13.
Pl.de la Llana 16 Ⓜ Jaume I Ⓣ 932 776 827, Ⓦ thepansclub.com. Daily 10am–9.30pm.

A small place full to the brim of healthy vegetarian dishes made from local produce. Amazing quiche and a great selection of salads, you can also grab a sandwich or a bagel to go and follow it with an excellent smoothie.

Senyor Parellada

MAP P.70, POCKET MAP E13.
C/Argenteria 37 Ⓜ Jaume I Ⓣ 933 105 094, Ⓦ senyorparellada.com. Daily 1–4pm & 8–11.30pm.

A gorgeous renovation of an eighteenth-century building is the mellow background for genuine Catalan food – home-style cabbage rolls, duck with figs, a *papillote* of beans with herbs – served from a long menu that doesn't bother dividing starters from mains. Most mains cost €8–19.

El Xampanyet

MAP P.70, POCKET MAP F13.
C/de Montcada 22 Ⓜ Jaume I Ⓣ 933 197 003. Mon 7–11pm, Tue–Fri noon–3.30pm & 7–11pm, Sat noon–3.30pm; closed two weeks in Aug.

Traditional blue-tiled bar doing a roaring trade in sparkling cava, cider and traditional tapas (anchovies are the speciality). The drinks are cheap and the tapas turn out to be rather pricey, but there's usually a good buzz about the place.

El Xampanyet

Bars

Espai Barroc

MAP P.70, POCKET MAP F13.
Palau Dalmases, C/de Montcada 20 Ⓜ Jaume I Ⓣ 933 100 673, Ⓦ palaudalmases.com. Daily 7pm–1.30am. Map

The handsome Baroque mansion of Palau Dalmases is open in the evenings for wine, champagne or cognac in refined surroundings or, once a week, the billowing strains of live opera (Thu at 11pm; €20, first drink included).

La Fianna

MAP P.70, POCKET MAP F13.
C/Manresa 4 Ⓜ Jaume I Ⓣ 933 151 810, Ⓦ www.lafianna.com. Daily 6pm–2am.

Flickering candelabras, rough plaster walls and deep colours set the Gothic mood in this stylish lounge-bar. Relax on the chill-out beds and velvet sofas, or book ahead to eat – the fusion-food restaurant is open from 8.30pm.

Marlowe

MAP P.70, POCKET MAP F14.
C/del Rec 24 Ⓜ Barceloneta Ⓣ 650 188 117. Mon–Thur 6.30pm–2.30am, Fri & Sat 6.30pm–3am.

A slightly noir atmosphere - yes, the bar is named after the famous Chandlerian character. There is no set drink menu, just talk to the creative bartenders and their professional hands will mix something just for you.

Mudanzas

MAP P.70, POCKET MAP F14.
C/Vidriería 15 Ⓜ Barceloneta Ⓣ 933 191 137. Daily 10am–2.30am, Aug opens at 6pm.

Locals like the relaxed atmosphere, while those in the know come for the wide selection of rums, whiskies and vodkas from around the world.

La Vinya del Senyor

MAP P.70, POCKET MAP F14.
Pl. Santa Maria 5 Ⓜ Jaume I Ⓣ 933 103 379. Mon–Thu noon–1am, Fri & Sat noon–2am, Sun noon–midnight.

A great wine bar with front-row seats onto the lovely church of Santa María del Mar. The wine list is really good – with a score available by the glass – and there are oysters, smoked salmon and other classy tapas available.

Parc de la Ciutadella

While you might escape to Montjuïc or the Collserola hills for the air, there's no beating the city's green lung, Parc de la Ciutadella (open daily 10am until dusk), for a break from the downtown bustle. Though the park holds a full set of attractions, on lazy summer days you may simply want to stroll along the garden paths and row lazily across the ornamental lake. The name of the park recalls a Bourbon citadel which used to occupy the site, the building of which caused the brutal destruction of a great part of La Ribera neighbourhood. This symbol of authority survived uneasily until 1869; after this the area was made into a park. It was subsequently chosen as the site of the 1888 Universal Exhibition, from which period dates a series of eye-catching buildings and monuments by the city's pioneering *modernista* architects.

Arc de Triomf

MAP P.77, POCKET MAP G11.
Pg. Lluís Companys Ⓜ Arc de Triomf.

A giant brick arch announces the architectural splendours to come in the park itself. Conceived as a bold statement of Catalan intent, it's studded with ceramic figures and motifs and topped by two pairs of bulbous domes. The reliefs on the main facade show the City of Barcelona welcoming visitors to the 1888 Universal Exhibition, held in the park to the south. Connecting

Cascada, Parc de la Cuitadella

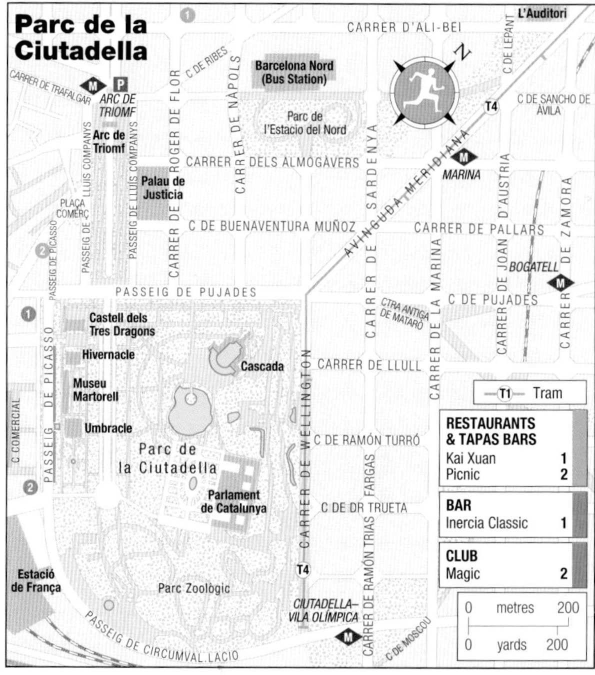

the arch to the park is a gorgeous promenade flanked by linden and palm trees and ornate lamp posts. Just before the park's entrance on Passeig de Pujades stands the monument to Francisco de Paula Rius i Taulet, the four-time mayor of Barcelona credited with helping bring the Universal Exhibition to the city.

Cascada

MAP P.77, POCKET MAP K6.
Parc de la Ciutadella Ⓜ Arc de Triomf.

The first of the major projects undertaken inside the park was the Cascada, the monumental fountain in the northeast corner. It was designed by Josep Fontseré i Mestrès, the architect chosen to oversee the conversion of the former citadel grounds into a park, and his assistant was the young Antoni Gaudí, then a student. The Baroque extravagance of the Cascada is suggestive of the flamboyant decoration that was later to become Gaudí's trademark. The best place to contemplate the fountain is from the small open-air café-kiosk. Near here you'll also find a small lake, where you can rent a rowing boat and paddle about among the ducks.

Hivernacle and Umbracle

MAP P.77, POCKET MAP G13.
Pg. de Picasso Ⓜ Arc de Triomf. Under renovation at the time of writing. Free.

The two unsung glories of Ciutadella are its plant houses, arranged either side of the Museu Martorell. The larger Hivernacle (conservatory) features enclosed greenhouses separated by a soaring glass-roofed terrace. If anything, the Umbracle (palmhouse) is even more imposing, with a vaulted wood-slat roof supported by cast-iron pillars, which allows shafts of light to play across the assembled palms and ferns. Traditionally, there's always been a café-bar in the Hivernacle, set among the plants and trees, though it was closed at the time of writing while restoration work continued on the building.

Museu de Ciències Naturals

MAP P.77, POCKET MAP G12 & G13. Pg. de Picasso Ⓜ Arc de Triomf Ⓦ museuciencies.bcn.cat.

The city's Natural Science Museum has its public showcase, the Museu Blau, over at the Diagonal Mar Fòrum site, but its genesis lies in two interesting buildings in Ciutadella park that are currently undergoing major renovation (and will be for some time). The Neoclassical **Museu Martorell**, which opened in 1882, was actually the first public museum to be built in the city, designed by leading architect of the day Antoni Rovira i Trias. For decades this housed the city's geological collections; the new permanent exhibition here will concentrate on the development of the natural sciences in Barcelona. The other building has always been a city favourite, a whimsical red-brick confection that was long the zoology museum. It's universally known as the **Castell dels Tres Dragons** (Three Dragons Castle), designed by *modernista* architect Lluís Domènech i Montaner and originally intended for use as the café-restaurant for the 1888 Universal Exhibition. It's going to become the research, study and conservation centre for the Natural Science Museum's geology and zoology collections, and will be known as the Laboratori de Natura (Laboratory of Nature).

Parc Zoològic

Parc Zoològic

MAP P.77, POCKET MAP J7–K7. C/de Wellington Ⓜ Ciutadella-Vila Olímpica Ⓣ 902 457 545, Ⓦ zoobarcelona.com. Daily: Jan–mid-March & late Oct–Dec 10am–5.30pm; mid-March–mid-May & mid-Sept–late Oct 10am–7pm; mid-May–mid-Sept 10am–8pm. €21.40.

Ciutadella's most popular attraction by far is the city zoo, which takes up most of the southeastern part of the park (main entrance on C/Wellington, signposted from Ⓜ Ciutadella-Vila Olímpica). It boasts more than 2000 animals from over 400 different species – which is seen by some as too many for a zoo that is still essentially nineteenth century in character, confined to the formal grounds of a public park. Nonetheless it's hugely popular with families, as there are mini-train and pony rides, a petting zoo and daily dolphin shows alongside the main animal attractions. The many endangered species on show include the Iberian wolf, and big cats such as the Sri Lankan leopard, snow leopard and the Sumatran tiger. The zoo's days in its current form are numbered: over the next few years parts of it will be completely remodelled as it attempts to expand its facilities and modernize.

Restaurants and tapas bars

Kai Xuan

MAP P.77, POCKET MAP J5.
C/Roger de Flor 74 Ⓜ Arc de Triomf Ⓣ 932 450 359, Ⓦ kaixuan.es. Daily 9am–midnight.

Forget the Raval's so-called Barrio Xino, the city's real Chinatown is in the streets near this family restaurant. Specializing in hand-pulled lamian noodles and featuring a buffet of astonishing value (€6), *Kai Xuan* fills up fast every day with Chinese people and in-the-know locals.

Picnic

MAP P.77, POCKET MAP G12.
C/Comerç 1 Ⓜ Arc de Triomf Ⓣ 935 116 661, Ⓦ picnic-restaurant.com. Mon 10.30am–4.30pm, Tue & Wed 10.30am–4.30pm & 7pm–2am, Thu & Fri 10.30am–4.30pm & 7pm–2am, Sat 10.30am–2am, Sun 10.30am–5pm.

Just a short stroll from the park, this lovely little spot serves classic brunch food such as eggs Benedict, pancakes and French toast, plus more creative dishes like duck hash and fried green tomatoes (brunch Fri–Sun; €5.50–14). The dinner menu focuses on tapas, with offerings that include oysters in tempura, grilled kangaroo and Myanmar pickled tea-leaf salad. There's also a weekday lunch menu (Tue–Thu; from €12), as well as thirst-quenching drinks such as the refreshingly tart pink lemonade.

Bar

Inercia Classic

MAP P.77, POCKET MAP G12.
Pg. Picasso 20 Ⓜ Barceloneta Ⓣ 933 107 207. Daily 10am–7pm.

During the summer heat, a cold drink on the shaded *terrassa* – which sits under the arcaded walkway of Passeig de Picasso across from the park – is just the ticket. It's a great spot to start the evening before diving into Born's vibrant nightlife.

Club

Magic

MAP P.77, POCKET MAP G13.
Pg. Picasso 40 Ⓜ Barceloneta Ⓣ 933 107 267, Ⓦ magic-club.net. Thu–Sat 11pm–6am.

A Barcelona classic that's been rocking out since the mid-1970s. While first and foremost a rock 'n' roll club, *Magic* doesn't take itself too seriously. The usual suspects (Ramones, AC/DC and Iggy Pop) are played alongside hits from the likes of the Beastie Boys, the Violent Femmes and more.

Picnic

Montjuïc

For art and gardens you need to head across the city to the verdant park area of Montjuïc, site of the 1992 Olympics. The hill is topped by a sturdy castle and anchored around the heavyweight art collections in the Museu Nacional d'Art de Catalunya (MNAC). Two other superb galleries also draw visitors, namely Caixa Forum and the celebrated Fundació Joan Miró, not to mention a whole host of family-oriented attractions, from the open-air Poble Espanyol (Spanish Village) to the cable car ride to the castle. Meanwhile, the various gardens that spill down the hillsides culminate in Barcelona's excellent botanical gardens. For Caixa Forum, Poble Espanyol and MNAC use Metro Espanya; the Telefèric del Port (cable car from Barceloneta) and Funicular de Montjuïc (from Metro Paral.lel) drop you near the Fundació Joan Miró.

Plaça d'Espanya

MAP P.82, POCKET MAP C4.

Ⓜ Espanya.

Montjuïc's characteristic gardens, terraces, fountains and monumental buildings were established for the International Exhibition of 1929. Gateway to the Exhibition was the vast Plaça d'Espanya and its huge Neoclassical fountain, with striking twin towers, 47m high, standing at the foot of the imposing Avinguda de la Reina Maria Cristina. This avenue heads up towards Montjuïc, and is lined by exhibition halls used for trade fairs. At the end, monumental steps (and modern escalators) ascend the hill to the Palau Nacional (home of MNAC), past water cascades and under the flanking walls of two grand Viennese-style pavilions. The higher you climb, the better the views, while a few café-kiosks put out seats on the way up to MNAC.

Plaça d'Espanya

Monument de les Quatre Columnes

MAP P.82, POCKET MAP C4.

Ⓜ Espanya.

The simplest of architect Josep Puig i Cadafalch's ideas for the ceremonial gateway to Montjuïc at Plaça d'Espanya were four 20m-high columns, erected in 1919 on a raised site below the future Palau Nacional. Who could possibly object? The authoritarian government of General Primo de Rivera, as it

Font Màgica

happened, knowing perfectly well that the architect, a Catalan nationalist, meant the four columns to represent the four stripes of the Catalan flag. Down they came in 1928, to be replaced by the Magic Fountain, and not until 2010 were the columns reconstructed (using the original plans) to be seen again in public – erected across from the fountain by the city government as "an act of memory" and symbol of freedom and democracy.

Caixa Forum

MAP P.82, POCKET MAP C4.
Av. Francesc Ferrer i Guàrdia 6–8 Ⓜ Espanya Ⓣ 934 768 600, Ⓦ fundacio.lacaixa.es. Sept–June daily 10am–8pm; July & Aug Thu–Tue 10am–8pm, Wed 10am–11pm. €4.

The former Casaramona textile factory (1911) at the foot of Montjuïc conceals a terrific arts and cultural centre. The exhibition halls were fashioned from the former factory buildings, whose external structure was left untouched – girders, pillars, brickwork and crenellated walls appear at every turn. The undulating roof (signposted "terrats") offers unique views, while the high Casaramona tower, etched in blue and yellow tiling, is as readily recognizable as the huge Miró starfish logos emblazoned across the building. The contemporary art collection focuses on the period from the 1980s to the present, and works are shown in partial rotation alongside an excellent programme of changing exhibitions across all aspects of the arts. There's also the Mediateca multimedia space, plus an arts bookshop, children's activities and a 400-seat auditorium for music, art and literary events.

Font Màgica

MAP P.82, POCKET MAP C5.
Pl. de Carles Buigas Ⓜ Espanya. March, Nov & Dec Thu, Fri & Sat 8pm–9pm, April & May Thu, Fri & Sat 9pm–10pm, June–Sept Wed–Sun 9.30-10.30pm. Free.

On selected evenings, the "Magic Fountain" at the foot of the Montjuïc steps becomes the centrepiece of an impressive, if slightly kitsch, sound-and-light show, as the sprays and sheets of brightly coloured water dance to the music.

Pavelló Mies van der Rohe

MAP P.82, POCKET MAP C5.
Av. Francesc Ferrer i Guàrdia 7 Ⓜ Espanya Ⓣ 934 234 016, Ⓦ miesbcn.com. Daily 10am–6pm; guided visits in English Sat 10am. €5.

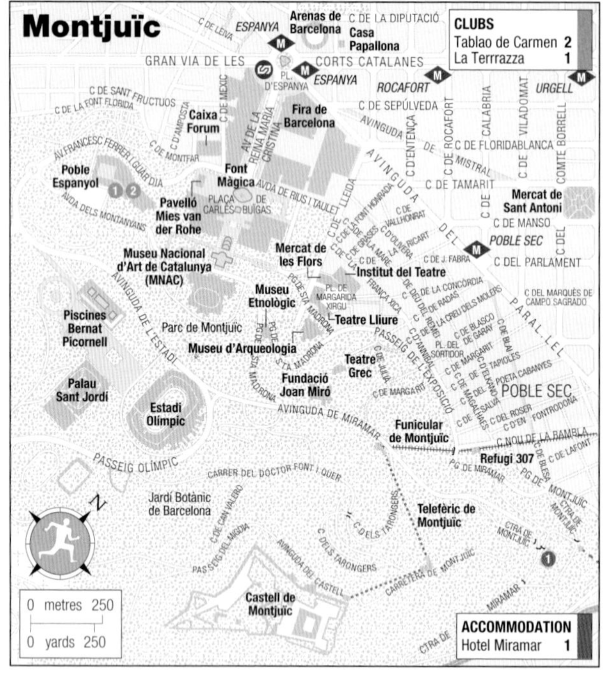

The German contribution to the 1929 International Exhibition was a pavilion designed by Mies van der Rohe (and reconstructed in 1986 by Catalan architects). It's considered a major example of modern rationalist architecture – a startling conjunction of dark-green polished onyx, shining glass and watery surfaces. Unless there's an exhibition in place (a fairly regular occurrence) there is little to see inside, though you can buy postcards and books from the small shop and debate quite how much you want a Mies mousepad or a "Less is More" T-shirt.

Poble Espanyol

MAP P.82, POCKET MAP B5.
Av. Francesc Ferrer i Guàrdia 13 Ⓜ Espanya Ⓣ 935 086 300, Ⓦ poble-espanyol.com. Mon 9am–8pm, Tue–Thu & Sun 9am–midnight, Fri 9am–3am, Sat 9am–4am. €14, family ticket €36, night ticket €7, combined ticket with MNAC €20.

"Get to know Spain in one hour" is what's promised at the Spanish Village – an open-air park of reconstructed Spanish buildings, such as the medieval walls of Ávila, through which you enter. The echoing main square is lined with cafés, while the surrounding streets and alleys contain around forty workshops, where you can witness crafts like engraving, weaving and pottery. Inevitably, it's one huge shopping experience, and prices are inflated, but children will love it (they can run free as there's no traffic) and there are plenty of family activities. Get to the village early to enjoy it in relatively crowd-free circumstances – once the tour groups arrive, it becomes a bit of a scrum. You could always come instead at the other end of the day, to venues like *Tablao de Carmen* or *La Terrrazza*, when the village transforms into a vibrant centre of Barcelona nightlife.

Museu de Carrosses Fúnebres

MAP P.82, POCKET MAP A8.
C/Mare de Déu de Port 56–58. Bus #21 from Ⓜ Paral.lel ⓣ 934 841 999, Ⓦ cbsa.cat. Mon–Fri 7.45am–7pm, Sat & Sun 7.45am–3pm. Free.

One of the city's more esoteric attractions, the Funerary Carriage Museum is fittingly located at the entrance to Montjuïc cemetery. The horse-drawn carriages on display were used for city funeral processions from the 1830s until the service was mechanized in the 1950s, when the silver Buick (also on display) came into use. Most of the carriages and hearses are extravagantly decorated, and some carried dignitaries, politicians and big-name bullfighters to their final resting places. There are also plenty of old photographs of them in use in the city's streets, alongside antique uniforms, mourning wear and formal riding gear.

Museu Nacional d'Art de Catalunya (MNAC)

MAP P.82, POCKET MAP C5/6.
Palau Nacional Ⓜ Espanya ⓣ 936 220 376, Ⓦ mnac.cat. Tue–Sat 10am–8pm (Oct–April until 6pm), Sun & hols 10am–3pm. €12, ticket valid 48hr, first Sun of the month free; special exhibitions, varied charges apply.

Catalunya's national art gallery is one of Barcelona's essential visits, showcasing a thousand years of Catalan art in stupendous surroundings. For first-time visitors it can be difficult to know where to start, but if time is limited it's recommended you concentrate on the medieval collection. It's split into two main sections, one dedicated to Romanesque art and the other to Gothic – periods in which Catalunya's artists were pre-eminent in Spain.

The collection of Romanesque frescoes in particular is the museum's pride and joy – removed from churches in the Catalan Pyrenees, and presented in a reconstruction of their original setting. MNAC also boasts an unsurpassed nineteenth- and twentieth-century Catalan art collection (until the 1940s – everything from the 1950s onwards is covered by MACBA in the Raval). It's particularly strong on *modernista* and *noucentista* painting and sculpture, the two dominant schools of the period, while there are some fascinating diversions into subjects like *modernista* interior design, avant-garde sculpture and historical photography.

Blockbuster exhibitions, and special shows based on the museum's archives are popular (separate charges may apply).

Museu Etnològic

MAP P.82, POCKET MAP C6.
Pg. Santa Madrona 16–22 Ⓜ Espanya Ⓦ ajuntament.barcelona.cat/museuetnologic. Tue–Sat 10am–7pm, Sun & hols 10am–8pm.

The Ethnological Museum boasts extensive global cultural collections and puts on excellent exhibitions, which usually last for a year or two and focus on a particular

Museu Nacional d'Art de Catalunya

subject or geographical area. Refreshingly, pieces close to home aren't neglected, which means that there's also often a focus on local and national themes, such as rural life and work or Spanish carnival celebrations.

Museu d'Arqueologia

MAP P.82, POCKET MAP C6.
Pg. Santa Madrona 39–41 Ⓜ Espanya Ⓣ 934 232 129, Ⓦ mac.cat. Tue–Sat 9.30am–7pm, Sun & hols 10am–2.30pm. €4.50, free last Tue of each month Oct–June.

The city's main archeological collection spans the centuries from the Stone Age to the time of the Visigoths, with the Roman and Greek periods particularly well represented. Finds from Catalunya's best-preserved archeological site – the Greek remains at Empúries on the Costa Brava – are notable, while on an upper floor life in Barcino (Roman Barcelona) is interpreted through a vivid array of tombstones, staTue, inscriptions and friezes.

La Ciutat del Teatre

MAP P.82, POCKET MAP C5–D6.
Mercat de les Flors Ⓜ Poble Sec Ⓣ 932 562 600, Ⓦ mercatflors.cat; Teatre Lliure Ⓣ 932 289 747, Ⓦ teatrelliure.cat; Institut del Teatre Ⓣ 932 892 770, Ⓦ teatrelliure.com.

At the foot of Montjuïc the theatre area known as La Ciutat del Teatre ("Theatre City") occupies a corner of the old working-class neighbourhood of Poble Sec. Here, off C/de Lleida, you'll find the **Mercat de les Flors** – once a flower market, now a centre for dance and the "movement arts" – and the progressive **Teatre Lliure** ("Free Theatre"), while the sleek **Institut del Teatre** brings together the city's major drama and dance schools.

Poble Sec

MAP P.85, POCKET MAP D5–E6.
Ⓜ Poble Sec.

The Poble Sec neighbourhood provides a complete contrast to the landscaped slopes of Montjuïc. The name ("Dry Village") is derived from the fact that this working-class neighbourhood originally had no water supply. Today, the hillside grid of streets is lined with down-to-earth grocery stores and good-value restaurants, while Poble Sec is also emerging as an "off-Raval" nightlife destination, with its fashionable bars and music clubs – pedestrianized Carrer de Blai is the epicentre of the scene. It has its own metro station, or it's an easy walk from El Raval, while the Montjuïc funicular has its lower station at nearby Ⓜ Paral.lel.

La Ciutat del Teatre

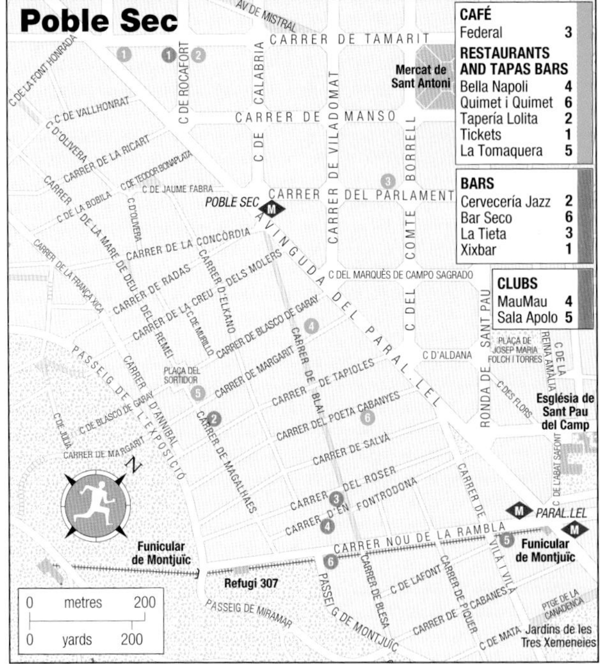

Refugi 307

MAP P.82, POCKET MAP D7/8.
C/Nou de la Rambla 175 Ⓜ Paral.lel ⓣ 932 562 100, ⓦ museuhistoria.bcn.cat. Guided tours Sun at 10.30am, 11.30am & 12.30pm. €3.40.

For a fascinating look at one of the city's hidden corners, visit Poble Sec's old Civil War air-raid shelter, dug into the hillside by local people in 1936.

The tunnels could shelter up to 2000 people from Franco's bombs – you follow your guide into the labyrinth to the sound of screaming sirens, which at the time gave the locals just two minutes to get safely underground. Storyboards and photographs by the entrance explain the gripping history of the Civil War in Barcelona. Tours are in Spanish or Catalan, though someone usually speaks English, and you can just turn up on the day.

Estadi Olímpic

MAP P.82, POCKET MAP B6.
Museu Olímpic i de l'Esport, Av. de

Teatre Grec and the Barcelona Festival

Centrepiece of Barcelona's annual summer cultural festival (ⓦ grec.bcn.cat) is the **Teatre Grec** (Greek Theatre), cut into a former quarry on the Montjuïc hillside. Starting in late June (and running throughout July and sometimes early Aug), the festival incorporates drama, music and dance, with some of the most atmospheric events staged in the Greek theatre, from Shakespearean productions to shows by avant-garde performance artists.

Fundació Joan Miró

l'Estadi 60 Ⓜ Espanya ⓣ 932 925 379, Ⓦ museuolimpicbcn.cat. Tue–Sat 10am–6pm (April–Sept until 8pm), Sun & hols 10am–2.30pm. €5.10.

The 65,000-seater Olympic Stadium was the ceremonial venue for the 1992 Barcelona Olympics. From the front, a vast *terrassa* provides one of the finest vantage points in the city, while the space-age curve of Santiago Calatrava's communications tower dominates the skyline.

Around the other side, across the road from the stadium, the history of the Games – and Barcelona's successful hosting – are covered in the Olympic and Sports Museum. It's a fully interactive experience, with lots of sports gear and memorabilia displayed, but even so it's probably one for hardcore Olympics fans only.

Fundació Joan Miró

MAP P.82, POCKET MAP C6.
Parc de Montjuïc Ⓜ Espanya ⓣ 934 439 470, Ⓦ fundaciomiro-bcn.org. Tue–Sat 10am–8pm (winter until 6pm), Thu until 9pm, Sun & hols 10am–3pm. €12, exhibitions from €7.

Barcelona's most adventurous art museum houses the life's work of the great Catalan artist Joan Miró (1893–1983). Inside the stark white building is a permanent collection of works largely donated by Miró himself and covering the period from 1914 to 1978. The paintings and drawings in particular are instantly recognizable, being among the chief links between Surrealism and abstract art, while there's also a selection of fascinating original sketches – Miró's enormous tapestries and outdoor sculptures, for example, often started life as a doodle on a scrap of notepaper. The museum's Sala K provides a rapid appraisal of Miró's entire *oeuvre* in a representative selection of works. Elsewhere are pieces by other artists in homage to Miró, and exhibitions by young experimental artists in the Espai 13 gallery.

The museum sponsors temporary exhibitions, film shows, lectures and children's theatre. There's also a café-restaurant with outdoor tables on a sunny patio – and you don't need a museum ticket to go in.

Funicular de Montjuïc

MAP P.82, POCKET MAP D6.
Av. del Paral.lel Ⓜ Paral.lel Ⓦ tmb.cat. Every 10min, Mon–Fri 7.30am–8pm, Sat, Sun & hols 9am–8pm (April–Oct daily until 10pm). €2.15, transport tickets and passes valid.

The quickest way to reach the lower heights of Montjuïc is to take the funicular, from inside the station at Ⓜ Paral.lel. At the upper station you can switch to the Montjuïc cable car, or you're only a few minutes' walk from the Fundació Joan Miró.

Telefèric de Montjuïc

MAP P.82, POCKET MAP D7.
Av. de Miramar Ⓜ Paral.lel, then Funicular Ⓦ tmb.cat. Daily: April, May & Oct 10am–7pm; June–Sept 10am–9pm; Nov–March 10am–6pm. €7.50 one way, €10.80 return.

The cable car up to the castle and back is an exciting ride, and the views, of course, are stupendous. There's an intermediate station, called Mirador, where you can get out and enjoy more sweeping vistas.

Castell de Montjuïc

MAP P.82, POCKET MAP C7/8.
Carretera de Montjuïc Ⓣ 932 564 445, Ⓦ bcn.cat/castelldemontjuic. Daily 10am–8pm.

Barcelona's fortress served as a military base and prison for decades, and was where the last president of the prewar Catalan government, Lluís Companys, was executed on Franco's orders on October 15, 1940. However, in 2008 the castle was symbolically handed over to the city and restoration work is transforming the site into a combined peace museum, memorial space and Montjuïc interpretation centre. Exhibitions take place here in the meantime, and the cable car ride and dramatic location merit a visit in their own right. The rampart views are magnificent, while below the walls the panoramic **Camí del Mar** pathway looks out over port and ocean. It runs for one kilometre to the Mirador del Migdia viewpoint, where there's a great open-air bar called *La Caseta* (weekends from noon, plus summer weekend DJ nights).

Jardí Botànic de Barcelona

MAP P.82, POCKET MAP B7.
C/Dr Font i Quer 2 Ⓜ Espanya Ⓣ 932 564 160, Ⓦ museuciencies.bcn.cat. Daily: April, May, Sept,Oct 10am–7pm; Nov–March 10am–6pm, June, July, Aug 10am–8pm. €3.50, or combined ticket with Museu Blau €7; free Sun after 3pm & first Sun of the month.

Principal among Montjuïc's many gardens is the city's Botanical Garden, laid out on terraced slopes offering fine views over the city. The Montjuïc buses run here directly, or it's a five-minute walk around the back of the Olympic Stadium. The beautifully kept contemporary garden has landscaped zones representing the flora of the Mediterranean, Canary Islands, California, Chile, South Africa and Australia. Just try to avoid arriving in the full heat of a summer day, as there's very little≈shade.

Jardí Botànic de Barcelona

Café

Federal

MAP P.85, POCKET MAP E5.
C/del Parlament 39 Ⓜ Sant Antoni Ⓣ 931 873 607, Ⓦ federalcafe.es. Mon–Thu 8am–11pm, Fri 8am–1am, Sat 9am–1am, Sun 9am–5.30pm.

Australian-style brunch has broken into Barcelona via this cosy corner café with a great little roof garden. Whether you're looking for a flat white and French toast, a bacon butty and a glass of New Zealand Sauvignon Blanc or a dandelion soy latte, you can guarantee that there's nowhere else quite like this in town.

Restaurants and tapas bars

Bella Napoli

MAP P.85, POCKET MAP E6.
C/Margarit 14 Ⓜ Poble Sec Ⓣ 934 425 056, Ⓦ bellanapoli.es. Daily 1.30–4pm & 8.30pm–midnight.

Authentic Neapolitan pizzeria serving some of the city's finest pizzas straight from a beehive-shaped oven. Or there's a huge range of pastas, risottos and veal *scaloppine* (most dishes between €9 and €15).

Tickets

Quimet i Quimet

MAP P.85, POCKET MAP E6.
C/Poeta Cabanyes 25 Ⓜ Paral.lel Ⓣ 934 423 142.Mon–Fri noon–4pm & 7–10.30pm, Sat noon–4pm; closed Aug.

Poble Sec's cosiest tapas bar is a place of pilgrimage where classy finger food (dishes €3–10) is served from a minuscule counter.

Tapería Lolita

MAP P.85, POCKET MAP D5.
C/Tamarit 104 Ⓜ Poble Sec Ⓣ 934 245 231, Ⓦ lolitataperia.com. Tue–Thu 7pm–midnight, Fri 7pm–2.30am, Sat 1–4pm & 7pm–2.30am.

A hip bar which serves classic tapas to tuned-in city folk and in-the-know tourists. You'll eat for around €25 – don't miss the signature-dish *patatas bravas* or the deep-fried *bombas* (meatballs) and *croquetas.*

Tickets

MAP P.85, POCKET MAP D5.
Av. Paral.lel 164 Ⓜ Poble Sec Ⓦ elbarri.com. Online reservations only. Tue–Fri 6.30–10.30pm, Sat 1–3pm & 7–10.30pm. Open to non-reservation holders.

Star-studded tapas bar by *El Bulli*'s Albert Adrià and his even-more-famous brother Ferran Adrià, where terrifically inventive dishes (€5–20 each; expect to spend €70) mix impeccably sourced ingredients with flights of fancy. Online reservations are taken up to three months in advance and seats are hard to get.

La Tomaquera

MAP P.85, POCKET MAP D6.
C/Margarit 58 Ⓜ Poble Sec Ⓣ 675 902 389. Tue–Thu 1pm–3.45pm & 8.15–11pm, Fri & Sat 1–3.45pm & 8.30–11.30pm, Sun 1–3.45pm; closed Sun in June & July; closed Aug.

Chatter-filled traditional tavern where the chefs hack steaks and chops from great hunks of meat. It's not for the faint-hearted, but the grilled chicken is sensational and the *entrecôtes* enormous (most mains €8–15).

Bars

Cervecería Jazz

MAP P.85, POCKET MAP D6.
C/Margarit 43 Poble Sec 934 433 259, cerveceriajazz.com. Tue–Sat 7pm–3am.
Grab a stool at the carved bar and shoot the breeze over a Catalan craft beer. It's an amiable joint with great music, from jazz to reggae, and locals swear that the burgers are the best in town.

Bar Seco

MAP P.85, POCKET MAP E6.
Pg. Montjuïc 74 Paral.lel 933 296 374. Mon–Thu 10am–4pm & 7.30pm–1am (Fri & Sat until 2am), Sun 10am–5pm.
The "Dry Bar" is a local hit, with its mellow vibe, fresh juices and artisan beers.

La Tieta

MAP P.85, POCKET MAP E6.
C/de Blai 1 Paral.lel 931 863 595. May–Nov Mon 6pm–midnight, Tue–Thu noon–midnight, Fri & Sat noon–1am; Dec–April Tue–Thu noon–midnight, Fri & Sat noon–2am, Sun noon–4pm.
Small but perfectly formed, "The Aunt" is a cool drinks and tapas place with an open window onto the street and just enough room for a dozen or so good friends.

Xixbar

MAP P.85, POCKET MAP D5.
C/Rocafort 19 Poble Sec 934 234 314, xixbar.com. Mon 6.30pm–2.30am, Tue & Wed 6pm–2.30am, Thu 5pm–2.30am, Fri & Sat 5pm–3am.
An old *granja* (milk bar) turned candlelit cocktail bar. It's big on gin, boasting over a hundred varieties.

Clubs

MauMau

MAP P.85, POCKET MAP E6.
C/Fontrodona 33 Paral.lel 934 418 015, maumaunderground.com. Thu–Sat 9pm–2.30am.

Sala Apolo

Underground lounge-club, cultural centre and chill-out space, with nightly video projections, all sorts of exhibitions and guest DJs playing deep, soulful grooves.

Sala Apolo

MAP P.85, POCKET MAP A13.
C/Nou de la Rambla 113 Paral.lel 934 414 001, sala-apolo.com. Daily midnight–5am.
Old-time ballroom turned hip concert venue with gigs on two stages (local acts to big names) and an eclectic series of club nights, from punk or Catalan rumba sounds to the weekend's long-running *Nitsa Club* (www.nitsa.com). Gigs €10–35, club nights €10–15.

Tablao de Carmen

MAP P.82, POCKET MAP B5.
Poble Espanyol Espanya 933 256 895, tablaodecarmen.com. Tue–Sun, shows at 6pm & 8.30pm.
Poble Espanyol's famous flamenco club features a variety of shows from seasoned performers and new talent. From €41, rising to €70 for the show plus dinner. Reservations required.

La Terrrazza

MAP P.82, POCKET MAP B5.
Poble Espanyol Espanya 932 724 980, laterrrazza.com. May–Oct Thu–Sat 11.45pm–6am.
Open-air summer club for nonstop dance, house and techno. Don't get there until 3am and be prepared for the style police. Admission €15–20.

Port Olímpic and Poble Nou

The main waterfront legacy of the 1992 Olympics was the Port Olímpic, the marina development which lies fifteen minutes' walk along the promenade from Barceloneta. Locals make full use of the beach and boardwalks, descending in force at the weekends for a leisurely lunch or late drink in one of the scores of restaurants and bars. There are also fine beaches further north near the old working-class neighbourhood of Poble Nou, while the impressive Museu Blau anchors the waterside zone known as the Parc del Fòrum. Access to the area is by metro to Ciutadella-Vila Olímpica or Poble Nou, or bus #59 runs from the Ramblas through Barceloneta and out to Port Olímpic.

Port Olímpic

MAP P.91, POCKET MAP K8–M8.

Ⓜ Ciutadella-Vila Olímpica.

Approaching the Olympic port, the golden mirage above the promenade slowly reveals itself to be a huge **copper fish** (courtesy of Frank Gehry, architect of the Bilbao Guggenheim). It's the emblem of the seafront development constructed for the 1992 Olympics, incorporating the port itself – site of many of the Olympic watersports events – which is backed by the city's two tallest buildings, the **Torre Mapfre** and the steel-framed **Hotel Arts Barcelona**, both 154m high. Two wharves contain the bulk of the action: the Moll de Mestral has a lower deck by the marina lined with

Port Olímpic

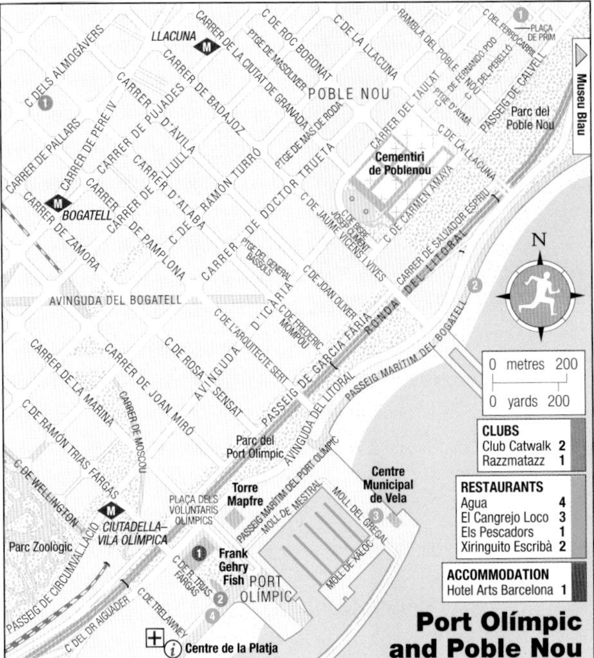

bars, while the Moll de Gregal sports a double-decker tier of seafood restaurants. The beach, meanwhile, turns into a full-on summer resort, backed by class-conscious clubs along Passeig Marítim appealing to local rich kids and A-list celebs.

City beaches

MAP P.91, POCKET MAP L8–M8.

From Ⓜ Ciutadella-Vila Olímpica it's a 15 min walk along the promenade to Bogatell beach.

A series of sandy beaches stretches for four kilometres north of Port Olímpic. Split into different named sections (Nova Icària, Bogatell etc), which boast showers, playgrounds and open-air café-bars, it's a pretty extraordinary facility to find so close to a city centre. A sunny day, even in winter, brings the locals out in force, and the sands are regularly swept and replenished.

Centre de la Platja

MAP P.91, POCKET MAP K8.

Pg. Marítim Ⓜ Ciutadella-Vila Olímpica ⓣ 932 210 348, Ⓦ bcn.cat/platges. June–Sept Tue–Sun 10am–7pm; Oct–May Tue–Sun 10am–2pm.

On the boardwalk arcade, in front of the Hospital del Mar, the city council has opened a beach visitor centre. There's a full programme of walks, talks and sports, as well as buckets and spades for kids, and frisbees, volleyball and beach tennis gear available for pick-up games on the sands.

Rambla del Poble Nou

MAP P.91.

Ⓜ Poble Nou.

A twenty-minute walk up the beach from Port Olímpic, the Rambla de Poble Nou runs through the most attractive part of **Poble Nou** ("New Village"). The old industrial neighbourhood is at the heart of a huge city regeneration scheme,

Edifici Fòrum

but the local avenue remains unchanged – a run of modest shops, cafés and restaurants, including the classic juice and milk bar of *El Tio Che* (Rambla de Poble Nou 44–46).

Cementiri del Poble Nou

MAP P.91, POCKET MAP M7.
Av. d'Icaria Ⓜ Bogatell. Daily 8am–6pm.
This vast nineteenth-century mausoleum has its tombs set in walls 7m high. With birdsong accompanying a stroll around the flower-lined pavements, quiet courtyards and chapels, this village of the dead is a rare haven of peace in the city.

Museu Blau

MAP P.91, POCKET MAP M7.
Pl. Leonardo da Vinci 4–5, Parc del Fòrum Ⓜ El Maresme Fòrum, or tram T4 Ⓣ 932 566 002, Ⓦ www.museuciencies.bcn.cat. March–Sept Tue–Sat 10am–7pm, Sun 10am–8pm; Oct–Feb Tue–Fri 10am–6pm, Sat 10am–7pm, Sun 10am–8pm. €7, includes entrance to Montjuïc botanical garden; first Sun of the month free & every Sun after 3pm.
The Natural Science Museum's million-strong collection of rocks, fossils, plants and animals has a state-of-the-art home in the visually stunning Blue Museum, housed in the Fòrum building, whose permanent exhibition – Planeta Vida (Planet Life) – plots a journey through the history of life on earth. It's heavily focused on evolutionary, whole-earth, Gaia principles, with plenty of entertaining, interactive bells and whistles to guide you through topics as diverse as sex and reproduction and conservation of the environment.

Diagonal Mar

The waterfront district north of Poble Nou was developed in the wake of the Universal Forum of Cultures Expo (held in 2004). It's promoted as **Diagonal Mar**, anchored by the Diagonal Mar shopping mall (Ⓜ El Maresme Fòrum or tram T4) and with several classy hotels, convention centres and exhibition halls grouped nearby. The dazzling **Edifici Fòrum** building is the work of Jacques Herzog (architect of London's Tate Modern), while the main open space is claimed to be the second-largest square in the world after Beijing's Tiananmen Square. This immense expanse spreads towards the sea, culminating in a giant solar-panelled canopy that overlooks the marina, beach and park areas. In summer, temporary bars, dancefloors and chill-out zones are established at the **Parc del Fòrum**, and the city authorities have shifted some of the bigger annual music festivals and events down here to inject a bit of life outside convention time. At other times it can be a bit soulless, but it's definitely worth the metro or tram ride if you're interested in heroic-scale public projects.

Restaurants

Agua

MAP P.91, POCKET MAP K8.
Pg. Marítim 30 Ⓜ Ciutadella-Vila Olímpica Ⓣ 932 251 272, Ⓦ grupotragaluz.com. Mon–Thu & Sun noon–11.30pm, Fri & Sat noon–12.30am. Breakfast 9am–noon.
The nicest boardwalk restaurant on the strip, with a contemporary Mediterranean menu, from salads to grills. Prices are pretty fair (most dishes €10–25), so it's usually busy.

El Cangrejo Loco

MAP P.91, POCKET MAP L8.
Moll de Gregal 29–30 Ⓜ Ciutadella-Vila Olímpica Ⓣ 932 210 533, Ⓦ elcangrejoloco.com. Daily noon–11pm.
The terrace at the "Crazy Crab" offers ocean views, and the food is first rate. A mixed fried-fish plate is a typically Catalan starter, and the rice dishes are thoroughly recommended. From around €40.

Els Pescadors

MAP P.91.
Pl. Prim 1 Ⓜ Poble Nou Ⓣ 932 252 018, Ⓦ elspescadors.com. Daily 1–4pm & 8–11pm; closed 2 weeks in Dec.
The best fish restaurant in Barcelona? It's a tough call, but many would choose this hideaway place in a pretty Poble Nou square. The menu offers daily fresh fish dishes, and plenty more involving rice, noodles or salt cod. Don't go mad and you'll escape for around €60.

Xiringuito Escribà

MAP P.91, POCKET MAP M8.
Ronda del Litoral 42, Platja Bogatell Ⓜ Ciutadella-Vila Olímpica Ⓣ 932 210 729, Ⓦ xiringuitoescriba.com. Daily 1–10.30pm.
Beachfront restaurant (really a glorified beach shack) that's enough off the beaten track (a 15min walk from Port Olímpic) to mark you out as in the know. High points are paellas and daily fish specials (around €20), followed by sensational cakes and pastries from the Escribà family patisserie.

Clubs

Club Catwalk

MAP P.91, POCKET MAP K8.
C/Ramon Trias Fargas 2–4 Ⓜ Ciutadella-Vila Olímpica Ⓣ 932 216 161, Ⓦ clubcatwalk.net. Mon–Wed 11.30pm–5am, Thu–Sat 11.30pm–6am, Sun 7pm–6am.
Portside club of choice playing house, funk, soul and RnB for well-heeled locals and visitors. It's under the *Hotel Arts*; admission €12–15.

Razzmatazz

MAP P.91, POCKET MAP L5.
C/Pamplona 88 Ⓜ Bogatell Ⓣ 933 208 200, Ⓦ salarazzmatazz.com. Thu (Razz club only), Fri & Sat 6pm–6am times vary depending on the event).
Razzmatazz hosts the biggest in-town rock gigs, and at weekends turns into "five clubs in one", spinning mixed sounds in variously named bars. Admission €18.

Club Catwalk

Dreta de l'Eixample

The nineteenth-century street grid north of Plaça de Catalunya is the city's main shopping and business district. It was designed as part of a revolutionary urban plan – the Eixample in Catalan ("Extension" or "Widening") – that divided districts into regular blocks, whose characteristic wide streets and shaved corners survive today. Two parallel avenues, Passeig de Gràcia and Rambla de Catalunya, are the backbone of the Eixample, with everything to the east known as the Dreta de l'Eixample (the right-hand side). It's here that the bulk of the city's famous *modernista* (Catalan Art Nouveau) buildings are found, along with an array of classy galleries and some of the city's most stylish shops. Start your exploration from either Metro Passeig de Gràcia or Metro Diagonal.

Passeig de Gràcia

MAP P.96, POCKET MAP H1/4.
Ⓜ Passeig de Gràcia.

The prominent avenue, which runs northwest from Plaça de Catalunya, was laid out in its present form in 1827. It later developed as a showcase for *modernista* architects, eagerly commissioned by status-conscious merchants and businessmen. Walk the length of Passeig de Gràcia from Plaça de Catalunya to Avinguda Diagonal (a 25min stroll) and you'll pass some of the city's most extraordinary architecture, notably the famous group of buildings (including casas Amatller and Batllò) known as the Mansana de la Discòrdia, or "Block of Discord", as they show off wildly varying manifestations of the *modernista* style and spirit. Further up is Antoni Gaudí's iconic apartment building La Pedrera, while, in between, wrought-iron Art Nouveau street lamps, fashion stores and designer hotels set the tone for this resolutely upscale avenue.

Passeig de Gràcia

Museu del Perfum

MAP P.96, POCKET MAP H3.
Pg. de Gràcia 39 Ⓜ Passeig de Gràcia
Ⓣ 932 160 121, Ⓦ museodelperfume.com.
Mon–Fri 10.30am–8pm, Sat 11am–2pm. €5.

At the back of the Regia perfume store is a private collection of over five thousand perfume and essence bottles from Egyptian times onwards. There are some exquisite pieces, including Turkish filigree-and-crystal ware and bronze and silver Indian elephant flasks, while

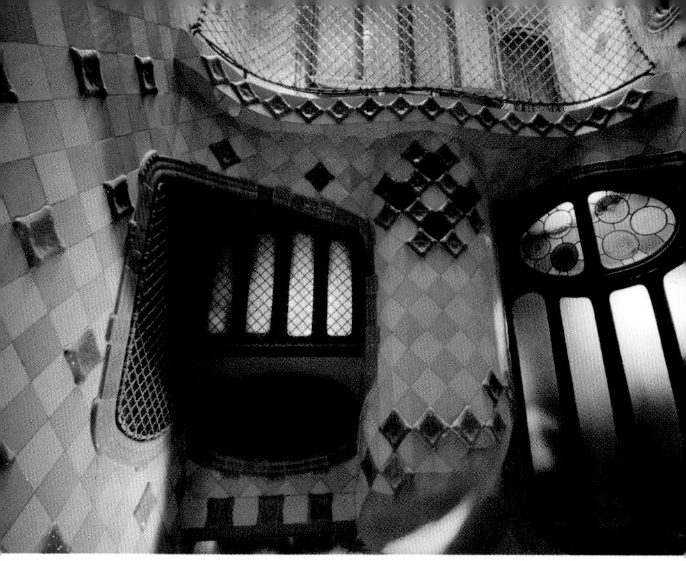

Casa Batlló

more modern times are represented by scents made for Brigitte Bardot, Grace Kelly and Elizabeth Taylor.

Casa Amatller

MAP P.96, POCKET MAP G3. Fundació Amatller, Pg. de Gràcia 41 Ⓜ Passeig de Gràcia Ⓦ amatller.org.

Josep Puig i Cadafalch's striking Casa Amatller (1900) was designed for Antoni Amatller, a Catalan chocolate manufacturer, art collector, photographer and traveller. It's awash with coloured ceramic decoration, while inside the hallway twisted stone columns are interspersed with dragon lamps. Guided tours are occasionally available (check website for details) while renovation works continue and usually include a visit to Amatller's photographic studio as well as chocolate-tasting in the original kitchen. The house also displays temporary exhibitions under the auspices of the Amatller Institute of Hispanic Art.

Casa Batlló

MAP P.96, POCKET MAP G3. Pg. de Gràcia 43 Ⓜ Passeig de Gràcia Ⓣ 932 160 306, Ⓦ casabatllo.es. Daily 9am–9pm, access occasionally restricted. €18.50.

The most extraordinary creation on the "Block of Discord" is the Casa Batllò, designed for the industrialist Josep Batllò and finished in 1907. Antoni Gaudí created an undulating facade that Salvador Dalí later compared to "the tranquil waters of a lake". The sinuous interior, meanwhile, resembles the inside of some great organism, complete with meandering, snakeskin-patterned walls. Self-guided audio tours show you the main floor, the patio and rear facade, the ribbed attic and celebrated mosaic rooftop chimneys. Advance tickets are recommended (by phone, in person or online); the scrum of visitors can be a frustrating business at peak times.

Fundació Antoni Tàpies

MAP P.96, POCKET MAP G3. C/Aragó 255 Ⓜ Passeig de Gràcia Ⓣ 934 870 315, Ⓦ fundaciotapies.org. Tue–Thu & Sat 10am–7pm (Fri 9pm), Sun 10am–3pm. €7.

Dreta de l'Eixample
RESTAURANTS AND TAPAS BARS
2254 5
Au Port de la Lune 8
La Bodegueta 2
El Mussol 3, 11
El Nacional Barcelona 9
Tapas, 24 7
Tragaluz 1
CAFÉS
Cafè del Centre 6
Forn de Sant Jaume 4
Laie Llibreria Café 10
SHOPS
Bulevard dels Antiquaris 4
Casa del Libro 3
Cubiña 2
Mango 6
Purificacion Garcia 1
Reserva Ibérica 5
ACCOMMODATION
Casa Bonay 6
Equity Point Centric 4
Hostal Girona 8
Hostal Goya 7
Hotel Condes de Barcelona 3
Hotel Omm 1
Mandarin Oriental 5
Praktik Bakery Hotel 2
the5rooms 9
GRÀCIA
Mercat Abaceria Central
Casa Fuster
Casa Comalat
Palau Robert
Palau Baró de Quadras
Casa de les Punxes
La Pedrera
Casa Thomas
Palau Montaner
Fundació Antoni Tàpies
Museu Egipci
La Concepció
Mercat de la Concepció
Casa Batllò
Casa Amatller
Museu del Perfum
Jardins de les Torres de les Aigües
Museu del Modernisme Català
Casa Calvet
Palau de la Música Catalana
PLAÇA DE CATALUNYA
DIAGONAL
PASSEIG DE GRÀCIA
GIRONA
CATALUNYA
URQUINAONA
CARRER DE CORSEGA
CARRER DEL ROSSELLÒ
CARRER DE PROVENÇA
AV DIAGONAL
CARRER DE MALLORCA
CARRER DE VALENCIA
CARRER D'ARAGÓ
CARRER DEL CONSELL DE CENT
CARRER DE LA DIPUTACIÓ
GRAN VIA DE LES CORTS CATALANES
CARRER DE CASP
CARRER D' AUSIAS MARC
RONDA DE SANT PERE
PASSEIG DE GRÀCIA
RAMBLA DE CATALUNYA
CARRER DE PAU CLARIS
CARRER DE ROGER DE LLÚRIA
CARRER DEL BRUC
CARRER DE GIRONA
CARRER DE BAILÉN
VIA LAIETANA
CARRER DE BONAVISTA
C DE LA LLIBERTAT
C DEL PERILL
C DE TORDERA
C DE SIRACUSA
C DEL DILUVI
C DEL PENEDÈS
C DE S DOMÈNEC
C DE LUIS ANTÚNEZ
C DE GOYA
C DEL DR RIZAL
C DE SENECA
PLAÇA D'URQUINAONA
CARRER DE ORTIGOSA
CARRER DE TRAFALGAR
C DE SANT PERE MES ALT
PLAÇA DE LLUIS MILLET
PL DE JOAN CARLES I
PTGE DE LA CONCEPCIÓ
PTGE DE PERMANYER
0 metres 200
0 yards 200

Modernisme

The Catalan offshoot of Art Nouveau, **modernisme**, was the expression of a renewed upsurge in Catalan nationalism in the 1870s. Its most famous exponent was **Antoni Gaudí i Cornet** (1852–1926), whose buildings are apparently lunatic flights of fantasy, which at the same time are perfectly functional. His architectural influences were Moorish and Gothic, while he embellished his work with elements from the natural world. The imaginative impetus he provided inspired others like **Lluís Domènech i Montaner** (1850–1923) – perhaps the greatest *modernista* architect – and **Josep Puig i Cadafalch** (1867–1957), both of whom also experimented with the use of ceramic tiles, ironwork, stained glass and stone carving. This combination of traditional methods with modern technology became the hallmark of *modernisme* – producing some of the most exciting architecture to be found anywhere in the world.

The definitive collection of the work of Catalan abstract artist Antoni Tàpies i Puig (who died in 2012) is housed in *modernista* architect Lluís Domènech i Montaner's first important building, the Casa Montaner i Simon (1880). You can't miss it – the foundation building is capped by Tàpies's own striking sculpture, *Núvol i Cadira* ("Cloud and Chair", 1990), a tangle of glass, wire and aluminium. The artist was born in Barcelona in 1923 and was a founding member (1948) of the influential avant-garde Dau al Set ("Die at Seven") artists' group. Tàpies's abstract style matured in the 1950s, with underlying messages and themes signalled by the inclusion of everyday objects and symbols on the canvas. Changing exhibitions focus on selections of Tàpies's work, while other shows highlight works by various contemporary artists.

Museu Egipci de Barcelona

MAP P.96, POCKET MAP H3.
C/de València 284 Ⓜ Passeig de Gràcia
Ⓣ 934 880 188, Ⓦ museuegipci.com.
Mon–Fri 10am–2pm & 4–8pm (summer: Mon–Sat 10am–10pm), Sun 10am–2pm.
€12.

Barcelona's Egyptian Museum is an exceptional private collection of over a thousand ancient artefacts, from amulets to sarcophagi – there's nothing else in Spain quite like it. Visitors are given a detailed English-language guidebook, but the real pleasure is a serendipitous wander, turning up items like cat mummies or the rare figurine of a spoonbill (ibis) representing an Egyptian god. There are temporary exhibitions, plus a good shop and terrace café, while the museum also hosts children's activities and themed events.

Museo Egipci de Barcelona

Palau Montaner

Jardins de les Torres de les Aigües

MAP P.96, POCKET MAP H3.
C/Roger de Llúria 56, between C/Consell de Cent and C/Diputació Ⓜ Girona. Daily 10.30am–dusk. €1.55

The original nineteenth-century Eixample urban plan – by utopian architect Ildefons Cerdà – was drawn up with local inhabitants very much in mind. Space, light and social community projects were part of the grand design, and something of the original municipal spirit can be seen in the Jardins de les Torres de les Aigües, an enclosed square (reached down a herringbone-brick tunnel) centred on a Moorish-style water tower. It has been handsomely restored by the city council, who turn it into a backyard family beach every summer, complete with sand and paddling pool. Another example of the old Eixample lies directly opposite, across C/Roger de Llúria, where the cobbled **Passatge del Permanyer** cuts across an Eixample block, lined by candy coloured, single-storey townhouses.

Mercat de la Concepció

MAP P.96, POCKET MAP J3.
Between C/de Valencia and C/d'Aragó Ⓜ Girona Ⓦ laconcepcio.com. Mon & Sat 8am–3pm, Tue–Fri 8am–8pm (summer: Mon–Sat 8am–3pm); florists 24/7.

Flowers, shrubs and plants are a Concepció speciality (the florists on C/Valencia are open 24 hours a day), and there are some good snack bars inside the market and a few outdoor cafés to the side. The market takes its name from the nearby church of **La Concepció** (entrance on C/Roger de Llúria), whose quiet cloister is a surprising haven of slender columns and orange trees.

Palau Montaner

MAP P.96, POCKET MAP H3.
C/de Mallorca 278 Ⓜ Passeig de Gràcia Ⓣ 933 177 652, Ⓦ rutadelmodernisme.com. Guided visits: for groups only; reservations required. Tickets from €7.

The Palau Montaner (1896) has a curious history – after the original architect quit, Lluís Domènech i Montaner took over halfway through construction, and the top half of the facade is clearly more elaborate than the lower part. Meanwhile, the period's most celebrated craftsmen were set to work on the interior, which sports rich mosaic floors, painted glass, carved woodwork and a monumental staircase.

The building is now the seat of the Madrid government's delegation to Catalunya, but it is possible to arrange **guided tours** that explain something of the house's history and show you the lavish public rooms, grand dining room and courtyard. It's unusual to be able to get inside a private *modernista* house of the period, so it's definitely worth the effort.

La Pedrera

MAP P.96, POCKET MAP H2.

Pg. de Gràcia 92, entrance on C/Provença Ⓜ Diagonal Ⓣ 902 400 973, Ⓦ lapedrera.com. Daily: March–Nov 9am–8.30pm; Dec–Feb 9am–6.30pm.Tickets from €15. Nits d'estiu: last week June to first week Sept Thu–Sat 9–11pm; €25, advance sales online.

Antoni Gaudí's weird apartment building at the top of Passeig de Gràcia is simply not to be missed – though you can expect queues whenever you visit. Popularly known as La Pedrera, "the stone quarry", its rippled facade, curving around the street corner in one smooth sweep, is said to have been inspired by the mountain of Montserrat, while the apartments themselves resemble eroded cave dwellings. Indeed, there's not a straight line to be seen – hence the contemporary joke that the new tenants would only be able to keep snakes as pets. The self-guided visit includes a trip up to the extraordinary *terrat* (roof terrace) to see at close quarters the enigmatic chimneys – you should note that the roof terrace is often closed if it's raining. In addition, there's an excellent exhibition about Gaudí's life and work installed under the 270 curved brick arches of the attic. **El Pis** ("the apartment"), on the building's fourth floor, re-creates the design and style of a *modernista*-era bourgeois apartment in a series of extraordinarily light rooms that flow seamlessly from one to another. The apartment is filled with period furniture and effects, while the moulded door and window frames, and even the brass door handles, all follow Gaudí's sinuous building design. During the **Nits d'estiu** ("summer nights" – advance booking essential) you can enjoy the amazing rooftop by night with a complimentary glass of cava and music, while other concerts are also held at La Pedrera at various times.

Through the grand main entrance of the building there's access to the Pedrera **exhibition hall**, which hosts temporary art shows of works by major international artists.

Palau Robert

MAP P.96, POCKET MAP H2.

Pg. de Gràcia 107 Ⓜ Diagonal Ⓣ 932 388 091, Ⓦ gencat.cat/palaurobert. Mon–Sat 9am–8pm, Sun 9am–2.30pm. Free.

Visit the information centre for the Catalunya region for regularly changing exhibitions on all matters

La Pedrera

Catalan, from art to business. There are several exhibition spaces, both inside the main palace – built as a typical aristocratic residence in 1903 – and in the old coach house. The centre is also an important concert venue for recitals and orchestras, while the gardens around the back are a popular meeting point for local nannies and their charges.

Palau Baró de Quadras

MAP P.96, POCKET MAP H2.
Av. Diagonal 373 Ⓜ Diagonal Ⓣ 934 678 000, Ⓦ llull.cat. Mon 9am–5pm, Tue–Thu 9am–5.30pm, Fri till 2pm.

The beautifully detailed Palau Baró de Quadras (a Josep Puig i Cadafalch work from 1904) now serves as the headquarters of the Institut Ramon Llull, an organization that promotes Catalan language studies at universities worldwide. Though most of the building is closed to the public, visitors can look around its stunningly ornate ground floor during the institute's opening hours. If you first see the building from the Avinguda Diagonal side, be sure to walk around to Carrer del Rosselló – this side of the building is decorated in a more subdued, but very lovely, *modernista* style.

Casa de les Punxes

MAP P.96, POCKET MAP H2.
Av. Diagonal 416–420 Ⓜ Diagonal. Ⓦ casadelespunxes.com. Daily 10am–7pm.

Cadafalch's largest work, the soaring Casa Terrades, is more usually known as the Casa de les Punxes ("House of Spikes") because of its red-tiled turrets and steep gables. Built in 1903 for three sisters, and converted from three separate houses spreading around an entire corner of a block, the crenellated structure is almost northern European in style, reminiscent of a Gothic castle.

Passatge Permanyer

MAP P.96, POCKET MAP H3.
Passatge Permanyer Ⓜ Girona

If this elegant, leafy alleyway cut into one of the monolithic blocks of the Eixample reminds you of London, it's no coincidence. Ildefons Cerdà, who planned this part of the city's expansion, took inspiration from Regent's Park and included green spaces in the centre of his squares. Most of them were built over immediately – if they were built at all – and now contain car parks and retail space, but 46 alleys (*passatges*), of which Permanyer is the best preserved, break up the urban grid and lend a glimpse of what could have been.

Palau Baró de Quadras

Shops

Antonio Miró

MAP P.114, POCKET MAP G3.
Enric Granados 46 Ⓜ Diagonal Ⓦ antoniomiro.es. Mon–Sat 10.30am–8.30pm.
The showcase for Barcelona's most innovative designer, now also branding accessories and household design items.

Bulevard dels Antiquaris

MAP P.96, POCKET MAP H3.
Pg. de Gràcia 55–57 Ⓜ Passeig de Gràcia Ⓦ bulevarddelsantiquaris.com. Mon–Sat 10am–8.30pm; closed Sat in Aug.
An arcade with over seventy shops full of antiques - from toys and dolls to Spanish ceramics and African art.

Casa del Libro

MAP P.96, POCKET MAP H3.
Pg. de Gràcia 62 Ⓜ Passeig de Gràcia Ⓦ casadellibro.com. Mon–Sat 9.30am–9.30pm.
Barcelona's biggest book emporium, with lots of English-language titles and Catalan literature in translation.

Cubiñà

MAP P.96, POCKET MAP H3.
C/Mallorca 291 Ⓜ Verdaguer Ⓦ cubinya.es. Mon–Fri 10am–2pm & 4.30–8.30pm.
The building is stupendous – Domènech i Montaner's *modernista* Casa Thomas – while inside holds the very latest in household design.

Estanc Duaso

MAP P.112, POCKET MAP G2.
C/Balmes 116 Ⓜ Diagonal/FGC Provença Ⓣ 932 151 330, Ⓦ duaso.com. Mon–Fri 9am–8pm, Sat 10am–2pm.
Arnold Schwarzenegger shops for his stogies in this cigar-smokers' paradise that features a walk-in humidor, in-store rolling demonstrations and expert advice.

Mango

MAP P.96, POCKET MAP H3, H4.
Pg. de Gràcia 36, plus others Ⓜ Passeig de Gràcia Ⓦ mango.com. Mon–Sat 10am–9.30pm.
Barcelona is where high-street fashion chain Mango began. For last season's gear at unbeatable prices, head to Mango Outlet (C/ Girona 37).

Purificacion Garcia

MAP P.96, POCKET MAP H2.
C/de Provença 292 Ⓜ Diagonal Ⓦ purificaciongarcia.es. Mon–Sat 10am–8.30pm.
A hot designer with an eye for fabrics – Garcia's first job was in a textile factory. She's also designed clothes for film and theatre, and her costumes were seen at the opening ceremony of the Barcelona Olympics.

Reserva Ibérica

MAP P.96, POCKET MAP G3.
Rambla de Catalunya 61 Ⓜ Passeig de Gràcia Ⓣ 902 112 641, Ⓦ reservaiberica.com. Mon–Fri 9.30am–9pm, Sat 10am–9pm.
A ham wonderland specializing in *jamón ibérico de bellota*, the finest of all the Spanish cured hams, which comes from acorn-fed pigs. Pick up pre-packaged samplers or tuck into a plate of paper-thin slices at one of the marble-topped tables.

Antonio Miró

Cafés

Cafè del Centre

MAP P.96, POCKET MAP J3.
C/Girona 69 Ⓜ Girona Ⓣ 934 881 101. Tue–Thu & Sun 11.30am–11pm, Fri & Sat 11.30am–1.30pm; closed Aug.

This quiet coffee stop is only four blocks from the main drag of Passeig de Gràcia. It's been here since 1873 (a plaque outside honours its service to the city) and, with its timeworn *modernista* decor, it seems largely unchanged.

Forn de Sant Jaume

MAP P.96, POCKET MAP G3.
Rambla de Catalunya 50 Ⓜ Passeig de Gràcia Ⓣ 932 160 229. Mon–Fri 8.30am–9pm, Sat & Sun 9am–9pm.

Uptown *pastisseria* whose glittering windows are piled high with croissants, cakes, pastries and sweets. The small adjacent café has *rambla* seats, or you can take away your goodies for later.

Cafè del Centre

Laie Llibreria Café

MAP P.96, POCKET MAP H4.
C/Pau Claris 85 Ⓜ Passeig de Gràcia Ⓣ 933 027 310, Ⓦ laie.es. Mon–Fri 9am–9pm, Sat 10am–9pm (August 10am–8pm).

The city's first and best bookshop-café (buy a book downstairs and take it to the café to read) is known for its popular weekday buffet breakfast spread, set lunch deals and à la carte dining.

Restaurants and tapas bars

2254

MAP P.96, POCKET MAP G3.
C/del Consell de Cent 335 Ⓜ Passseig de Gràcia Ⓣ 935 286 002, Ⓦ 2254restaurant.com. Sun–Thu 11.am–midnight, Fri & Sat noon–1am.

The name of the restaurant stands for the number of kilometres between Barcelona and Palermo - the birthplace of the restaurant owner and chef, Nuncio Cona. Creative, tasty tapas and splendid desserts (tiramisu 2254, €7.50). Try some of their signature tapas (between €8.95 and €13) influenced by not just Spanish, but also Italian and French cuisine.

Au Port de la Lune

MAP P.96, POCKET MAP H4.
C/Paul Claris 103 Ⓜ Passseig de Gràcia Ⓣ 934 122 224. Mon–Fri 8am–5pm & 6.30–11.30pm, Sat 10am–5pm & 6pm–midnight, Sun 11am–5pm.

This no-nonsense French bistro is a favourite of local foodies. The decor borders on cliché, but the cooking is the real deal: fresh oysters, ripe cheese and a killer cassoulet. A sign reading "There's no ketchup, no Coca-Cola, no Coca-Cola light, and there never will be" sets the tone. The €15 lunch menu and €25, four-course evening menu are unbeatable value.

La Bodegueta

MAP P.96, POCKET MAP G2.
Rambla Catalunya 100 Ⓜ Diagonal Ⓣ 932 154 894, Ⓦ labodegueta.cat. Mon–Fri 7am–1.45am, Sat 8am–1.45am, Sun & hols 6.30pm–1.45am; closed mornings in Aug.

This long-established *bodega* offers cava and wine by the glass, as well as ham, cheese, anchovies and other tapas to soak it up.

El Mussol

MAP P.96, POCKET MAP G3, E10.
C/Aragó 261 Ⓜ Passeig de Gràcia Ⓣ 934 876 151; branch at C/de Casp 19 Ⓣ 933 017 610. Daily 8am–1am (C/de Casp branch from 1pm).

Chain of big rustic diners, known for their meat and vegetables *a la brasa* (on the grill), most of which run between €6 and €12. They're good places to sample hearty Catalan country cooking, with snails and wild mushrooms on the menu all year round and *calçots* (big spring onions) a spring speciality.

El Nacional Barcelona

MAP P.96, POCKET MAP H4.
Pg. de Gràcia 24 Bis Ⓜ Passeig de Gràcia Ⓣ 935 185 053, Ⓦ elnacionalbcn.com. Daily noon–1am.

A massive one-stop-shop for Spanish cuisine. In this gorgeous, high-ceilinged space you'll find a fish restaurant, grill, tapas bar, snack bar, oyster bar, wine bar, cocktail bar and most other bars you can think of. Check it out on the cheap with a quick snack or go for broke with a massive extra-aged rib-eye steak from the wood grill.

Tapas, 24

MAP P.96, POCKET MAP H4.
C/Diputació 269 Ⓜ Passeig de Gràcia Ⓣ 934 880 977, Ⓦ carlesabellan.com. Mon–Sat 9am–midnight.

Star chef Carles Abellan gets back to his roots at this basement tapas bar. There's a reassuringly traditional feel that's echoed in the menu, which features *patatas bravas*, Andalucian-style fried fish, meatballs, chorizo sausage and fried eggs. But the kitchen updates the classics too, so there's also *calamares romana* (fried squid) dyed black with squid ink or a burger with foie gras. Most tapas cost €4–16. There's always a rush and a bustle at meal times, so be aware you might have to queue.

Tapas, 24

Tragaluz

MAP P.96, POCKET MAP G2.
Ptge. de la Concepció 5 Ⓜ Diagonal Ⓣ 934 870 621, Ⓦ grupotragaluz.com/restaurante/tragaluz. Daily 1.30–4pm & 8pm–11.30pm.

A stylish uptown standby that attracts beautiful people by the score, and the classy Mediterranean-with-knobs-on cooking, served under a glass roof (*tragaluz* means "skylight"), doesn't disappoint. The menu ranges from seasonal salads to grilled sea bass, with mains costing €16–30. It's a relaxing stop for those fresh off the *modernista* trail (La Pedrera is just across the way).

Sagrada Família and Glòries

If there's one building that is an essential stop on any visit to Barcelona it's Antoni Gaudí's great church of the Sagrada Família (Metro Sagrada Família). Most visitors make a special journey out to see it and then head back into the centre, but it's worth sticking around to visit Lluís Domènech i Montaner's *modernista* Hospital de la Santa Creu i de Sant Pau. A few blocks south of Sagrada Família you'll find the Glòries area and a further set of attractions, including the city's main concert hall and music museum, and Catalunya's flagship national theatre building.

Sagrada Família

MAP P.106, POCKET MAP K2.
C/Mallorca 401 Ⓜ Sagrada Família Ⓣ 935 132 060, Ⓦ sagradafamilia.org. Daily: April–Sept 9am–8pm; Oct & Mar 9am–7pm, Nov–Feb 9am–6pm. Tours in English April–Oct 11.15am, 12.30pm, 1.45pm & 3pm; Nov–Mar 10.15am, 12.15pm & 3pm. Tickets from €15 (under-10s free), or €24 including tour; combination ticket with Casa-Museu Gaudí at Parc Güell €24.

The metro drops you right outside the overpowering church of the Sagrada Família ("Sacred Family"). Begun in 1882 on a modest scale, the project changed the minute that 31-year-old architect Antoni Gaudí took charge in 1884 – he saw in the Sagrada Família an opportunity to reflect his own deepening spiritual feelings. Gaudí spent the rest of his life working on the church and was adapting the plans right up to his untimely death. Run over by a tram on June 7, 1926, his death was treated as a Catalan national disaster, and all of Barcelona turned out for his funeral.

Sagrada Familia

Hospital de la Santa Creu i Sant Pau

Although the building survived, Gaudí's plans were mostly destroyed during the Spanish Civil War. Nevertheless, work restarted in the 1950s amid great controversy, and has continued ever since – as have the arguments. Some maintained that the Sagrada Família should be left incomplete as a memorial to Gaudí, others that the architect intended it to be the work of several generations. Either way, based on reconstructed models and notes, the project is now moving towards completion (within the next ten years, it's said), and the building is beginning to take its final shape.

The size alone is startling (Gaudí's original plan was to build a church to seat over 10,000 people), while the carved spires, monumental bronze doors and vibrant facades are an imaginative and symbolic *tour de force*. Gaudí made extensive use of human, plant and animal models to exactly produce the likenesses he sought – the spreading stone leaves of the roof in the church interior, for example, were inspired by the city's plane trees. A **lift** (€4.50) up one of the towers provides an unforgettable close-up view of the work, while in the **crypt** (where Gaudí is buried) a fascinating museum traces the construction of the church – you can also view sculptors and model-makers still at work today.

Hospital de la Santa Creu i de Sant Pau

MAP P.106, POCKET MAP M1.
C/de Sant Antoni Maria Claret 167 Ⓜ Sant Pau Dos de Maig Ⓣ 935 537 801, Ⓦ santpaubarcelona.org. Mon–Sat 9.30am–6.30pm (Nov–Mar until 4.30pm), Sun & hols 9.30am–2.30pm. English-language tours Mon–Fri 10.30am–noon & 1pm, Sat & Sun noon & 1pm. €14, free first Sun of month; tours €19.

Lluís Domènech i Montaner's *modernista* public hospital is possibly the one building that can touch the Sagrada Família for size and invention. It's hard to believe that its whimsical pavilions and towers, which are adorned with sculpture, mosaics, stained glass and ironwork, were once a working hospital, but it remained fully functional until 2009. A massive cleanup project has restored the historical complex's glory, while the business of curing the sick has moved to an ugly modern complex next door. The original building is now home to health and sustainability NGOs, not recovering patients. Interesting tours of the old hospital run regularly and the breathtaking

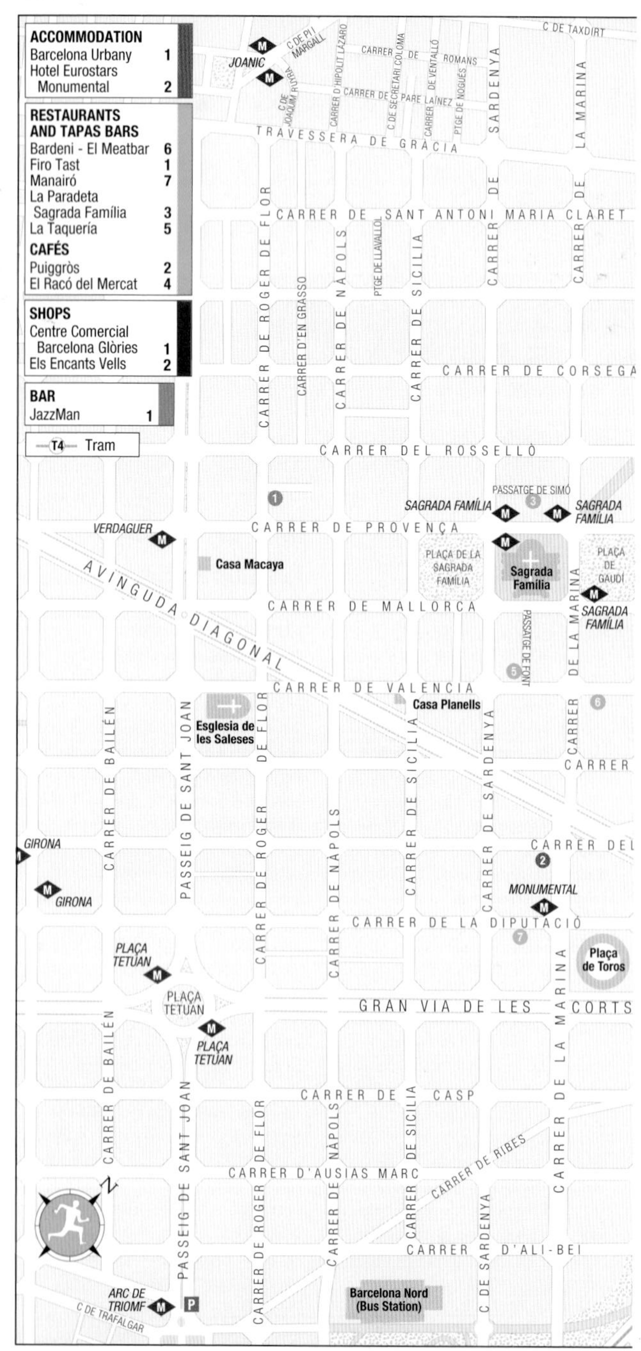
ACCOMMODATION
Barcelona Urbany 1
Hotel Eurostars Monumental 2
RESTAURANTS AND TAPAS BARS
Bardeni - El Meatbar 6
Firo Tast 1
Manairó 7
La Paradeta Sagrada Família 3
La Taquería 5
CAFÉS
Puiggròs 2
El Racó del Mercat 4
SHOPS
Centre Comercial Barcelona Glòries 1
Els Encants Vells 2
BAR
JazzMan 1
T4 Tram
JOANIC
TRAVESSERA DE GRÀCIA
CARRER DE SANT ANTONI MARIA CLARET
CARRER DE CORSEGA
CARRER DEL ROSSELLÓ
CARRER DE PROVENÇA
CARRER DE MALLORCA
CARRER DE VALENCIA
CARRER DE LA DIPUTACIÓ
GRAN VIA DE LES CORTS
CARRER DE CASP
CARRER D'AUSIAS MARC
CARRER D'ALI-BEI
CARRER DE RIBES
CARRER DE ROGER DE FLOR
CARRER DE NÀPOLS
CARRER DE SICILIA
CARRER DE LA MARINA
CARRER DE BAILÉN
PASSEIG DE SANT JOAN
SARDENYA
AVINGUDA DIAGONAL
SAGRADA FAMÍLIA
VERDAGUER
Casa Macaya
PLAÇA DE LA SAGRADA FAMÍLIA
Sagrada Família
PLAÇA DE GAUDÍ
Casa Planells
Esglesia de les Saleses
GIRONA
MONUMENTAL
Plaça de Toros
PLAÇA TETUAN
ARC DE TRIOMF
Barcelona Nord (Bus Station)

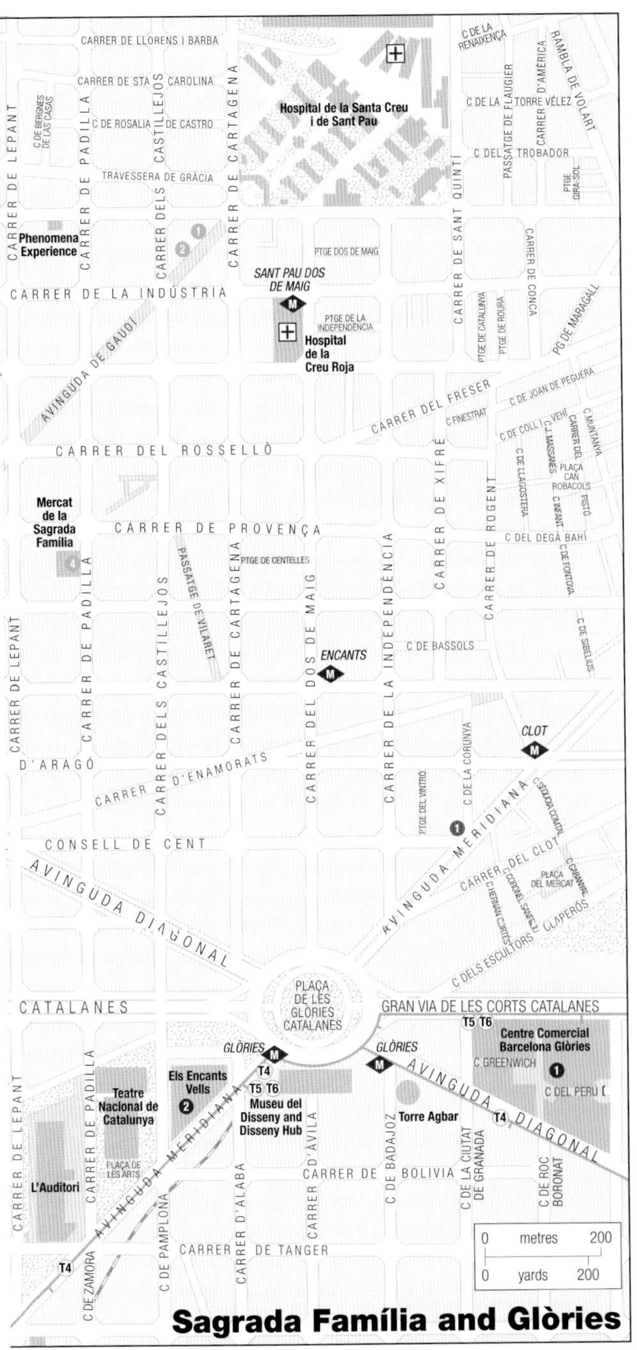

Sagrada Família and Glòries

Casa Macaya

central courtyard is a popular venue for outdoor concerts and fashion shows. It's an easy stroll up here from the Sagrada Família.

Casa Macaya

MAP P.106, POCKET MAP J2.
Pg. de Sant Joan 108 Ⓜ Verdaguer.

Just four blocks from the Sagrada Família, Josep Puig i Cadafalch's Casa Macaya (1898–1900) is well known for its imaginative exterior carvings by craftsman Eusebi Arnau – look for the angel holding a camera or the sculptor himself on his way to work by bike.

Plaça de les Glòries Catalanes

MAP P.106, POCKET MAP M4.
Ⓜ Glòries.

Barcelona's major avenues all meet at Plaça de les Glòries Catalanes, dedicated to the Catalan "glories", from architecture to literature. Glòries is at the centre of the city's latest bout of regeneration. Signature buildings are Jean Nouvel's cigar-shaped **Torre Agbar**, a remarkable aluminium-and-glass tower inspired by Montserrat, and the sleek, zinc-plated Disseny Hub (Design Hub). Nearby **Parc del Clot** shows what can be done in an urban setting within the remains of a razed factory site. Trams speed down Avinguda Diagonal to the Diagonal Mar district, passing the **Parc del Centre del Poble Nou** (10min walk, or tram stop Pere IV), another park on an old industrial site.

Casa Planells

MAP P.106, POCKET MAP K3.
Av. Diagonal 332 Ⓜ Verdaguer

This 1924 residential building by lesser-known *modernista* architect Josep Maria Jujol is understated and austere by the standards of his contemporaries but still features organic, flowing lines. Jujol was given a free hand to do whatever he wanted with the small space available and came up with an anachronistic design that remains unique. Its interior is closed to the public but the exterior oval windows and intricate cast-iron railings are worth seeing.

Església de les Saleses

MAP P.106, POCKET MAP K3.
Passeig de Sant Joan 86–92 Ⓜ Tetuan ⓣ 934 587667, Ⓦ parroquiaconcepciobcn.org. Mon–Fri 7.30am–1pm & 5–9pm, Sun 7.30am–2pm & 5–9pm.

This fine neo-Gothic church and former convent was designed by Joan Martorell i Montells. His student, one Antoni Gaudí, may also have worked on it during its construction, which was between 1882 and 1885. The beginnings of Catalan *modernisme* can be seen in the church's ornate details, but it suffered damage during the Setmana Trágica (Tragic Week) of 1909. It was also set alight in 1936 during the Spanish Civil War, when the bodies of nuns were pulled from its crypts and gruesomely displayed on the street. Today, the church has been extensively restored and the monastery is now a school.

Museu del Disseny and Disseny Hub

MAP P.106, POCKET MAP M4. Pl. de les Glòries Catalanes 37–38 Ⓜ Glòries Ⓦ ajuntament.barcelona.cat/museudeldisseny. Tue–Sun 10am–8pm. Disseny Hub Ⓣ 932 566 713, Ⓦ dhub.cat. Mon 4–9pm, Tue–Sun 9am–9pm. Hub free.

The new Museu del Dissney brings together Barcelona's applied art collections inside the Disseny Hub building. In addition to the museum, the Hub is also home to temporary exhibition spaces, a public library and the headquarters of local design institutions such as the Foment de les Arts i del Disseny (FAD).

Teatre Nacional de Catalunya

MAP P.106, POCKET MAP L4/5. Pl. de les Arts 1 Ⓜ Glòries Ⓣ 933 065 700, Ⓦ tnc.cat.

Catalunya's National Theatre features an enterprising programme of classics, original works and productions by guest companies. The building itself makes a dramatic statement, presenting a soaring glass box encased within a Greek temple, and there are guided **tours** for anyone interested in learning more (currently Wed & Thu; €8; reservations required).

L'Auditori

MAP P.106, POCKET MAP L5. C/Lepant 150 Ⓜ Glòries Ⓣ 932 479 300, Ⓦ auditori.cat. Museu de la Música, C/Padilla 155 Ⓣ 932 563 650, Ⓦ museumusica.bcn.cat. Tue, Wed & Fri 10am–6pm, Thu 9pm, Sat & Sun 10am–7pm. €5, free first Sun of the month and every Sun after 3pm.

The city's main contemporary concert hall is home to the Barcelona Symphony Orchestra (OBC), though the programme includes chamber, choral, jazz and world concerts too. There's also the entertaining Museu de la Música (Music Museum), which displays a remarkable collection of historic instruments and musical devices.

Phenomena Experience

MAP P.106, POCKET MAP L1. C/Sant Antoni Maria Claret 168 Ⓜ Sant Pau Dos de Maig Ⓣ 932 527 743, Ⓦ phenomena-experience.com.

Fall in love again with the great movies of the 70s, 80s and 90s, plus selected recent blockbusters (all in their original language), at this independent cinema. You can also try a "beer and pizza night" in the company of fellow movie geeks. The seats are comfortable, the screen is wide and the sound is state-of-the-art. Tickets €6–8.

Museu del Disseny and Torre Agbar

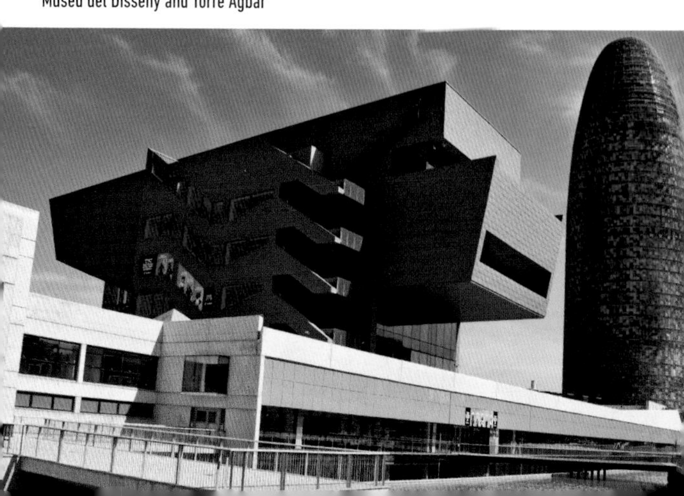

Shops

Centre Comercial Barcelona Glòries

MAP P.106, POCKET MAP M4.
Av. Diagonal 208 Ⓜ Glòries Ⓦ lesglories.com. Mon–Sat 9.30am–10pm.

Anchoring the neighbourhood is this huge 230-store mall with all the national high-street fashion names represented (H&M, Zara, Bershka, Mango) as well as a big Carrefour supermarket and an eight-screen cinema complex.

Els Encants Vells

MAP P.106, POCKET MAP L4.
Av. Meridiana 69 Ⓜ Glòries Ⓦ encantsbcn.com. Mon, Wed, Fri & Sat 9am–8pm.

The city's flea market has a shiny new home next to the Teatre Nacional de Catalunya. The site sports multiple levels of open-air treasure-hunting – you name it, you can buy it – all protected by a large canopy whose metallic underside reflects the bustling market below. You can also find surprisingly good food in the top-floor snack bars.

Els Encants Vells

Cafés

Puiggròs

MAP P.106, POCKET MAP L1.
Av. Gaudí 77 Ⓜ Sant Pau Dos de Maig Ⓣ 934 362 304. Daily 9am–9.30pm.

Open since 1922, this family bakery has recently been stylishly renovated. Take your pick from tempting pastries, fresh bread and excellent coffee, then grab a seat on the terrace or inside to watch the bakers in their glass-walled workshop.

El Racó del Mercat

MAP P.106, POCKET MAP L2.
Mercat de la Sagrada Família, C/de Padilla 255 Ⓜ Sagrada Família Ⓣ 934 363 452, Ⓦ mercatsagradafamilia.com. Tue–Thu 7am–2.30pm & 5.30–8.30pm, Fri 7am–8.30pm, Sat 7am–2pm.

Only two blocks east of the Sagrada Família – and not a tourist in sight. Browse the stalls, pick up your picnic lunch, and make for the stand-up market bar, which has pastries, tapas and sandwiches at local prices.

Restaurants and tapas bars

Bardeni – el Meatbar

MAP P.106, POCKET MAP L3.
C/Valencias 454 Ⓜ Sagrada Família Ⓣ 932 314 511, Ⓦ caldeni.com/bardeni. No reservations. Tue–Sat 1.30–3.10pm & 8.30–10.30pm.

Former Catalan chef of the year Dani Lechuga (whose surname ironically means "lettuce") is from a family of butchers and meat experts, so *Bardeni*'s raw materials are first rate. Beefy tapas like oxtail cannelloni and hamburgers (all priced around €7) is served, plus a few refined specials from *Caldeni*, its excellent fine dining sister restaurant next door.

Firo Tast

MAP P.106, POCKET MAP L1.
Av. Gaudí 83 Ⓜ Sant Pau Dos de Maig Ⓣ 934 507 454. Mon & Sun 12.30–4pm, Tue–Sat 12.30–4.30pm & 7.30–11.30pm.
Three *Firo* food businesses cluster together here; the superb Chocofiro chocolatiers is flanked by *El Petit Firo* (a quality tapas bar) and *Firo Tast*, a sit-down restaurant. Together they form a bright spot in a street full of mediocre tourist restaurants. *Firo Tast* serves a solid set menu of Catalan classics for €15, and a weekend tasting menu for €27.

Manairó

MAP P.106, POCKET MAP K4.
C/Diputació 424 Ⓜ Sagrada Família Ⓣ 932 310 057, Ⓦ manairo.com.
Jordi Herrera doesn't look like the kind of guy who cooks delicate dishes but the bearded, motorbike-riding former rugby player has carved out a reputation as one of the city's top fine dining chefs. His creations combine technical wizardry with big, bold flavours. The signature steak, cooked on a patented bear trap-like system of spikes over a stove-top bonfire (€32), is one of the best you'll ever eat. Tasting menus cost €70 and €90.

La Paradeta Sagrada Família

MAP P.106, POCKET MAP K2.
Ptge. Simó 18 Ⓜ Sagrada Família Ⓣ 934 500 191, Ⓦ laparadeta.com. No reservations. Tue–Thu 8–11.30pm, Fri–Sun 8pm–midnight.
One of a chain of similar *La Paradeta* restaurants across the city, "the market stall" looks like its name suggests. Join the queue and check out the fish and shellfish on ice, priced by weight. Point to the prawns, cockles, mussels, clams, crabs and lobsters you want and they'll be cooked for you there and then. Listen for your number being called, collect the food from the hatch and tuck into some of the best-priced fresh seafood in town. Expect to pay about €20–25.

La Paradeta

La Taquería

MAP P.106, POCKET MAP K3.
Ptge. del Font 5 Ⓜ Sagrada Família Ⓣ 931 261 359, Ⓦ lataqueria.eu. Tue–Sun 1–4.30pm & 8.30–11.30pm (Fri & Sat until midnight).
When it comes to Mexican food in Europe, throwing the word "authentic" around can get you in trouble with the purists, but it's an apt description for the menu here, which ranges from *tacos al pastor* to freshly made guacamole (€5–10).

Bars

JazzMan

MAP P.106, POCKET MAP K2.
C/Roger de Flor 238 Ⓜ Sagrada Família Ⓣ 667 618 593, Ⓦ jazzmanbarcelona.blogspot.com.es. Mon–Thu 9pm–2.30am, Fri 8pm–3am, Sat 10pm–3am.
Everything you'd want from a cosy jazz club: low lights, live music, good drinks and a cool, intimate vibe. When there's no one on stage, expect to hear classics from *JazzMan*'s impeccable vinyl and CD collection.

Esquerra de l'Eixample

The long streets west of Rambla de Catalunya as far as Barcelona Sants station are perhaps the least visited on any city sightseeing trip. With all the major architectural highlights found on the Eixample's eastern (or right-hand) side, the Esquerra de l'Eixample (left-hand side) was intended by its nineteenth-century planners for public buildings and institutions, many of which still stand. However, the Esquerra does have its moments of interest – not least a couple of excellent museums and an eye-catching public park or two – while it's here that some of the city's best bars and clubs are found, particularly in the gay-friendly streets of the so-called Gaixample district, near the university.

Universitat de Barcelona

MAP P.114, POCKET MAP F4–G4.
Gran Via de les Corts Catalanes 585, at Pl. de la Universitat Ⓜ Universitat.

Built in the 1860s, the grand neoclassical university building is now largely used for ceremonies and administration purposes, but you can visit the main hall or the fine arcaded courtyards and extensive gardens. The traditional student meeting point is the *Bar Estudiantil*, outside in Plaça Universitat, where you can usually grab a pavement table.

Museu del Modernisme Català

MAP P.114, POCKET MAP G3.
C/Balmes 48 Ⓜ Passeig de Gràcia Ⓣ 932 722 896, Ⓦ mmcat.cat. Mon–Fri 10.30am–2pm & 4–7pm, Sat, Sun & hols closed. €10.

Barcelona's traditional "gallery district", around C/Consell de Cent, is a fitting location

Universitat de Barcelona

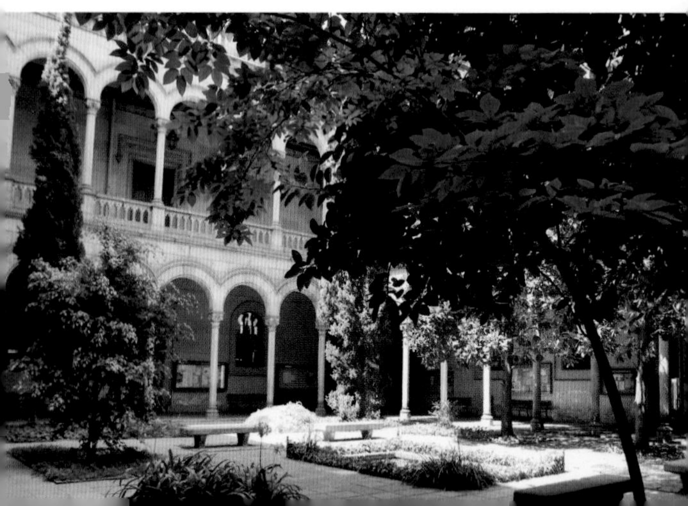

for the stupendous *modernista* collection housed in the Museu del Modernisme Català. It's the private enterprise of the celebrated Gothsland antiques gallery, and displays a collection forty years in the making – including the famous marble decorative vase by craftsman Eusebi Arnau that was the gallery's symbol for over thirty years. This is just one of 350 works on show across two exhibition floors in a restored former textile warehouse – the grand, vaulted basement contains paintings and sculpture while on the ground floor is *modernista* furniture, from screens to sofas. There are paintings and works by many famous names, from oils by Ramon Casas i Carbó to sinuous mirrors and tables by Antoni Gaudí (originally made for the casas Batlló and Calvet). But above all, this is a rare opportunity to examine extraordinary Art Nouveau fixtures and fittings by less familiar artists: wonderful creations by pioneering cabinetmaker Joan Busquets i Jané, for example; the dramatic carved headboards of Gaspar Homar i Mezquida; or the expressive terracotta sculptures of Lambert Escaler i Milà. As a crash course in the varied facets of Catalan *modernisme*, beyond the iconic buildings themselves, it's invaluable.

Museu del Modernisme Català

Mercat del Ninot

MAP P.114, POCKET MAP F2-3.
C/Mallorca 133 Ⓜ Hospital Clínic Ⓣ 934 536 512, Ⓦ mercatsbcn.com. Mon–Sat 8am–9pm, outdoor Mon–Fri 9am–8pm, Sat 9am–2pm.

One of the oldest markets in the city has recently undergone a major refurbishment. The "new" Ninot is a treat for hungry shoppers, full of stallholders selling ready-to-eat dishes as well as fresh produce. The restaurant at the rear, *El Ninot Cuina*, is an understated gem. Around the back of the hospital, it's also worth having a look at the **Escola Industrial**, formerly a textile mill, which boasts a 1920s chapel by Joan Rubió i Bellvér, who worked with Antoni Gaudí. Students usually fill the courtyards, and you're free to take a stroll through to view the highly decorative buildings.

Casa Golferichs

MAP P.114, POCKET MAP E4.
Gran Via de les Corts Catalanes 491 Ⓜ Rocafort Ⓣ 933 237 790, Ⓦ golferichs.org. Mon–Fri 10am–8pm, Sat 10am–2pm (Jul closed on Sat).

In 1900, when road engineer and wood trader Macari Golferichs wanted to show off his success with a *modernista* mansion in the Eixample, he turned to the young architect Joan Rubió i Bellver, one of Antoni Gaudí's closest collaborators. The result, known as El Xalet ("The Chalet") was a Gothic-tinged oddity, full of dark wood, ornate ceramics and soaring vertical lines. It is now a venue for intimate concerts, presentations and exhibitions.

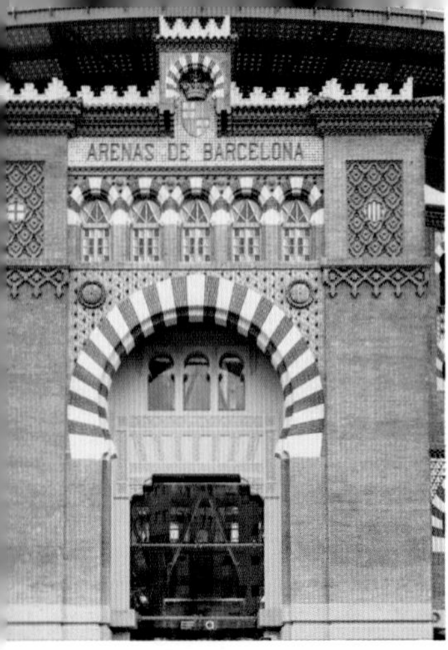

ARENAS DE BARCELONA

Arenas de Barcelona

Parc Joan Miró

MAP P.114, POCKET MAP C3-4–D3-4.
C/de Tarragona Ⓜ Tarragona. Daily 10am–dusk.

Parc Joan Miró was laid out on the site of the nineteenth-century municipal slaughter-house. It features a raised piazza whose only feature is Joan Miró's gigantic mosaic sculpture *Dona i Ocell* ("Woman and Bird"), towering above a shallow reflecting pool. The rear of the park is given over to games areas and landscaped sections of palms and firs, with a kiosk café and some outdoor tables among the trees. The children's playground here is one of the best in the city.

Arenas de Barcelona

MAP P.114, POCKET MAP C4.
Gran Via de les Corts Catalanes 373–385, at Pl. d'Espanya Ⓜ Espanya Ⓣ 932 890 244, Ⓦ arenasdebarcelona.com. Daily 10am–10pm (Oct–May 9am–9pm).

The landmark building on the north side of Plaça d'Espanya is the fabulous Moorish-style bullring, the Arenas de Barcelona, originally built in 1900 but reimagined as a swish shopping and leisure centre that opened in 2011. On top is a walk-

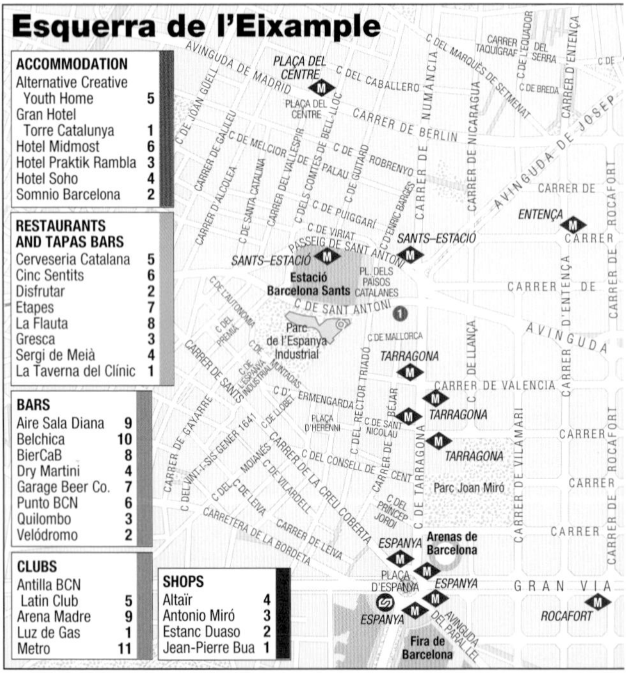

Esquerra de l'Eixample
ACCOMMODATION
Alternative Creative Youth Home 5
Gran Hotel Torre Catalunya 1
Hotel Midmost 6
Hotel Praktik Rambla 3
Hotel Soho 4
Somnio Barcelona 2
RESTAURANTS AND TAPAS BARS
Cerveseria Catalana 5
Cinc Sentits 6
Disfrutar 2
Etapes 7
La Flauta 8
Gresca 3
Sergi de Meià 4
La Taverna del Clínic 1
BARS
Aire Sala Diana 9
Belchica 10
BierCaB 8
Dry Martini 4
Garage Beer Co. 7
Punto BCN 6
Quilombo 3
Velódromo 2
CLUBS
Antilla BCN Latin Club 5
Arena Madre 9
Luz de Gas 1
Metro 11
SHOPS
Altaïr 4
Antonio Miró 3
Estanc Duaso 2
Jean-Pierre Bua 1
AVINGUDA DE MADRID
PLAÇA DEL CENTRE
C DEL CABALLERO
CARRER DE BERLIN
C DE ROBRENYO
C DE PUIGGARÍ
C DE VIRIAT
PASSEIG DE SANT ANTONI
SANTS-ESTACIÓ
Estació Barcelona Sants
PL. DELS PAÏSOS CATALANES
C DE SANT ANTONI
Parc de l'Espanya Industrial
C DE MALLORCA
TARRAGONA
CARRER DE VALENCIA
C D'ERMENGARDA
PLAÇA D'HERENNI
C DEL CONSELL DE CENT
CARRER DE SANTS
CARRER DE LA CREU COBERTA
CARRETERA DE LA BORDETA
Parc Joan Miró
Arenas de Barcelona
ESPANYA
PLAÇA D'ESPANYA
AVINGUDA DEL PARAL·LEL
Fira de Barcelona
GRAN VIA
ROCAFORT
ENTENÇA
AVINGUDA DE JOSEP
CARRER DE NICARAGUA
CARRER DE NUMÀNCIA
CARRER DE VILAMARI
CARRER DE ROCAFORT
CARRER D'ENTENÇA
C DE LLANÇA
C DEL MARQUÈS DE SENTMENAT

On the Miró trail

When you've seen one Miró – well, you start to see them everywhere in Barcelona, starting with the large ceramic mural visible on the facade at the airport. The towering *Dona i Ocell* in the Parc Joan Miró is unmissable, but you should also look down at your feet on the Ramblas for the pavement mural at Plaça de la Boqueria. Miró also designed the *Caixa de Pensions* starfish logo splashed across the Caixa Forum arts centre. In many ways, it's a Miró city, whatever Picasso fans might think.

around promenade circling the **dome** that offers 360-degree views, while inside are four floors of shopping and entertainment, including cinema, gym and various restaurants (some on the top-floor promenade).

Parc de l'Espanya Industrial

MAP P.114, POCKET MAP B2-3 & C2-3. C/de Sant Antoni Ⓜ Sants Estació. Daily 10am–dusk.

If you have time to kill at Barcelona Sants station, nip around the south side to Basque architect Luis Peña Ganchegui's urban park. Built on the site of an old textile factory, there's a line of concrete lighthouses contrasting with an incongruously classical Neptune, as well as boating lake, café kiosk, playground and sports facilities. It's a decent attempt at reconciling local interests with the otherwise mundane nature of the surroundings, typical of the city's approach to revitalizing unkempt urban corners.

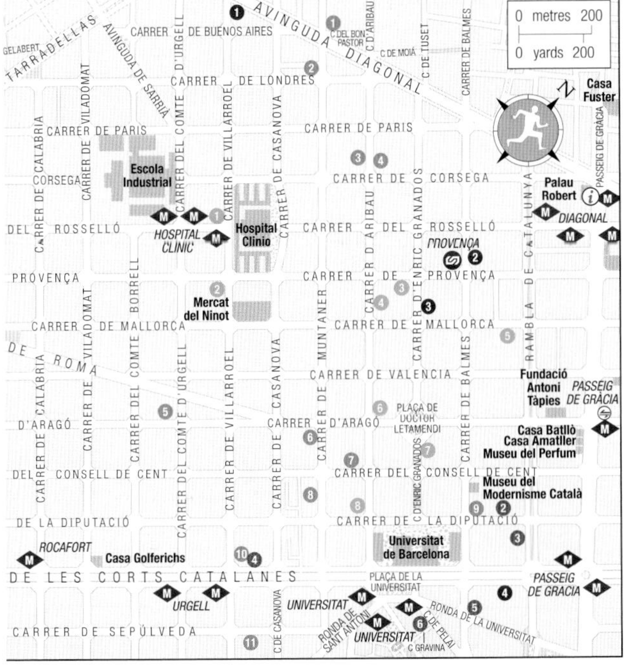

Shops

Altaïr

MAP P.114, POCKET MAP G4.
Gran Via de les Corts Catalanes 616 Ⓜ Passeig de Gràcia Ⓦ altair.es. Mon–Sat 10am–8.30pm.

Europe's biggest travel superstore has a massive selection of travel books, guides, maps and world music, plus a programme of travel-related talks and exhibitions.

Jean-Pierre Bua

MAP P.114, POCKET MAP F1.
Av. Diagonal 469 Ⓜ Hospital Clínic Ⓦ jeanpierrebua.com. Mon–Sat 10am–8.30pm.

The city's high temple for fashion victims: a postmodern shrine for Yamamoto, Gaultier, Miyake, Galliano, McQueen, McCartney, Westwood and other international stars.

Restaurants and tapas bars

Cerveseria Catalana

MAP P.114, POCKET MAP G3.
C/Mallorca 236 Ⓜ Passeig de Gràcia Ⓣ 932 160 368. Daily 9am–1.30am.

A place that is serious about its tapas and beer – the counters are piled high, supplemented by a blackboard list of daily specials, while the walls are lined with bottled brews from around the world. It gets busy after work and at meal times, and you might have to wait for a table.

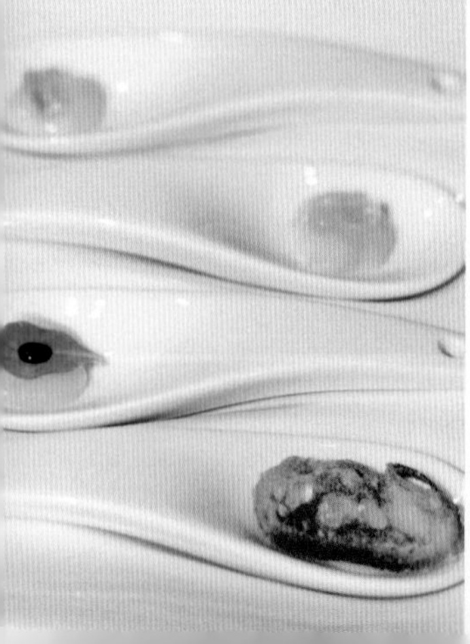

Cinc Sentits

Cinc Sentits

MAP P.114, POCKET MAP F3.
C/Aribau 58 Ⓜ Universitat Ⓣ 933 239 490, Ⓦ cincsentits.com. Tue–Fri 1.30–2.30pm & 8.30–9.30pm, Sat 1.30–10pm; closed 2 weeks in Aug.

Jordi Artal's "Five Senses" wows diners with its contemporary Catalan cuisine – and it has a Michelin star to boot, so you'll need to book. Three tasting menus (€55, €95 and €125, wine pairings available) use rigorously sourced ingredients (wild fish, mountain lamb, seasonal vegetables, farmhouse cheeses) in elegant, pared-down dishes that are all about flavour.

Disfrutar

MAP P.114, POCKET MAP F2.
C/Villarroel 163 Ⓜ Hospital Clínic Ⓣ 933 486 896, Ⓦ disfrutarbarcelona.com. Mon 9am–2.30pm & 8–9.30pm, Tue–Fri 1–2.30pm & 8–9.30pm.

A recipe for the hottest ticket in town: take three head chefs from the former "world's best restaurant" *El Bulli*, add a labyrinthine Barcelona location, season with the smiles of happy customers and decorate with an instant Michelin star. €100 gets you 28 courses of *Disfrutar*'s magical creations and a lot of lasting memories.

Etapes

MAP P.114, POCKET MAP G3.
C/Enric Granados 10 Ⓜ Universitat Ⓣ 933 236 914, Ⓦ etapes.cat. Mon–Fri 1–3.30pm & 8–11pm, Sat & Sun 8–11pm.

This family-owned restaurant is fuelled by an unusual combination of simplicity and sophistication.

The food ticks both boxes: it's refined but steers clear of anything too fancy. Instead, you'll get home-cooked cakes from *yaya* (grandma) after things like scallops and pork belly, and prawn tartare. The service is excellent and the lunch menu (€15.50) is a steal. In the evenings, there are tasting menus at €35 and €60.

La Flauta

MAP P.114, POCKET MAP F4.
C/Aribau 23 Ⓜ Universitat ⓣ 933 237 038. Mon–Sat 7am–1.30am, closed 3 weeks in Aug.

One of the city's best-value lunch menus sees diners queuing for tables early – get there before 2pm to avoid the rush. While the name is a nod to the house speciality gourmet sandwiches (a *flauta* is a crispy baguette) there are also tapas-style meals served day and night (dishes €4–10).

Gresca

MAP P.114, POCKET MAP G2.
C/Provença 230 Ⓜ Diagonal ⓣ 934 516 193, ⓦ gresca.net. Mon–Fri 1.30–3.30pm & 8.30–10.30pm, Sat & Sun 1.30–3.30pm.

Local food writers have unsuccessfully campaigned for years for chef Rafa Penya to have a Michelin star. But what's bad news for him is good news for diners: you get to keep eating his superb food at bargain prices. The €19 lunchtime menu is a winner but, if funds permit, the €38–70 tasting menus are even more spectacular, and showcase creative, technical cooking of the highest standard.

Sergi de Meià

MAP P.114, POCKET MAP F2.
C/Aribau 106 Ⓜ Universitat ⓣ 931 255 710, ⓦ restaurantsergidemeia.cat. Tue–Sat 9.30–11.30am, 1.30–3.30pm & 8–10.30pm.

In the morning, Sergi's mother cooks hearty, old-fashioned Catalan breakfasts that stick to your ribs. Later in the day, Sergi (after whom the restaurant is named) takes all-local, all-sustainable ingredients

La Taverna del Clínic

and elevates things a notch, refining rustic dishes like wild duck and truffle rice. The €21 lunch menu draws crowds of locals and the full tasting menu is €50.

La Taverna del Clínic

MAP P.114, POCKET MAP F2.
C/Rosselló 155 Ⓜ Hospital Clínic ⓣ 934 104 221, ⓦ latavernadelclinic.com. Mon–Sat 1–4pm & 8–11.30pm.

Named for the hospital over the road, this is a gourmet tapas spot that concentrates on regional produce. Snack at the solid marble bar or sit down for serious food, accompanied by artisan olive oil and a high-class wine list, at one of the ten tables (book in advance). Quality is high but the bill runs up quickly at €10–30 a dish, from crispy suckling pig to sea urchins artfully arranged atop mounds of sea salt.

Bars

Aire Sala Diana

MAP P.114, POCKET MAP G3.
C/de Valencia 236 Ⓜ Passeig de Gràcia ⓣ 934 878 342, ⓦ arenadisco.com. Thu–Sat 11pm–2.30am.

The hottest, most stylish lesbian bar in town is a relaxed place for a drink and a dance to pop, house

Dry Martini

and retro sounds. Gay men are welcome too.

Belchica

MAP P.114, POCKET MAP F4.
C/Villaroel 60 Ⓜ Urgell Ⓣ 625 814 001, Ⓦ belchica.be. Tue–Thu 6pm–3am, Fri–Sat 8pm–3am.

Barcelona's first Belgian beer bar guarantees a range of decent brews (including Trappist beers) that you can't get anywhere else. It's a cosy haunt, playing electronica, new jazz, lounge, reggae and other left-field sounds, and there are music and poetry nights.

BierCaB

MAP P.114, POCKET MAP F3.
C/Muntaner 55 Ⓜ Universitat Ⓣ 644 689 045, Ⓦ biercab.com. Mon–Sat 3.30–10pm, summer: Mon–Thu 4pm–midnight, Fri & Sat 4pm–2am; closed in August.

Thirty international craft beers on tap, constantly updated via large screens, means that there's an ale to slake all thirsts here. The staff are enthusiastic and well-informed, and you can try before you buy. Prices, like most craft beer bars in Barcelona, are steep so save some euros to pick up a bottle of your favourite from the adjoining shop.

Dry Martini

MAP P.114, POCKET MAP F2.
C/Aribau 166 Ⓜ Provença Ⓣ 932 175 072, Ⓦ drymartinibcn.com. Mon–Fri 1pm–2.30am (opens 6.30pm in Aug), Sat & Sun 6.30pm–3am.

White-jacketed bartenders, dark wood and brass fittings, a self-satisfied air – it could only be Barcelona's legendary uptown cocktail bar. To be fair, though, no one in town mixes drinks better.

Garage Beer Co.

MAP P.114, POCKET MAP F3.
C/Consell de Cent 261 Ⓜ Universitat Ⓣ 935 285 989, Ⓦ garagebeer.co. Mon–Thu & Sun 5pm–midnight, Fri & Sat 5pm–3am.

This friendly brewpub was an early fixture on Barcelona's "beer mile" – the craft beer bar-filled area that's boomed in recent years. There are no frills, just great ales, simple snacks, wooden benches and a glass wall onto the microbrewery out back.

Punto BCN

MAP P.114, POCKET MAP F3.
C/Muntaner 63–65 Ⓜ Universitat Ⓣ 934 878 342, Ⓦ arenadisco.com. Daily 6pm–2.30am.

Gaixample classic that attracts a lively crowd for drinks, chat and music. Wednesday happy hour is a blast, while Friday night is party night.

Quilombo

MAP P.114, POCKET MAP F2.
C/Aribau 149 Ⓜ Provença Ⓣ 934 395 406. Mon–Thu 9.30pm–2.30am, Fri & Sat 8.30pm–3am.

Unpretentious music bar that's rolled with the years since 1971, featuring live guitarists, Latin American bands and a clientele that joins in enthusiastically, maracas in hand.

Velódromo

MAP P.114, POCKET MAP F1.
C/Muntaner 213 Ⓜ Hospital Clínic Ⓣ 934 306 022. Daily 6am–3am.

A gleaming facelift has put the glam back into this lofty, Parisian-style Art Deco gem. It's ideal for swish drinks and cocktails, though with a breakfast, tapas and bistro menu by renowned chef Jordi Vilà, it's also made for early starts and later dinners.

Clubs

Antilla BCN Latin Club

MAP P.114, POCKET MAP E3.
C/Aragó 141–143 Ⓜ Urgell Ⓣ 934 514 564, Ⓦ antillasalsa.com. Wed 10pm–5am, Thu 11pm–5am, Fri & Sat 11pm–6am, Sun 7pm–3am.

Latin and Caribbean tunes galore – rumba, son, salsa, merengue, mambo, you name it – for out-and-out good-time dancing. There are live bands, killer cocktails and dance classes most nights.

Arena Madre

MAP P.114, POCKET MAP G4.
C/Balmes 32 Ⓜ Passeig de Gràcia Ⓣ 934 878 342, Ⓦ arenadisco.com.

The "mother" club sits at the helm of *Arena*'s gay empire, all within a city block (pay for one, get in to all) – frenetic house at *Arena Madre* (daily 12.30–5am), high-disco antics at *Arena Classic* (C/de la Diputació 233; Fri & Sat 2–6am), more of the same plus dance, RnB, pop and rock at the more mixed *Arena VIP* (Gran Via de les Corts Catalanes 593; Fri & Sat 00.30–6am), and vintage chart hits at *Arena Dandy* (same address and hours). Admission is usually €6 on weekdays and €12 on Saturdays.

Luz de Gas

MAP P.114, POCKET MAP F1.
C/Muntaner 246 Ⓜ Provença Ⓣ 932 097 711, Ⓦ luzdegas.com. Daily midnight–5am, occasional gigs from 9.30pm.

Smart live-music venue, housed in a former ballroom, which is popular with a slightly older crowd and hosts live bands (rock, blues, soul, jazz and covers) every night around midnight. Foreign acts appear regularly too, mainly jazz-blues types but also old soul acts and up-and-coming rockers. Admission up to €20.

Metro

MAP P.114, POCKET MAP A10.
C/Sepúlveda 158 Ⓜ Universitat Ⓣ 933 235 227, Ⓦ www.metrodiscobcn.com. Daily 12.15–5am (Fri & Sat until 6.30am).

A gay institution in Barcelona, with cabaret nights and other events midweek, and extremely crowded club nights at weekends in its two rooms playing either current dance and techno or retro disco.

Arena Madre

Gràcia and Parc Güell

Gràcia was a village for much of its early existence, before being annexed as a suburb in the late nineteenth century. It still feels set apart from the city in many ways, and though actual sights are few and far between it's well known for its cinemas, bars and restaurants. The one unmissable attraction, meanwhile, just on the neighbourhood fringe, is nearby Parc Güell, an extraordinary flight of fancy by architectural genius Antoni Gaudí. To get to Gràcia take the FGC train from Plaça de Catalunya to Gràcia station, or the metro to either Diagonal (south) or Fontana (north). From any of the stations, it's around a 500m walk to Gràcia's main square, Plaça del Sol, hub of the neighbourhood's renowned nightlife.

Mercat de la Llibertat

MAP P.121, POCKET MAP G1

Pl. Llibertat 27 Ⓜ Fontana Ⓣ 932 170 995, Ⓦ mercatsbcn.com. Mon–Fri 8am–8.30pm, Sat 8am–3pm.

You may as well start where the locals start, first thing in the morning, shopping for bread and provisions in the neighbourhood market. The red-brick and iron structure has been beautifully restored and at *El Tast de Joan Noi* (next to the Joan Noi fish counter) you can sample the breakfast of champions – oysters, grilled razor clams and a glass of cava.

Casa Vicens

MAP P.121.

C/de les Carolines 24 Ⓜ Fontana. No public access.

Antoni Gaudí's first major private commission (1883–85) took its inspiration from the Moorish style,

Casa Vicens

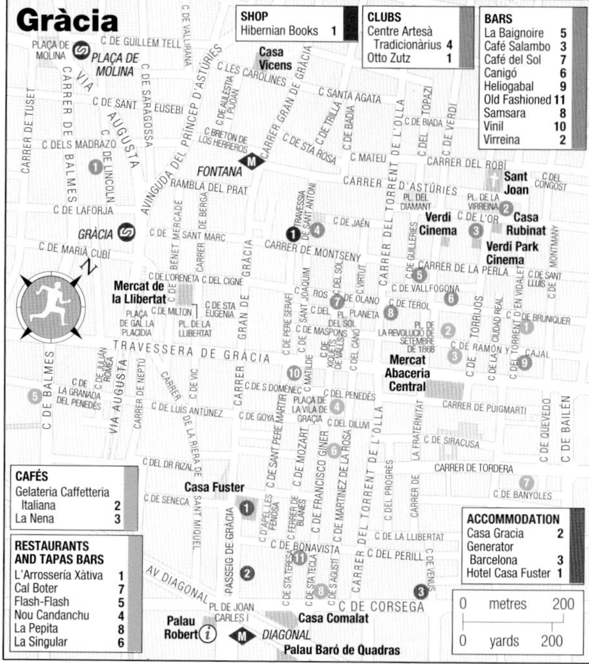

covering the facade of the house in green and white tiles with a flower motif. The decorative iron railings are a reminder of Gaudí's early training as a metalsmith (and he also designed much of the mansion's original furniture).

Plaça de la Virreina

MAP P.121.

Fontana.

This pretty square, backed by the parish church of Sant Joan, is one of Gràcia's favourites, with a couple of bars providing a place to rest and admire the handsome houses, most notably the Casa Rubinat (1909). Nearby streets, particularly **Carrer Verdi**, contain many of the neighbourhood's most fashionable boutiques, galleries and cafés.

Verdi and Verdi Park

MAP P.121.

C/Verdi 32 and C/Torrijos 49 Fontana 932 387 990, cines-verdi.com.

These art-house cinemas have sister locations in adjacent streets, with nine screens showing original-language movies from around the world. Tickets are €9 at the weekend, €6 on Monday and €8 from Tueday to Friday (€7 for the first screening of the day).

Plaça de la Vila de Gràcia

MAP P.121, POCKET MAP H1.

Diagonal.

The 30m-high clock tower in the heart of Gràcia was a rallying point for nineteenth-century radicals – whose twenty-first-century counterparts prefer to meet for brunch at the square's popular café *terrassas*.

Parc Güell

MAP P.122.

C/d'Olot Vallcarca/Lesseps 902 200 302, parkguell.cat. Daily: April 8am–8.30pm; May–Aug 8am–9.30pm; Sept & Oct 8am–8.30pm; Nov–March

Park Güell

8.30am–6.15pm. €7 online or €8 ticket office/ATMs at Lesseps and Vallcarca metro stations. Advance bookings recommended. Gaudí's Parc Güell (1900–14) was his most ambitious project after the Sagrada Família, conceived as a "garden city" of the type popular at the time in England, but opened as a public park instead in 1922. Laid out on a hill, which provides fabulous views back across the city, the park is an almost hallucinatory expression of the imagination. Pavilions of contorted stone, giant decorative lizards, meandering rustic viaducts, a vast Hall of Columns, carved stone trees – all combine in one manic swirl of ideas and excesses, like the famous ceramic bench that snakes along the edge of the terrace above the columned hall. Your ticket grants access to these sites, now part of the **monumental zone**. Only 400 visitors are allowed inside this zone each half-hour. The area outside the monumental zone is free. Some areas might be closed due to restoration works.

The most direct route to Parc Güell is on bus #24 from Plaça de Catalunya, Passeig de Gràcia or

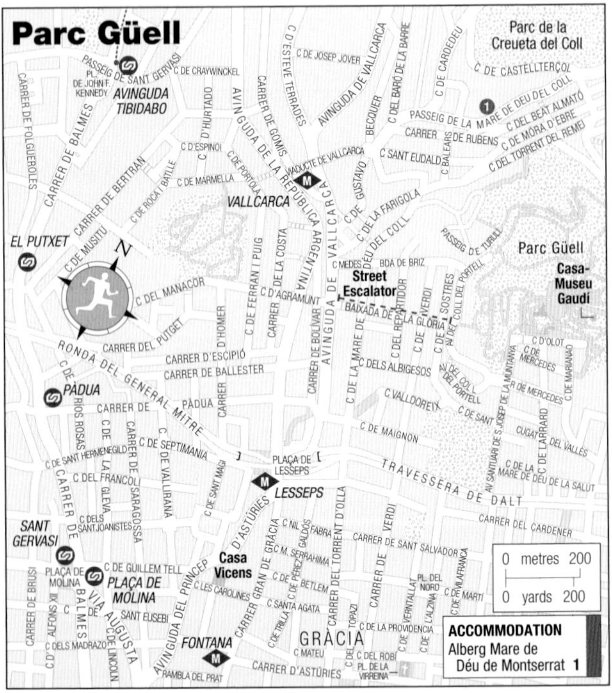

Parc Güell

0 metres 200
0 yards 200

ACCOMMODATION
Alberg Mare de Déu de Montserrat 1

C/Gran de Gràcia, which drops you at the eastern side gate. From Ⓜ Vallcarca, walk a few hundred metres down Avinguda de Vallcarca until you see the mechanical escalators on your left, ascending Baixada de la Glòria – follow these to the western-side park entrance (15min in total). From Ⓜ Lesseps, turn right along Travessera de Dalt and then left up steep C/Larrard, which leads (10min) straight to the main entrance on C/Olot.

Casa Museu Gaudí

MAP P.122.

Parc Güell Ⓜ Vallcarca/Lesseps Ⓣ 932 193 811, Ⓦ casamuseugaudi.org. Daily: April–Sept 9am–8pm; Oct–March 10am–6pm. €5.50, combination ticket with Sagrada Família €18.30.

One of Gaudí's collaborators, Francesc Berenguer, designed and built a turreted house within Parc Güell for the architect (though he only lived in it intermittently). This contains a diverting collection of some of the furniture Gaudí designed for other projects – a typical mixture of wild originality and brilliant engineering – as well as plans and objects related to the park and to Gaudí's life. His study and bedroom have been preserved and there's an inkling of his personality, too, in the displayed religious texts and pictures, along with a silver coffee cup and his death mask, made at the Santa Pau hospital where he died.

Parc de la Creueta del Coll

MAP P.122.

Pg. de la Mare de Deu del Coll 89 Ⓜ Vallcarca. Daily 10am–dusk. Free.

For a different kind of experience altogether, combine a trip to Gaudí's extravagant park with this contemporary urban space laid out on the site of an old quarry, whose sheer walls were retained in the landscaping. You're greeted at the top of the park steps by an Ellsworth Kelly metal spike, while suspended by steel cables over water is a massive concrete claw by the Basque artist Eduardo Chillida. There are also palms, promenades and a kiosk-café.

Bus #V17 from near Plaça de Catalunya at Via Laietana and Ⓜ Urquinaona, stops 100m from the park, or you can walk from Ⓜ Vallcarca in about twenty minutes (there's a map of the neighbourhood at the metro station). It's worth knowing that if you visit Creueta del Coll first and then take the main Passeig de la Mare de Deu del Coll, there are signposts leading you into Parc Güell the back way.

Casa Museu Gaudí

Hibernian Books

Shop

Hibernian Books

MAP P.121.
C/Montseny 17 Ⓜ Fontana Ⓦ hibernian-books.com. Mon 4–8.30pm, Tue–Sat 11am–8.30pm (in August hours might differ).

Barcelona's only secondhand English bookstore has around 40,000 titles in stock – you can part-exchange, and there are always plenty of giveaway bargains available.

Cafés

Gelateria Caffetteria Italiana

MAP P.121, POCKET MAP H1.
Pl. de la Revolució 2 Ⓜ Fontana Ⓣ 932 102 339. Mon–Thu 9.30pm–midnight, Fri & Sat 9.30pm–1.30 am.

Stroll around a pretty square in the sun with a real hand-made Italian ice cream (they've been churning it out since 1881). Expect queues at peak times and then more waiting as you struggle to choose from the twenty-odd flavours.

La Nena

MAP P.121, POCKET MAP J1.
C/Ramon i Cajal 36 Ⓜ Joanic Ⓣ 932 851 476.Mon–Fri 1–4pm & 7.30–midnight, Sat, Sun & hols 1pm–midnight; closed Aug.

Great for home-made cakes, waffles, quiches, organic ice cream, squeezed juices and the like. But parents also like the "little girl" as it's very child-friendly, from the changing mats in the loos to the small seats, games and puzzles.

Restaurants and tapas bars

L' Arrossería Xàtiva

MAP P.121, POCKET MAP J1.
C/Torrent d'en Vidalet 26 Ⓜ Joanic Ⓣ 932 848 502, Ⓦ grupxativa.com. Daily 1–4pm & 7.30pm–midnight.

The microwaved and burnt offerings that pass for paella in most Barcelona restaurants enrage proud Valencians. For the real thing, try one of the two *Xàtiva* restaurants (the other is in Les Corts). There's also a full range of Catalan rice dishes including creamy *arros melos*, and the lunch menu (€14.50) is a great way to fill up before exploring the area.

Cal Boter

MAP P.121, POCKET MAP J1.
C/Tordera 62 Ⓜ Verdaguer Ⓣ 934 588 462, Ⓦ restaurantcalboter.com. Daily 9am–noon & 1–4pm & 9pm–midnight, Sun & Mon lunch only.

This old-school bistro is perpetually packed with everyone from hipsters to those in need of hip replacements. Survive the queue (or arrive when it opens) and you'll be rewarded with rib-sticking stews, meatballs, snails and other classic dishes at knockdown prices (€11.20 lunch menu; à la carte mains €8–16).

Flash-Flash

MAP P.121, POCKET MAP G1.
C/de la Granada del Penedès 25 Ⓜ Diagonal ⓣ 932 370 990, Ⓦ flashflashbarcelona.com. Daily 1pm–1.30am (bar open 11am–2am).

A classic 1970s survivor with a keen sense of style, *Flash-Flash* does tortillas (€6–9) served any time you like, any way you like, from plain and simple to elaborately stuffed, with sweet ones for dessert. If that doesn't grab you, try the reasonably priced salads, steaks, burgers and fish. The original white leatherette booths and monotone photo-model cutouts are very Austin Powers.

Nou Candanchu

MAP P.121, POCKET MAP H1.
Pl. de la Vila de Gràcia 9 Ⓜ Diagonal ⓣ 932 377 362. Mon, Wed, Thu & Sun 7am–1am, Fri & Sat 7am–2am.

Good for lunch on a sunny day or a leisurely night out on a budget, when you can sit beneath the clock tower and soak up the atmosphere in the ever-entertaining local square. There's a wide menu – tapas and hot sandwiches, but also steak and eggs, steamed clams and mussels, or cod and hake cooked plenty of different ways, all for €8–12.

La Pepita

MAP P.121, POCKET MAP H2.
C/Còrsega 343 Ⓜ Diagonal/Verdaguer ⓣ 932 384 893, Ⓦ lapepitabcn.com. Bar Mon–Sat 1pm–1.30am, kitchen open Mon 7.30pm–midnight, Tue–Sat 1–4pm & 7.30pm–midnight.

There's usually a queue out the door, and deservedly so. The tapas, like roasted chicken croquettes with romesco sauce (€4) or aubergine fritters with goats' cheese, honey and apples (€8), are fantastic, and the atmosphere is chatty and convivial. Hundreds of "love notes" scrawled by customers on the white-tiled walls hint at its popularity. It's a good place for a drink if you show up outside of kitchen hours, too.

La Singular

MAP P.121, POCKET MAP H1.
C/Francesc Giner 50 Ⓜ Diagonal ⓣ 932 375 098, Ⓦ lasingular-barcelona.com. Mon–Thu 1–4pm & 8.30–11.30pm, Fri 1–4pm & 8.30pm–12.30am, Sat 8.30pm–12.30am.

The tiny kitchen turns out refined Mediterranean food at moderate prices (most dishes €5–15) – think aubergine and smoked fish salad or chicken stuffed with dates and ham. There's always something appealing on the menu for veggies, too. It's a cornerstone of the neighbourhood, with a friendly atmosphere, but there are only nine tables, so go early or reserve.

Bars

La Baignoire

MAP P.121, POCKET MAP H1.
C/Verdi 6 Ⓜ Fontana ⓣ 932 843 967. Daily 7pm–1am (Fri & Sat until 3am).

Cosy little wine bar offering a small corner of sophistication on an otherwise busy street – Ella Fitzgerald on CD, a dozen goodwines by the glass and cheesy nibbles.

Flash-Flash

Café Salambo

MAP P.121.
C/Torrijos 51 Ⓜ Fontana Ⓣ 932 186 966, Ⓦ cafesalambo.com. Mon–Thu noon–1am, Fri & Sat noon–3am, Sun noon–midnight.
Where the pre- and post-cinema crowd meets (both Verdi cinemas are on the doorstep). It's a long-standing neighbourhood hangout, with something of a colonial feel, and there are lots of wines and cava by the glass, and good food too.

Café del Sol

MAP P.121, POCKET MAP H1.
Pl. del Sol 16 Ⓜ Fontana Ⓣ 934 155 663, Ⓦ cafedelsol.cat. Mon–Thu 1–3.30pm & 9–11pm (Fri & Sat until 3am).
The grandaddy of the Plaça del Sol scene sees action day and night. On summer evenings, when the square is packed with people, there's not an outdoor table to be had, but even in winter this is a popular drinking den – the pubby interior has a back room and gallery, often rammed to the rafters.

Canigó

MAP P.121, POCKET MAP H1.
C/Verdi 2 Ⓜ Fontana Ⓣ 932 133 049, Ⓦ barcanigo.com. Mon–Tue 10am–2am, Fri 10am–3am, Sat 8pm–3am.
Family-run neighbourhood bar now entering its third generation. It's not much to look at, but the drinks are cheap and it's a Gràcia institution with a loyal following, packed out at weekends especially with a young, largely local crowd.

Heliogabal

MAP P.121, POCKET MAP J1.
C/Ramon i Cajal 80 Ⓜ Joanic Ⓦ heliogabal.com. Daily 9pm–midnight.
Not much more than a boiler room given a lick of paint, but filled with a cool, twenty-something crowd, here for the live poetry and music – expect something different every night (Catalan versifying, jazz jam sessions and earnest singer-songwriters), starting at 10pm. Admission is usually €5–10, depending on the act, and drinks aren't expensive.

Old Fashioned

MAP P.121, POCKET MAP H2.
Santa Teresa 1 Ⓜ Diagonal Ⓣ 933 685 277, Ⓦ cocktailsbarcelona.oldfashionedbcn.com/wp/. Mon & Sun 5pm–2am, Tue–Thu noon–2am, Fri noon–3am, Sat 4pm–3am.
Step inside and back in time to the roaring 20s, with waiters in white tuxes, old-school decor and a swinging soundtrack. The expert bartenders will mix a perfect classic cocktail or something more modern for around €8–12.

Samsara

MAP P.121, POCKET MAP H1.
C/Terol 6 Ⓜ Fontana Ⓣ 932 853 688, Ⓦ samsarabcn.com. Mon–Thu 8.30pm–1am, Fri 7.30pm–1am, Sat 1–4pm & 7.30pm–2am, Sun 12.30–3.30pm & 7.30pm–1am.
It's totally Gràcia – low tables, low lighting and painted concrete walls, plus a chill-out soundtrack and a projection screen above the bar. There's also contemporary tapas and *platillos* (little plates) but it's a bar first and foremost, with DJs cracking out house and techno sets at the weekend.

Vinil

MAP P.121, POCKET MAP H1.
C/Matilde 2 Ⓜ Diagonal Ⓣ 669 177 945. Mon–Wed 9pm–2am, Thu 9pm–2.30am, Fri & Sat 9pm–3.30am.
Wear a beret, surgically attached to your iPad? Favour *Blade Runner*, Jeff Buckley and Band of Horses? This bar's for you – a dive bar with the lighting set at perpetual dusk, where time slips easily away.

Virreina

MAP P.121.
Pl. de la Virreina 1 Ⓜ Fontana Ⓣ 932 379 880. Mon–Fri 9am–1am, Sat 10am–2am, Sun 10am–midnight.
Another real Gràcia favourite, on one of the neighbourhood's prettiest squares, with a very

popular summer *terrassa*. Cold beer and sandwiches are served to a laidback crowd – it's one of those places where you drop by for a quick drink and find yourself staying for hours.

Clubs

Centre Artesà Tradicionàrius

MAP P.121.
Trav. de Sant Antoni 6–8 Ⓜ Fontana ⓣ 932 184 485, ⓦ tradicionarius.cat.
The best place in town for folk, traditional and world music by Catalan, Spanish and visiting performers, including some occasional big names. Admission is usually €5–15, and you can expect anything from Basque bagpipes to Brazilian singers. There are also music and instrument workshops, while CAT sponsors all sorts of outreach concerts and festivals, including an annual international folk and traditional dance festival between January and April.

Otto Zutz

MAP P.121.
C/de Lincoln 15 Ⓜ Fontana ⓣ 932 380 722, ⓦ ottozutz.com. Wed–Sat 11.45pm–6am.
It first opened in 1985, and has lost some of its erstwhile glam cachet, but this three-storey former textile factory still has a shedload of pretensions. The sounds are basically hip-hop, r'n'b and house, and with the right clothes and face you're in (you may or may not have to pay, depending on how impressive you are, the day of the week, the mood of the door staff, etc).

Otto Zutz

Camp Nou, Pedralbes and Sarrià-Sant Gervasi

On the northwestern edge of the centre, the city's famous football stadium, Camp Nou, draws locals and visitors alike, both to the big game and to the FC Barcelona museum. Nearby, across Avinguda Diagonal, the Palau Reial de Pedralbes is home to serene public gardens (the lush vegetation hides an early work by Gaudí), while a half-day's excursion can be made by walking from the palace, past the Gaudí dragon gate at Pavellons Güell, to the calm cloister at the Gothic monastery of Pedralbes. You can complete the day by returning via Sarrià, to the east, more like a small town than a suburb, with a pretty main street and market to explore. At night, the focus shifts to the bars and restaurants of neighbouring Sant Gervasi in the streets north of Plaça de Francesc Macià.

Avinguda Diagonal

MAP P.130, POCKET MAP E1.
Ⓜ Maria Cristina.

The uptown section of Avinguda Diagonal runs through the heart of Barcelona's flashiest business and shopping district. The giant **L'Illa** shopping centre flanks the avenue – the stepped design is a prone echo of New York's Rockefeller Center. Designer fashion stores are ubiquitous, particularly around **Plaça de Francesc Macià** and Avinguda Pau Casals – at the end

Camp Nou

of the latter, **Turó Parc** (daily 10am–dusk) is a good place to rest weary feet, with a small children's playground and a café-kiosk. Meanwhile, behind L'Illa, it's worth seeking out **Plaça de la Concordia**, a surprising survivor from the past amid the uptown tower blocks – the pretty little square is dominated by its church bell tower and ringed by local businesses (florist, pharmacy, hairdresser), with an outdoor café or two for a quiet drink.

Camp Nou and FC Barcelona

MAP P.130.

Av. Arístides Maillol Ⓜ Collblanc/Maria Cristina Ⓣ 902 189 900 or Ⓣ 934 963 600 from outside Spain, Ⓦ fcbarcelona.com. Match tickets (€50–100) also from Ticketmaster Ⓦ ticketmaster.es.

In Barcelona, football is a genuine obsession, with support for the local giants FC (Futbol Club) Barcelona raised to an art form. "More than just a club" is the proud boast, and during the dictatorship years the club stood as a Catalan symbol around which people could rally. Arch rivals, Real Madrid, on the other hand, were always seen as Franco's club. The swashbuckling team – past European champions and darling of football neutrals everywhere – plays at the magnificent Camp Nou football stadium, built in 1957, and enlarged for the 1982 World Cup semifinal to accommodate 98,000 spectators. A new remodelling (by architect Norman Foster) plans to update the stadium over the next few years, but even today Camp Nou provides one of the world's best football-watching experiences.

The **football season** runs from August until May, with league games usually played on Sundays. Tickets are relatively easy to come by, except for the biggest games, and go on general sale up to a month before each match – buy them online or at the ticket office.

FC Barcelona Museu

The stadium complex hosts basketball, handball and hockey games with FC Barcelona's other professional teams, and there's also a public ice rink, souvenir shop and café.

Camp Nou Experience

MAP P.130.

Camp Nou, Av. Arístides Maillol, enter through Gates 7 & 9 Ⓜ Collblanc/Maria Cristina Ⓣ 902 189 900 or Ⓣ 934 963 600, Ⓦ fcbarcelona.com. April & mid-Oct to Dec Mon–Sat 10am–6.30pm, Sun & hols 10am–2.30pm; May to mid-Oct daily 9.30am–7.30pm (may vary each season); tours until 1hr before closing. €25, children 6–13 years €20.

No soccer fan should miss the Camp Nou stadium tour and museum, billed as the "Camp Nou Experience". The self-guided tour winds through the changing rooms, onto the pitch and up to the press gallery and directors' box for stunning views. The museum, meanwhile, is jammed full of silverware and memorabilia, while displays and archive footage trace the history of the club back to

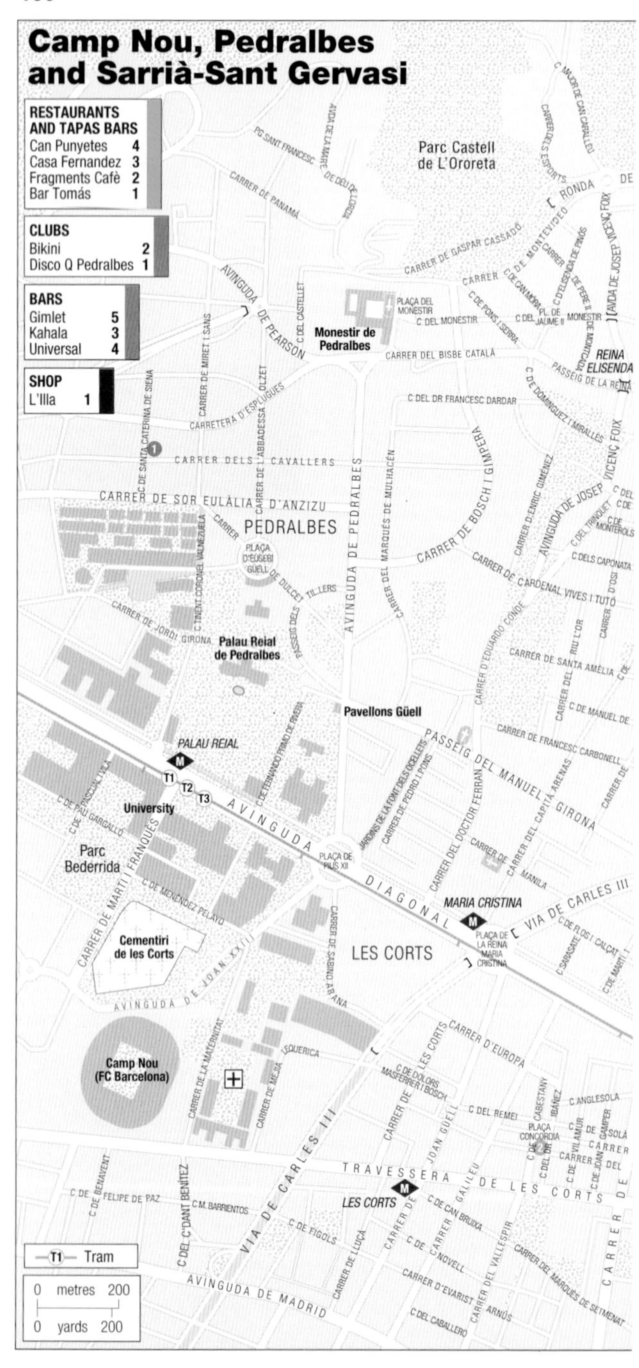
Camp Nou, Pedralbes and Sarrià-Sant Gervasi
RESTAURANTS AND TAPAS BARS
Can Punyetes 4
Casa Fernandez 3
Fragments Cafè 2
Bar Tomás 1
CLUBS
Bikini 2
Disco Q Pedralbes 1
BARS
Gimlet 5
Kahala 3
Universal 4
SHOP
L'Illa 1
Parc Castell de L'Ororeta
Monestir de Pedralbes
PLAÇA DEL MONESTIR
C DEL MONESTIR
CARRER DEL BISBE CATALÀ
REINA ELISENDA
PASSEIG DE LA REINA
AVINGUDA DE PEARSON
CARRETERA D'ESPLUGUES
CARRER DELS CAVALLERS
CARRER DE SOR EULÀLIA D'ANZIZU
PEDRALBES
PLAÇA D'EUSEBI GÜELL
AVINGUDA DE PEDRALBES
CARRER DE BOSCH I GIMPERA
AVINGUDA DE JOSEP VICENÇ FOIX
CARRER DE CARDENAL VIVES I TUTÓ
CARRER DE JORDI GIRONA
Palau Reial de Pedralbes
Pavellons Güell
CARRER DE SANTA AMÈLIA
CARRER DE FRANCESC CARBONELL
PASSEIG DEL MANUEL GIRONA
PALAU REIAL
M
T1
T2
T3
University
Parc Bederrida
AVINGUDA DIAGONAL
PLAÇA DE PIUS XII
MARIA CRISTINA
PLAÇA DE LA REINA MARIA CRISTINA
VIA DE CARLES III
C DE MENÉNDEZ PELAYO
CARRER DE MARTÍ I FRANQUÈS
Cementiri de les Corts
LES CORTS
AVINGUDA DE JOAN XXIII
CARRER DE SABINO ARANA
CARRER D'EUROPA
Camp Nou (FC Barcelona)
CARRER DE LA MATERNITAT
TRAVESSERA DE LES CORTS
C DE FELIPE DE PAZ
C DEL C'DANT BENÍTEZ
AVINGUDA DE MADRID
CARRER D'EVARIST ARNÚS
C DEL CABALLERO
T1 Tram
0 metres 200
0 yards 200

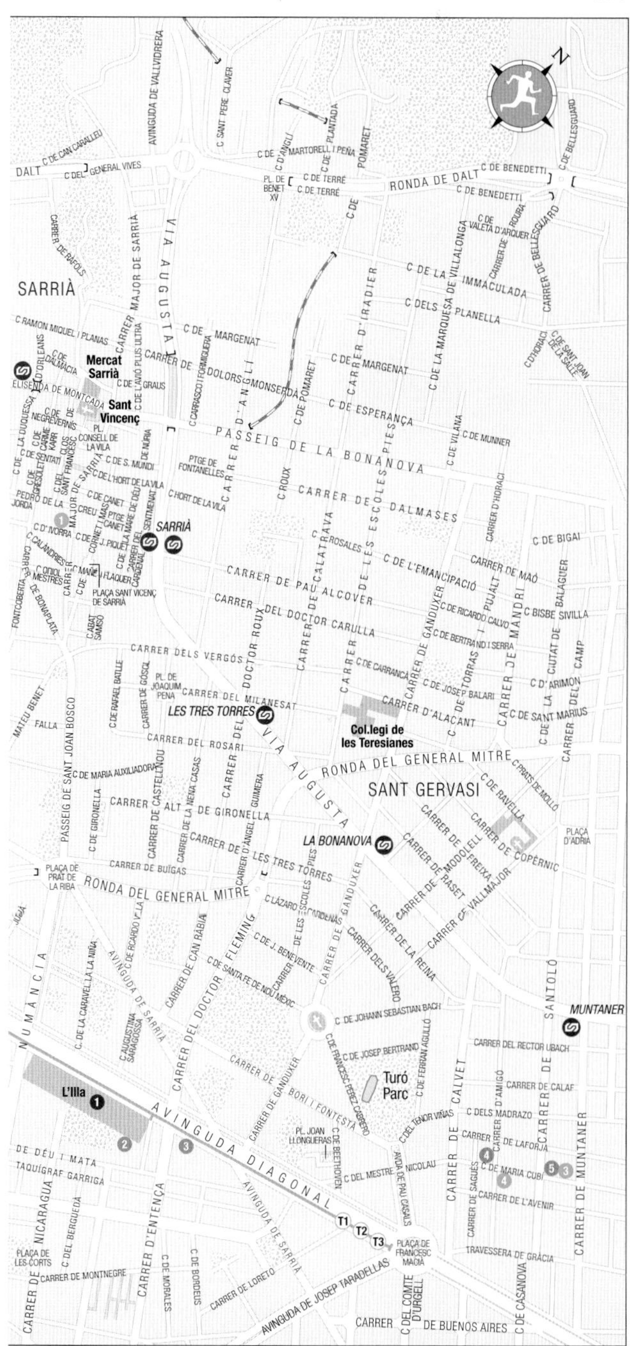
SARRIÀ
Mercat Sarrià
Sant Vicenç
SARRIÀ
LES TRES TORRES
Col.legi de les Teresianes
SANT GERVASI
LA BONANOVA
MUNTANER
Turó Parc
L'Illa
RONDA DE DALT
VIA AUGUSTA
PASSEIG DE LA BONANOVA
CARRER DE DALMASES
CARRER DE PAU ALCOVER
CARRER DEL DOCTOR CARULLA
CARRER DELS VERGÓS
CARRER DEL MILANESAT
CARRER DEL ROSARI
RONDA DEL GENERAL MITRE
CARRER ALT DE GIRONELLA
CARRER DE LES TRES TORRES
CARRER DE BUÏGAS
AVINGUDA DIAGONAL
AVINGUDA DE SARRIÀ
AVINGUDA DE JOSEP TARADELLAS
CARRER DE BUENOS AIRES
TRAVESSERA DE GRÀCIA
CARRER DE MUNTANER
CARRER DE CALVET
CARRER DE GANDUXER
CARRER DE BORI I FONTESTÀ
CARRER DEL DOCTOR FLEMING
CARRER DE CAN RÀBIA
CARRER D'ENTENÇA
NUMÀNCIA
PLAÇA DE FRANCESC MACIÀ
PASSEIG DE SANT JOAN BOSCO
CARRER MAJOR DE SARRIÀ
AVINGUDA DE VALLVIDRERA
CARRER D'IRADIER
CARRER DE MARGENAT
C DE LA IMMACULADA
C DELS PLANELLA
C DE ESPERANÇA
C DE L'EMANCIPACIÓ
CARRER DE MAÓ
C DE BIGAI
CARRER D'ALACANT
CARRER DE MODOLELL
CARRER DE VALLMAJOR
CARRER DE LA REINA
C DE JOHANN SEBASTIAN BACH
CARRER DEL RECTOR UBACH
CARRER DE CALAF
C DELS MADRAZO
CARRER DE LAFORJA
C DE MARIA CUBÍ
CARRER DE L'AVENIR
CARRER DE MONTNEGRE
CARRER DE LORETO
PLAÇA DE PRAT DE LA RIBA
PLAÇA D'ADRIÀ
T1
T2
T3

Palau Reial de Pedralbes

1901. Finally, you're directed into the massive **FC Botiga**, where you can buy anything from a replica shirt to a branded bottle of wine.

Palau Reial de Pedralbes

MAP P.130.

Av. Diagonal 686 Ⓜ Palau Reial. Gardens daily 10am–dusk. Free.

Opposite the university on Avinguda Diagonal, formal grounds stretch up to the Italianate Palau Reial de Pedralbes – basically a large villa with pretensions. It was built for the use of the royal family on their visits to Barcelona, with funds raised by public subscription, and received its first such visit in 1926. However, within five years the king had abdicated and the palace somewhat lost its role. Franco kept it on as a presidential residence and it later passed to the city. The rooms had been used to show off the city's applied art collections, but those collections have now moved to the new Museu del Disseny near Plaça de les Glòries Catalanes. Although the palace is now closed to the public, the gardens – a breezy oasis of Himalaya cedar, strawberry trees and bougainvillea – are worth a visit. Hidden in a bamboo thicket, to the left-centre of the facade, is the "Hercules fountain" (1884), an early work by Antoni Gaudí. He also designed the parabolic pergola, which is covered in climbing plants and is a nice place to sit and rest your feet. In late June, a music festival (Ⓦ festivalpedralbes.com) takes place in the palace's gardens.

Pavellons Güell

MAP P.130.

Av. de Pedralbes 7 Ⓜ Palau Reial Ⓣ 933 177 652, Ⓦ rutadelmodernisme.com. Daily 10am–4pm; tours 10.15am, 11.15am & 3pm in English, 12.15pm in Catalan & 1.15pm in Spanish. €4.

As an early test of his capabilities, Antoni Gaudí was asked by his patron, Eusebi Güell, to rework the entrance, gatehouse and stables of the Güell summer residence. The resultant brick and tile buildings are

Here be dragons

The slavering beast on Gaudí's dragon gate at the Pavellons Güell is not the vanquished dragon of Sant Jordi (St George), the Catalan patron saint, but the one that appears in the Labours of Hercules myth, a familiar Catalan theme in the nineteenth century. Gaudí's design was based on a work by the Catalan renaissance poet Jacint Verdaguer, a friend of the Güell family, who had reworked the myth in his epic poem, *L'Atlàntida* – thus, the dragon guarding golden apples in the Gardens of Hesperides is here protecting instead an orange tree (considered a more Catalan fruit). Gaudí's gate indeed can be read as an homage to Verdaguer, with its stencilled roses representing those traditionally given to the winner of the Catalan poetry competition, the Jocs Floral, which the poet won in 1877.

frothy, whimsical affairs, though it's the gateway that's the most famous element. An extraordinary winged dragon of twisted iron snarls at passers-by, its razor-toothed jaws spread wide in a fearsome roar. During the week you can't go any further than the gate, but guided visits show you the grounds and Gaudí's innovative stables, now used as a library by the university's historical architecture department.

Sarrià

MAP P.130.

FGC Sarrià, or bus #64 from Pl. Universitat or Pedralbes.

The Sarrià district was once an independent small town and still looks the part, with a narrow, traffic-free main street – C/Major de Sarrià – at the top of which stands the much-restored church of Sant Vicenç. The church flanks the main Passeig de la Reina Elisenda de Montcada, across which lies the neighbourhood market, Mercat Sarrià, housed in a 1911 *modernista* red-brick building. You'll find a few other surviving old-town squares down the main street, prettiest of which is Plaça Sant Vicenç de Sarrià (off C/Mañe i Flaquer), where there's a statue of the saint.

Monestir de Pedralbes

MAP P.130.

Biaxada del Monestir Ⓜ Palau Reial and 20min walk, or FGC Reina Elisenda and 10min walk, or bus #64 from Pl. Universitat Ⓣ 932 563 434, Ⓦ monestirpedralbes.bcn.cat/en. April–Sept Tue–Fri 10am–5pm, Sat 10am–7pm, Sun 10am–8pm; Oct–Mar Tue–Fri 10am–2pm, Sat & Sun 10am–5pm. €5, admission free Sun after 3pm.

Founded in 1326 for the nuns of the Order of St Clare, this is in effect an entire monastic village set within medieval walls on the outskirts of the city. The cloisters in particular are the finest in Barcelona, built on three levels and adorned by the slenderest of columns. Side rooms and chambers give a clear impression of medieval convent life, and also display a selection of the monastery's treasures, while the adjacent church contains the carved marble tomb of the convent's founder, Elisenda de Montcada, wife of King Jaume II. After 600 years of isolation, the monastery was sequestered by the Generalitat during the Civil War. It was turned into a museum in 1983, and a new adjacent convent was built, where the Clare nuns still reside.

Monestir de Pedralbes

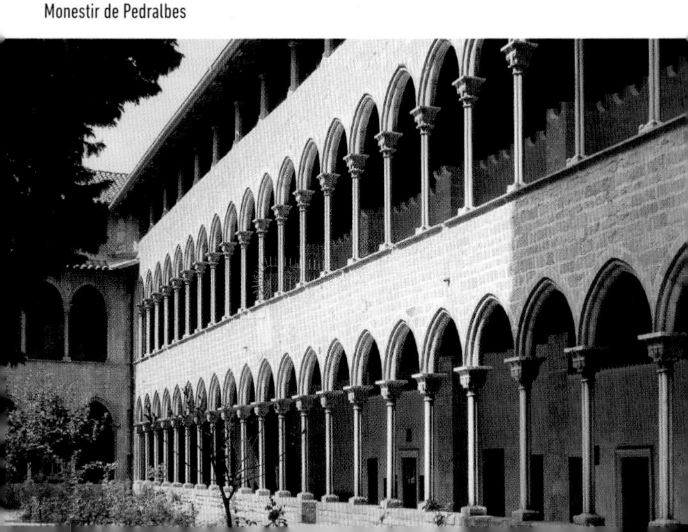

Shops

L'Illa

MAP P.130.

Av. Diagonal 555–559 Ⓜ Maria Cristina Ⓦ lilla.com.Oct–May Mon–Sat 9.30am–9pm, June–Sept till 10pm.

The landmark uptown shopping mall is stuffed full of designer fashion, plus Camper (shoes), FNAC (music, film and books), Sfera (cosmetics), Decathlon (sports), El Corte Inglés (department store), Caprabo (supermarket), food hall and much more.

You can get here by metro (Maria Cristina) or tram (from Pl. de Francesc Macià), or on the **Tomb Bus shopping line service**, which also visits other uptown stores on a circular route from Plaça de Catalunya (departures every 6–8min; tickets available on board).

Restaurants and tapas bars

Casa Fernandez

MAP P.130.

C/Santaló 46, FGC Muntaner Ⓣ 932 019 308, Ⓦ casafernandez.com. Mon–Sat 1–5pm & 8pm–midnight, Sun noon–midnight.

The long kitchen hours are a boon for the bar-crawlers in this neck of the woods. It's a contemporary place featuring market cuisine, though they are specialists in – of all things – fried eggs, either served straight with chips or with Catalan sausage, garlic prawns or other variations. Most dishes are in the range of €6 to €15.

Can Punyetes

MAP P.130.

C/Marià Cubí 189, FGC Muntaner Ⓣ 932 009 159, Ⓦ canpunyetesbarcelona.com. Daily noon–3.45pm & 8pm–midnight.

Traditional grillhouse-tavern that offers diners a taste of older times. Simple salads and tapas, open grills turning out *botifarra* (sausage), lamb chops, chicken and pork – accompanied by grilled country bread, white beans and char-grilled potato halves. It's cheap (almost everything under €10) and locals love it.

Fragments Cafè

MAP P.130.

Pl. de la Concórdia 12 Ⓜ Les Corts Ⓣ 934 199 613, Ⓦ fragmentscafe.com. Tue & Wed 1pm–1am, Thu 1pm–1.30am, Fri 1pm–2.30am, Sat noon–2.30am, Sun noon–12.30am; closed 2 weeks in Aug.

A classy yet casual bistro popular with locals for its fresh, classic food that's served in the charming dining room or in the shaded garden. The lunch menu is good value (€12), with the rest of the dishes, from tapas to fresh pasta, around €5–14.

Bar Tomás

MAP P.130.

C/Major de Sarrià 49, FGC Sarrià Ⓣ 932 031 077. Mon–Sat noon–4pm & 6–10pm; closed Aug.

The best *patatas bravas* in Barcelona? Everyone will point you here, to this unassuming, white-Formica-table bar in the suburbs (a 12min train ride from Plaça de Catalunya FGC) for their unrivalled spicy fried potatoes with garlic mayo and *salsa picante*. It's not all they serve, but it might as well be.

They fry noon to 3pm and 6pm to closing, so if it's *patatas bravas* you want, be sure to take a note of the hours.

Bars

Gimlet

MAP P.130.

C/Santaló 46, FGC Muntaner Ⓣ 932 015 306, Ⓦ gimletbcn.com. Mon–6pm–1am, Thu 6pm–2.30am, Fri & Sat 6pm–3am.

This favoured cocktail joint is especially popular in summertime, when the streetside tables offer a great vantage point for watching the party unfold. There are also two or three other late-opening bars on the same stretch.

Kahala

MAP P.130.
Avgda. Diagonal 537 Ⓜ Maria Cristina Ⓣ 934 309 026, Ⓦ kahalabarcelona.com. Daily 6pm–3am, Fri & Sat till 3.30am.
Open since 1971, this Hawaiian-themed bar is a treasure-trove of Polynesian kitsch: gurgling waterfalls, bamboo furniture and grimacing tiki masks abound. The drinks – from the Perla de Vicio ("Pearl of Vice") to the classic Mai Tai – pack quite the punch and are certain to ready you for an evening of island – pardon – *club* hopping.

Universal

MAP P.130.
C/Marià Cubí 182, FGC Muntaner Ⓣ 934 136 362, Ⓦ universalbcn.com. Thu–Sat 11.45pm–5am.
A classic designer music bar that's been part of the Barcelona style scene since 1985. Sounds range from house to back-to-the-80s, but be warned: drinks are fairly pricey and they operate a strict door policy; if your face doesn't fit you might not get in.

Clubs

Bikini

MAP P.130.
C/Deu i Mata 105 Ⓜ Les Corts Ⓣ 933 220 800, Ⓦ bikinibcn.com. Thu–Sat midnight–5am.
This traditional landmark of Barcelona nightlife (behind the L'Illa shopping centre) offers a regular diet of great indie, rock, roots and world gigs followed by club sounds, from house to Brazilian, according to the night. Admission usually €15–25, though some big-name gigs up to €40.

Disco Q Pedralbes

MAP P.130.
C/Santa Caterina de Siena 28 Ⓜ Passeig de Gracia es Corts Ⓣ 932 051 203, Ⓦ discoqpedralbes.com. Thu 7pm–2am, Fri & Sat 11.30pm–6am, Sun 6-11pm (closed on Sun in August).
Offers pop and rock'n'roll or live music on Thursdays, 80s and 90s hits on Fridays and Saturdays and 80s disco fever on Sundays. On Fridays and Saturdays "dinner + disco" is available, with a regular menu for €23 and premium menu for €29 (disco entrance is, of course, included in the price). You can buy both types of menu up front on the website if you do not want to stand in a queue once you arrive at the club.

Gimlet

Tibidabo and Parc de Collserola

The views from the heights of Tibidabo (550m), the peak that signals the northwestern boundary of the city, are legendary. On a clear day you can see across to the Pyrenees and out to sea even as far as Mallorca. However, while many make the tram and funicular ride up to Tibidabo's amusement park, few realize that beyond stretches the Parc de Collserola, an area of peaks, wooded river valleys and hiking paths – one of Barcelona's best-kept secrets. You can walk into the park from Tibidabo, but it's actually better to start from the park's information centre, across to the east above Vallvidrera, where hiking-trail leaflets are available. Meanwhile, families won't want to miss CosmoCaixa, the city's excellent science museum, which can easily be seen on the way to or from Tibidabo.

Parc d'Atraccions

MAP P.137.

Pl. del Tibidabo 932 117 942, tibidabo.cat. Days and hours vary, but basically June–Sept Wed–Sun, Aug daily, rest of the year Sat, Sun & hols only; closed Jan & Feb. Park open from noon until 7–11pm depending on season. Skywalk ticket €12.70, full admission €28.50, plus family/discount tickets.

Barcelona's self-styled "magic mountain" amusement park takes full advantage of its hillside location to offer jaw-dropping perspectives over the city. Some of the most famous rides (like the aeroplane – spinning since 1928 – and the carousel) are grouped under the discounted "Skywalk" ticket. Summer weekends finish

Parc d'Atraccions

with parades, concerts and a noisy *correfoc*, a theatrical fireworks display.

Sagrat Cor

MAP P.137.

Elevator operates daily 10am–2pm & 3–7pm. €2.

Next to Tibidabo's amusement park climb the shining steps of the Templo Expiatorio de España – otherwise known as the Sagrat Cor (Sacred Heart). This is topped by a huge statue of Christ, and inside the church an elevator climbs to a viewing platform from where the city, surrounding hills and shimmering sea glisten in the distance.

Torre de Collserola

MAP P.137.

Carretera de Vallvidrera al Tibidabo ⓣ 932 117 942, ⓦ torredecollserola.com. March, April, Nov & Dec Sat & Sun noon–1.45pm & 3.30–5.45pm; May & Oct Sat & Sun noon–1.45pm & 3.30– 6.45pm; July–Sept Wed–Sun noon–1.45pm & 3.30–7.45pm. €5.60.

Follow the road from the Tibidabo car park and it's only a few minutes' walk to Norman Foster's soaring communications tower, built for the 1992 Olympics. This features a glass elevator that whisks you up ten storeys (115m) for extensive views – 70km, they claim, on a good day. Note that there's a combo ticket for the tower available at the Tibidabo amusement park.

Parc de Collserola

MAP P.137.

Centre d'Informació, FGC Baixada de Vallvidrera (on the Sabadell or Terrassa line from Pl. de Catalunya; 15min) ⓣ 932 803 552, ⓦ parcnaturalcollserola.cat. Daily 9.30am–3pm.

Given a half-decent day, local bikers, hikers and outdoor enthusiasts all make a beeline for the city's ring of wooded

Getting to Tibidabo

Reaching the heights of Tibidabo takes up to an hour, all told, from the city centre. First, take the FGC train (line 7) from Plaça de Catalunya station to **Avinguda Tibidabo** (the last stop), where you cross the road to the tram/bus shelter (the Bus Turístic stops here too). The **Tramvia Blau**, an antique tram service (Jan–April & mid-Oct to Dec Sat, Sun & hols 10am–6pm; May, June & mid-Sept to mid-Oct Sat, Sun & hols 10am–7.30pm; July to mid-Sept & Easter week daily 10am–7.30pm; €4.20 one way) then runs you up the hill to Plaça Doctor Andreu; out of season there's a bus service instead during the week. Here, you change to the **Funicular del Tibidabo**, with connections every 15min to Tibidabo (operates when the Parc d'Atraccions is open; €7.70 without park admission, €4.10 with park admission). Alternatively, the **Tibibus** runs direct to Tibidabo from Plaça de Catalunya, outside El Corte Inglés (from 10.15am every day the park is open; €2.95, reimbursed with park admission).

hills beyond Tibidabo. The park information centre lies in oak and pine woods, an easy ten-minute walk up through the trees from the FGC Baixada de Vallvidrera train station. There's a bar-restaurant here with an outdoor terrace, plus an exhibition on the park's history, flora and fauna, while the staff hand out English-language leaflets detailing the various park walks.

Parc de Collserola

Some of the well-marked paths – like the oak-forest walk – soon gain height for marvellous views over the tree canopy, while others descend through the valley bottoms to springs and shaded picnic areas. Perhaps the nicest short walk from the information centre is to the **Font de la Budellera** (1hr 15min return), a landscaped spring deep in the woods. If you follow the signs from the *font* to the Torre de Collserola (another 20min), you can return to Barcelona on the funicular from the nearby suburban village of **Vallvidrera** (daily 6am–midnight; every 6–10min), which connects to Peu del Funicular, an FGC train station on the line from Plaça de Catalunya.

Museu-Casa Verdaguer

MAP P.137.

Villa Joana, Carretera de l'Església 104 T 932 047 805, W verdaguer.cat. Tue 10am–1.30pm & 5–7pm, Wed–Sun 10am–1.30pm (April–Oct also 5–7pm). Free.

If you're up at the park, it's worth having a quick look inside the country house just below the Collserola information centre. Jacint Verdaguer (1845–1902), the Catalan Renaissance poet, lived here briefly before his death, andthe

CosmoCaixa

house has been preserved as an example of well-to-do nineteenth-century Catalan life.

CosmoCaixa

MAP P.137.

C/Isaac Newton 26 932 126 050, cosmocaixa.com. Tue–Sun 10am–8pm. €4, under-16s free.

A dramatic refurbishment in 2005 turned the city's science museum into a must-see attraction, certainly if you've got children in tow – it's an easy place to spend a couple of hours and can break the journey on your way to or from Tibidabo. Partly housed in a converted *modernista* hospice, the museum retains the original building but has added a light-filled public concourse and a huge underground extension with four subterranean levels, where hands-on experiments and displays investigate life, the universe and everything, "from bacteria to Shake-speare". The two big draws are the hundred tonnes of "sliced rock" in the Geological Wall and, best of all, the Bosc Inundat – nothing less than a thousand square metres of real Amazonian rainforest, complete with croc-filled mangroves, anacondas and giant catfish. Other levels of the museum are devoted to children's and family activities, which tend to be held at weekends and during school holidays; pick up a schedule when you arrive. There are also daily shows in the planetarium (in Spanish and Catalan only), a great gift shop and a café-restaurant with outdoor seating.

The easiest way to reach CosmoCaixa is by FGC train from Plaça de Catalunya to Avinguda del Tibidabo station, and then walk up the avenue, turning left just before the ring road (10min) – or the Tramvia Blau or Bus Turístic can drop you close by.

Bar

Mirablau

MAP P.137.

Pl. del Dr. Andrea, Av. Tibidabo 934 185 879. Daily 11am–5am.

Unbelievable city views from a chic bar near the Tibidabo funicular that fills to bursting at times. By day, a great place for coffee, by night a rich-kid disco-tunes stomping ground.

Montserrat

The mountain of Montserrat, with its rock crags, vast monastery and hermitage caves, stands just 40km northwest of Barcelona. It's the most popular day-trip from the city, reached in around ninety minutes by train and then cable car or rack railway for a thrilling ride up to the monastery. Once there, you can visit the basilica and monastery buildings and complete your day with a walk around the woods and crags, using the two funicular railways that depart from the complex. There are cafés and restaurants at the monastery, but they are relatively pricey and none too inspiring – you may wish to take a picnic instead.

Aeri de Montserrat

MAP P.140.
Montserrat Aeri ⓣ 938 350 005, ⓦ aeridemontserrat.com. Departures around every 15min, Mar–Oct daily 9.40am–7pm; Nov–Feb daily 10.10am–5.45pm, weekends and hols 9.40am–6.15pm.

For the cable car service, get off the train from Barcelona at Montserrat Aeri station (52min). You may have to wait in line fifteen minutes or so, but then it's only a five-minute swoop up the sheer mountainside

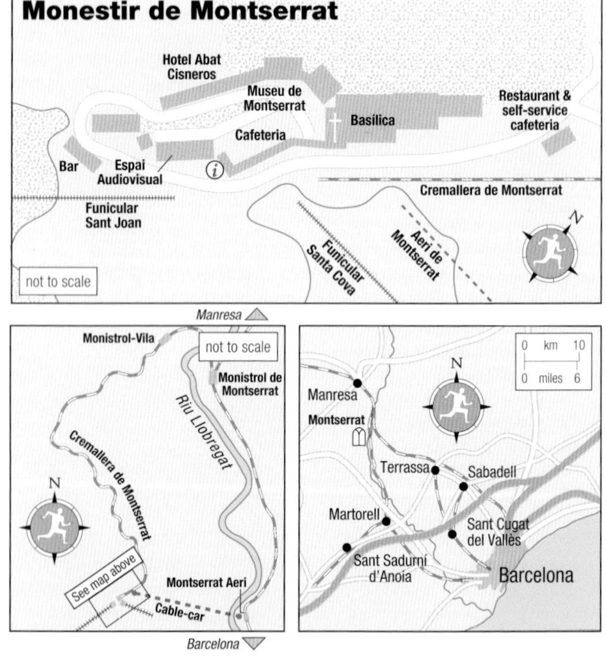

to a terrace just below the monastery – probably the most exhilarating ride in Catalunya. Returning to Barcelona, the line R5 trains depart hourly from Montserrat Aeri (from 9.37am).

Cremallera de Montserrat

MAP P.140.
Monistrol de Montserrat ⓣ 932 051 515, ⓦ cremallerademontserrat.com. Departures every hour, daily 8.48am–5.38/7.38pm (later services at weekends Apr–Oct, plus daily Jul–Sep).

The alternative approach to the monastery is by the Montserrat rack railway, which departs from Monistrol de Montserrat station (the next stop after Montserrat Aeri, another 4min), and takes twenty minutes to complete the climb. The original rack railway on Montserrat ran between 1892 and 1957, and this modern replacement re-creates the majestic engineering that allows the train to climb 550m in 4km. Returning to Barcelona, the line R5 trains depart at least hourly from Monistrol de Montserrat (from 9.21am).

Monestir de Montserrat

MAP P.140.
Visitor centre ⓣ 938 777 701, ⓦ montserratvisita.com. Daily 9am–5.30pm (Sat, Sun & July–Sept until 6.45pm). Walking maps and accommodation advice available.

Monestir de Montserrat

Legends hang easily upon the monastery of Montserrat. Fifty years after the birth of Christ, St Peter is said to have deposited an image of the Virgin (known as La Moreneta), carved by St Luke, in one of the mountain caves. The icon was lost in the early eighth century after being hidden during the Moorish invasion, but reappeared in 880, accompanied by the customary visions and celestial music. A chapel was built to house it, and in 976 this was superseded by a Benedictine monastery, set at an altitude of nearly 1000m.

Getting to Montserrat

To reach the Montserrat cable car/rack railway stations, take the **FGC train** (line R5, direction Manresa), which leaves daily from **Plaça d'Espanya** (Ⓜ Espanya) at hourly intervals from 8.36am. All fare options are detailed at Plaça d'Espanya, including return through-tickets from Barcelona (around €20) either for the train/cable car or train/rack railway. There are also two combination tickets available: the **Trans Montserrat** (€27.50), which includes all transport services, including unlimited use of the mountain funiculars, and the audiovisual show; and the **Tot Montserrat** (€43.70), which includes the same, plus monastery museum and a cafeteria lunch. Both tickets are also available at the Plaça de Catalunya tourist office.

Miracles abounded and the Virgin of Montserrat soon became the chief cult image of Catalunya and a pilgrimage centre second in Spain only to Santiago de Compostela – the main pilgrimages to Montserrat take place on April 27 and September 8.

The monastery's various outbuildings – including hotel, post office, souvenir shop and bar – fan out around an open square, and there are extraordinary mountain views from the terrace. The best restaurant is inside the *Hotel Abat Cisneros* (meals around €40), though the finest views are from the cliff-edge *Restaurant de Montserrat* (around €25) – the self-service cafeteria, one floor up, is where you eat with the all-inclusive *Tot Montserrat* ticket.

Basílica

MAP P.140.

Basílica daily 7.30am–8pm. Access to La Moreneta 8–10.30am & noon–6.30pm (mid-July to Sept also 7.30–8pm). Free.

Of the religious buildings, only the Renaissance basilica, dating largely from 1560 to 1592, is open to the public. **La Moreneta** stands above the high altar – reached from behind, by way of an entrance to the right of the basilica's main entrance. The approach to this beautiful icon reveals the enormous wealth of the monastery, as you queue along a corridor leading through the back of the basilica's rich side-chapels. Signs at head height command "SILENCE" in various languages, but nothing quietens the line which waits to kiss the image's hands and feet.

The best time to be here is when Montserrat's world-famous **boys' choir** sings (Mon–Fri 1pm, Sun noon; performance times may vary during school holidays at Christmas/New Year and from late June to mid-Aug). The boys belong to the Escolania, a choral school established in the thirteenth century and unchanged in musical style since its foundation.

Museu de Montserrat

MAP P.140.

T 938 777 745, W museudemontserrat.com. Daily 10am–5.45pm, summer and weekends 10am–6.45pm. €7.

The monastery museum presents a few archeological finds brought

Basílica, Monestir de Monstserrat

Funicular, Montserrat

back by travelling monks, together with valuable painting and sculpture dating from the thirteenth century onwards, including works by Old Masters, French Impressionists and Catalan *modernistas*. There's also a collection of Byzantine icons, though other religious items are in surprisingly short supply, as most of the monastery's valuables were carried off by Napoleon's troops who sacked the complex in 1811. For more on the history, and to learn something of the life of a Benedictine community, visit the **Espai Audiovisual** (Mon–Fri 9am–5.30pm, Sat & Sun 9am–6.45pm; €5), near the information office.

Mountain walks

Funicular departures vary by season, but mostly every 20min, daily 10am–6pm, weekends only Oct–March. Santa Cova €3.50 return, Sant Joan €9 return, combination ticket €10.

Following the mountain tracks to the caves and hermitages, you can contemplate Goethe's observation of 1816: "Nowhere but in his own Montserrat will a man find happiness and peace." The going is pretty good on all the tracks and the signposting is clear, but you do need to remember that you are on a mountain. Take water if you're hiking far and keep away from the edges.

Two separate funiculars run from points close to the cable car station. One drops to the path for **Santa Cova**, a seventeenth-century chapel built where the Moreneta icon is said to have been found. It's an easy walk of less than an hour there and back. The other funicular rises steeply to the hermitage of **Sant Joan**, from where it's a tougher 45 minutes' walk to the **Sant Jeroni** hermitage, and another 15 minutes to the Sant Jeroni summit at 1236m. Several other walks are also possible from the Sant Joan funicular, perhaps the nicest being the 45-minute circuit around the ridge that leads all the way back down to the monastery.

Sitges

The seaside town of Sitges, 36km south of Barcelona, is definitely the highlight of the local coast – a great weekend escape for young Barcelonans, who have created a resort very much in their own image. It's also a noted gay holiday destination, with an outrageous annual carnival (February/March) and a summertime nightlife to match. During the heat of the day, though, the tempo drops as everyone hits the beach. Out of season Sitges is delightful: far less crowded, and with a temperate climate that encourages promenade strolls and Old Town exploration.

The beaches

MAP P.145

There are clean sands on either side of the Old Town, though they become extremely crowded in high season. For more space keep walking west from Passeig de la Ribera along Passeig Marítim promenade, past eight interlinked beaches that run a couple of kilometres down the coast as far as the *Hotel Terramar*. Many of the handsome, nineteenth-century seafront mansions were built by successful local merchants (known as "Americanos") who had returned from Cuba and Puerto Rico.

The old town

MAP P.145

The knoll overlooking the town beaches is topped by the landmark Baroque parish church dedicated to Sant Bartolomeu, whose festival is celebrated in the last week of August. The views from the terrace sweep along the coast, while behind in the narrow streets of the Old

Sitges beach

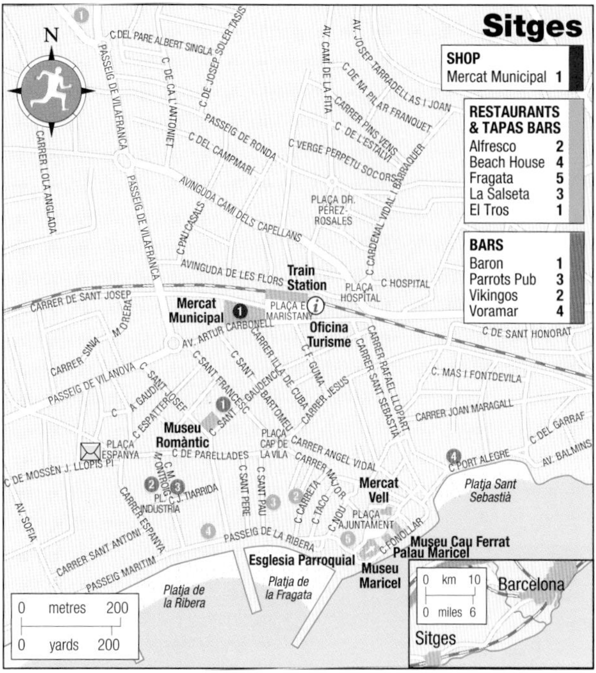

Sitges

SHOP

Mercat Municipal 1

RESTAURANTS & TAPAS BARS

Alfresco 2
Beach House 4
Fragata 5
La Salseta 3
El Tros 1

BARS

Baron 1
Parrots Pub 3
Vikingos 2
Voramar 4

Town you'll find whitewashed mansions, as well as the town hall and the **Mercat Vell** (Old Market), the latter now an exhibition hall. The pedestrianized shopping street, **Carrer Major**, is the best place for browsing boutiques.

Cau Ferrat, Maricel and Romàntico museums

MAP P.145

Mar–Jun Tue–Sun 10am–7pm; Jul–Sep Tue–Sun 10am–8pm; Nov–Feb Tue–Sun 10am–5pm. €10 each.

Three museums showcase the town's artistic heritage, not least the renovated **Museu Cau Ferrat** (C/Fonollar), the former house of *modernista* artist Santiago Rusiñol (1861–1931). Next door, the **Museu de Maricel** (also renovated) contains minor art works, ceramics and sculpture, while in July and August (usually two evenings a week) the main part of the mansion itself is open for guided tours and concerts. Occupying a stately bourgeois house of 1793, the **Museu Romàntico** (C/Sant Gaudenci 1) shows the lifestyle of a rich, nineteenth-century Sitges family (temporarily closed for renovation works).

Museu de Maricel

Museu Romàntico

Exuding romance – from its tucked-away location off a stepped alley to its trellised patio – this restaurant serves Catalan cuisine with Asian influences (green Thai curry, duck breast with glass noodles), with meals for €25–35.

Beach House

MAP P.145.
C/Paseo de la Ribera 33 ⓣ 935 168 136. Daily 9am–11pm.
Aussie owners have created a highly relaxed seafront restaurant, offering both lunch and dinner menus (from €13 and €20) of the best Mediterranean-Asian fusion food, with dishes such as black rice with squid and bonito fish flakes. It's a cocktail joint too, while the open-air terrace adds a touch of seaside romance.

Fragata

MAP P.145
Pg. de la Ribera 1 ⓣ 938 941 086, ⓦ restaurantefragata.com. Mon–Thu 1–4.15pm & 8–11.15pm, Fri & Sat 1–4.45pm & 8–11.45pm, Sun 1–4.45pm.
Fragata is typical of the new wave of classy seafood places in town, where catch-of-the-day choices like grilled scallops or wild sea bass cost €17 to €28.

La Salseta

MAP P.145
C/Sant Pau 35 ⓣ 938 110 419, ⓦ lasalseta.com. Tue–Sat 1.15–3.30pm, Wed–Sat 8.15–11pm.

Shop

Mercat Municipal

MAP P.145
Av. Artur Carbonell ⓣ 938 949 777. Mon, Wed & Sat 8.30am–2pm, Tue, Thu & Fri 8.30am–2pm & 5.30–8.30pm.
The town market is a great place to put together a picnic of cured meats, olives, cheese, fresh bread and fruit.

Restaurants and tapas bars

AlFresco

MAP P.145.
C/Pau Barrabeitg 4 ⓣ 938 940 600, ⓦ alfrescorestaurante.es. Daily 8pm–midnight (May–Jun closed Mon).

Sitges information

Trains to Sitges leave Passeig de Gràcia or Barcelona Sants stations every twenty minutes, more frequently at peak times (destination Vilanova/St Vicenç), and it's a thirty- to forty-minute ride depending on the service. The main Oficina Turisme (Pl. Eduard Maristany 2 ⓣ 938 944 251, ⓦ sitgestur.cat; Mon–Fri 10am–2pm & 4–6.30pm, Sat 10am–2pm & 4–7pm, Sun 10am–2pm) is adjacent to the train station. Note that Monday isn't the best day to come, as the museums and many restaurants are closed. As well as Carnival, Sitges is known for its celebrated annual sci-fi, horror and fantasy fest, the Festival Internacional de Cinema (ⓦ sitgesfilmfestival.com) every October.

The LGBTQ scene and Carnival

The Sitges LGBTQ scene is frenetic and ever-changing, but the bulk of the nightlife is centred on Plaça de l'Industria. Summer, of course, sees one long nonstop party, but Carnival time (Feb/March) is also notoriously riotous, with a full programme of parades, masked balls, concerts and beach parties. Highlights are Sunday night's Debauchery Parade and Tueday's Extermination Parade, in which exquisitely dressed drag queens twirl lacy parasols, while bar doors stand wide open and the celebrations go on till dawn. The other big bash is Gay Pride Sitges (gaypridesitges.com), a weekend of events plus street parade every July.

Classic, unpretentious Catalan food (cod with garlic confit, seafood paella) made from locally sourced ingredients at reasonable prices have kept this 23-year-old restaurant's cosy dining room full of tourists and locals alike.

El Tros

MAP P.145

C/Sant Pere de Ribes 12 938 110 696. Mon–Fri 7am–7pm, Sat 8am–7pm.

A family run little restaurant with a friendly atmosphere that offers tasty food at very good prices. Have a Spanish omelette for breakfast or come to get some lunch at around 1.30pm - try the menú del dia (around €12) with some delicious coffee.

Bars

Baron

MAP P.145.

C/Sant Gaudenci 17. Daily 7pm–2.30am, Fri & Sat up to 3am.

Definitely not a stylish bar, but this old tavern is a real slice of Sitges nonetheless. It's nowhere near the sea, so there's more of a down-to-earth local crowd.

Parrots Pub

MAP P.145

Pl. de l'Industria 938 941 350, parrotspub.com. Daily 5pm–2.30am.

The stalwart of the gay bar scene in Sitges, with front-row seats on all the action.

Vikingos

MAP P.145

C/Marqués de Montroig 7–9 938 949 687, losvikingos.com. Mon–Thu 1pm–1am, Fri 1pm–1.30am, Sat 11pm–2am, Sun 11pm–1am.

Long-standing party-zone bar with a huge air-conditioned interior and streetside terrace. This and the similar *Montroig* next door serve drinks, snacks and meals from morning until night to a really mixed crowd.

Voramar

MAP P.145.

C/Port Alegre 55. Daily 9pm–12.30am (Sat & Sun until 12.30am); closed Wed.

Charismatic seafront bar, away from the main crowds, just right for an ice-cold beer or sundowner cocktail.

Carnival

ACCOMMODATION

Hotel Arts Barcelona

Accommodation

Finding a hotel vacancy in Barcelona at any time of year can be very difficult, so it's best to book in advance. The absolute cheapest rooms in a simple family-run *hostal* or *pensión*, sharing a bathroom, cost around €50 (singles from €30), though if you want private facilities €70–80 a night is more realistic. There's a fair amount of choice around the €100 mark, while up to €200 gets you the run of decent hotels in most city areas. For Barcelona's most fashionable hotels count on €250–400 a night, while dorm beds in youth hostels go for €20 to €30 depending on the season. An eight-percent tax (IVA) is added to all accommodation bills (though it's sometimes included in the quoted price), and a new "tourist tax" adds €0.65 to €2.25 per person per night to your bill for stays of up to seven days. Under-17s are exempt, and most tourist establishments in Barcelona fall into the lowest tax band. Breakfast isn't usually included, unless specifically stated in the reviews. Credit cards are accepted almost everywhere (though American Express isn't always). There's a lot of street noise in Barcelona, so bring earplugs if you're at all concerned. You can reserve accommodation online with the city tourist board (ⓦ hotelsbcn.com) or make same-day bookings in person only at their tourist offices (ⓦ barcelonaturisme.com) at Plaça de Catalunya, the airport and elsewhere. Many agencies offer apartment rental, which can be good value for couples and friends.

Along the Ramblas

EXE RAMBLAS BOQUERÍA MAP P.26, POCKET MAP C12. **Ramblas 91–93 Ⓜ Liceu ⓣ 933 435 461, ⓦ exeramblasboqueria.com.** Snappy little boutique rooms in a small three-star hotel right outside the Boqueria market. There's not much space, but all you need is on the doorstep, and the soundproofing is good so you get a street view without the racket. **€143**

HOSTAL BENIDORM MAP P.26, POCKET MAP C13. **Ramblas 37 Ⓜ Drassanes ⓣ 933 022 054, ⓦ hostalbenidorm.com.** Refurbished *pensión* that offers real value for money, hence the tribes of young tourists. Rooms available for one to five people, and a balcony with a Ramblas view if you're lucky (and prepared to pay a bit more). **€89**

HOTEL 1898 MAP P.26, POCKET MAP C11. **Ramblas 109 Ⓜ Catalunya ⓣ 935 529 552, ⓦ hotel1898.com.** The former HQ of the Philippines Tobacco Company got an eye-popping boutique refit, adding four grades of rooms (the standard is "Classic") in deep red, green or black, plus sumptuous suites and dramatic public areas, including neocolonial lobby-lounge bar, heated rooftop pool and glam spa facilities. Special rates from €260. **€335**

HOTEL ORIENTE MAP P.26, POCKET MAP C13. **Ramblas 45 Ⓜ Liceu ⓣ 933 022 558, ⓦ atiramhotels.com.** For somewhere on the Ramblas that's traditional but not too pricey, this historic three-star hotel is your best bet – nineteenth-century style in the grand public rooms and tastefully updated bedrooms, some with Ramblas views (though the quieter ones face inwards). **€125**

HOTEL RIVOLI RAMBLAS MAP P.26, POCKET MAP D11. **Ramblas 128 Ⓜ Catalunya ⓣ 934 817 676, ⓦ hotelserhsrivolirambla.com.** The elegant rooms in this four-star hotel are imaginatively furnished (Art Deco to contemporary); all come with spacious bathrooms, while the front ones have floor-to-ceiling windows and classic Ramblas views. There's a lovely rooftop terrace and bar. Special rates from €99. **€160**

Barri Gòtic

HOTEL EL JARDÍ MAP P.34, POCKET MAP D12. **Pl. Sant Josep Oriol 1 Ⓜ Liceu ⓣ 933 015 900, ⓦ eljardi-barcelona.com.** Location is all – overlooking the charming Plaça del Pi – and though rooms can seem a bit bare and plain, some look directly onto the square (terrace or balcony rooms €105). You can have breakfast at the hotel, though the *Bar del Pi* below is nicer. **€90**

HOTEL RACÓ DEL PI MAP P.34, POCKET MAP D12. **C/del Pi 7 Ⓜ Liceu ⓣ 933 426 190, ⓦ hotelh10racodelpi.com.** A stylish three-star hotel in a great location. Rooms – some with balconies over the street – have wood floors and granite-and-mosaic bathrooms. There's a glass of cava on check-in and free coffee and pastries during the day in the bar. **€130**

ITACA HOSTEL MAP P.34, POCKET MAP E12. **C/Ripoll 21 Ⓜ Jaume I ⓣ 933 019 751, ⓦ itacahostel.com.** Bright and breezy hostel close to the cathedral offering spacious rooms with balconies. Dorms are mixed, though you can also reserve a private room or apartment (sleeps up to six; €120), and with a capacity of only 30 it feels more house party than hostel. **Dorms €25, rooms €100**

NERI HOTEL MAP P.34, POCKET MAP D12. **C/de Sant Sever 5 Ⓜ Liceu/Jaume I ⓣ 933 040 655, ⓦ hotelneri.com.** A delightful eighteenth-century palace close to the cathedral houses this stunning boutique hotel of just 22 rooms and suites, featuring swags of flowing material, rescued timber and granite-toned bathrooms. Catalan designers have created eye-catching effects, like a tapestry that falls four floors through the central atrium, while a beamed library and stylish roof terrace provide a tranquil escape. Breakfast is served bento-box style, either out in the courtyard in summer or in the fine contemporary Mediterranean restaurant. **€350**

PENSIÓ ALAMAR MAP P.34, POCKET MAP D13. **C/Comtessa de Sobradiel 1 Ⓜ Liceu/Jaume I ⓣ 933 025 012, ⓦ pensioalamar.com.** If you don't mind sharing a bathroom, this simply furnished *pensión* makes a convenient base. There are twelve rooms (including singles, doubles and triples), most with little balconies, and there's a friendly welcome, laundry service and use of a kitchen. No credit cards. **€45**

PENSIÓN MARI-LUZ MAP P.34, POCKET MAP D13. **C/del Palau 4, 2° Ⓜ Liceu/Jaume I ⓣ 933 173 463, ⓦ pensionmariluz.com.** This old mansion, on a quiet Barri Gòtic street, offers inexpensive rooms (most share bathrooms), plus a more personal touch than many other places of its kind. It can be a tight squeeze when full, but a dozen slick apartments (ⓦ www.apartmentsunio.com; €85) a few minutes' walk away in the Raval offer more space. **€75**

Port Vell and Barceloneta

H10 PORT VELL MAP P.46, POCKET MAP D14. **Pas de Sota Muralla 9 Ⓜ Barceloneta ⓣ 933 103 065, ⓦ h10hotels.com.** An elegant hotel set in a restored historic building. On the rooftop there is a lovely

What's the neighbourhood like?

If you hanker after a **Ramblas** view, you'll pay for the privilege – generally speaking, there are better deals to be had either side of the famous boulevard, often just a minute's walk away. Alongside some classy boutique choices, most of Barcelona's cheapest accommodation is found in the Old Town, principally the **Barri Gòtic** and **El Raval** neighbourhoods, which both still have their rough edges – be careful (without being paranoid) when coming and going after dark. North of Plaça de Catalunya, the **Eixample** – split into Right (**Dreta**) and Left (**Esquerra**) – has some of the city's most fashionable hotels. Those near **Sants** station are convenient for Montjuïc and the metro system, and those further north in **Les Corts** for the Avinguda Diagonal shopping district. For waterfront views look at **Port Vell** at the end of the Ramblas, and at the **Port Olímpic** southeast of the Old Town – while new four- and five-star hotels abound further out on the metro at the **Diagonal Mar** conference and events site. If you prefer neighbourhood living then **Gràcia** is the best base, as you're only ever a short walk away from its excellent bars, restaurants and clubs.

terrace with a bar, a swimming pool and a gorgeous view of the port. Well located and close to many popular restaurants, it can also boast of an excellent restaurant itself. **€230**

HOTEL DUQUESA DE CARDONA MAP **P.46, POCKET MAP D14. Pg. de Colom 12 Ⓜ Drassanes/Barceloneta ⓣ 932 689 090, ⓦ hduquesadecardona.com.** Step off the busy harbourfront highway into this soothing four-star haven, set in a remodelled sixteenth-century mansion. The rooms are calm and quiet, decorated in earth tones and immaculately appointed. Although not all of the rooms have harbour views, all guests have access to the stylish roof-deck overlooking the harbour. It's great for sundowner drinks, and boasts (if that's the word) probably the city's smallest outdoor pool. **€240**

SAFESTAY SEA MAP **P.46, POCKET MAP H8. Pl. del Mar 1–4 Ⓜ Barceloneta ⓦ safestay.com/barcelona-sea/; online bookings only.** The budget beachside choice is this neat little hostel with modern en-suite rooms sleeping four to eight people. The attached café looks right out onto the boardwalk. Breakfast included. **Dorms €26**

W BARCELONA MAP **P.46. Pl. de la Rosa dels Vents Ⓜ Barceloneta ⓣ 932 952 800, ⓦ w-barcelona.com.** Signature building on the Barceloneta seafront is the *W Barcelona*. No one calls it the "W", though; to locals it is the "Vela" (sail) because of its shape. Open-plan designer rooms have fantastic views and there's a hip, resort feel, with direct beach access and guest DJs on the see-and-be-seen rooftop lounge. Standout restaurant *Bravo 24* is courtesy of star Barcelona chef Carles Abellan but you can also chill out with cocktails, burgers and sand between your toes at the *Salt Beach Club*. **€350**

El Raval

BARCELÓ RAVAL MAP **P.54, POCKET MAP B12. Rambla del Raval 17–21 Ⓜ Liceu/Sant Antoni ⓣ 933 201 490, ⓦ barcelo.com.** Neighbourhood landmark is this glow-in-the-dark tower whose USP is the 360-degree top-floor terrace with plunge pool and city views. Sophisticated, open-plan rooms have a crisp, space-station-style sheen, plus iPod docks, coffee-makers and other cool comforts, while the slinky lobby "B-lounge" is the place for everything from breakfast to cocktails. **€160**

CASA CAMPER MAP P.54, POCKET MAP C11. C/Elisabets 11 Ⓜ Universitat/Liceu Ⓣ 933 426 280, Ⓦ casacamper.com. Synonymous with creative, comfy shoes, Barcelona-based Camper has taken a bold step into the hospitality business with this sleek, minimalist hotel. All the rooms are divided by a corridor: the "sleeping" side faces a six-storey tall vertical garden; the other part is a "mini-lounge" with a flat screen TV, hammock and street-facing balcony. Breakfast is included. **€240**

HOSTAL CÈNTRIC MAP P.54, POCKET MAP B10. C/Casanova 13 Ⓜ Universitat Ⓣ 934 267 573, Ⓦ hostalcentric.com. A good upper-budget choice a couple of minutes' walk from the Raval proper. The rooms offer plenty of light, plus a/c and private bathrooms. Some include balconies. **€115**

HOSTAL GRAU MAP P.54, POCKET MAP C10. C/Ramelleres 27 Ⓜ Catalunya Ⓣ 933 018 135, Ⓦ hostalgrau.com. A really friendly *pensión* with attractive, colour-coordinated rooms – superior rooms also have balconies and a touch of modern Catalan style (en suites €105). Two small private apartments in the same building (sleeping two to four, available by the night; €150) offer a bit more independence. **€100**

HOTEL ESPAÑA MAP P.54, POCKET MAP C13. C/de Sant Pau 9–11 Ⓜ Liceu Ⓣ 935 500 000, Ⓦ hotelespanya.com. This *modernista* icon has been sumptuously restored, and the gem-like interior – colourful mosaics, sculpted marble, iron swirls and marine motifs – has no equal in Barcelona. Guest rooms are a boutique blend of earth tones and designer style, with rain-showers, iPod docks and the like, while the handsome house restaurant – known as *Fonda España* – offers contemporary Catalan bistro dishes by renowned chef Martín Berasategui. **€160**

HOTEL ONIX LICEO MAP P.54, POCKET MAP B13. C/Nou de la Rambla 36 Ⓜ Liceu/Drassanes Ⓣ 934 816 441, Ⓦ onixliceohotel.com. Steps from Palau Güell, this four-star hotel features minimalist decor that melds nicely with the building's older architectural elements, such as the grand marble staircase that curves up from the lobby to the second floor. There's a tropical patio and big-for-Barcelona pool on the ground floor and an airy Mozarab-influenced lounge area. **€60**

HOTEL PENINSULAR MAP P.54, POCKET MAP C13. C/de Sant Pau 34 Ⓜ Liceu Ⓣ 933 023 138, Ⓦ hotelpeninsular.net. The interesting old building originally belonged to a priestly order, which explains the slightly cell-like rooms. However, there's nothing spartan about the galleried courtyard (around which the rooms are ranged), hung with tumbling houseplants, while breakfast (included) is served in the arcaded dining room. **€80**

HOTEL SANT AGUSTÍ MAP P.54, POCKET MAP C12. Pl. Sant Agusti 3 Ⓜ Liceu Ⓣ 933 181 658, Ⓦ hotelsa.com. Barcelona's oldest hotel occupies a former convent, with front balconies overlooking a restored square and church. It's of three-star standard, with the best rooms located in the attic, from where there are rooftop views. **€140**

MARKET HOTEL MAP P.54, POCKET MAP E5. C/Comte Borrell 68, at Ptge. Sant Antoni Abad Ⓜ Sant Antoni Ⓣ 933 251 205, Ⓦ markethotel.com.es. The designer-budget *Market* makes a splash with its part-Japanese, part-neocolonial look – think jet-black rooms with hardwood floors and boxy wardrobes topped with travel trunks. **€110**

Sant Pere

PENSIÓ 2000 MAP P.64, POCKET MAP E11. C/Sant Pere Més Alt 6, 1° Ⓜ Urquinaona Ⓣ 933 107 466, Ⓦ pensio2000.com. As close to a traditional family-style B&B as Barcelona gets – seven rooms in a welcoming mansion apartment strewn with books, plants and pictures. A third person could easily share most rooms (€20 extra). **€80**

La Ribera

CHIC & BASIC MAP P.70, POCKET MAP G13. C/de la Princesa 50 Ⓜ Jaume I Ⓣ 932 954 652, Ⓦ chicandbasic.com. From the babbling blurb ("it's fresh, it's cool, it's fusion") to the all-in-white rooms with adjustable mood lighting, everything is punchily boutique and in-your-face. Chic, certainly – basic, not at all, though the concept eschews room service, minibars and tonnes of staff at your beck and call. There's a more budget *Chic & Basic* on C/ dels Tallers (near Pl. Universitat, El Raval) and apartments peppered around the cily centre too (details on the website). **€110**

EQUITY POINT GOTHIC MAP P.70, POCKET MAP E13. **C/Vigatans 5 Ⓜ Jaume I Ⓦ equity-point.com; online bookings only.** Backpacker heaven, not far from the Picasso museum. There's a great roof terrace, and all sorts of tours available, while each bunk bed gets its own cabinet and reading light. Breakfast included. **Dorms €25**

HOSTAL NUEVO COLÓN MAP P.70, POCKET MAP G14. **Av. Marquès de l'Argentera 19, 1° Ⓜ Barceloneta Ⓣ 933 195 077, Ⓦ hostalnuevocolon.com.** Run by a friendly family, featuring 24 spacious rooms painted yellow and kitted out with directors' chairs and double glazing. Sunny front rooms all have side views to Ciutadella park, while França station is opposite. Pay more for en suites (€70) or an apartment (€155). **€82**

HOTEL BANYS ORIENTALS MAP P.70, POCKET MAP E13. **C/de l'Argenteria 37 Ⓜ Jaume I Ⓣ 932 688 460, Ⓦ hotelbanysorientals.com.** Funky boutique hotel with 43 minimalist rooms, plus some duplex suites in a nearby building (suites €143). Hardwood floors, sharp marble bathrooms and urban-chic decor – not to mention bargain prices for this sort of style – make it a hugely popular choice. The attached restaurant, *Senyor Parellada*, is a great find too. **€130**

Montjuïc

HOTEL MIRAMAR MAP P.82, POCKET MAP E7. **Pl. Carlos Ibañez 3 Ⓜ Paral.lel and Funicular de Montjuïc Ⓣ 932 811 600, Ⓦ hotelmiramarbarcelona.com.** The remodelled *Miramar* has 75 stylish rooms with sweeping views over the city. From the architecture books in the lounge to the terrace jacuzzis, you're in designer heaven, augmented by a stunning pool and tranquil gardens. **€220**

Port Olímpic

HOTEL ARTS BARCELONA MAP P.91, POCKET MAP K8. **C/Marina 19–21 Ⓜ Ciutadella-Vila Olímpica Ⓣ 932 211 000, Ⓦ hotelartsbarcelona.com** Effortlessly classy rooms feature enormous marble bathrooms and fabulous views. The upper floors belong to *The Club* – an exclusive hotel-within-a-hotel with a luxurious lounge and concierge service. You're only a hop from the beach, but seafront gardens also have a swimming pool and hot tub. Dining options include the two-Michelin-starred *Enoteca* and the open-air gourmet tapas terrace *Arola*. **€456**

Dreta de l'Eixample

CASA BONAY MAP P.96, POCKET MAP G3. **Gran Via de Les Corts Catalanes 700 Ⓜ Passeig de Gràcia Ⓦ casabonay.com; online bookings only.** This hotel is set in a neoclassical historical building, it offers a cosy and yet elegant interior. After the renovation of the 1896 building the main attention grabbing features were preserved - like floor tiles. The omnipresent potted plants add a lot of charm to the place. Some of the rooms offer private terraces which will give you a secluded place of rest in the centre of the bustling city. **€150**

EQUITY POINT CENTRIC MAP P.96, POCKET MAP G3. **Pg. de Gràcia 33 Ⓜ Passeig de Gràcia Ⓦ equity-point.com; online bookings only.** The biggest hostel in the city occupies a refurbished *modernista* building in a swish midtown location. Private twins, doubles, triples and quads available, all with shower room, balcony and views, while dorms (all en suite) sleep up to fourteen. Excellent facilities include a spectacular roof terrace with views of the famous boulevard. Breakfast included. **Dorms €22, rooms €90**

HOSTAL GIRONA MAP P.96, POCKET MAP G10. **C/Girona 24, 1° Ⓜ Urquinaona Ⓣ 932 650 259, Ⓦ hostalgirona.com.** Delightful family-run *pensión* with a wide range of cosy, traditional rooms (some sharing a bathroom, others with a shower or full bath; en suites €85) – the best and biggest have balconies, though you can expect some noise. **€90**

HOSTAL GOYA MAP P.96, POCKET MAP **E10. C/de Pau Claris 74, 1° Ⓜ Urquinaona Ⓣ 933 022 565, Ⓦ hostalgoya.com.** Boutique-style *pensión* that offers stylishly decorated rooms on two floors of a mansion building. There's a fair range of options, with the best rooms opening onto a balcony or terrace (€110). Comfortable sitting areas, and free tea and coffee, are available on both floors. **€120**

HOTEL CONDES DE BARCELONA MAP **P.96, POCKET MAP H3. Pg. de Gràcia 73–75 Ⓜ Passeig de Gràcia Ⓣ 934 450 000, Ⓦ condesdebarcelona.com.** Straddling two sides of C/Mallorca, the *Condes* is fashioned from two former palaces. Its rooms are classily turned out in contemporary style, some with a balcony or private terrace, some with views of Gaudí's La Pedrera. There's a roof terrace with a plunge pool, plus *Alaire*, a hip rooftop cocktail bar. Multi-Michelin-starred Basque chef Martín Berasategui oversees upmarket bistro *Loidi* and the more casual *Loidi Bar&Tapas* (both closed Sun). **€170**

HOTEL OMM MAP P.96, POCKET MAP **H2. C/Rosselló 265 Ⓜ Diagonal Ⓣ 934 454 000, Ⓦ hotelomm.es.** The glam designer experience that is *Omm* means stark but sensational rooms, elegant staff and a Spaciomm "relaxation centre". The Roca brothers serve Michelin-starred fine dining at *Roca Moo* restaurant (closed Sun & August), plus slightly less far-out fare at its baby brother, *Roca Bar*. Expect live jazz on the roof terrace, where beautiful people gather to sip cocktails. **€250**

MANDARIN ORIENTAL MAP P.96, **POCKET MAP H3. Pg. de Gràcia 38–40 Ⓜ Passeig de Gràcia Ⓣ 931 518 888, Ⓦ mandarinoriental.com/barcelona.** The sleek *Mandarin Oriental* fills the premises of a former bank building with a soaring white atrium and a selection of extremely thick-walled rooms made from old vaults. The suites are among the finest in Barcelona. There are the obligatory superstar restaurants, *Moments* and *Bistreau*, and the super-cool *Banker's Bar*, which has live music and some of the best cocktails in town. **€625**

PRAKTIK BAKERY HOTEL MAP **P.96, POCKET MAP H2. C/Provença 279 Ⓜ Diagonal Ⓣ 934 880 061, Ⓦ hotelpraktikbakery.com.** Minimalist, all-white designer rooms and a great location aren't the reason for the queue that constantly stretches out of this hotel's door and onto the street. That would be the hotel's bakery run by Baluard, makers of some of Barcelona's best bread. Breakfast doesn't get much better than the buffet of butter croissants, cakes, buns and pastries that await you here each morning. **€120**

THE5ROOMS MAP P.96, POCKET MAP **E10. C/Pau Claris 72, 1° Ⓜ Urquinaona Ⓣ 933 427 880, Ⓦ thefiverooms.com.** The owner's impeccable taste and fashion background are evident in gorgeous contemporary-styled B&B rooms that are spacious and light-filled, with original artwork above each bed, exposed brick walls and terrific bathrooms. Breakfast is served whenever you like, drinks are always available, and Jessica is happy to sit down and talk you through her favourite bars, restaurants and galleries. Suites and apartments are also available (apartments €159 for two people). **€130**

Sagrada Família and Glòries

BARCELONA URBANY MAP P.106, POCKET **MAP M3. Av. Meridiana 97 Ⓜ Clot Ⓣ 932 458 414, Ⓦ barcelonaurbany.com.** Bumper steel-and-glass 400-bed hostel that's a bit off the beaten track, but on handy metro and airport train routes and with amazing views of Torre Agbar. The rooms are like space-shuttle pods – boxy en-suites with pull-down beds (sleeping two to eight), power-showers and key-card lockers – that are just as viable for couples on a budget as backpackers (private rooms from €50). There's a bar and terrace, plus free gym, jacuzzi and pool entry in the same building. Breakfast is included. **Dorms €18**

HOTEL EUROSTARS MONUMENTAL MAP P.106, POCKET MAP K3. **C/Consell de Cent 498–500 Ⓜ Monumental Ⓣ 932 320 288, Ⓦ eurostarshotels.com.** An excellent-value four-star choice within walking distance of the Sagrada Família. The 45 rooms are crisply appointed in dark wood and earth tones, staff are really helpful and the top-floor suites (€200) boast terrace views of the Gaudí church. **€143**

Esquerra de l'Eixample

ALTERNATIVE CREATIVE YOUTH HOME MAP P.114, POCKET MAP G4. **Ronda Universitat 17 Ⓜ Universitat/Catalunya Ⓣ 635 669 021, Ⓦ alternative-barcelona.com.** The hostel hangout for an art crowd who love the laidback vibe, projection lounge, cool music and city-savvy staff. The regular hostel stuff is well designed too, with a walk-in kitchen and a maximum of 24 people spread across three small dorms. **Dorms €20**

GRAN HOTEL TORRE CATALUNYA MAP P.114, POCKET MAP C2. **Av. Roma 2–4 Ⓜ Sants Estació Ⓣ 936 006 966, Ⓦ torrecatalunya.com.** The landmark four-star deluxe hotel outside Sants station features sweeping views from all sides. Breakfast on the 23rd floor is a buzz; there's also a spa with indoor pool, and guests can use the nearby sister *Expo* hotel's outdoor pool. You'll pay €30 more for superior rooms. **€120**

MIDMOST HOTEL BARCELONA MAP P.114, POCKET MAP C10. **C/Pelai 14 Ⓜ Universitat Ⓣ 935 051 100, Ⓦ hotelmidmost.com.** The boutique little three-star sister to the Dreta's *Hotel Majestic* has harmoniously toned rooms and snazzy bathrooms. Space is at a premium, but some rooms have cute private terraces, others street-side balconies, while best of all are the romantic roof terrace and pool. **€200**

HOTEL PRAKTIK RAMBLA MAP P.114, POCKET MAP G4. **Rambla de Catalunya 27 Ⓜ Passeig de Gràcia Ⓣ 933 436 690, Ⓦ hotelpraktikrambla.com.** This new boutique hotel in a converted *modernista* mansion keeps the design touches toned down and lets the architecture do the talking. Big, high-ceilinged rooms (especially the deluxe doubles, about €30 extra) look out onto a tranquil terrace, complete with burbling fountain, where you can enjoy the sunshine in peace. **€105**

SOHO HOTEL MAP P.114, POCKET MAP G4. **Gran Via de les Corts Catalanes 543-545, Ⓜ Urgell Ⓣ 935 529 610, Ⓦ hotelsohobarcelona.com.** The decor here is very modern and sophisticated and the hotel itself is a stone's throw away from public transit. The rooftop pool may not be one of the biggest you've seen, but it offers enough cool serenity to calm you down after a long day of busy sightseeing. The terrace is quite spacious, however, and eating your breakfast with a view of Barcelona's rooftops could prove quite an experience. **€110**

SOMNIO BARCELONA MAP P.114, POCKET MAP G4. **C/Diputació 251 2° Ⓜ Passeig de Gràcia Ⓣ 932 725 308, Ⓦ somniohostels.com.** Sisters Lauren and Lee from Chicago bring their passion for Barcelona right into their upscale *pensión*, dropping "tips for the day" into your room each morning. Simple but smart rooms with wood-block floors cater for singles (€44), couples and friends. There are four spacious twin rooms, four double rooms (two en suite; €87) and a single. Some have balconies. **€60**

Gràcia and Parc Güell

ALBERG MARE DE DÉU DE MONTSERRAT MAP P.122, **Pg. de la Mare de Déu del Coll 41–51 Ⓜ Vallcarca Ⓣ 932 105 151, reservations on Ⓣ 934 838 363, Ⓦ xanascat.cat.** A popular hostel, set in a converted mansion with gardens, terrace and great city views, with dorms sleeping six, eight or twelve. It's a long way from the centre (though it's close to Parc Güell) – from the metro, follow Av. República d'Argentina, C/Viaducte de Vallcarca and then the signs, while buses (#V17 from Plaça d'Urquinaona, plus night buses) stop just across the street. Reception open 8am–11pm; main door closes at midnight, but opens every 30min thereafter. Breakfast included. **Dorms €24**

CASA GRACIA MAP P.121, POCKET MAP H2. **Pg. de Gràcia 116** Ⓜ **Diagonal** Ⓣ **931 740 528,** Ⓦ **casagraciabcn.com.** A vibrant and stylish space spread over six floors in a *modernista* building, with bonuses like a concierge, themed dinners and evening concerts. The rooms (from dorms to doubles to six-bed private rooms) have a/c and are en suite, while the deluxe suite pampers with a spa bath, slippers and bathrobes. Though *Casa Gracia* is technically a hostel, you'll feel like you're staying in a (pretty good) hotel. Breakfast is included. **Dorms €25, rooms €130**

GENERATOR BARCELONA MAP P.121, POCKET MAP H2. **C/de Corsega 373** Ⓜ **Diagonal** Ⓣ **932 200 377,** Ⓦ **generatorhostels.com.** Big, bright and abuzz with people having fun, the *Generator* lounge frequently features live music, DJ sets and art performances, as well as a pool table and large-screen TV. Rooms are clean and modern and there's 24-hour reception and free, fast wi-fi. Splash out on the penthouse apartment (€200). **Dorms €9, rooms €40**

HOTEL CASA FUSTER MAP P.121, POCKET MAP H1. **Pg. de Gràcia 132** Ⓜ **Diagonal** Ⓣ **932 553 000,** Ⓦ **hotelcasafuster.com.** *Modernista* architect Lluís Domènech i Montaner's magnificent Casa Fuster (1908) is the backdrop for five-star deluxe luxury with service to match. Rooms are in earth tones, with huge beds, smart bathrooms, and remote-controlled light and heat, while public areas make full use of the architectural heritage – from the magnificent pillared lobby bar, the *Café Vienés*, to the panoramic roof terrace and pool. There's also a contemporary restaurant, *Galaxó*, plus fitness centre, sauna and 24hr room service. **€320**

Tibidabo

GRAN HOTEL LA FLORIDA MAP P.137, **Carretera Vallvidrera a Tibidabo 83–93, 7km from the centre** Ⓣ **932 593 000,** Ⓦ **hotellaflorida.com.** This five-star place on Tibidabo mountain re-creates the glory days of the 1950s, when *La Florida* was at the centre of Barcelona high society. Its terraces and pools have amazing views, while some of the seventy rooms and suites have private gardens or terraces and jacuzzis. Jazz sessions in the club are not to be missed. There's also a spa, restaurant, poolside bar and shuttle-bus service to town. Cheaper if you book in advance online (from €198).**€300**

ESSENTIALS

Montjuïc cable car

Arrival

In most cases, you can be off the plane, train or bus and in your central Barcelona hotel room within the hour. Note that many Ryanair flights (and some others) to Barcelona are actually to Girona (90km north) or Reus (110km south), and though there are reliable connecting bus and train services this means up to a 90-minute journey from either airport to Barcelona city centre.

By air

Barcelona's airport (T 902 404 704, W aena.es) is 18km southwest of the city. A **taxi** to the centre costs up to €30, including the airport surcharge (plus other surcharges for travel after 9pm, at weekends or for luggage in the boot). Far cheaper is the **airport train** (5.42am–11.38pm; journey time 18min; €6.30; info on T 902 240 202), which runs every thirty minutes to Barcelona Sants station (see "By train") and then continues on to Passeig de Gràcia (best stop for Eixample, Plaça de Catalunya and the Ramblas). It departs from Terminal T2, and there's a free shuttle bus to the station from T1 which takes around ten minutes. City travel passes and the Barcelona Card (available at the airport) are valid on the airport train.

Alternatively, the **Aerobús** service (Mon–Sat 5.30am–1am; €5.90, €10.20 return, departures every 5–10min; W aerobusbcn.com) from T1 and T2 stops in the city at Plaça d'Espanya, Gran Via–Urgell, Plaça Universitat and Plaça de Catalunya (travel time 30min). Aerobus departures back to the airport leave from in front of El Corte Inglés in Plaça de Catalunya – note that there are separate services to terminals T1 and T2.

By bus

The main bus terminal is the **Estació del Nord** (T 902 260 606, W barcelonanord.com; M Arc de Triomf) on C/Ali-Bei, three blocks north of Parc de la Ciutadella. Various companies operate services across Catalunya, Spain and Europe from here – it's a good idea to reserve a ticket in advance on long-distance routes (a day before at the station is usually fine, or buy online). Some intercity and international services also make a stop at the bus terminal behind Barcelona Sants station. Either way, you're only a short metro ride from the city centre.

By train

The national rail service is operated by RENFE T 912 320 320, W renfe.com). The city's main station is **Barcelona Sants**, 3km west of the centre, with a metro station (M Sants Estació) that links directly to the Ramblas (M Liceu), Plaça de Catalunya and Passeig de Gràcia. The high-speed AVE line between Barcelona and Madrid has cut the fastest journey between the cities to under three hours. These services also arrive at and depart from Barcelona Sants, though a second high-speed station is under construction in the north of the city.

Some Spanish intercity services and international trains also stop at **Estació de França**, 1km east of the Ramblas and close to M Barceloneta.

Regional and local commuter train services are operated by Ferrocarrils de la Generalitat de Catalunya, or **FGC** (T 932 051 515, W fgc.cat), with stations at **Plaça de Catalunya**, at the top of the Ramblas (for trains from coastal towns north of the city); **Plaça d'Espanya** (for Montserrat); and **Passeig de Gràcia** (Catalunya provincial destinations).

Getting around

Barcelona has an excellent integrated transport system which comprises the metro, buses, trams and local trains, plus a network of funiculars and cable cars. The local transport authority has a useful website (W tmb.cat, English-language version available) with full timetable and ticket information, while a city transport map and information is posted at major bus stops and all metro and tram stations.

The metro

The quickest way of getting around Barcelona is by **metro**, which currently runs on six main lines. A few stations on lines L9, L10 & L12 are also now open – on its completion, this will be the longest underground line in Europe (almost 50km) and will run between the airport, city centre and high-speed Sagrera train station.

There's a limited network of stations in the Old Town, but you can take the metro directly to the Ramblas (Catalunya, Liceu or Drassanes), and to the edge of the Barri Gòtic, El Raval and La Ribera.

Metro entrances are marked with a red diamond sign with an "M". Its **hours of operation** are Monday to Thursday, plus Sunday and public holidays 5am to midnight; Friday 5am to 2am; Saturday and the day before a public holiday, 24hr service. The system is safe, but some of the train carriages are heavily graffitied, and buskers and beggars are common.

Tickets and travel passes

On all the city's public transport (including night buses and funiculars), you can buy a **single ticket** every time you ride (€2.15), but it's much cheaper to buy a **targeta** – a discount ticket card. They are available at metro, train and tram stations, but not on the buses.

Best general ticket deal is the T-10 ("tay day-oo" in Catalan) *targeta* (€10.20), valid for ten separate journeys, with changes between methods of transport allowed within 75 minutes. This card (also available at newsagents' kiosks) can be used by more than one person at a time – simply validate it the same number of times as there are people travelling.

Other useful (single-person) *targetes* include the T-Dia (1 day's unlimited travel; €8.60), and there are also multiday combos (HolaBCN!) for up to five days (€35). Prices given are for passes valid as far as the Zone 1 city limits, which in practice is everywhere you're likely to want to go except Montserrat and Sitges. For trips to these and other out-of-town destinations, buy a specific ticket.

Trams

The **tram** system (W tram.cat) runs on six lines, with departures every eight to twenty minutes throughout the day from 5am to midnight. Lines **T1, T2 and T3** depart from Plaça Francesc Macià and run along the uptown part of Avinguda Diagonal to suburban destinations in the northwest – useful tourist stops are at L'Illa shopping and the Maria Cristina and Palau Reial metro stations. **Line T4** operates from Ciutadella-Vila Olímpica (where there's also a metro station) and runs up past the zoo and TNC (the National Theatre) to Glòries, before running down the

Emergency numbers

Call T 112 for emergency ambulance, police and fire services; for the national police service call T 091.

lower part of Avinguda Diagonal to Diagonal Mar and the Fòrum site. You're unlikely to use the more suburban lines T5 and T6.

Buses

Most **buses** operate daily, roughly from 4am or 5am until 10.30pm, though some lines stop earlier and some run on until after midnight. Night bus services fill in the gaps on all the main routes, with services every twenty to sixty minutes from around 10pm to 4am. Many bus routes (including all night buses) stop in or near Plaça de Catalunya, but the full route is marked at each bus stop, along with a timetable.

City tours

The number of available tours is bewildering, and you can see the sights on anything from a Segway to a hot-air balloon. A good place to start is the official Barcelona Turisme website (ⓦ barcelonaturisme.com), which has a dedicated tours section offering online sales and discounts.

Highest profile are the two tour-bus operators with daily board-at-will, open-top services (1 day €30, 2 days €40), which drop you outside every attraction in the city. The choice is between **Barcelona City Tour** (ⓦ barcelonatours.es) or the **Bus Turístic** (ⓦ barcelonaturisme.com), with frequent departures from Plaça de Catalunya and many other stops – tickets are available on board.

Advance booking is advised (at Pl. de Catalunya tourist office) for **Barcelona Walking Tours**' two-hour historical Barri Gòtic tour (daily all year, in English at 9.30am; €15.50). There are also "Picasso", "*Modernisme*" and "Gourmet" walking tours on selected days.

Long-time resident Nick Lloyd's **Spanish Civil War** tours (ⓦ iberianature.com/barcelona/contact/) weave human stories with the historical events that shaped the city. Delivered in English, these absorbing half-day tours cost €25.

The Food Lovers Company **Barcelona Tapas Tour** (ⓦ foodloverscompany.com), led in English by locals Nuria and Margherita, takes in the city's best traditional tapas spots and costs €70 for three hours.

Bike tours now infest the city, with follow-the-leader cycle packs careering through the Old Town alleys. There are flyers and bike outfits everywhere and you'll pay around €25 for a guided 3hr tour.

At any time of year, the sparkling harbour waters invite a cruise and **Las Golondrinas** (ⓣ 934 423 106, ⓦ lasgolondrinas.com) daily sightseeing boats depart (at least hourly June–Sept, less frequently Oct–May) from the quayside opposite the Columbus statue, at the bottom of the Ramblas (Ⓜ Drassanes). Two of the services visit either the port (40min; €7.70), or port and local coast (1hr 30min; €15.20).

There are also afternoon catamaran trips around the port with **Catamaran Orsom** (ⓦ barcelona-orsom.com; Easter week & June–Sept daily; May & Oct Mon, Thurs–Sun; €15.50) plus summer evening jazz cruises (daily June–Aug; €17.50).

Cycling and bike rental

The city council is investing heavily in cycle lanes and bike schemes, notably the **Bicing** pick-up and drop-off scheme (ⓦ bicing.cat), which is touted as Barcelona's new public transport system. You'll see the red bikes and bike stations all over the city, but Bicing is not available to tourists, only to locals who are encouraged to use the bikes for short trips. To rent a bike you need to be registered as a Barcelona resident.

There are plenty of other **bike rental** outfits aimed at tourists. Rental costs around €25 a day with companies all over town, including Un Coxte Menys (W bicicletabarcelona.com), Donkey Republic (W donkey.bike) and Biciclot (W biciclot.coop).

Currently there are around 200km of **cycle paths** throughout the city, with plans to double the network in the future. Not all locals have embraced the bike yet, and some cycle paths are still ignored by cars or clogged with pedestrians, indignantly reluctant to give way to two-wheelers. But, on the whole, cycling around Barcelona is not the completely hairy experience it was just a few years ago, while you can always get **off-road** in the Parc de Collserola, where there are waymarked trails through the woods and hills.

Funiculars and cable cars

As well as the regular city options, Barcelona also has some fun transport trips and historic survivors. A few **funicular railways** are still widely used, particularly up to Montjuïc and Tibidabo, while summer and year-round weekend visits to Tibidabo also combine a funicular trip with a ride on the clanking antique tram, the **Tramvia Blau**. Best of all, though, are the two **cable car** (*telefèric*) rides: from Barceloneta across the harbour to Montjuïc, and then from the top station of the Montjuïc funicular right the way up to the castle.

Taxis

There are taxi ranks outside major train and metro stations, in main squares, near large hotels and at places along the main avenues. To call a taxi in advance (few of the operators speak English, and you'll be charged an extra €3 or €4), try: Barna Taxis T 933 222 222; Radio Taxi T 933 033 033; Servi-Taxi T 933 300 300; or Taxi Amic T 934 208 088.

A fun way to get around the Old Town, port area and beaches is by **Trixi** (W trixi.com), a kind of love-bug-style bicycle-rickshaw. They tout for business between 11am and 8pm near the Columbus statue at the bottom of the Ramblas, and outside La Seu cathedral in the Barri Gòtic, though you can also flag them down if one cruises by. Fares are fixed (from €6 for 15min, longer tours also available) and the *trixistas* are an amiable, multilingual bunch for the most part.

Trains

The FGC **commuter train line** has its main stations at Plaça de Catalunya and Plaça d'Espanya, used when going to Sarrià, Vallvidrera, Tibidabo and Montserrat. The national rail service, RENFE, runs all the other services out of Barcelona, with local lines designated as **Rodiales/Cercanías**. The hub is Barcelona Sants station, with services also passing through Plaça de Catalunya (heading north) and Passeig de Gràcia (south). Arrive in plenty of time to buy a ticket, as queues are often long, though for most regional destinations you can use the automatic vending machines instead.

Directory A–Z

Addresses

The main address abbreviations are Av. (for Avinguda, avenue), C/ (Carrer, street), Pg. (Passeig, boulevard/street), Bxda. (Baixada, alley), Ptge. (Passatge, passage) and Pl. (Plaça, square). The address "C/Picasso 2, 4°" means: Picasso street, number two, fourth floor.

Crime

Take all the usual precautions and be on guard when on public transport or on the crowded Ramblas and the medieval streets to either side. Easiest place to report a crime is the Gùardia Urbana (municipal police) for each district (T 092, W bcn.cat/guardiaurbana; 24hr, English spoken). For a police report for your insurance go to C/Nou de la Rambla 80, El Raval (M Paral.lel English speaking line T 902 102 112, inside Spain T 092).

Electricity

The electricity supply is 220v and plugs come with two round pins – bring an adapter (and transformer) to use UK and US mobile phone chargers etc.

Embassies and consulates

Australia, Av. Diagonal 433, Eixample, M Diagonal T 933 623 792, W spain.embassy.gov.au; UK, Av. Diagonal 477, Eixample, M Hospital Clínic T 902 109 356, or from outside Spain T 913 342 194, W ukinspain.fco.gov.uk; Canada, Pl. Catalunya 9, M Catalunya T 934 127 263, W canadainternational.gc.ca; Republic of Ireland, Gran Via Carlos III 94, Les Corts, M Maria Cristina/Les Corts T 934 915 021, W dfa.ie; New Zealand, Trav. de Gràcia 64, Gràcia, FGC Gràcia, T 932 095 048, W nzembassy.com; USA, Pg. de la Reina Elisenda 23, Sarrià, FGC Reina Elisenda, T 932 802 227, W es.usembassy.gov.

Health

The following central hospitals have 24hr accident and emergency services: Centre Perecamps, Av. Drassanes 13–15, El Raval, M Drassanes T 934 410 600; Hospital Clínic i Provincial, C/Villaroel 170, Eixample, M Hospital Clínic T 932 275 400. EU citizens receive free or reduced cost treatment if they bring their EHIC card and passport.

Usual pharmacy hours are 9am to 1pm and 4 to 8pm. At least one in each neighbourhood is open 24hr (and marked as such).

LGBTQ travellers

Epicentre of the gay scene is the so-called Gaixample, an area of a few blocks near the university in the Esquerra de l'Eixample. The annual Pride festival runs for ten days in June (W pridebarcelona.org). General listings magazine *Guia del Ocio* can put you on the right track for bars and clubs. The single best English-language website is W 60by80.com/Barcelona. For other information, contact the lesbian and gay city telephone hotline on T 900 601 601 (daily 6–10pm only).

Lost property

Anything recovered by police, or left on public transport, is sent to the Oficina de Troballes (municipal lost property office) at Pl. Carles Pi Sunyer 8–10, Barri Gòtic M Jaume I/Catalunya (Mon–Fri 9am–2pm; T 010). You could also try the transport office at M Universitat.

Money

Spain's currency is the euro (€), with notes issued in denominations of 5, 10, 20, 50, 100, 200 and 500 euros, and coins in denominations of 1, 2, 5, 10, 20 and 50 cents, and 1 and 2 euros. Normal banking hours are Monday to Friday from 8.30am to 2pm, and there are out-of-hours exchange offices down the Ramblas, as well as at the airport, Barcelona Sants station and the Pl. de Catalunya tourist office. ATMs are available all over the city, and you can usually withdraw up to €300 a day.

Museums and passes

Many museums and galleries offer free admission on the first or last Sunday of the month, and most museums are free on the saints' days of February 12, April 23 and September 24, plus May 18 (International Museum Day). The useful Barcelona Card (3 days €45, 4 days €55 or 5 days €60; W barcelonaturisme.com) offers free public transport, plus museum and attraction discounts. The Articket (€30; valid three months; articketbcn.org) covers free admission into six major art galleries, while the *Ruta del Modernisme* (€12; valid one year; rutadelmodernisme.com) is an excellent English-language guidebook and discount-voucher package that covers 116 *modernista* buildings, plus other benefits.

Opening hours

Basic working hours are Monday to Saturday 9.30 or 10am to 1.30pm and 4.30 to 8 or 9pm, though many offices and shops don't open on Saturday afternoons. Local cafés, bars and markets open from around 7am, while shopping centres, major stores and large supermarkets tend to open all day from 10am to 9pm, with some even open on Sunday. Museums and galleries often have restricted Sunday and public holiday hours, while on Mondays most are closed all day.

Phones

Public telephones accept coins, credit cards and phone cards (the latter available in various denominations in tobacconists, newsagents and post offices). The cheapest way to make an international call is to go to a *locutorio* (phone centre); these are scattered throughout the old city, particularly in the Raval and Ribera. You'll be assigned a cabin to make your calls, and afterwards you pay in cash.

Post

The main post office (Correus) is on Pl. d'Antoni López, at the eastern end of Pg. de Colom, in the Barri Gòtic (Mon–Fri 8.30am–9.30pm, Sat 8.30am–2pm; Barceloneta/Jaume I). For stamps it's easier to visit a tobacconist (look for the brown-and-yellow *tabac* sign), found on virtually every street.

Public holidays

Official holidays are: Jan 1 (Cap d'Any, New Year's Day); Jan 6 (Epifanía, Epiphany); Good Friday & Easter Monday; May 1 (Dia del Treball, May Day/Labour Day); June 24 (Dia de Sant Joan, St John's Day); Aug 15 (L'Assumpció, Assumption of the Virgin); Sept 11 (Diada Nacional, Catalan National Day); Sept 24 (Festa de la Mercè, Our Lady of Mercy, Barcelona's patron saint); Oct 12 (Dia de la Hispanidad, Spanish National Day); Nov 1 (Tots Sants, All Saints' Day); Dec 6 (Dia de la Constitució, Constitution Day); Dec 8 (La Imaculada, Immaculate Conception); Dec 25 (Nadal, Christmas Day); Dec 26 (Sant Esteve, St Stephen's Day).

Tickets

You can buy concert, sporting and exhibition tickets with a credit card using the ServiCaixa (servicaixa.com) automatic dispensing machines in branches of La Caixa savings bank. You can also order tickets online through ServiCaixa or TelEntrada (telentrada.com). For advance tickets for all city council (Ajuntament) sponsored concerts visit the Palau de la Virreina, Ramblas 99.

Time

Barcelona is one hour ahead of the UK, six hours ahead of New York and Toronto, nine hours ahead of Los Angeles, nine hours behind Sydney and eleven hours behind Auckland. This applies except for brief periods during the change-overs to and from daylight saving (in Spain the clocks go forward in the last week in March, back again in the last week of Oct).

Tipping

Locals leave only a few cents or round up the change for a coffee or drink, and a euro or two for most meals, though fancier restaurants will expect ten to fifteen percent. Taxi drivers normally get around five percent.

Tourist information

The city's tourist board, Turisme de Barcelona (T 807 117 222 from within Spain, T 932 853 834 from abroad, W barcelonaturisme.com), has its main office in Plaça de Catalunya (daily 9.30am–9.30pm; M Catalunya), down the steps in the southeast corner of the square, where there's a tours service and accommodation desk. There's also an office in the Barri Gòtic at Plaça de Sant Jaume, entrance at C/Ciutat 2 (Mon–Fri 8.30am–8.30pm, Sat 9am–7pm, Sun & hols 9am–2pm; M Jaume I), and staffed information booths dotted across the city. The city's T 010 telephone enquiries service (available 24hr; some English-speaking staff available) can help with questions about transport, public services and other matters. The city hall (Ajuntament; W bcn.cat) and regional government (Generalitat; W gencat.cat) websites are also mines of information about every aspect of cultural, social and working life in Barcelona. Concerts, exhibitions and festivals are covered in full at the walk-in office of the Institut de Cultura at the Palau de la Virreina, Ramblas 99, M Liceu (T 933 161 000, W bcn.cat/cultura; daily 10am–8.30pm). The most useful listings magazine is the Spanish-language *Guia del Ocio* (out every Thursday; W guiadelociobcn.es), available at any newspaper kiosk.

Travelling with children

Taking your children to Barcelona doesn't pose insurmountable travel problems. There's plenty to do, whether it's a day at the beach or a daredevil cable-car ride, while if you coincide with one of Barcelona's festivals, you'll be able to join in with the local celebrations, from sweet-tossing and puppet shows to fireworks and human castles. For ideas, check out the English-language resource and support site W kidsinbarcelona.com, which is packed with information on everything from safe play areas to babysitting services. Most establishments are baby-friendly in the sense that you'll be made very welcome if you turn up with a child in tow. Many museum cloakrooms, for example, will be happy to look after your pushchair as you carry your child around the building, while restaurants will make a fuss of your little one. However, specific facilities are not as widespread as they are in the UK or US. Baby-changing areas are relatively rare, except in department stores and shopping centres, and even where they do exist they are not always up to scratch. By far the best is at El Corte Inglés, though most major shopping centres now have pull-down changing tables in their public toilets. Local restaurants tend not to offer children's menus (though they will try to accommodate specific requests), highchairs are rarely provided and restaurants open relatively late for lunch and dinner. Despite best intentions, you might find yourself eating in one of the international franchise restaurants, which tend to be open throughout the day. You'll pay from around €15–25/hr for babysitting if arranged through your hotel; or contact Barcelona Babysitter (from €20/hr; enquiries Mon–Sat 9am–9pm; T 622 511 675, W bcnbabysitter.com), who can provide English-speaking nannies and babysitters.

Travellers with disabilities

Barcelona's airport and Aerobús are fully accessible to travellers in wheelchairs. On the metro lines 2, 9, 10 and 11 are fully accessible and others are being adapted, with elevators at major stations (including Pl. de Catalunya, Universitat, Pg. de

Celebrating Catalan-style

Central to any traditional Barcelona festival is the parade of *gegants*, five-metre-high giants with papier-mâché or fibreglass heads. Also typically Catalan is the *correfoc* ("fire-running"), where drummers, dragons and demons cavort in the streets. Meanwhile, teams of *castellers* – "castle-makers" – pile person upon person to see who can construct the highest tower.

Gràcia and Sagrada Família) from the street to the platforms. However, all city buses have been adapted for wheelchair use, while the city information line – ⓣ 010 – has accessibility information for museums, galleries, hotels, restaurants, museums, bars and stores. Many Old Town attractions have steps, cobbles or other impediments to access.

Water

Water from the tap is safe to drink, but generally doesn't taste very nice. You'll be given bottled mineral water in a bar or restaurant.

Festivals and events

Almost any month you visit Barcelona you'll coincide with a festival, event or holiday. The best are picked out below, but for a full list check out the Ajuntament (city hall) website ⓦ bcn.cat/cultura.

Festes de Santa Eulàlia

Mid-February ⓦ bcn.cat/santaeulalia
Winter festival around February 12 in honour of the young Barcelona girl who suffered a beastly martyrdom at the hands of the Romans. There are parades, concerts, fireworks and *sardana* dancing.

Carnaval/Carnestoltes

Week before Lent (Feb or March)
Costumed parades and other carnival events across every city neighbourhood. Sitges, down the coast, has the most outrageous celebrations.

Dia de Sant Jordi

April 23
St George's Day celebrates Catalunya's patron saint, with hundreds of book and flower stalls down the Ramblas and elsewhere.

Primavera Sound

Usually late May
ⓦ primaverasound.com
The city's hottest music festival attracts top names in the rock, indie and electronica world.

Sónar

June ⓦ sonar.es
Europe's biggest, most cutting-edge electronic music, multimedia and urban art festival presents three days of brilliant noise and spectacle.

Verbena/Dia de Sant Joan

June 23/24
The "eve" and "day" of St John herald a "night of fire", involving bonfires and fireworks (particularly on Montjuïc) and watching the sun come up on the beach.

Festival de Barcelona Grec

From end June to August ⓦ grec.bcn.cat
This is the city's main performing arts festival, with many events staged at Montjuïc's Teatre Grec.

Festes de la Mercè

End September **bcn.cat/merce**
The city's main festival is celebrated for a week around September 24, with costumed giants, firework displays and human tower competitions.

Festival Internacional de Jazz

October/November
barcelonajazzfestival.com
The annual jazz festival attracts big-name artists to the clubs, as well as smaller-scale street concerts.

Chronology

c230 BC Carthaginians found the settlement of "Barcino", probably on the heights of Montjuïc.

218–201 BC Romans expel Carthaginians from Iberian peninsula in Second Punic War. Roman Barcino is established around today's Barri Gòtic.

304 AD Santa Eulàlia – the city's patron saint – is martyred by Romans for refusing to renounce Christianity.

c350 AD Roman city walls are built, as threat of invasion grows.

415 Visigoths sweep across Spain and establish temporary capital in Barcino (later "Barcelona").

711 Moorish conquest of Spain. Barcelona eventually forced to surrender (719).

801 Barcelona retaken by Louis the Pious, son of Charlemagne. Frankish counties of Catalunya become a buffer zone, known as the Spanish Marches.

878 Guifré el Pelós (Wilfred the Hairy) declared first Count of Barcelona, founding a dynastic line that was to rule until 1410.

985 Moorish sacking of city. Sant Pau del Camp – the city's oldest surviving church – built after this date.

1137 Dynastic union of Catalunya and Aragón established.

1213–76 Reign of Jaume I, "the Conqueror", expansion of empire and beginning of Catalan golden age.

1282–1387 Barcelona at the centre of an aggressively mercantile Mediterranean empire. Successive rulers construct most of Barcelona's best-known Gothic buildings.

1348 The Black Death strikes, killing half of Barcelona's population.

1391 Pogrom against the city's Jewish population.

1410 Death of Martí el Humà (Martin the Humane), last of Catalan count-kings. Beginning of the end of Catalan influence in the Mediterranean.

1469 Marriage of Ferdinand of Aragón and Isabel of Castile.

1479 Ferdinand succeeds to Catalan-Aragón crown, and Catalunya's fortunes decline. Inquisition introduced to Barcelona, leading to forced flight of the Jews.

1493 Christopher Columbus received in Barcelona after his triumphant return from New World. The shifting of trade routes away from Mediterranean and across the Atlantic further impoverishes the city.

1516 Spanish crown passes to Habsburgs and Madrid is established as capital of Spanish empire.

1640–52 The uprising known as the "Wars of the Reapers" declares Catalunya an independent republic. Barcelona is besieged and eventually surrenders to the Spanish army.

1714 After War of Spanish Succession, throne passes to Bourbons. Barcelona subdued on September 11 (now Catalan National Day); Ciutadella fortress built, Catalan language banned and parliament abolished.

1755 Barceloneta district laid out – gridded layout is an early example of urban planning.

1778 Steady increase in trade; Barcelona's economy improves.

1814 After Peninsular War (1808–14), French finally driven out, with Barcelona the last city to fall.

1859 Old city walls demolished and Eixample district built to accommodate growing population.

1882 Work begins on Sagrada Família; Antoni Gaudí takes charge two years later.

1888 Universal Exhibition held at Parc de la Ciutadella. *Modernista* architects start to make their mark.

1893 First stirrings of anarchist unrest. Liceu opera house bombed.

1901 Pablo Picasso's first public exhibition held at *Els Quatre Gats* tavern.

1909 Setmana Trágica (Tragic Week) of rioting. Many churches destroyed.

1922 Parc Güell opens to the public.

1926 Antoni Gaudí is run over by a tram; Barcelona stops en masse for his funeral.

1929 International Exhibition held at Montjuïc.

1936–39 Spanish Civil War. Barcelona at the heart of Republican cause, with George Orwell and other volunteers arriving to fight. City eventually falls to Nationalists on January 26, 1939.

1939–75 Spain under Franco. Generalitat president Lluís Companys executed and Catalan language banned. Emigration encouraged from south to dilute Catalan identity. Franco dies in 1975.

1977 First democratic Spanish elections for 40 years.

1978–80 Generalitat re-established and Statute of Autonomy approved. Conservative nationalist government elected.

1992 Olympics held in Barcelona. Rebuilding projects transform Montjuïc and the waterfront.

1995 MACBA (contemporary art museum) opens, and signals the regeneration of El Raval district.

2006 New Statute of Autonomy agreed with Spain.

2014 Constitutional Court of Spain deems the Catalan government's 2013 declaration of sovereignty to be unconstitutional.

2017 On 17 August 2017 in a jihadist attack, a man drove a van into the crowd of pedestrians on Las Ramblas, killing 13 people and injuring 130.

2017 In a referendum deemed illegal and violently suppressed by the Spanish government, Catalonians vote in favour of the region becoming an independent state. The Catalonian parliament declares independence and is promptly dismissed by the Spanish government, which then dissolves the Catalonian parliament and calls for new regional elections, won again by pro-independence parties.

Catalan

In Barcelona, Catalan (Català) has more or less taken over from Castilian (Castellano) Spanish as the language on street signs and maps. On paper it looks like a cross between French and Spanish and is generally easy to read if you know those two. Few visitors realize how important Catalan is to those who speak it: never commit the error of calling it a dialect. Despite the preponderance of the Catalan language you'll get by perfectly well in Spanish as long as you're aware of the use of Catalan in timetables, on menus, and so on. However you'll generally get a good reception if you at least try communicating in the local language.

Pronunciation

Don't be tempted to use the few rules of Spanish pronunciation you may know – in particular the soft Spanish Z and C don't apply, so unlike in the rest of Spain, the city is not Barthelona but Barcelona, as in English.

a as in hat if stressed, as in alone when unstressed.

e varies, but usually as in get.

i as in police.

ig sounds like the "tch" in the English scratch; lleig (ugly) is pronounced "yeah-tch".

o a round, full sound, when stressed, otherwise like a soft U sound.

u somewhere between the U of put and rule.

ç sounds like an English S; plaça is pronounced "plassa".

c followed by an E or I is soft; otherwise hard.

g followed by E or I is like the "zh" in Zhivago; otherwise hard.

h is always silent.

j as in the French "Jean".

l.l is best pronounced (for foreigners) as a single L sound; but for Catalan speakers it has two distinct L sounds.

ll sounds like an English Y or LY, like the "yuh" sound in million.

n as in English, though before F or V it sometimes sounds like an M.

ny corresponds to the Castilian Ñ.

qu before E or I sounds like K; before A or O, or if the U has an umlaut (Ü), sounds like KWE, as in quit.

r is rolled, but only at the start of a word; at the end it's often silent.

t is pronounced as in English, though sometimes it sounds like a D; as in viatge or dotze.

v at the start of a word sounds like B; in all other positions it's a soft F sound.

w is pronounced like a B/V.

x is like SH or CH in most words, though in some, like exit, it sounds like an X.

z is like the English Z in zoo.

Words and phrases

Basics

Yes, No, OK Si, No, Val

Please, Thank you Si us plau, Gràcies

Hello, Goodbye Hola, Adéu

Good morning Bon dia

Good afternoon/night Bona tarde/nit

See you later Fins després

Sorry Ho sento

Excuse me Perdoni

I (don't) understand (No) Ho entenc

Do you speak English? Parleu anglès?

Where? When? Dónde? Cuando?

What? How much? Què? Quant?

Here, There Aquí, Allí/Allá

This, That Això, Allò

Open, Closed Obert, Tancat

With, Without Amb, Sense
Good, Bad Bo(na), Dolent(a)
Big, Small Gran, Petit(a)
Cheap, Expensive Barat(a), Car(a)
I want Vull (pronounced "vwee")
I'd like Voldria
Do you know? Vostès saben?
I don't know No sé
There is (Is there?) Hi ha(?)
What's that? Què és això?
Do you have...? Té...?
Today, Tomorrow Avui, Demà

Accommodation

Do you have a room? Té alguna habitació?
...with two beds//double bed ...amb dos llits/llit per dues persones
...with shower/bath ...amb dutxa/bany
It's for one person (two people) Per a una persona (dues persones)
For one night (one week) Per una nit (unasetmana)
It's fine, how much is it? Esta bé, quant és?
Don't you have anything cheaper? En té de més bon preu?

Directions and transport

How do I get to...? Per anar a...?
Left, Right A l'esquerra, A la dreta
Straight on Tot recte
Where is...? On és...?
...the bus station ...l'estació de autobuses
...the train station ...l'estació
...the nearest bank ...el banc més a prop
...the post office ...l'oficina de correus
...the toilet ...la toaleta
Where does the bus to...leave from? De on surt el autobús a...?
Is this the train for Barcelona? Aquest tren va a Barcelona?
I'd like a (return) ticket to... Voldria un bitlet (d'anar i tornar) a...
What time does it leave (arrive in)? A quina hora surt (arriba a)?

Days of the week

Monday dilluns
Tuesday dimarts
Wednesday dimecres
Thursday dijous
Friday divendres
Saturday dissabte
Sunday diumenge

Months of the Year

January Gener
February Febrer
March Març
April Abril
May Maig
June Juny
July Juliol
August Agost
September Setembre
October Octobre
November Novembre
December Desembre

Numbers

1 un(a)
2 dos (dues)
3 tres
4 quatre
5 cinc
6 sis
7 set
8 vuit
9 nou
10 deu
11 onze
12 dotze
13 tretze
14 catorze
15 quinze
16 setze
17 disset
18 divuit
19 dinou
20 vint
21 vint-i-un
30 trenta
40 quaranta
50 cinquanta
60 seixanta
70 setanta
80 vuitanta
90 novanta
100 cent
101 cent un
200 dos-cents (dues-centes)

500 cinc-cents
1000 mil

Menu reader

Basic words

Esmorzar To have breakfast
Dinar To have lunch
Sopar To have dinner
Ganivet Knife
Forquilla Fork
Cullera Spoon
Taula Table
Ampolla Bottle
Got Glass
Carta Menu
Sopa Soup
Amanida Salad
Entremesos Hors d'oeuvres
Truita Omelette
Entrepà Sandwich
Torrades Toast
Tapes Tapas
Mantega Butter
Ous Eggs
Pa Bread
Olives Olives
Oli Oil
Vinagre Vinegar
Sal Salt
Pebre Pepper
Sucre Sugar
El compte The bill
Sóc vegetarià/ I'm a vegetarian

Catalan specialities

Amanida Catalana Salad served with sliced meats (sometimes cheese)
Arròs a banda Rice with seafood, the rice served separately
Arròs a la marinera Paella: rice with seafood and saffron
Arròs negre "Black rice", cooked in squid ink
Bacallà a la llauna Salt cod baked with garlic, tomato and paprika
Botifarra (amb mongetes) Grilled Catalan pork sausage (with stewed haricot beans)
Calçots Large char-grilled spring onions
Canelons Cannelloni, baked pasta with ground meat and béchamel sauce
Conill all i oli Rabbit with garlic mayonnaise
Crema Catalana Crème caramel, with caramelized sugar topping
Escalivada Grilled aubergine/eggplant, pepper/capsicum and onion
Espinacs a la Catalana Spinach cooked with raisins and pine nuts
Esqueixada Salad of salt cod with peppers/capsicums, tomatoes, onions and olives
Estofat de vedella Veal stew
Faves a la Catalana Stewed broad beans, with bacon and botifarra
Fideuà Short, thin noodles (the width of vermicelli) served with seafood
Fuet Catalan salami
Llenties guisades Stewed lentils
Mel i mató Curd cheese and honey
Pa amb tomàquet Bread (often grilled), rubbed with tomato, garlic and olive oil
Pollastre al cava Chicken with cava sauce
Pollastre amb gambes Chicken with prawns
Postres de músic Cake of dried fruit and nuts
Salsa Romesco Spicy sauce (with chillis, nuts, tomato and wine), often served with grilled fish
Samfaina Ratatouille-like stew (onions, peppers/capsicum, aubergine/eggplant, tomato), served with salt cod or chicken
Sarsuela Fish and shellfish stew
Sípia amb mandonguilles Cuttlefish with meatballs
Suquet de peix Fish and potato casserole
Xató Mixed salad of olives, salt cod, preserved tuna, anchovies and onions

Cooking terms

Assortit Assorted
Al forn Baked
A la brasa Char-grilled
Fresc Fresh
Fregit Fried
A la romana Fried in batter
All i oli Garlic mayonnaise
A la plantxa Grilled
En escabetx Pickled
Rostit Roast
Salsa Sauce
Saltat Sautéed
Remenat Scrambled

Del temps Seasonal
Fumat Smoked
A l'ast Spit-roasted
Al vapor Steamed
Guisat Stewed
Farcit Stuffed

Desserts/Postres

Pastís Cake
Formatge Cheese
Flam Crème caramel
Gelat Ice cream
Arròs amb llet Rice pudding
Tarta Tart
Yogur Yoghurt

Drinks

Cervesa Beer
Vi Wine
Xampan/cava Champagne
Cafè amb llet Large white coffee
Cafè tallat Small white coffee
Descafeinat Decaf
Te Tea
Xocolata Drinking chocolate
Granissat Crushed ice drink
Llet Milk
Orxata Tiger nut drink
Aigua Water
Aigua mineral Mineral water
Zumo Juice

Fish and seafood/Peix i marisc

Anxoves/Seitons Anchovies
Calamarsets Baby squid
Orada Bream
Cloïses Clams
Cranc Crab
Sipia Cuttlefish
Lluç Hake
Llagosta Lobster
Rap Monkfish
Musclos Mussels
Pop Octopus
Gambes Prawns
Navalles Razor clams
Salmó Salmon
Bacallà Salt cod
Sardines Sardines
Llobarro Sea bass
Llenguado Sole
Calamars Squid
Peix espasa Swordfish
Tonyina Tuna

Fruit/Fruita

Poma Apple
Plàtan Banana
Raïm Grapes
Meló Melon
Taronja Orange
Pera Pear
Maduixes Strawberries

Meat and poultry/Carn i aviram

Bou Beef
Embotits Charcuterie
Pollastre Chicken
Xoriço Chorizo sausage
Pernil serrà Cured ham
Llonganissa Cured pork sausage
Costelles Cutlets/chops
Ànec Duck
Pernil dolç Ham
Xai/Be Lamb
Fetge Liver
Llom Loin of pork
Mandonguilles Meatballs
Porc Pork
Conill Rabbit
Salsitxes Sausages
Cargols Snails
Bistec Steak
Llengua Tongue
Vedella Veal

Vegetables/Verdures i llegums

Carxofes Artichokes
Albergínia Aubergine/eggplant
Faves Broad/lima beans
Carbassó Courgette/zucchini
All Garlic
Mongetes Haricot beans
Llenties Lentils
Xampinyons Mushrooms
Cebes Onions
Patates Potatoes
Espinacs Spinach
Tomàquets Tomatoes
Bolets Wild mushrooms

Publishing Information

Fifth edition 2019

Distribution
UK, Ireland and Europe
Apa Publications (UK) Ltd; sales@roughguides.com
United States and Canada
Ingram Publisher Services; ips@ingramcontent.com
Australia and New Zealand
Woodslane; info@woodslane.com.au
Southeast Asia
Apa Publications (SN) Pte; sales@roughguides.com
Worldwide
Apa Publications (UK) Ltd; sales@roughguides.com
Special Sales, Content Licensing and CoPublishing
Rough Guides can be purchased in bulk quantities at discounted prices. We can create special editions, personalised jackets and corporate imprints tailored to your needs. sales@roughguides.com.
roughguides.com
Printed in China by RR Donnelley Asia Printing Solutions Limited

A catalogue record for this book is available from the British Library

Rough Guide Credits

Editor: Tatiana Wilde
Cartography: Katie Bennett
Managing editor: Rachel Lawrence
Picture editor: Aude Vauconsant
Cover photo research: Aude Vauconsant
Original design: Richard Czapnik
Senior DTP coordinator: Dan May
Head of DTP and Pre-Press: Rebeka Davies

Reader's updates

Thanks to all the readers who have taken the time to write in with comments and suggestions (and apologies if we've inadvertently omitted or misspelt anyone's name).

Help us update

We've gone to a lot of effort to ensure that this edition of the **Pocket Rough Guide Barcelona** is accurate and up-to-date. However, things change – places get "discovered", opening hours are notoriously fickle, restaurants and rooms raise prices or lower standards. If you feel we've got it wrong or left something out, we'd like to know, and if you can remember the address, the price, the hours, the phone number, so much the better.

Please send your comments with the subject line "**Pocket Rough Guide Barcelona Update**" to mail@uk.roughguides.com. We'll credit all contributions and send a copy of the next edition (or any other Rough Guide if you prefer) for the very best emails.

Photo Credits

(Key: T-top; C-centre; B-bottom; L-left; R-right)

A Tu Bola 61
Afagundes/Dreamstime.com 114
Alamy 5, 6, 11T, 13C, 17T, 19T, 19C, 21B, 22/23, 31, 42, 43, 44, 50, 58, 59, 60, 69, 71, 74, 75, 97, 98, 101, 102, 103, 110, 111, 116, 127
Chris Christoforou/Rough Guides 16B, 18T, 19B, 21T, 25, 49, 52, 56, 62, 63, 66, 67, 71, 83, 87, 92, 108, 112, 118, 119, 129, 135, 139, 148/149
Christian Schriefer/Picnic 79
Getty Images 2CR, 28, 68, 89, 144, 146
iStock 1, 2T, 2BR, 4, 10, 11B, 12/13T, 17B, 20B, 24, 32, 37, 65, 80, 86, 99, 104, 105, 120, 133, 138, 141, 142, 143, 147
Jordan Banks/4Corners Images 2BL
Kalman89/Dreamstime.com 158/159
Marta Perez/Epa/REX/Shutterstock 12B
Nito100/Dreamstime.com 16T, 109
Quique Garcia/Epa/REX/Shutterstock 29
Ramon Casas i Carbó/Museu del Modernisme Català 112
REX/Shutterstock 12/13B
Roger Mapp/Rough Guides 14B, 15T, 20C, 21C, 27, 30, 32, 40, 41, 45, 47, 51, 53, 57, 73, 78, 81, 90, 93, 95, 100, 122, 124, 125, 132
Shutterstock 14T, 15B, 18MC, 19C, 20T, 36, 38, 39, 46, 76, 84, 94, 122/123, 128, 145
Taverna del Clinic 117
Tickets 88
Tim Kavenagh/Rough Guides 136

Cover: Casa Amatller **Shutterstock**

Index

D

E

F

G

H

I

ROUGH
GUIDES

COLOUR THE WORL
BEST DAY ON
EARTH
THE WORLD'S MOST EXTRAORDINARY EXPERIENCES
FROM DAWN TILL AFTER DARK
1000 ULTIMATE TRAVEL EXPERIENCES
MAKE THE
MOST OF YOUR
TIME ON
EARTH

Young Founders

1870:

Not with Our Blood

Elizabeth Massie

A TOM DOHERTY ASSOCIATES BOOK
NEW YORK

YOUNG FOUNDERS #1: 1870: NOT WITH OUR BLOOD

A Tor Book
Published by Tom Doherty Associates, LLC
175 Fifth Avenue
New York, NY 10010

www.tor.com

ISBN: 0-812-59092-9

First edition: March 2000

Printed in the United States of America

0 9 8 7 6 5 4 3 2 1

To Jeni Hurst, a very special person

Introduction

LEELAND IS A fictional mill town, but the cotton textile mills were a very real part of New England in the 1800s, cranking out tons of material to be used across the growing United States. Many of these mills were along the Merrimack River, from Manchester, New Hampshire, to Lowell and Lawrence, Massachusetts. And many of the workers who poured their energies and life's blood into the mills were countless immigrants who had come to America seeking a better life.

During the Civil War the agricultural South had endured much destruction and devastation. Reconstruction was a painful and expensive proposition. But the North, an area already more dependant on industry than farming, had suffered little damage during the war and had little to rebuild. It was a time of rapid growth. Mills and other factories began to flourish. In 1840 manufacturing accounted for less than a fifth of all U.S. production, but by the late

1800s, the United States had become the largest and most competitive industrial nation in the world. Not only did the United States supply goods for its own westward-expanding population, it exported a good deal of its materials across the seas. The need for workers to run the machines in the factories was great.

It was to the United States, the country of opportunity, that many immigrants flocked seeking plentiful jobs, good farmland, and political and religious freedom. They came from Ireland, Germany, Poland, Scandinavia, and Eastern Europe during the mid-1800s. The largest movement of the Irish to the United States occurred between 1840 and 1850, when a famine in their homeland caused a potato crop failure so severe that many had to leave or face starvation and economic ruin. In 1847 alone, 100,000 Irish sailed to the United States to begin anew. And while some founded homesteads in the west, many others believed that by moving to the cities, where the industries were located, they would have a greater chance at gaining the good life.

Today, around five million young Americans between the ages of fourteen and eighteen work at some time during the year. In the 1800s, part-time work would have been considered a luxury that most families couldn't afford. In the 1800s it was not enough for immigrant parents to work while the children went to school or had free time with friends. As more immigrants arrived looking for work, the competition for mill jobs grew fierce. Immigrants were willing to work for less pay in order to secure jobs, which lowered wage levels. For a family to survive, even under the roughest of conditions in the worst slum housing, everyone of age ("of age" meaning anyone older than ten years old) was needed to work. And in spite of the fact that entire families worked hard in hopes of making their lives better, many remained in poverty.

Prejudices against the immigrants grew as the industries grew. Some Americans, even those whose parents had been immigrants, blamed the new arrivals for problems such as poor wages, crime, overcrowding, and even immoral influences. The American Party, sometimes called the Know-Nothing Party, wanted to halt immigration and make it difficult for immigrants to become citizens.

Not everyone saw the immigrants as evil, however. Labor unions and "radical" journalists hoped to end long hours, terrible working conditions, and child labor in the factories by making society and lawmakers aware of these issues. In 1860, Pemberton Mills in Lawrence, Massachusetts, collapsed. The weight of the machines proved to be too much for the structure and many workers were killed or seriously maimed by the falling machinery. This disaster brought media attention to poorly constructed, poorly planned buildings. Newspapers published shocking, graphically vivid articles. But it took a long time before factories started improving conditions and longer still before the changes were consistent throughout New England and the rest of the country.

And so, in 1870, people still lived in crowded, rundown tenement apartments. They rose before dawn and walked to the mills where they were locked in rooms filled with dust, lint, and the relentless pounding of machinery. The mills were places where materials were produced and tragic accidents occurred. There was a short break in the day so that workers could eat in the aisles between the machines. They returned home after the day after twelve or fourteen hours of work. They went to sleep, only to rise as the mill bell clanged to begin the routine once more.

1

July 6, 1863

Something is wrong. Mother hasn't come back from the barn. Abigail and Liam pestered me all afternoon to go out and see her, but Mother told me that we all must stay in the house. And so we have.

It's been nine hours. What is she doing out there?

I think Abigail and Liam are asleep now. I can't hear them talking anymore. They were both crying and crying and it made my head hurt so bad that I gave them some leftover stew for supper and sent them off to their mattresses in the loft. Liam went right away, but Abigail argued with me. She said she was nine and not a baby, so she didn't have to do as I said. I told her Father is dead now, so she has to listen to me, because I was the man of the house now, even if I was a year younger than she. I threw a biscuit at her and it hit her on the head and she stamped her foot, screamed at me, then climbed the ladder to the loft.

I cleaned up the bowls, but I couldn't eat any stew myself. My stomach hurts bad.

It's dark and Mother is still in the barn. From the table where I sit I can see out across the dark yard. Her lantern is burning in there.

This morning we got word that Father was killed in a battle at Gettysburg. They are bringing the body home for burial in a few days.

Gettysburg. It seems so far away. Father has been away nearly a year now. Mother hated to see him go. 'It's not your fight,' she had said.

Father told her he could not abide a system in which one man was made the master of another. He said, being Irish, he'd had enough of that with the English.

'This war is every man's fight,' he said.

I wanted to join the Union Army with Father. But he said 'no.' I was too young. And he needed me to help with the farm. He rustled my hair and smiled. 'There will be plenty of chores to do when I get back.'

Now, he's never coming back.

Mother thanked the man who brought the message, then turned to the three of us and told us to stay in the house. She didn't cry. She told us we best not cry, either. Then she put on her shawl, took a lantern, and went to the barn. Nugget tried to go in the barn with her, but she pushed him out with her foot.

Widow Muncy is dead. It happened last year when her husband was killed in the war. They found her all puffed up and purple in the rafters of her cabin. I wonder if she has hanged herself from grief.

Father is dead, too. If I think of it, I can't bear it. And now Mother may be dead as well. So many have died already. When will it end?

The politicians promised it would be a short fight. That was two years ago. And it doesn't appear that the rebel soldiers are ready to quit.

It hasn't gone well for the Union. People are growing tired of the fight. But I support President Lincoln. Slavery is an abomination. No man has the right to make a slave of another. Father said that.

And I believe him. What are we going to do now? I am the oldest. I am supposed to know, but I don't. We do not own this farm. We lease it with money we make from raising our chickens and cows. I can't raise them by myself. We will lose our home! What am I supposed to do?

2

PATRICK THOMAS O'NEILL put his paper and pen away inside the cupboard, gave one more glance out the window at the barn, then climbed the ladder to join his sister and brother for sleep. In the darkness he felt his way along the rough wooden floor to his own mattress. He kicked off his shoes, leaned over, and opened the loft window to let in a cool Pennsylvania breeze. Then he lay down and drew his legs up beneath his quilt.

But sleep didn't come for many hours.

July 12, 1863
We buried Father today. A wagon arrived at the farm this morning, with a private and a lieutenant named Marshall. Mother came outside when the wagon pulled into the yard. Lt. Marshall nodded and lifted off his hat. Mother looked over his shoulder to the wagon. When Mother saw the pine box I heard her inhale deeply, but she said not a word.

"What is it?" asked Liam. "It's Father," I said. "Now hush."

Mother called to me then. "Patrick, bring your Father off that wagon and up that hill just below the oak."

Abigail began to cry softly. Mother turned and glared at her coldly.

Lt. Marshall stepped aside. The private tumbled down from the wagon and helped me slide the coffin out the back. It was not heavy. "This way," I said. Our eyes met, and I realized he was not that much older than me.

We carried the box across the small meadow and lay it down under the shade of a sprawling oak. A hole had been dug. I guess Mother had attended to it. We stood around the box in a silent circle as the lieutenant read a few prayers from an old leather Bible. It did not seem possible that Father was actually inside the box. Dead. That I would never see him again.

It was like a strange dream I was in.

The lieutenant closed his book, and he and the private remounted their wagon and drove away. After an awkward silence, I steered Abigail and Liam back to the house. In the doorway, I turned to look back at Mother.

She lingered at the grave a long time, like a stone statue in the shade of the great oak, its limbs spread over her as if in comfort. Then her shoulders began to shake, and she dropped slowly to her knees.

I stepped inside the house, and closed the door.

When Patrick awoke, there was a puddle of morning sunlight on the loft floor. Patrick rubbed his eyes and sat up. Abigail and five-year-old Liam were still sleeping. Patrick wasn't surprised. Yesterday had been hell. *Today,* he thought, *might be even worse.*

Patrick stretched his shoulders and clutched his quilt around himself. The quilt was a special one, made for him by his mother the year he was born, embroidered with his name and his birthday and all sorts of animals and flowers. Usually the quilt offered comfort. But not today. And even though it was stuffy in the loft, Patrick was cold.

Mother must still be in the barn, he thought, shivering as much from fear of what had happened as with the cold. *It's been almost a week now. What can she do doing?*

Quietly he slipped into his clothes and went down the ladder. He stoked the coals in the hearth from yesterday's fire but only got a few red sparks. He would have to go outside for wood if he was going to fix a breakfast or heat water for washing linens.

But Mother had said to stay in the house.

He opened the door.

Nugget raced in, wagging his tail and dancing on his paws as if happy to be remembered. Patrick gave the brown mutt a quick pat on the head, then looked out the door, across the wide garden to the barn.

I have to find out what's going on, he told himself. *I have to see what Mother's done.*

He went out onto the covered porch, closing the door behind him. The air was warm. Soon it would be stiflingly hot. The broad leaves of the cornstalks in the garden stood motionless; the pole beans were ripe and heavy on the tangle of woven sticks. Patrick straightened his suspenders, set his jaw, and marched across the lumpy ground of the garden to the barn. If she was dead, he couldn't think what he would do.

Creeping to the open door, he took a breath. He looked at his feet. He looked at the sky. And then he looked into the barn.

Lucy O'Neill was there, alive and bustling. Her sleeves were rolled up and her apron was twisted slightly askew. There was a hammer in her hand. Dust swirled in golden sparkles of the filtered sunshine. There were nails clamped in Lucy's lips and a scowl of determination on her face.

She was repairing the old wagon. Patrick watched for a few minutes, then went back to the house.

Abigail and Liam were up, still in nightclothes, watching from the porch. Abigail hadn't brushed her hair. Liam's hair stuck up like the brush of a rooster.

"She's fixing the wagon," Patrick said.

"What for?" asked Abigail.

"I don't know."

"We going somewhere?" asked Liam.

"I don't know," said Patrick. "Let's have some oatmeal."

By noon, as Abigail was hanging out clothes to dry and Liam and Patrick were in the garden weeding, Mother came out of the barn. She strolled straight to the porch, called her three children to her, and explained that they would leave the farm and go to New Jersey.

"My brother Robert lives there," she said, weariness tugging on the sides of her mouth. "You don't remember my brother, but that is no matter. He will help us. That is what family is for. I will write him and let him know that we will work for our board. They needn't worry that we'll be a burden. They have cows and goats. You children know about animal care. You'll do as you are told, be the command from me or anyone in that household."

"New Jersey?" Abigail asked, pressing her hand to the bodice of her dress as if she was going to be ill.

"Yes," said Mother. "There will be no mourning for what we have lost here, because longing does no good. We must go on."

Liam began to cry, and Mother let him. But when Abigail's eyes teared up and Patrick put his fist to his mouth, she snapped, "I do not need this of you! I need your help and your strength. Change doesn't have to be a bad thing. Now, Patrick! I want you to write a flyer this very afternoon, telling of our need to sell. Then take it to the mercantile and tack it on the wall for all to see."

Patrick did as he had been told. He also secretly sold his father's good boots to the man at the next farm and kept the money hidden in the well-worn leather haversack his father had carried with him during the war.

Two months later, the O'Neill family left the farm with the wagon and horse and dog, two chairs, mattress ticks, and a chest, heading for Robert Norman's New Jersey farm.

3

December 21, 1864

I'm sick of this place. It hasn't gotten better, only worse. Nugget ran away. Nobody likes us. We O'Neills are just a bother to the Normans. I have to tell my stories and jokes to Abigail and Liam when no one else is around because they think a child should be seen and not heard. Back in Pennsylvania, before Father went to war, he taught me to read and write. Although there are many men who have never had the chance to learn their letters, my father believed it was one thing a man needed to know in order to do better in life. My favorite books were Robinson Crusoe *and* Gulliver's Travels, *two tales of adventure! But here they have only a few books, and would be angry if they knew I borrowed them to read at night. They know nothing of adventure.*

I think grouchy old adults shouldn't have to be seen or *heard.*

The work here on the Normans' farm is not hard,

only dull. The animals here in New Jersey are just like the ones we had back in Pennsylvania. But even though I've tried for some time now, I still hate Uncle Robert and Aunt Sadie. I hate them! Mother says we have to obey, and we do. We only have one cramped bedroom for all of us, and we have to smile and say thank you for every crumb. Uncle Robert never speaks to children except to yell, and Aunt Sadie is afraid of her own shadow. She spooks Liam and Abigail at night, telling them tales of ghosts in the attic and in the well.

The story that scares them the most is one she tells about the old woman who used to live at a farm nearby. The old woman had white hair and white eyes. The old woman would wait until she could see children from her upstairs window, then would beckon them with her bony fingers to come over for cakes. When the children got close enough, she would reach down her arms, which could stretch ten feet, and grab the children. She would then cook them for dinner.

A few nights ago, I went outside when everyone was asleep and held a mop covered with a white cloth up to Aunt Sadie's bedroom window and tapped on the glass lightly. She awoke, saw the mop in the moonlight, and screamed that the demons were after her. I hid in the shed while everyone searched the yard for the demon. I laughed, but couldn't share the trick with anyone else or I'd be in serious trouble. When Liam is older, I'll tell him.

It would be more fun if Uncle Robert and Aunt Sadie had children to play with, but Mother says God hasn't blessed them.

Good news. The War may soon be over. General

Grant is chasing Lee back through Virginia. It's only a matter of time now. Then it will be over.

I wonder what will happen then? Uncle Robert grumbles about falling prices for farm goods, now that the war is coming to an end. I heard him talking with a neighbor about something called a "depression." I'm not sure I know what that means. When I asked Uncle Robert, he barked, "It means hard times are coming!"

The Negroes are free. Thank God. It makes me think Father's death was not in vain. He would be so proud. What would he think of me then? Sometimes I wonder if freedom means so much when you are poor. Like us. This journal paper is poor quality, but it is all I can get. Father used to buy me paper when he would go to town, but, of course, he is gone. I used the money I got from selling his boots to get these sheets and this ink. I feel bad about it because I never told Mother I had the money, but I had to be able to get paper. I have to be able to write.

I am going to be a real writer someday. I'll make up stories of adventure and excitement! One day I'll be paid for my stories and my poems. I'll be famous, and will help my family buy a new farm. My father will know it, even though he is dead. And Liam will be so proud of me. I'm twelve now. How old does one need to be before he can be a real writer?

I wonder.

It will be Christmas soon. I think it might be a dreary holiday this year. Father used to make Christmas a jolly time.

I pray there are beautiful candles and wonderful food in heaven at Christmastime.

4

BY LATE 1867, talk of the war was beginning to fade. Patrick had read in newspapers that the South was having a hard time rebuilding homes and lives due to the great destruction and lack of industry. But in New Jersey, people worked and farmed and went to church as usual. Aunt Sadie, who had said she would never be able to have children, bore twins, two little girls with red hair and squinty baby eyes. Sadie swore to anyone close enough to listen that the pain of the birth had nearly killed her.

It was then that Uncle Robert made it clear that the strain of too many people on too little land was making Sadie's tribulation even greater. By the end of the harvest in August, the O'Neills packed up and prepared to leave in search of yet another, stranger life.

"We need housing and jobs," Mother said. She was sitting with her children in their narrow bedroom at the back of the Normans' house the night before they left. All four were on Mother's bed, the bedside lantern battling feebly with the night gloom, a moth battling feebly with the lantern. Mother had a newspaper, and was pointing at an announcement. "There are many textile mills in Massachusetts which are in need of workers. You children are strong and healthy. We'll do well."

"What's a textile mill?" asked Liam.

"Makes cloth," said Mother.

"How?"

"I don't know," she said. "Doesn't matter. They'll show you. Article here says that many mills up north let go thousands of workers during the war, thinking they couldn't run their mills to profit. Now that the war's done, they're running full again, selling not only to our own country but other countries. There is much money to make in the mills, and they need workers. They're filling up with immigrants, but there may well be room for a Pennsylvania family."

"If we have to move, I want to move south," said Abigail. "Father had a cousin in Virginia. Can't we go there? I don't want to work in a mill."

"The South is poor," said Mother. "One reason they lost the war is because they didn't have factories to make what they needed in bulk for their soldiers. Clothes. Weapons. And now the little they did have has been burned or knocked down. The southern plantations are producing cotton, but the money's not there, it is in the cloth the cotton produces. And the cloth is made in the factories. We'd be worse off than we are now if we went south. Our only hope is in the North."

"I don't like the sound of it all," said Abigail.

Mother said, "We're going to find us a mill."

"What mill, Mother?" asked Liam, leaning into Patrick, and Patrick putting his arm about his little brother's shoulder. "Where is the mill?"

Lucy didn't answer. It was clear she was thinking this over. Patrick said to his sister and brother, "This will be good. We can go and make some real money. We'll start over, and soon we'll be able to get a new farm, all our own."

"Really?" asked Liam.

"Of course really," said Patrick.

"We'll go to Leeland," said Lucy at last, as if she hadn't heard Patrick. Then she turned down the lantern, shooed the children off the bed, and said no more.

The next morning, after a hurried breakfast and good-byes, the O'Neills steered their horse and wagon onto the rain-rutted dirt path, heading northward.

Leeland, Massachusetts, which was on the Merrimack River just southwest of Lawrence, was different from other towns Patrick had seen. It was not a farming town. It was an industrial town. When they first rounded the bend in the road and looked down the gentle slope of the hill, Mother pulled the horse up short and all four of the family stared, eyes wide. Abigail, sitting in front with her mother, caught her breath audibly. In the back, Liam and Patrick got up on their knees.

The first thing that struck Patrick was the smokestacks. They were dark and tall, pointing to the sky. They were part of the enormous factory compound along the river. Within the walled compound were several single-story brick buildings, a tall bell tower, and one main brick building, which was four stories high and quite long. Windows dotted the tall building's sides. Even from the top of the knoll where the O'Neills sat, the huge building seemed to groan with its mysterious inner workings. Two canals and a train track ran through gateways into the compound.

Patrick held his breath and clutched his journal to his chest. He had been writing in the wagon whenever there had been a stretch of straight road, but much of what he'd written was a jumbled, scratched mess.

"I don't like it," said Liam to his mother.

Patrick tried to picture his family working here, making lots of money and becoming rich. It was hard to imagine. The place was so stark.

"Train brings in cotton and takes away the cloth when it's done," said Mother matter-of-factly to her children in the wagon.

"I see," Liam said. He snuggled against Patrick as if he didn't really want to see at all.

Outside the wall of the compound and up the hillside were several rows of smaller, single-story wooden buildings. Squinting in the sunlight, Patrick could see clothes on lines behind these buildings.

He wrote quickly in the journal.

Do the workers live here in these little houses? They aren't very welcoming, but at least they are close to the mill. Maybe workers can live there for free. That would be good. We could save our money up faster, my family can buy a new farm, and I can go to college and become a writer! We won't have to stay here long!

Across the river from the mill compound was the town of Leeland. The sky that hung over it was not crisp and bright like the sky over the farmland. It was blue, but a tainted blue.

A dirty blue.

Lucy clucked to the horse to get him going again. Patrick glanced at Abigail. Abigail glanced back at Patrick. The road was rutted, and reluctantly Patrick put his journal aside.

The wagon descended the knoll, moving by the mill compound and across a community bridge. The Merrimack River below the bridge was brown and rippling. Parallel to the community bridge, about one hundred feet down the river, was a covered bridge that led from the town across to the mill compound. A workers' bridge, Patrick imagined. No one was on that bridge now. Patrick tried to picture himself strolling that bridge, but couldn't. Even his good imagination was struggling here, trying to place himself and his family in this town. In that mill.

At an open-air market in town, women argued and men shouted and children laughed and cried, their voices all becoming a blurred, discordant melody. Vegetables sat in baskets and buckets; salted meats hung on hooks. Clearly this produce was far from fresh. Patrick stared as the wagon rattled by. He watched the faces of those in the market, hoping to see someone turn and smile at him, bidding him welcome. But they were all too busy with their own chores.

"That's all right," he said to himself. "We'll get along just fine."

"What did you say?" asked Liam.

"I asked if you saw those apples. Aren't they fine now?" said Patrick. Liam nodded.

They stopped on a side street, and Lucy told the children to stay put. She climbed out and spoke to a woman who was pouring a bucket of soapy water into the street. The woman pointed to a tall, wooden building on the other side of the road. Lucy knocked on the door and a man came out. Patrick strained to listen to what the man was saying to his mother.

"Twenty years ago you'd get your boarding in a decent house. The company would provide it. But the cotton mill has expanded so much they can't do that no more. You got to live wherever you can find space. If you can find it at all."

Lucy stood straight and adjusted her shawl. "Those homes behind the mill?"

"Those are the old boardinghouses," said the man, pulling at one end of his greasy mustache. "But they're filled. No chance there. Now workers rent from private tenement owners here in the town proper. Like me. Used to be it was mostly farm girls in the mills, back in the forties. Girls who needed money to send their families, and some who just wanted to be a bit more independent than their farming sisters. These girls would live in them boardinghouses and have meals cooked for them. Disciplined, they were, going to church regularly, and in at proper hours. Mills knew what to do to keep them in line. You won't find that now, though. The company ain't got time to worry 'bout girls out after ten at night. Ain't got the desire to pay matrons to watch over the girls and cook meals. Those were good days, yes, sir."

Lucy said, "We don't care about twenty years ago."

"Of course," said the man suddenly, his face twitching as though he was trying not to laugh. "There's the shanties outside town, up west end. There's Irish out there, and the French-Canadians, too. You want I should find you some boards for making a shanty shack?"

Lucy pressed, "Is there work here now, and are there lodgings?"

"Work, most likely, but boarding, I don't know. I'll have to check."

"Thank you," said Lucy.

Lucy came back over the road and climbed into the wagon. The man walked ahead, on foot.

"Who is that?" asked Liam.

"Landlord," said Lucy. Slapping the reins on the horse's flanks, Lucy went silent again.

The wagon went down a street with a marker reading "Charlotte Road" and then down an alley and around the back of a four-story wooden building full of open windows and noisy tenants. Clothing and bed linens hung from the windows and were draped on the railings of the stair landings. A child leaned out of a fourth-floor window and emptied a bucket of excrement.

The landlord skipped out of the way as the human waste hit the alley with a wet splat. Patrick gawked. "Got to watch out for that," the landlord said.

The flat offered to the O'Neills was on the third floor. Lucy hobbled the horse, and the family ascended two flights of rickety exterior steps, then through an open doorway into a dim, musty hall.

The landlord unlocked the door and everyone stared inside. Liam was the only one to pinch his nose and say, "Stinks!"

"It certainly does," Patrick whispered to his brother. Patrick was used to the scents of a farm, of cow manure and mud and straw and sunshine. But this smelled of the people who had lived here before them. It smelled of sickness and decay.

The flat consisted of only two rooms, a kitchen with a window overlooking the alleyway below, and a bedroom with no window at all. There was a cast-iron cookstove provided, which seemed to satisfy Lucy. Wood, the landlord said, could be purchased at the market or from a cart that came around every morning on Charlotte Road. The flat's walls were thin, and Patrick could hear an argument next door. Riding the sunlight that filtered through the kitchen window was thick, airborne mill grit.

"You have the Keiths across from you, and the Pattersons next to you," said the landlord. "You'll meet them shortly, I suppose."

Lucy nodded. "Neighbors," she said.

Patrick studied the warped wood of the floor of the kitchen and whispered to Abigail, "We'll make it here. We'll be all right." Abigail looked at him and shook her head.

The landlord accepted the wagon and horse as payment for three months' rent.

"We'll make do," Lucy had said as the wagon and horse were led away and the O'Neills watched from the landing on the steps. "We have our arms and legs to work."

That night, when everyone seemed to have settled down to sleep, Patrick went outside and sat on the wooden steps with his pad and pen.

October 3, 1867

Neighbors? The landlord says we have neighbors, but I'd argue with him if I could! Neighbors live in houses down roads, not in stinky boxes next to each other! How can we call this home? How can anyone? I'd hoped this would be better than living with Uncle Robert and Aunt Sadie, but now I don't know.

We are here, in Leeland. I don't like it.

It's very strange here.

I can see the stars overhead. They are blurry and pale, but they are there, nonetheless.

I'm fourteen, almost a man. My mother needs me. So does Abigail, and especially Liam. I know I will do what I have to so we can get by. And I'll keep on writing. I'll never give that up. Father wouldn't have wanted me to give it up. He always knew I wanted to be a writer, even when I was just a little boy.

Some things will never change. Like the stars. Like me.

Tomorrow I will look for work at the mill.

The Leeland Mills
1870

5

WHEN THE GREAT machines in the mill shuddered to a halt for the noon dinner break, Patrick heard the child's scream. His fingers drew up from the cloth he was folding into wooden crates for shipment. His neck tightened; his heart pounded. Around his face, dust flew like insects.

The cry had come from beyond the storage room door where Patrick and the other cloth packers worked, out where the early September sun cast spots of light through the overcast sky, where the train tracks lay along the mill yard, awaiting the cars that would carry away the crates of cotton cloth.

"Hear that?" Patrick asked Mr. Steele, the old man who packed crates next to him.

"What?"

"The child."

"No."

It might be Liam, Patrick thought. *It can't be Liam, not again!*

Patrick moved quickly to the open door. He squeezed through the towering stacks of crates with their Leeland Mills trademark emblem stenciled on the lids and the mountainous bolts of fabric that had been brought in on hardcarts from the finishing rooms. He swiped at his eyes as he went, trying to dislodge the grime that made clear sight difficult.

Of course it's not Liam injured. So many children work here. It could be any one of them.

"Where you going there, boy!" This was Mr. Depper, the second hand. He had been scolding another packer for some infraction Patrick could only guess was slow work, but when the second hand saw Patrick pass, he stopped short and frowned.

"I need some air."

"Air?" called Mr. Depper. His voice was as irritating as a mosquito's buzz. "You got plenty air in here! You ain't up in one of them spinning or weaving rooms where the windows are nailed shut, are you? What you got to complain about?"

Patrick didn't turn around, but he didn't talk back either. It would do no good to get in trouble for insubordination.

"Don't you go outside, boy. You know the train ain't here yet!"

Patrick stopped at the door and looked out at the mill yard. It was hard to see at first. Squinting, he put his hand up to shield his eyes. Then he saw them. Standing beside the tracks was a man and a crying boy. Every few seconds the man would shake the boy and the boy would scream. He was small, about Liam's size. He wore short, ragged pants, a dirty white shirt, suspenders, and cracked leather shoes. The boy held his right hand in his left. Most likely he had been wounded by one of the machines.

"Patrick O'Neill!" shouted Mr. Depper.

"Just a moment!" Patrick shouted back.

There was a piece of cloth around the boy's hand, bound tightly. The unbleached cloth was now scarlet. The boy was hurt badly. Somehow his hand had been smashed.

Patrick's stomach twisted. He remembered Liam losing his left forefinger the year before. He'd been cleaning the floors in Carding Room #1, collecting lint with a broom. When he'd lost his balance, he had stumbled, catching his finger in the gears of a sharp-toothed machine. The finger had been amputated at the second knuckle.

Patrick did not know this wounded boy, not that there was any reason he would. Liam talked about different children he knew at the mill, some of whom worked as doffers in Spinning Room #4 on the third floor, but Patrick had never put names to faces because he never really saw the worker children's faces. He only saw them in a blur, running messages or carting fluff and dust down from the weaving and spinning rooms, and in particular, wheeling the handcarts in from the finishing room so the men could crate the material for shipment on the next train.

Outside, the man shook the boy one more time, then stalked away, his boots sending up dusty divots. The boy hung his head and walked off in the direction of the mill's offices.

If he's too badly hurt, Patrick thought, *he'll be dismissed. It will be his own bad luck.*

Shaking his head, Patrick walked back to his work station. He could hear another packer say quietly as he passed, "A shame, truly, that child out there. Another crime ignored by this man-eating business."

Mr. Steele was seated on a crate, eating a roll. "Let it go, boy," he said. "It's not for you to worry about the problems of another."

Patrick looked at the old man. Mr. Steele was tall, pale, and bald. The only hairs he had grew like wild gray weeds on his chin and upper lip. His arms were knotted and sweat-slicked.

"Maybe," Patrick said. He picked up the leather haversack in which he carried his lunch and took out an apple. He took a bite, carried his cup to the bucket by the wall and filled it with water, then went back and sat on the crate next to Mr. Steele.

"How old are you now, boy?"

"Sixteen," said Patrick. He swallowed the apple bite and washed it down with the coppery-tasting water.

"You been here how long?"

"'Bout four years."

"Thought so," said Mr. Steele. "And you're old enough to know that you have your own matters to tend to. We can't save the world. A man's got to work and earn his keep, and you can't do much more than that."

Patrick didn't answer. He didn't care to have conversations with Mr. Steele, because the man was always trying to tell him what to do. He acted as though he thought he was Patrick's father even though he was not married and had no children. Mr. Steele claimed to have been an overseer in a mill up in Lawrence when he was a younger man, but Patrick didn't believe him. Why would an overseer be reduced to the tedious job of packer here in Leeland? It made no sense, and Mr. Steele was not inclined to explain.

I wish it was Wednesday, Patrick thought. On Wednesdays, with the permission of Mr. Spilman, the packing room overseer, Patrick was allowed to hurry up the outer staircase to the third floor to dine with Abigail and Liam, both of whom worked in Spinning Room #4. This was a rare and for the most part unheard-of practice. Most workers were confined to their space for the many relentless hours of work, forbidden to even take a breath of fresh air through a door or window. But each week Patrick secretly gave Mr. Spilman a few pennies from his pay, and Liam was liked well enough by his own Mr. Gilbert to allow the practice to go on. But today was Friday and so he would eat alone, as long as Mr. Steele kept his thoughts to himself and stayed on his own crate.

Dinner today was the usual, cheese and a hard roll. Water was taken from the buckets in the corner of the room, drawn and brought in by storage-room errand boys.

As he finished the apple and pulled out a piece of hard cheese, Patrick wondered about the family of the injured boy.

"He will go home and mend," Patrick whispered to the cheese in his hand. "If he's lucky, he can return as Liam did, to clean or sweep or doff the bobbins. If he can keep up the pace and not be slowed by the injury, he shouldn't lose pay for it."

Suddenly the machines on the mill thundered back into gear. Patrick stood, brushed cheese crumbs from his legs, stretched his neck to pull out a cramp, and lifted a bolt of cloth to fold.

6

IT WAS NEARING eight-thirty when Patrick, Abigail, and Liam crossed the covered mill workers' bridge over the Merrimack River and plodded up rocky Burris Street on their way home. Most of the shops on the street were closed. The only store open was the company store, Leeland Supplies, just off the bridge by the river. A few operatives came out with their purchases, but none of the O'Neills had either the money or the energy to shop. There were very few other pedestrians.

Although it was already September, fall was hard to detect in the middle of town. Not a cool breeze found the street tonight, not a hint of the cinnamon smell of autumn. The few scraggly maple trees at roadside had not a single red or orange leaf to share with passersby.

The three O'Neills walked close together. It was a good idea, since an occasional children's gang might decide to attack and rob lone people out after dark.

Abigail, a willowy girl of eighteen with light brown hair, braided and pinned, held her broadcloth skirt and apron up to keep them from dragging in the puddles on the road. Liam, nearly thirteen, with Patrick's dark brown hair and bright blue eyes, wearily threw pebbles into the puddles to watch them splash.

Gaslights hissed on the street corners, throwing shadows back into alleyways.

The tenement in which the O'Neills lived was a good mile from the river, up the long stretch of Burris Street, then south down narrow Charlotte Road. On both sides of Charlotte Road were three- and four-story tenements. The shadows were black as tar, as no streetlights had been erected here. Except for occasional spots from oil lamps and candles in unshaded windows, Patrick, Abigail, and Liam walked in the darkness. They stepped carefully to keep from twisting ankles or stepping in horse manure.

"You haven't said a word since we left the mill, Patrick," said Liam. "What's wrong?" He punched his brother lightly on the arm.

"Oh, nothing," said Patrick.

"It's something," Liam said. "Usually you tell us jokes or stories. Something."

"I don't have any jokes tonight," said Patrick.

"Why not?"

Patrick sighed. He loved his little brother's admiration and his sister's respect. But tonight he kept thinking of the injured boy. He kept thinking about Mr. Steele's comments. It made him feel tired and discouraged. He hated that feeling.

"Then tell us a story you've told before. Tell the

one you made up about the overseer who falls in the river and is caught by the giant crayfish," said Liam.

Patrick shook his head.

"Then the one about the farmer who invents a spinning machine to spin honeysuckle vines into cloth, but then can't get the machine to stop and his house and farm are swallowed up."

"No," said Patrick.

"But why not?"

"A boy was hurt today," said Patrick. "Did you hear about it?"

"No," said Liam.

"Did you, Abigail?"

Abigail said, "I think so. But I don't know who it was. Some careless child, I suppose. I heard it happened right before the noon dinner break in one of the weaving rooms upstairs. The boy should have been watching out for himself, but clearly he didn't. Why should he have sympathy? I heard no word about him after that. I suppose he must have been all right."

"I don't think he was all right," Patrick mumbled. "And I don't want to talk about it."

"Do you wonder what it would be like to travel on that railroad across the whole country?" asked Liam, his voice rising with the new topic of conversation. He paced his steps with Patrick, taking big strides like his older brother. Abigail had fallen a few yards behind, watching her steps. "Polly told me today that she is going to go to California with her parents as soon as they have the money. There is gold there, and so much land. Isn't she lucky?"

"I suppose she is," said Patrick. Polly Bruce was a

fourteen-year-old girl who worked in Spinning Room #4 with Abigail and Liam. She was a gangly thing with a terrible cough. Her father was one of the drunkards who littered the streets at night. Her mother had a severe case of consumption, which flooded her lungs with mucus and made breathing difficult. Patrick had once heard Polly tell another operative that her father had saved General Ulysses Grant's life in the battle of Shiloh. Of course, just a day earlier, Polly had told Patrick that her father had never set foot outside of Massachusetts because he didn't dare be too far away from his father-in-law, who had thousands of dollars and would not give him a cent if he ever left the bedside of Polly's mother.

Patrick shook his head. Liam was smart but young and easily swayed by exciting stories.

"All right," Patrick said at last. "I'll give you a story. A new one." Anything at this point was better than having to listen to wild tales of Polly Bruce. Patrick began making up a story as he walked. "There once was a flea. He lived on a shaggy little mutt. But one day the owner of the mutt decided it would be so much fancier if he were shaved muzzle to tail tip. Of course, this left the flea without a home."

Liam skipped a step and hooked his thumbs under his suspender straps. "Good! Keep on!"

"The flea was out of his place now, and didn't know what to do. Certainly there were other dogs, but they weren't home. And so the flea decided he would somehow need to go about gluing hair back onto his now bald flat."

Suddenly Abigail grabbed Patrick's shoulder. "The

witch woman is watching us again!" she whispered.

Patrick's head snapped left. There, in a second-floor tenement window, with pale light outlining her, were the head and shoulders of an old woman. The tangled hairs on her head stood out against the light like old cobwebs. One gnarled hand was held up to the window, fingers scrabbling and twitching as if they were cursing the O'Neills. The shadows of the hand on the street at Patrick's feet looked like an enormous, deadly spider.

"Don't look at her!" hissed Liam.

Patrick stopped dead in the street. He stared at the old woman in the window. This was the fourth night in a row she had been waiting, it seemed, for the O'Neills to come home from the mill; the fourth night she had watched them, glaring at them.

"It's like Aunt Sadie's witch!" said Liam. "She wants to suck out our souls!"

"Patrick, run!" said Abigail. She came around Patrick and shook him by the arm. "Now!"

"She'll put a spell on us! She'll let down her hair and catch us!" said Liam.

The woman tilted her head and her wild, white hair rippled. Gooseflesh raced up the backs of Patrick's arms and neck. His heart kicked into a fast, painful rhythm. But still, he could not look away.

"Patrick!" snapped Abigail.

The old woman's other hand came up and linked fingers with the first, making a single bony, wrinkled knot. Her mouth opened slowly.

"She's cursing us!" screeched Liam. "Put your hands over your ears!"

All three did so, and they raced the rest of the distance up Charlotte Road, away from the demon-woman to their own brick tenement and their own tiny third-floor flat.

7

September 7, 1870

Lucky. Mr. Steele said the boy who was hurt today would be lucky if he could return to work like Liam did after his accident. Lucky used to have a different meaning. Before coming to Leeland, lucky meant finding a lost coin in the cabin floor or the river not rising all the way to the barn after a long, hard rain. Lucky was how I felt when I watched the birth of a healthy new foal or finding that Mother had made an apple pie for supper.

Now lucky means staying alive.

I keep thinking of the boy who was hurt today. Did he have a mother who will cry? A father who will curse the mill and the men who owned it? Will a sister want to strike on the boy's behalf, or a brother write a letter to a newspaper about the horrors of the factories?

No, probably not. Well, the mother will cry, but the sister won't strike and the brother won't write an article. The sister needs her work; the brother is illiterate.

The father may curse in private, but he knows his family should stay where they are and not raise a ruckus. Survival is at stake.

Today would have been my father's birthday. Today he would have been thirty-nine. He didn't survive the war. I wonder what it would have been like if he had lived. What would we have been doing tonight?

I am different from my father in some ways. I can't picture myself a soldier as I know I don't have the temperament for battle as he did. But I often fancy I favor him in looks. It would have been no disgrace. His hair was as dark as the riverbank mud, his eyes blue as a clear stream. I would wear whiskers such as his if Mother would allow, but she still sees me as too young, in spite of my upcoming seventeenth birthday this December. Many boys younger than I sport manly beards. The last time I tried to grow whiskers I got by four days, then Mother said I looked like a pincushion and off they came. I think she's forgotten that Father had his beard when he was seventeen and they fell in love.

Sometimes I think that Abigail, Liam, and Mother don't remember Father well. To them it has been a lifetime since the war. Abigail and Liam do their mill work, Mother does her housework at the Clatterbucks'. They don't talk about the past.

But to me, there are times when Father's death seems like only yesterday. I want to reach back to that day, grab my father by his straps in the heat of that dread battle, and shout at him, "Stay low! Watch out! Be careful, and come back to us at our farm near Duncannon." Then I become aware again of where I am, and of the years gone. And I set my mind on my work *and my duties, so I can help my family up from our poverty. So I can save enough that someday I can quit the mill. I have, as of this day, put away $19, of which my mother knows nothing. It is hidden behind a loose wall board in our bedroom. This shall go to pay my college fees someday.*

College. It is there I'll become a writer.

But some nights, sorrow hangs on my back like an old jacket too tight to shed, like pine sap in my hair, too thick and old to wash away, like the stings of hornets, red and hot, swelling up more each time I scratch at them. Tonight college seems like a ridiculous fantasy, as slippery as a catfish.

The Leeland moon is watching me now. It is a cold, unblinking eye, so unlike the kind moon of the country. I think it can read my journal over my shoulder.

I hope someday to become a writer and make his spirit proud.

Father, I miss you.

8

PATRICK PUT HIS journal aside and pushed it back against the crumbling brick wall of his tenement so the random winds wouldn't catch the pages and spin them like dead leaves to the alley. Paper was a treasure, and he couldn't afford to lose a single sheet. He had to tell his mother he made fewer cents than he really did at the mill so he could squirrel away a precious yet small amount to save for college and also buy paper for his journal. There were a lot of things he had learned since his father had died. One thing was the importance of his family, because he could not imagine making it through this mill life alone. Another was how to lie about little things.

Patrick sat with his legs dangling off the landing on the back stairs, his arms laced through the balusters, staring at the garbage-littered alley two floors below. The alley was dark but not silent. There were the growling sounds of stray cats, seeking out scraps of food among trash and discarded boards, and the argument of drunk men in the building next door. Every so often there would be the snorting of a feral pig, scampering through the night. Then there would be the whistles and hoots of child gangs in the shadows of nearby streets. These groups of children, many as young as Liam, had deserted their poverty-stricken families or had been abandonded by them. They made their living in the cloak of night, rolling men for pay and robbing shops of anything they could lay hands on.

Mother and Abigail were sleeping, and Liam at last quieted down. According to the mantel clock that Mother kept on a tiny table near her cot, it was nearing midnight. Patrick knew he should be sleeping. It wasn't wise to stay up, knowing that the factory whistle would blow at five in the morning. But as often as he could, he would come out to the steps to breathe the night air, to watch for the sneaky moon, to think. And to write.

Two cats, now visible in a silvery sliver of moonlight, began a brawl beneath the steps. They dove, snarling and hissing, latching onto each other's necks and dissolving into a rolling, tangled mass of fur. Patrick pressed his face between the slats and watched. He'd seen boys act like this many times. Snarling, yelling, fighting over nothing more than a look or a word or a bit of space on the street corner.

Patrick closed his eyes and thought of the Pennsylvania farm. He remembered working up potato hills while Abigail and Mother hung clothes up on the line and Liam tossed a stick to their dog. The soil was rich and red, and smelled fine and earthy.

Worms and grubs wriggled and curled in each shovelful of soil. Sunlight sparkled on the tiny bits of quartz in the dirt. Somewhere in the trees beyond the garden, mockingbirds called to each other. Father came out of the barn, holding a pitchfork, laughing and shaking hay out of his dark hair.

"Patrick, you digging your way clear through the world, boy?" Father said with a wink. "You know, you keep going, you'll either hit the devil or a Chinaman on the head with that spade."

Patrick grinned and said, "I suspect the Chinaman will be a gentleman about it, but not the devil. Maybe I could bribe him with some of those huge trout you caught this morning. That will assure me safe passage, do you think?"

Father chuckled, picked up a handful of soil, and flung it at his son. Patrick ducked in time. The trout Father had caught that morning had been pitifully small things, more like minnows than anything else. They'd joked about those fish for more than a week.

His father said, "You're a bright boy, Patrick. You'll do something fine with your life. I'm proud of you."

Why can't we go back and change things? Patrick thought. *Why must time always go forward and never backward?*

"Patrick Thomas O'Neill, if I see correctly. And what are you doing out late like this? Isn't this past your bedtime?"

Patrick opened his eyes. Down where the cats had been moments earlier stood James Greig, an eighteen-year-old boy with long, scraggly brown hair and clothes that were frayed remnants. He lived nowhere, having run off from his family, who lived with other Irish immigrants in the shanty outside of town. James stayed wherever he could find space for a night, a loner, not joining any gangs, more satisfied to be independent. He was wild and loud, and he was Patrick's friend.

"Oh," said Patrick. "I'm enjoying the view from this nice balcony. I'm planning my day tomorrow, which will be full of relaxation and recreation, as are all my Tuesdays."

James grinned, his bright eyes full of mischief. "Aye? And what did you do today, me rich friend?"

"Much the same as I'll do tomorrow," said Patrick, grinning broadly. "Sleep until ten. Dine on quail and cakes. Stroll through the shops up on the high ridge of town and buy whatever catches my attention. You should be jealous of me, James."

James laughed out loud. "Oh, yes, I'm jealous," he said. "Jealous that you work fourteen straight hours a day. Jealous that you don't see the sun except on long summer days and Sundays." James swung around the step beam and climbed the rickety stairs to Patrick. He sat down and raked a strand of hair behind his ear. The boy smelled of smoke and beer. "Jealous that you are always tired and your back aches you. Jealous that there is no future for you in all that, me friend."

Patrick's smile faded. "How can you talk of the future, James? How can you see anything?"

"Oh, easily," said James. He pulled a cigar from the pocket of his tattered brown shirt, struck a sulfur match on the rough wood of the landing, and puffed until smoke came through his lips. The glow circled his face, revealing the scar that ran from his left ear to his forehead. "I take care of meself, you know that. And I took care of you, if I remember correctly. You were attacked by that child gang last year and I rescued you, pulling you out from under just as a knife came at your throat. Anyone who is brave as me has a future, Patrick."

Patrick said, "Perhaps."

"Me future is clear in me mind," James continued. He took out the cigar and blew smoke toward the sky. "I wish you would share the vision. We really are one of a kind, aye, you and me. We're both the bottom of the barrel, both poor old cellar vermin. Looked down on by those with more money, but smarter than the lot of them. We won't be poor forever. I have a vision, and it's a fine one."

Patrick rubbed his chin and sighed. "Your vision. Nothing there but danger, I assure you."

"Aye! Danger and excitement. They go together. When was the last time you had excitement?"

Patrick shrugged.

"Should I guess, then?" said James. "Be it when Liam brought home his first, measly pay? Or when your mother was given permission to salvage the not-quite-wilted flowers from Mrs. Clatterbuck's house to arrange in your own flat in a pickle jar?"

Patrick felt heat rise on his neck. James was making fun of him, but he was right. Excitement was not something that existed in Patrick's life.

"Come with me tonight, Patrick," said James. He put his hand on his friend's shoulder. "You won't have to play a part, just be with us. I've got a new friend named Robbie. A free soul such as myself who approves of my kind of occupation. Come tonight, and you can be the watch. Robbie and me'll find you a gift. What do you say?"

"Where do you plan to go?"

James took the cigar from his mouth and tapped the ash. "Don't know yet. Sometimes we plan it, sometimes not. Theft is more fun that way. But, Paddy, whether we know ahead of time or not, it's always—"

"Exciting," finished Patrick.

"Aye."

There was a clatter in the alley, somewhere in the shadows to the right in front of the stoop to the tenement next door. Snarling followed. It was a dog, after a cat, perhaps, or its own shadow. It was a wild dog, alone and independent, like James.

Patrick looked back at James. "I can't chance it."

"Paddy, Paddy, Paddy." James offered the cigar, but Patrick shook his head. James put it back into his mouth. "You're a boy pretending to be a man. I'm a man pretending to be a boy. Me way's much more fun."

"I have family I have to be concerned with."

James made a snorting sound. "I had family. And as Irish immigrants, they ended up in that damn shanty outside of town. I won't have that, you know." James spit on the steps.

Patrick nodded. He knew. Indeed, as poorly as he and his brother and sister were treated and as little compensation as they received, those who weren't native-born had it even worse. The Irish and the French-Canadians had it worst. They were cheated in the stores, cursed in the streets, and even had their homes razed on occasion for fun. All this reminded Patrick of a book he'd read last year, *Uncle Tom's Cabin.* The book had been written before the war and told about the terrible conditions the blacks had at the hands of their masters in the South.

"Men never lack at finding other men to oppress," Patrick said.

"And so," said James, "I've learned that a man must be after his own concerns or he'll wither and die."

He sounds like Mr. Steele, Patrick thought. He said, "I'm sorry, James. I have to think of Liam, and Abigail, and Mother. If I was caught in trouble, I don't know what they would do. Besides, stealing is wrong."

James tugged the cigar from his mouth and studied it for a moment. Then he flung it out into the air. It flipped end over end as it flew, a tiny, glowing missile soon to die. It dropped into the darkness of the alley and vanished. James looked at Patrick, tipped his head, and grinned. "Don't worry a moment, friend. Maybe someday you'll consent to join us, and until then, I'll just have to convince you by giving you a little trinket or two. Here." He fished into his shirt pocket and pulled out several gumdrops. "Got these at Bronlin's shop. He never noticed."

The gumdrops were pressed into Patrick's hand. They were sticky and lint-covered from James's pocket, but that didn't matter. This was candy, rare and wonderful. Patrick put the drops to his nose and smelled their faint, sweet scents.

"Now." James hopped up, gave a little bow, and

clambered down the steps. When he reached the bottom, he called back up, "I'll be back in a night or two. Think it over. We might be born in different countries, but we're both Erin's sons. Your name gives you away, you know. We should stick together."

Patrick felt his mouth water at the smell of the candy.

"Three's a magic number," said James. "You, Robbie, and me. We could work wonders, I would think!"

Patrick raised his hand to wave, and James was gone, running down the street in the night.

Patrick rolled the drops around in his fingers. He picked up his journal and wrote.

These candies from James are stolen. Picked from the tall glass vase when Mr. Bronlin was busy, probably talking to another customer. I can't eat them.

"Liam would enjoy one," he said softly. "Abigail, as well. I can't think of the last time we had gumdrops."

But they are stolen.

With a heavy sigh, Patrick put the journal down. Then he flung the candy into the alley, where they landed somewhere in the darkness with James's cigar. Then he collected his journal, stretched, and went inside to get some sleep before the factory bell rang its early morning greeting.

9

THE LEELAND MILLS bell cut through the air, driving an ax into Patrick's dream of floating down a peaceful river on a wooden barge. His eyes fluttered open to the still dark morning and his hand went to his temple and pressed. Already a headache had begun beneath his skull.

I should have been up a half hour ago! he thought.

He sat up quickly, the fragments of the river dream falling away. Abigail's cot was empty, as was Mother's. Even Liam was out of the bed he shared with Patrick. From the sounds in the kitchen, it was clear that everyone was ready to go off to work but Patrick.

"Why did you let me sleep?" Patrick demanded through the half-open door to the kitchen as he slipped into his trousers. The stifling air of the bedroom had him already bathed in sweat, and he wiped his brow with the back of his hand.

"You won't be late, Patrick," Abigail said over the

rattling of tin plates. "Goodness, you complain over a gift of sleep! I've got a breakfast for you here to carry with you."

Patrick pulled his suspenders up over his shoulders and buttoned them at the waistband of his trousers. He had slept in his shirt and would wear it to work. He pulled on his shoes, ran a comb through his dark hair, briefly touched the loose wall plank in which he kept his hidden college dollars, and went out into the kitchen, where at least a small breeze was stirring though the open window.

Seated at the small table, Liam wolfed down spoonfuls of runny egg. Abigail, wearing the same dress she'd worn the day before, stood at the iron cookstove, scraping egg and a slice of bread into a tin cup. An oil lamp blazed on the edge of the table, chasing away the remnants of night.

"Your drinking cup will have to prove itself as a breakfast plate today, Patrick," she said, smiling as she held it out.

Patrick caught the cup in his hand. "Thank you," he said. "But I wish you'd not let me sleep." Most mornings, with an extra few minutes, Patrick would scribble in his journal. This morning there was no time.

Abigail slipped her shawl over her shoulders as Liam put his dishes into the basin. "And why not? You don't think I know about your late nights out on the steps? Out there in the wee hours, talking to yourself on and on. If I didn't know better, I'd take you for a crazy man and have you sent to an asylum. But I know you're only my brother, with a lot of thoughts locked away and the need to get them out.

And so I thought one morning with ten extra minutes in bed couldn't be harmful."

Patrick said, "Thank you." Picking up the haversack from the counter, he stuck in a half apple, some cheese, some hard bread, and his tin cup. Abigail and Liam already had their noon meals in their pails. Then, on impulse, he went back into the bedroom and stuck his journal inside his shirt. If there was a minute during lunch today, he would write.

Out in the hall, other tenants were shaking off sleep and mumbling to each other. Patrick said "Good morning" to the Patterson family as they passed on their way to the stairs outside. The Pattersons were a silent lot except for the eldest son, Richard, who always gave Patrick a smile and a pleasantry when they passed each other. "I understand the Boston company has decided to give us all a bonus today!" he said. "All the free lint we can carry to stuff our pillows at home!"

Liam, Patrick, and Abigail followed the Pattersons to the wooden steps and down to the alley. Mill operatives were already filling the narrow road, many spitting thick, fiber-filled phlegm onto the street, most chatting, a few laughing.

"Like horses to the plow," Patrick said to himself. He picked bits of egg and bread from his cup as he walked, putting them in his mouth and trying to savor the taste.

"Patrick, you stepped in horse manure yet again," said Liam. "That's the fourth time this morning. Aren't you looking where you are going?"

"Blast," Patrick said, looking down as he stepped out of the fresh, warm pile. "It's leaked in through the cracked sole of my shoe and is all the way up the cuff of my trousers."

Liam laughed out loud, his blue eyes crinkling. *Thank God Liam is able to hold on to his sense of humor,* Patrick thought.

The sun was rising, bathing the grit in the road with sparkles. The mill workers' feet pounded the bright grit into the air, making those with chronic coughs cough more, making those who rarely coughed go into temporary fits. So many operatives came to work in the mill with reasonably good health. So many left sick or dying, with their lungs destroyed and their energy drained away. Yet every morning they got up and they went to work. Day after day after day.

Abigail said suddenly, "There's Sarah! I best catch up with her. I have a lot to talk about. I'll see you boys later!"

She was off, her skirt whipping and her tin cup bouncing from her apron strings. Patrick watched as she linked up with several other girls, all of whom worked with Abigail and Liam in Spinning Room #4. The girls drew together, bending over and talking with animation, but still moving ahead.

"They're talking about Mr. Lance," said Liam, answering Patrick's unasked question. "The new second hand in our room. The girls think he's handsome, and he's not married. There is talk he has money and would be a good husband."

"A second hand with a lot of money? I can't imagine."

"That's what they say. The girls do their work, but whenever he is around they watch him out of the corners of their eyes. Sometimes they primp and giggle. Maybe he has money. Some people have money tucked away, you know. Polly Bruce says Mr. Lance has a lot of money."

Patrick frowned. "Money alone doesn't make for a good husband."

"Maybe not," said Liam. "But maybe so."

Up ahead, the girls linked arms and moved together to Burris Street. They disappeared around the bakery on the corner.

"I heard Abigail say Mr. Lance seemed dreadfully green," said Liam. "What does that mean?"

Patrick shrugged. "I suppose he is shy around girls. Maybe he doesn't quite know how to talk to them."

"Are you green?"

"Me?" Patrick didn't know how to answer Liam. Certainly there were girls who had caught his attention at the mill, but—like Mr. Lance—Patrick didn't really know how to talk to them, either. There was a girl he'd watched a few times in the mornings on the way to work. She was red-haired and had a happy face. But Patrick never knew what to say to her to get her attention. He was afraid he would sound like a fool.

I suppose I am green at that, he thought.

And then Liam said, "Oh, Patrick! She's there again, looking at us!"

Patrick glanced up and saw once again the old woman, seated at her tenement window, staring down at the street over the heads of the other workers and straight at the O'Neill boys. But Patrick didn't look away.

"Now she's watching us in the morning, too!" Liam whispered urgently. "Patrick, I'm scared of her!"

"Then go on," Patrick told his brother. "Just go on. I want to see what she is all about."

"No, Patrick!" Liam grabbed his arm.

"I'll come after you," said Patrick. He looked at the old woman in her window. Her face, cloaked in shadow, was just as hard to decipher in the early morning. But her fingers rose as he watched, and began their strumming and beckoning.

"Patrick!"

"Just go on, Liam! I'll be with you soon! Go!"

His face contorting, Liam spun on his heel and ran off to the end of the block, sending up divots of dust with each footfall, disappearing in the flow of workers. Patrick licked his lip, caught his breath, then forced his gaze back to the old woman's second-floor window.

Come here, the woman's twitching fingers seemed to say. *Come closer!*

Patrick walked slowly over to the dank-smelling brick wall of the tenement. Taking a deep breath, he called, "What do you want?"

The woman looked down. Her cheeks were sunken and hollow, like deflated bellows. The hands stopped their clutching. It made Patrick think of a spider on its web, pausing and waiting to strike.

"What do you want of us?" Patrick repeated.

The head angled even more, and now the nose was visible. It was sharp and big.

"Leave us alone!" Patrick shouted. "Stop watching us!"

And then, suddenly, with another shift of the head, the eyes were visible. Deep, sunken, black eyes, red-rimmed and rheumy. Wide. Staring down. Unblinking.

Patrick gasped.

But then there was something fluttering down from the window, drifting like an oak leaf on a fall breeze. Patrick watched it as it fell and landed on the toe of his boot.

It was a piece of paper.

A note. A note from the witch woman.

Patrick glanced from the note back to the window. But the old woman was gone.

10

YOU'RE SWEATING MIGHTILY today," said Mr. Steele as he slung another load of folded cotton cloth into a crate and picked up a handful of nails. He hammered the wooden lid down on the crate, pushed it aside, and picked up cloth to fold into another. "You ain't getting a fever, are you, boy?"

Patrick straightened from his own folding and pressed his hand to the small of his back. Around and above them, machines thumped and pounded. "No," he said.

"You're pale," said Mr. Steele.

"I'm fine," said Patrick.

"Good, then," said Mr. Steele, pausing to hawk a thick string of saliva on the floor, then brush at it with his shoe. "We can't be slowing down because you get sick. The river's running strong, the canals all full and fast, and the looms are turning out a lot of cloth. There are orders to fill, boy, and fill them, we must. Farms don't run this country now. Mills do. Machines do. We have to keep up."

"I know."

"The train to ship the cloth will be in soon. It won't wait on sick boys."

"I know." Patrick turned his back on the old man and went back to work: folding, lifting, packing, hammering crates shut, and stacking the crates. He couldn't stop thinking about the note in his pocket.

At lunch he rubbed his aching shoulders, filled his cup with water, then sat on a crate to chew his bread. He had not read the note. Maybe it was better just to tear it up and in this way prove to himself whatever the crazy old woman had to say meant nothing to him.

But he knew he would read it. His curiosity was too great.

Carefully, when Mr. Steele was turned the other way, he reached into his shirt pocket and pulled out the paper. He looked at the folded note. It was hot to the touch, perhaps from the heat of his own body, perhaps from the witch's curse. He opened it slowly.

The handwriting, lovely and fluid, caught Patrick by surprise. Surely a witch would have foul-appearing script. But the words were the most interesting of all:

I have seen you these past days. Walking home with your lovely family from a job at the mill, I surmise. My intent wasn't to frighten you, as I think I may have. You look so much like my son, Andrew, back when he was a mill boy. I'm an old woman at a lack for company. If you would ever have a spare moment, we could visit. Please forgive my forwardness. But you do look so much like Andrew.

Mrs. Randolph Wilson

Patrick's eyebrows drew together in disbelief. He read the note again.

If you would ever have a spare moment, we could visit . . . You do look so much like Andrew.

Patrick whispered, "The witch is inviting you to be her company!"

Please forgive my forwardness.

"She's not a witch," Patrick whispered. "She's just a lonely old woman in a second-floor tenement flat."

"What's that you're reading?" came a voice just over Patrick's head. He glanced up at Mr. Steele, who was wiping meat grease from his lips. Patrick quickly folded the paper and put it into his pocket.

"Nothing of interest," he said.

"Oh, is that so?" asked Mr. Steele. "I saw your eyes go big as bowls. What is it, then, a note of affection from a young lady?"

"It's nothing," said Patrick.

"Or is it a notice of termination? Are you let go from your employment here?"

"No."

"Then is it a petition for a turnout? Are you a rabble-rouser, ready to stop working and strike?"

Patrick felt his face flare red. "It's nothing!" he shouted. "Watch your lunch, Mr. Steele. I see a rat sniffing, ready to drag it away!"

Mr. Steele spun about and looked at his food on the crate. There was no rat, but the point was made.

Mr. Steele, grumbling and rubbing his hand across his bald pate, went back to eating.

Patrick went to a far corner of the room where other men chatted about their families and their aches and had no interest in a boy, and crouched down to write quickly in his journal.

•

Do I want to go visit an old woman I don't know just because I look like her son? What would I say? How could I explain this to Abigail or Liam? They would think I was insane.

Sometimes I feel like I am going insane. What is there in this mill town to keep me from losing my mind, with the constant work and constant pains in my body? Wouldn't a worker with half a mind be of more use than one with a whole mind? He wouldn't argue or think about problems, but would merely do as he is told.

Am I not at that point already?

At least I can still write.

The bell clanged, the looms and spinning frames upstairs roared into action, and it was time to go back to work.

11

September 15, 1870

Tonight Mother came home later than usual. It's Saturday, and tomorrow afternoon there is going to be a birthday party at the Clatterbuck house, where she works. She told us that she had spent the entire day cleaning nooks in the house she had not even known existed. Then she told me I would have to go there to help out during the party.

She said, "Mary Clatterbuck is turning fourteen. The serving boy who usually does the job has been hurt badly in a wagon accident and is unable to help. You'll be the waiter. They'll tell you what should be done. You be there, cleaned and fresh, ready to work at noon."

I wanted to argue, but she looked so weary. And then she leaned over and gave me a hug. It was strange. "We can use the money," she said. "And you'll do fine." Then she got up to heat some soup.

She didn't ask me if I wanted to, she just told me I would do it.

I'd rather spend the day scavenging the stables of Leeland, gathering scattered straw to restuff our mattresses. I'd rather muck out those stables than act as a serving boy!

I have only been to the Clatterbuck house twice, but never inside. I can't imagine the place, and I have a good imagination. Mother has never said anything unflattering about her employers, but I can't help but wonder what these people are truly like. Mr. Clatterbuck is one of the owners of Leeland Mills. I suspect a gruff man who would as soon spit at you as talk to you.

I think I would rather fall headlong in the manure I was mucking than serve there tomorrow.

12

IT WAS SUNDAY morning, and Abigail and Liam were out in the alley with other tenants, scrubbing down clothing and bed linens in large washbasins. Many operatives went to church on Sunday mornings; Leeland had no shortage of places of worship. There was a Presbyterian church, a Catholic church, a Unitarian church, and a Friends' meetinghouse. But Lucy excused her brood because she worked at the Clatterbucks' seven days a week and couldn't even go herself.

"Pray without stop," she would tell them. "To God, a heart is a church as much as a building."

"God," Patrick prayed as he walked through town, "let this day go by very quickly."

Patrick knew how to clean cotton, how to doff bobbins, how to shear and fold and pack cloth. But what did serving involve? He didn't have a clue.

The Clatterbuck home was on several acres of land by the river, a half mile east of the mill. Patrick's mother had told him all about the rich family for whom she worked. Their house had been built by the Boston company so George Clatterbuck could always be near the factory to keep a close eye on the goings-on. There were tall oak trees on the lane that passed the house, and shorter lilac and azalea shrubs beneath them. The dirt lane was kept scraped and level, unlike the rutted Charlotte Road. Lucy had told her children that a street washer came down the lane on hot, dusty days, sprinkling it with water from holes in a huge barrel on a wagon. There was a brick walkway leading from the lane to the Clatterbuck house. The picket fence and gate were freshly whitewashed.

Several other ornate, two-story houses shared the lane with the Clatterbuck house, owned by stockholders who could afford luxuries such as ornate fretwork and wicker porch furniture. Patrick's stride slowed as he approached the Clatterbucks'. The two times he'd been here, he had never gone any farther than the gate at the end of the brick walk. Each time he'd come to help his mother carry home castoffs that the lady of the house had given the O'Neills on the last two Christmases. The first time it was an armload of cast-off clothes. The second time the gift had been some dented pots that the cook refused to use, saying she couldn't cook fine food with less-than-fine kitchenware.

I don't want to do this, Patrick thought. *I feel like a fool.*

"I must think of the pay," he mumbled as he crossed the wide road to the walkway and the fenced Clatterbuck yard. "Pay I might be able to skim off to put in the wall with my college money. Pay that will buy some extra pork or chicken for the family."

A small, open-air carriage called a tea cart, drawn by a well-groomed and blinkered horse, rumbled by on the lane. A young couple sat in the cart, arm in arm, the woman in a velvet-trimmed hat and the man in black driving gloves. Patrick watched them go by, but they didn't watch him. They stared straight ahead, intent on their destination.

"I'll bet they're going somewhere where other boys will have to wait on them," muttered Patrick. "I'll bet the waiters smile at them, but they won't have a smile in return. A pleasant expression could be too much of a tip."

"Come on in, then, Patrick!" called Lucy O'Neill from the front porch of the house. Patrick spun around and saw her standing there in the shade, one hand on her hip, the other hand whirling impatiently. "We have much to do and there's no time for woolgathering!"

Patrick came through the gate and latched it back, then trotted up the walkway to the porch. He took the three front steps in a single stride. His mother was in her best clothes, a simple blue frock with a small white collar and scuffed black shoes. She opened the door for her son and then followed him into the front hall. Patrick was suddenly aware of his plain mother against this fancy background. Her gray hair was pinned flat, and her hands were gnarled and dry. Her waist, though not thick, was unshapely. Only rich women could afford corsets.

At first Patrick felt as if he couldn't catch his breath. It was the same sensation he'd had when he'd first set foot inside the Leeland Mills. He had never realized a house could be so crowded with things.

The hall was lined with narrow tables and two spindly coat stands. He and his mother had to walk single file in the hall toward the back and the kitchen, and as he passed the other rooms, he peered in and saw that they, too, were filled. Lamps, tidies, overstuffed chairs, display racks, cabinets, pillows of an array of fabrics and designs, and decorative benches took almost every bit of floor space. Lucy had told her children all about the fancy things here, but Patrick had never envisioned that there would be so much.

In just a moment Patrick and his mother were in the Clatterbuck kitchen with the two cooks and the matron of the house herself.

Mrs. Clatterbuck, a woman not much older than Mother, wore a serious expression on her chubby face. She was dressed for the afternoon party, which would begin in less than an hour. Her hair was swept high, and over her lace dress she wore a white shawl. There were lacy gloves with pearl buttons on her hands.

"So this is your boy, Mrs. O'Neill," Mrs. Clatterbuck said, pursing her lips. "Not really a boy, but nearly a man. I will hope for nothing less from him than a man's effort." She then turned to Patrick, who stood watching the cooks scurry and clamor around him, lifting pot lids and muttering to each other. "The job isn't hard, boy," the matron said. "Look at me!"

Patrick looked.

"There's no counting to do, nothing to read," the woman said sharply. "Just go where you are told and when you are told. Be careful and smile. Nothing is to be spilled. Nothing should even so much as teeter on a tray. Any questions?"

Patrick drove his teeth together and he said, "No questions, ma'am."

"Then I'll be off to greet the company," said Mrs. Clatterbuck. "It is noon. We will settle in the dining room at one, and you will listen for my bell then. This is my little Mary's fourteenth birthday party, and it will be a day to remember."

The cooks said, "Yes, ma'am." Lucy O'Neill said, "Yes, ma'am." Patrick felt his lip twitch as he said, "Yes, ma'am."

At least at the mill, he thought as he was given a white jacket to wear over his clothes, *people know I'm smart. They have seen me writing, and many of them can't even recite their letters. I don't have to play stupid. I do my work, and as long as I do it right, I'm left alone. I don't think I'll be left alone here.*

The kitchen burst into renewed activity. Dishes were set out to go around the dining table in the next room, and Lucy O'Neill quickly hurried them in through a swinging door. As Patrick buttoned his jacket, he tried to see into the dining room before the door swung closed, but couldn't. A cook caught his arm and spun him around to face her.

"You waiting for a proper invitation before you begin your job?" she asked. She was much shorter than Patrick, with a thick neck and arms that seemed full of enough muscle to bind and toss bales of raw cotton at the mill. Her hair was pure white like old cobwebs, combed and pinned against her skull. Her face was red with heat, and her eyes were tiny and keen.

"No, ma'am," Patrick said instinctively.

The second cook, a much younger woman with red hair, laughed as she ladled oysters from a large pan onto a platter. "You don't need to call her ma'am," she said. "We may be chickens with a pecking order in this kitchen, and the eldest can peck the hardest, but only women with enough money to wear gloves indoors require the title ma'am."

"Oh," said Patrick. "All right."

"Until serving time comes, boy," said the white-haired cook, "you will help us here. We have scraps to take out back. We have wood to bring in from the back porch to keep the stove going. And mind, keep that jacket clean."

Patrick thought it was unwise to carry garbage and wood in a white jacket, but he said nothing. He did as he was directed, carrying pans of vegetable scraps and ham fat to the compost pile out back and hauling split wood gingerly in a canvas slip for the two stoves.

On his third trip for wood, Patrick paused to scratch his neck in the backyard, and noticed the whitewashed barn just beyond the fence. He looked back to make sure a cook wasn't watching him from the kitchen window, then carried the armload of wood back to the fence.

The whitewashed barn was actually a five-stall stable. Four stalls appeared empty, but in the fifth, a small brown horse, a pony actually, had its head poking out and its large black eyes staring at Patrick.

"Hey, boy," Patrick said in a clear, quiet voice.

Instantly four more pony faces came to the windows of the four other stalls. Patrick smiled in surprise. "My goodness, you have friends."

Each pony was a different color: a bay, a dun with a large white blaze, a black, a chestnut, and the last one dapple gray. Such an assortment reminded Patrick of the rainbow candy displays in the window of Bronlin's shop on Burris Street.

"She don't care for them any more than she would a piece of dung in a ditch," said a voice nearby. Patrick whipped about to see an old man in dark pants and leather apron standing outside the paddock on a graveled path. He wore a flat hat and no shirt. A heavy leather harness was slung across his shoulder.

"Excuse me?" Patrick said.

The man shifted from one foot to the other; the metal on the harness jingled. "She don't care for them," he said, tipping his head toward the whitewashed stable and the five ponies. "Got 'em for her birthday last year. I heard her begging her father. 'I'll love them, Papa,' she said. 'Five ponies, one for each weekday. My friends and I can have rides, all at the same time. We can have a cart, and take trips up into town to shop!' "

Patrick said, "Who?"

"Why, Mary Clatterbuck," said the man. "George's youngest daughter. The spoiled thing that runs that household as if she was queen."

"Oh."

"She told her father if he got her those ponies for her birthday, she would help me care for them. You see, I'm the man in charge of the animals and the gardening. I ain't got time for five more! But Mary said, 'Oh, Papa, you know I'll help Jed.' That's me, Jed. She said, 'I'll remind him that my ponies need trimming and grooming and their stalls cleaned. I'll help him, too, Papa!' "

Patrick said, "They look healthy."

Jed snorted. He wiped sweat from the bridge of his nose. "You over there where you can't see and can't smell. Those ponies ain't been cleaned in over a week. She forgets, comes out every few weeks and looks 'em over. Never cleans 'em, though. Never feeds 'em except a sugar cube from the kitchen every so often. I swore to myself I wouldn't take care of 'em if she didn't care, but I just can't see them going lame on my account. They got thrush and grease heel, but I don't aim to let them founder. I try to keep up with 'em all."

"That's terrible."

"Mary had her fun for a while, then went off on another curiosity. Never seen a girl so taken with herself and nothing or nobody else. Sometimes I just think I should open the stalls and let 'em all go free."

Patrick nodded.

"You seem like a nice boy," said Jed. "You one of them Irish?"

"Not exactly. We're from Pennsylvania. My mother is a maid here."

"Company's arrived!" It was Lucy, shrieking from the back porch. "Patrick, what on earth is holding you up out there? It's ten till one! Get inside this moment!"

Giving Jed a quick nod, Patrick steadied his grip on the canvas sling handles and hurried across the yard to the porch, then up into the steaming kitchen.

13

LUCY BENT OVER Patrick's ear, her words a buzzing, angry whisper. "Don't dawdle. What are you trying to do, have me dismissed?"

"No," said Patrick. He didn't look at his mother. The flurry in the kitchen was about to explode into full-fledged business in which he would be swept up. He put the wood down by a stove and stood straight, flicking a bit of bark from his white jacket.

It did, indeed, look like the party was ready. The table in the center of the kitchen was crowded with dishes of aromatic foods. Beans, potato balls, roasted turkey, and ham baked in cider were ready for the guests. There were also large bowls of spinach, sweet potatoes, boiled rockfish, and several kinds of jellies. Patrick thought about pinching his nose to keep out the wonderful smells so his stomach wouldn't growl, but he knew that wouldn't be polite.

Suddenly the swinging door burst in, and a girl bounced into the kitchen. She was a few years younger than Patrick, with blond hair and bright green eyes. She was dressed in yellow, with a bodice of lace and satin bows in her hair. She wore white buttoned gloves like Mrs. Clatterbuck.

"Oh!" the girl shrieked, her loud voice unbecoming to her appearance. "Look at this! It is fine, I tell you! This is to be such a wonderful party. My friends will be jealous, and will all want such a party on their (sixteenth) fourteenth birthdays, as well. Perhaps, Emily and Lucy and Stella, I should hire you all out to them so they can celebrate in like fashion!"

The two cooks smiled and curtsied slightly. Lucy smiled on cue. Patrick's arms slipped behind his back, and one hand caught the other. He thought it would be best to stand still and not be noticed.

But it wasn't to be so. She noticed him almost immediately, and her head tilted in haughty curiosity. "Well, Emily, I see your Randolph couldn't help us today."

The red-haired cook said, "No, ma'am. He's broken his arm."

The girl crossed her arms and came around the food-bedecked table. "That's a pity," she said, without looking at the cook. But Patrick could hear no pity in her voice whatsoever. As she approached him, he felt an urge to back up.

"And what is your name, boy?" the girl asked.

"Patrick O'Neill," said Patrick. "What's yours?"

The girl's eyes widened, and she drew herself up. Emily and Stella glanced at each other. Lucy's brows pulled together.

"Have you no manners at all, boy?" said the girl. "Where on earth did they find the likes of you?"

Lucy said, "He's my son, ma'am. And I do apologize for his rudeness."

"Let him apologize himself," said the girl.

Patrick felt the words stinging his throat, but they came out in spite of himself. "I apologize."

The girl touched her lips with her finger and let out a disgusted puff of air. "I'm certain you'll remember your place, boy. Speak when spoken to. That will not be too hard to remember, will it?"

"No," said Patrick, thinking that Mary Clatterbuck was just like her mother.

The smile came back over Mary's face, so quickly it was startling. She laughed as though she'd been correcting a dog and was now cheerfully satisfied that the dog had learned the lesson. "Then I'll be off. We'll be ready soon. Listen for the bell and be quick! This will be a most extraordinary party!"

And then she was gone through the swinging door to the dining room from which many new voices drifted. It was to be a big party indeed.

"Patrick!" hissed Lucy. "What is on your mind, son, to speak out to the mistress? I told you last night that you were to be quiet and obedient!"

"But, Mother," began Patrick.

"Hush, now," said Lucy, turning away and snatching a starched towel from a countertop. She began to wash the utensils used to prepare the meal.

Emily walked over to Patrick. "Now, you listen," she said. "You're to be the only one going in and out of the dining room, so I best tell you the order in which the food is taken. The oysters are first, with the sauce, all on this silver tray. You see how well it fits? You hold the tray over their left shoulders, and spoon the oysters onto the plates with this spoon. Offer the sauce, which goes into the small white china bowls. The oysters are slippery things, so mind you don't let one escape into a lady's hair or a gentleman's lap."

Patrick nodded. He knew Emily was trying to make him laugh, or at least smile, but he couldn't.

A few minutes later, the bell rang. Patrick picked up the silver tray with the oysters and pushed through the swinging door into the dining room.

In the center of the room was a huge table covered in white linen and fine dishes. Well-dressed people sat with cloth napkins in their laps, hands folded properly. Mary Clatterbuck sat between two young girls and they giggled as they talked. Across from them was a mustached boy a little older than Patrick, and another girl, about seventeen, with brown hair and a blue dress. No one looked up as Patrick entered, and he felt a certain gratefulness for being an invisible serving boy.

He went around successfully, although his hands were sweating and he could feel the tray trembling just slightly in his grasp. Oysters were served without so much as a stumble. He hurried back into the kitchen for the next instructions.

Emily was testing the doneness of a cake. Stella was slicing fruit and arranging it. Lucy was gone, back to her more maidly duties, Patrick guessed.

"Let's see this," said Emily as she pulled a thin wooden stick from the center of the cake and frowned. "Another ten minutes," she muttered. "It best be done and garnished before the end of the meal or Mary will have a scene."

She glanced over at Patrick, who was unsure what to do next. "Listen for the bell, Patrick," she said. "Then it will be the turkey and ham, which go in the center near the master's chair so he can be in charge of them. You'll serve the potatoes and beans and other side dishes, as quickly and as carefully as you can. The same as it was for the oysters, over the left shoulders."

Patrick said, "I understand."

The next half hour of the meal went well. Every so often he felt the brown-haired girl looking at him, and his ears would go hot. Her name was Nancy, and she was a Clatterbuck, too. The conversation in the dining room was constant yet dignified; Patrick almost laughed out loud thinking how James would react to such civility.

But then it was time to bring in all five of Mary's birthday cakes. The first three cakes came in, a white cake, a chocolate cake, and one with pineapple pieces trimming the edges. Then Patrick went back to the kitchen for the fourth, but when he reentered the dining room, Mary was staring at him.

What does she want? he thought as he placed the coconut-covered cake on the table. *She didn't call me, did she? She didn't ask me a question that I didn't hear, did she?*

Then Mary said, over the hand-muffled giggling of her friends, "You are a mill rat, aren't you?"

Patrick's heart picked up speed. Everyone else in the dining room turned to listen. "What?" he managed to say.

The brown-haired girl said, "Mary, aren't these cakes lovely?"

But Mary ignored her older sister. "Are you deaf from the machinery noises, boy? Didn't you hear my question?" she asked. The girl on Mary's right ducked her head a little bit, obviously pleased with Mary's taunting but deliciously uncomfortable with the scene it was beginning to cause.

The boy across the table from Mary said, "Mary, we'll have that stop now. This is a party, not a competition of wits. I believe we would all have jollification as opposed to idle barbs tossed at a serving boy."

Mary tipped her head and flashed her eyes at the boy. "Listen to me, my dear brother John," she said. "Today the pleasures are mine, and I'll choose them as I see fit. If I want to talk with the serving boy, I'll do so." Mary looked back up at Patrick across the table. "I said, are you a mill rat?"

Patrick said, "I don't understand."

The girls on Mary's sides burst into uncontrollable, shaking giggles. Egged on by their approval, Mary said, "Mill rat. A rat from the mill. A smelly thing that crawls about in the factory, never coming out in the light of day. Eating crumbs in a hurry, scuttling in and out of the looms and spinning frames, getting dirty and not knowing or caring. My father tells me about them. He watches all of you. He tells what happens at the mill to those in Boston who own the majority of the shares."

Mr. Clatterbuck spoke up. "Mary, that isn't fair. People have different stations in life. We've taught you this. We are all equal in the eyes of God."

Mrs. Clatterbuck didn't seem to agree. "This is Mary's birthday," she said. "I won't have it fall apart and be ruined with an argument about your theories on equality."

I see Mary is her mother's daughter, Patrick thought.

Mary was determined to make her point. "Are you a mill rat? Answer me!"

He knew he had to answer, or he would be in trouble. Not only that, his mother would suffer the results. It didn't matter how he answered; it was addressing the question that was the degradation, the acknowledgment that someone could ask him such a thing, and that he had to respond.

"No," he said.

Mary said, "Hmmm. You smell like one. You do stink, you know. Have you no water with which to bathe?"

John said, "Mary, that's plenty from you on the matter."

"Yes, Mary," said Nancy. "Let us be on with our party."

"Hush," said Mary. "I said, boy, have you no water in your home?"

Patrick said nothing, and picked up an empty tray to carry it into the kitchen. Mary hooked her foot out and caught Patrick's ankle and he stumbled, dropping the tray and the remaining potatoes to the floor.

Mrs. Clatterbuck scowled.

Mary said, "Careless mill rat!"

Patrick snatched the tray up as quickly as he could regain his balance, but Mary caught him by the wrist and persisted with her questions.

"I asked you a question. You don't dare ignore me," she said coldly.

Patrick felt his nostrils flare and his wrist burn where she had touched him. He said, "We bring it in."

"Clearly not enough to do the job," Mary said, turning to her friends and giggling.

"Mary," said John, "stop it. Leave him alone. I aim to enjoy myself, and I won't have you making other folks irritable."

"What folks are irritable?" asked Mary. "Just you, Nancy, and Father."

John slammed his napkin on the tabletop. "I am embarrassed that my sister acts like a prissy, snotty child!"

"John!" shouted Mary.

"John!" said Mrs. Clatterbuck. "That is not appropriate. We have guests!"

John stood, throwing his chair back, and stalked from the room. Nancy looked at Patrick and said, "I hope there are more cakes in the kitchen. Please, I'd like to see what other good pastries we have to eat." She gave Patrick a small, apologetic smile, and Patrick went back for the cake.

After dinner, Patrick stayed to help clear the table and collect the garbage to go out of the house. He didn't speak to the cooks or to his mother except to answer questions with as little detail as possible. He was too angry to talk.

"Is this what money can do to people?" he whispered to himself. "I've never seen myself as less than anyone else before. What gives them the right to think they are better?"

He had never been so glad to get out of a place, not even the mill, as he was when he was excused from work at four-thirty that afternoon. Lucy waved him a curt good-bye, and he walked back into town.

But something led him in a different direction than home.

14

HE STOPPED ON Charlotte Road, amid the late Sunday afternoon pedestrians, horses, dogs, and rattling wagons. He squinted up at the second-floor window where the witch had sat and had tossed her note.

Don't be silly, go on home, one part of his mind instructed. But something even stronger said, *Visit her.*

He stood another few minutes, his veins still hot with fury, glancing between the tips of his scuffed shoes and the window. Then, before he could talk himself out of it, he took the steps two at a time and went inside the hallway.

For some reason, he had to meet her. It was a test, he supposed. A dare to himself. James dared himself all the time. Patrick sometimes felt like the boy James accused him of being. And today he'd had to be a boy, a sniveling little serving boy, enduring a rich girl's insults.

But not now.

Now he would meet the woman who had frightened his brother and sister. He would prove himself to himself.

It was the first door on the left. He knocked on the splintering wood, peeking over his shoulder in case someone might be there, ready to clock him on the head, believing he had something worth stealing.

I wonder if she has a gun, Patrick thought suddenly with horror. But then it was too late. The flat door creaked open. Patrick stepped out of the hall and into the old woman's home.

For a moment he stood, shocked and awed. Such a difference here from his own tenement flat. Yes, it was tiny, as small as the O'Neills', but there was something that he'd not seen since he'd left the farm back in Pennsylvania many years ago.

There was dignity.

It wasn't so much in the quality of things. The chairs were old, the table scratched and marred. There were dented cooking pots, several iron trivets, chipped teacups. But the difference was in the arrangement, the tidiness, the pride with which the few trinkets had been arranged.

In the center of the floor the old woman stood, her wrinkled hands folded against the bodice of her blue dress, her white hair tied back, her lips tugging in a hesitant smile.

"Hello," said Patrick.

The woman only nodded.

"I read your note," he said, feeling ridiculous, because of course she knew. Why else would he have come?

The woman nodded.

"My name is Patrick. And you're Mrs. Wilson."

The woman nodded. Then she eased herself down on a fabric-covered chair. She pointed to an upright wooden one, indicating Patrick should sit. He hesitated, then sat. *She's feebleminded,* he thought.

The woman was smiling, but Patrick suddenly realized that there was no insanity there. Only appreciation. Her eyes were bright and intelligent.

"Mrs. Wilson," said Patrick, "did you want to talk?"

Mrs. Wilson picked up a tablet from a chair-side stand and began to write with determined strokes. Patrick watched her.

"I thought you wanted to talk to me," Patrick said as the old woman continued to write. Then she leaned over, her back cracking, and handed the note to Patrick. It read, in the same cultured script as the first note:

Thank you for coming. Excuse me that I don't speak. I was working in the Pemberton Mill ten years ago in Lawrence when the mill building collapsed. So many were killed or maimed. My throat was crushed. I didn't die, but was left mute.

Patrick took a breath and looked up at the woman. "I'm sorry."

The woman smiled, then quickly wrote another note and passed it over.

It was a while ago. I get along. My son, Andrew, lives with me here, and my life is full.

"Andrew lives with you? Is he here now?"

The woman shook her head. She pointed out the window.

"He isn't home yet?"

Mrs. Wilson nodded.

"Where does Andrew work?"

Mrs. Wilson pointed at Patrick.

"At the mill? At Leeland Mills?"

Mrs. Wilson nodded.

"Oh," said Patrick. "I see. Is he an overseer or a second hand in one of the rooms?"

Mrs. Wilson wrote and passed the note.

Not anymore. He worked with me at Pemberton, when he was in his teens. He became an overseer at twenty-three. He was a fine one, a fair one. Opinionated, but I wouldn't have had him any other way. But he is no longer an overseer.

"Why not?"

Mrs. Wilson rocked back a little in her chair. She stretched her legs out, and Patrick could see they were in great need of a foot stool. The veins on her lower calves were dark blue and purple. One ankle was swollen with arthritis. She wrote:

He became involved in labor strikes. In turnouts. He detested the conditions at Pemberton. Such danger, such hours, can't be long tolerated. He led a turnout, but it was a failure. No one in charge cared to read his petition or hear his concerns. Not a week after the turnout, the mill collapsed.

Patrick put his elbows on his knees and leaned forward, reading. Mrs. Wilson and her son had certainly been through some hard times. He had tried to do what was right. And she had lost her voice because of the poorly constructed mill.

She gave him another note.

I was so injured I could no longer work. At least I had my legs and arms. Some workers had limbs ripped from their bodies by the falling machines. I'm lucky. I can still think. I can still write, thank God. But with the mill gone, workers had to go elsewhere. Andrew received a bad report from the Pemberton mill owners when he went to look for other work. And so when we came to Leeland the management gave him a low-paying job. He had to accept what they offered.

Patrick said, "I've worked at Leeland for three years now. I've seen bad things, too. When I lived on a farm I had no idea how money could corrupt people. How it could make employers care little or nothing for their workers. But I don't know if I could join a turnout. The owners have the reins, they make money, and we can do nothing except make it for them. I don't want to lose my job."

The woman nodded.

"I'm not much of a fighter," said Patrick.

Mrs. Wilson wrote:

There are many ways to fight, Patrick. I think you would stand up for your values if you had to.

Patrick couldn't answer.

The old woman stood up, put the tablet aside, and

hobbled to the window. She put her hands on the sill and looked out. Loose white hairs caught in an updraft and floated about her face. To anyone in the street below, she would appear to be a witch-woman. Patrick looked around the room, noticing for the first time a silver tea set on a shelf. *I hope James doesn't find out about that,* he thought. *He'd be here in an eye's wink.*

Then she turned back to Patrick. She poured a small cup of coffee from the single-eye cookstove and held it out. Patrick took it and sipped. It was bitter, but not much worse than the O'Neills' usual fare.

"Thank you," he said.

Mrs. Wilson sat and picked up the tablet again. She wrote and passed the paper over.

You have a brother and a sister?

Patrick sipped, then said, "Yes. Abigail and Liam. They work in the mill, too."

You do look like Andrew as a very young man. Except that Andrew had a beard.

"My mother doesn't think a beard is appropriate for me yet," said Patrick. "She still sees me as . . ." He hesitated. "She sees me as still a farm boy. I don't know when she'll understand that I'm nearly seventeen and grown."

What is it you want to do with your life, Patrick? Are you hoping to become an overseer in Leeland Mills?

"It may seem silly, but I want to go to college and be a writer."

How wonderful! There is a new university in New York, called Cornell. It opened two years ago, but this very year they are allowing women to attend. If I was young, I would go there! Writing is such a joy. I would have fancied being a journalist.

Mrs. Wilson went on to explain that she had been raised by educated parents in the South, but because they didn't believe in owning slaves, they weren't able to keep up with the neighboring planters and so lost most of their land. They moved north for a new start. But they never quite got on their feet as they'd hoped. She worked as one of the Lowell mill girls for a while, then was married. After her son was born, she kept on working just to keep the family from going into serious poverty.

But if I wasn't able to give a lot of fine things to my son as I'd had as a child, at least I taught him about the cruelty of owning others or treating them as if they were owned.

"I'm saving up for college," said Patrick, now excited by the conversation. "Our wages are low, and there are many things we have to buy. Also, Mother insists we have a family savings, and we each contribute to it on payday." He leaned over his knees, his fingers linking together. "But I've got nineteen dollars hidden in my bedroom in the wall. It's taken me three years, but I've got that much. It shouldn't be long before I have enough! I don't know what it would cost, but I'm guessing I'm close. Don't you think?"

Mrs. Wilson looked pensive, then she wrote:

The article said the tuition at Cornell is ten dollars a trimester.

"A what?"

That would be thirty dollars a year.

Patrick was shocked. "Thirty dollars a year? How long until I can save even another eleven dollars? All Liam and Abigail make goes to pay rent. My wages as well as Mother's pay for fuel and food. I give money to Mr. Spilman each week so I can have lunch with my sister and brother. And then there's the blasted family savings. Putting away pennies a week is all I can do!"

Mrs. Wilson shrugged and sighed.

"I'll be ninety before I have saved enough, and by then I'll be as senile as a stick!" Patrick stood up.

Mrs. Wilson pointed to Patrick and then to the floor, raising her eyebrows in a question.

"Will I come again?" asked Patrick. "I don't know. I'm busy with work, with my chores at home. I don't know. Thanks for the coffee."

Mrs. Wilson stood up and took Patrick's hand in her own. She squeezed it gently.

Patrick felt a sudden welling of tears in his eyes. His throat went tight. With a quick, nodded thank-you, he opened the door and went out to the step landing. He leaned on the railing, closing his eyes, taking deep breaths of squalid air.

Then, as quickly as one of Leeland's stray dogs, he slipped down to the street and back into the cloak of night.

15

September 16, 1870

Ever since we moved to Leeland, I've felt my soul changing. I've worked hard, but to what end? Doing right has never been a choice. It has been the only option. But recently I have felt a shift in my heart, a hardening of my spirit.

I don't like it.

I don't like it, but I don't know how to stop it.

My father said I would do something fine with my life. He said he would be proud of me. I don't think I know how to live up to that anymore.

Nineteen dollars. It's all I have, and it will be quite a long time before it grows to even twenty. What a fool I've been. A foolish dreamer all these years!

I felt sorry for the cooks at the Clatterbuck home at first, but now I think my sorrow was ill spent. These women realize they can't change themselves or their lot in life. Maybe accepting the lot is the only way to remain sane.

James has told me many times that there are two kinds of people. Those who take advantage, and those of whom advantage is taken. He says we are the poor, we are the betrayed. He justifies his stealing this way. He has no dream other than to get what he can while he can.

Me, a writer? What folly that was. I shall be a mill worker for my entire life.

He put his pen down and listened to the night sounds. Tonight, though, he didn't hear children or adults or cats or dogs.

I fancy I hear screaming ponies and screaming people, trapped in wooden buildings, rotting to death as machinery plays their terrible tunes.

Somehow, yet again, I have to get used to it all.

16

SO TELL ME. What was it like in your new profession?" asked James Greig. He had come up the steps and was seated beside Patrick, his fingers wrapped around his knees, the crumbs from a roll he'd just eaten spattering the front of his ragged coat.

Patrick shrugged, putting aside his journal, in which he had just put ideas for a new poem about ponies. "I was a waiter. I waited. I served. I removed rubbish and brought in wood. There was nothing to it."

"Will you quit the mill now, aye? Work full-time there with your mother?"

"No, they only needed me for a day. The usual boy was injured and couldn't work."

James sniffed, his nose twitching. "What are they like?"

"The Clatterbucks? Rich."

"Besides rich."

"Mrs. Clatterbuck and her daughter are intolerable. Rude. Selfish. Cruel. How my mother puts up with it all is beyond me. But she does. We put up with so much, don't we?"

"Not me. I put up with what I want to put up with," said James. He popped his knuckles, then said, "What is it like there, in that house?"

"I suppose it's like any other house belonging to people of means," said Patrick.

"But what exactly was it like? You came in the front door, right? What was there?"

Patrick scowled and scratched his face. "I don't want to think about it. It's over and done with. I waited. They paid me a quarter dollar."

James spat down the steps. "Quarter dollar!"

"I suppose that's fair," said Patrick.

"It's not fair if they could pay more," said James. "Now, think. What was inside the front door?"

"Why do you want to know?"

"Maybe I want to be their waiter someday, who knows?"

"Never," said Patrick, rolling his eyes at his friend.

"Humor me," said James. "Be a storyteller, for goodness' sake. Entertain me. We both know I can't afford to attend the theater or go down to a big city for the trotting races."

Patrick cleared his throat. "All right," he said. "There was a hall in the center. Gas lamps that smelled bad. Hot air from vents. There was a living room and parlor on the left, a dining room and library on the right."

"Details, me man. You ain't much of a storyteller."

Patrick smacked at a fly by his ear. "All right," he

said. "In the hall there was a tall mirror with a gold frame. There was a red runner all the way to the back of the house, and a matching red runner going up the stairs to the second floor."

"Persian runners?"

"I don't know. How would I know?"

"I need to know," said James. "There's an old white-haired rascal I know who pays me for much of what I take, and he then ships the items off elsewhere for sale. He's a crafty old thief, but we get along on the occasions when we do business. He taught me the value of things. Persian runners are the best. Now, have they got a dog?"

"I don't think so. I didn't see a dog. Why?"

"No matter. What else is there?"

"Narrow tables lining the hall, full of gimcracks and such."

"Now you're talking, Patrick. What kind of gimcracks?"

"Every sort you could imagine, and then some you probably couldn't. Figurines, little oil and gas lamps merely for decoration. Big mirrors. Tiny mirrors. Little paintings in frames. So much you could only walk in single file in the hall. And in the parlor, there was an upright piano with tidies lining the top, and vases on top of the tidies and another lamp shaped like a dragon."

James nodded, pulled a gumdrop from his pocket, and offered it to Patrick. Patrick hesitated, then put it in his mouth. "Amazing place, it seems," said James.

"Yes," said Patrick. "All the rooms were so furnished that you could barely turn around. Chairs, tables. I've never seen quite so much excess in one place at one time."

"Country boy." James smiled.

"Perhaps," said Patrick. "But at least we could walk about in our old house without worrying that we would break something for doing so!" He grinned. "And anything we had wasn't worth so much that we'd cry if it did break."

"I wonder if all large houses are decorated in such detail," said James.

"Why do you care?" asked Patrick. "Are you planning on becoming a respectable gentleman now, with a job as a clerk or policeman so you can marry well and buy a house? If so, you best make enough money to hire several cooks and a maid and a waiter on party days."

James said nothing, but the sudden change in his grin cleared up Patrick's confusion.

"James," said Patrick. "James, don't."

"Are you a mind reader as well as a waiter and mill worker, Patrick? Such skills could take you far," James said.

"No, James, you can't," Patrick said.

"What do you mean, Paddy?" James's cheeks twitched with glee. "I can do what I want."

"Please don't go to the Clatterbucks'. Leave them alone."

James stood up and stretched, his arms popping. "Now, Paddy, don't get yourself in a stew. I've honed me trade, and I won't be caught."

"Shh, speak more softly," said Patrick as he looked back over his shoulder, through the open door to where his family slept in the small flat. "It's not about being caught."

James popped another gumdrop into his mouth, chewed it silently, then said, "Aye, it is. It's not wrong if you don't get caught."

It's about Nancy. It's about John. James wouldn't only be taking advantage of the mother and daughter, but of the sister and brother as well. "Leave, James," said Patrick. "I don't want to talk about this anymore."

"Patrick, you know your way around in the house. You could be our eyes, Robbie's and mine. You think they'd miss anything we'd take? You yourself said you had never seen such excess. You yourself said you didn't like them."

"I didn't like what they were like," said Patrick. He remembered the ponies. He remembered the fallen tray, the angry dowager, the sting of fury he'd felt when Mary had said he smelled.

"We won't be long there," said James. "Just a few minutes at the most, but enough time to pick up some valuable items to sell. This, my friend, is something you can do for your mother. An extra income to supplement that pathetic mill pay."

Suddenly the September air seemed very cold indeed. Patrick began to shake.

"Hey, Paddy, we have to do what we have to do. We'll go tomorrow night, around midnight. What do you say?" James's hand came down on Patrick's shoulder, and Patrick was glad he didn't mention the trembling.

"Perhaps," Patrick said finally. "You might have a point."

"Aye! They won't miss a thing, and if they do, it

won't make them starve. It won't throw them into the streets for lack of it. They won't end up in a tenement building with no clean water and no heat, or in a shanty, trying to make a living working in a stinking mill for loss of a few gimcracks."

"Perhaps I will come with you. I don't know. Let me think on it."

James clapped Patrick on the back and said, "Think on it. I'll be off now, Paddy. Tomorrow I'll be by at midnight, and if you're here, the three of us will slip down to the river and the Clatterbucks' fancy house. We'll make it there by one. People are usually well asleep by then."

Patrick nodded, but his neck hurt in doing so. He was still shaking, and it wouldn't ease. "Perhaps."

"You'll be glad you decided to share the vision!" said James as he slipped down the steps and vanished into the night.

"Only time will tell," Patrick whispered to the empty space where James had sat. He rubbed his arms vigorously, trying to rid himself of the trembling before he collected his journal and pen and went in to bed.

17

PATRICK HAD SUGGESTED the three of them eat their noon meal together today, even though it was only Monday. Abigail had questioned it, but Liam had thought it was a fine idea. "Yes," he'd said as they'd walked across the workers' bridge with the other operatives at a quarter to six that morning. "Now we'll eat together on Mondays and Wednesdays."

"No, no, not two days a week," said Patrick. "Not an addition but a trade. Only this week."

"Why?" asked Liam. He picked up a stick and flung it through the bridge railing to the churning river below.

Because I don't know what is going to happen this evening, Patrick thought. *If I go with James to the Clatterbucks' tonight, who knows where I might be come morning?* But he said, "Just tell your Mr. Gilbert that I'll be coming up so he can unlock the door and let me in. He will, won't he?"

Abigail shrugged. The overseer in Spinning Room #4 liked Liam enough to let Patrick into the room on Wednesdays, but this might be too much. "I don't know, but I'll ask," she said.

"Thank you."

Several children raced past the O'Neills on the bridge, squeezing through the knot of adults and vanishing. Liam took off after them.

Abigail and Patrick walked together. Then Abigail said, "Patrick, you seem to have a lot on your mind."

"I always have a lot on my mind."

"But more than usual. I know you get up at night and go outside. Tell me, are you meeting a girl?"

"No!"

"Then you are writing a book, aren't you? You've always wanted to. You are writing a book and you are going to sell it for a lot of money. You just don't want to say anything yet. Am I right? You'll write a book and make so much money we won't have to work in the blasted mill any longer."

Patrick found himself almost smiling. Abigail believed he could do something with his writing. "Sure," he lied. "That's what I'm doing. But don't you tell anyone. It's a secret until it's done."

Abigail said, "I won't! That's wonderful, Patrick. I'd do anything to get out of the mill, and maybe this will be our answer."

They stepped off the bridge and passed through the gates of the mill yard, bumping along in the sea of workers. Before them and on both sides, the brick buildings of the complex stretched. In the center of the yard, Abigail would go right to climb the stairs to the spinning floor, and Patrick would go left, then around the building to the storage room next to the train tracks.

"Ask your overseer about today," Patrick reminded his sister as they parted.

The storage room was beginning to hum with activity. New crates that were stacked outside in the yard had to be brought inside and placed in rows. Men grumbled, stretching in preparation for the long day.

Patrick dipped his tin cup into the bucket of water for a quick sip before starting. Last night, in his bed, he'd calculated that he would need to save over one hundred more dollars if he was to go to college. He'd written:

I might as well dream of being the king of England. Today and every day from now on, work will be only that. Not for the future, but for the brain-numbing present. Food, rent, food, rent. A cycle of minimums, nothing more. I'm a horse walking circles, grinding my life away. I can't feel anything anymore. This is the worst day of my life, except for the day that Father died.

Patrick tossed the rest of the water onto the floor. Mr. Steele wiped his face with a dirty handkerchief and said, "Morning."

Patrick nodded in response, and then the first loads of cotton cloth came in on the carts and the day began.

18

PATRICK, ABIGAIL, AND Liam sat together for their noon dinner break in the filthy aisle next to Abigail's spinning frames. Mr. Spilman had agreed, to the dismay of Mr. Depper, to let Patrick trade a day for a day. And Liam had coaxed his own overseer, Mr. Gilbert, to unlock the doors when Patrick had pounded from outside on the stairs.

The spinning room was very large, filled with the long machines that made spools of thread from the coarser cotton fibers. When running, the machines had to be tended carefully; broken threads had to be tied and full spools replaced with empty ones in the blink of an eye. Windows were never opened, because the air needed to be warm and damp to prevent frequent thread breakage. If the room wasn't humid enough, it was sprayed down with water.

Making fabric wasn't a complex process, but it was backbreaking and tedious. The raw cotton came in on the trains, was combed free of tangles, dirt, and other impurities on the dreaded toothed carding machines, spun into thread on spools on the spinning machines, then woven on looms, cut, and packed for shipment. There was not a job within these walls that was without danger from bad air, vicious machines, or too much noise.

Seated all around the O'Neills were the workers who kept the spinning machines running and who took off full spools and put empty ones on. The operatives were primarily women because this job offered lower pay. Men, most people believed, were heads of their families and therefore should get better-paying jobs. The spinners talked among themselves and munched on whatever they'd packed in their pails. A good number of them paused to dip snuff from apron pockets. They claimed it helped reduce the irritating effects of lint in their throats.

Liam had dumped his pail out onto his lap, while both Abigail and Patrick ate one piece at a time out of their own pails.

"So tell us truly, Patrick," Abigail asked. "Why did you prefer Monday to Wednesday for our dinner together?"

He shrugged. It wasn't something he could explain. He took a bite of his pear half and couldn't taste it at all.

"You make no sense," she said.

"True. I don't."

"You keep making changes and they will stop our family lunches altogether. You know we can only do it because Mr. Gilbert has a liking for Liam. Others resent us at times and have said so."

"It's just this week. I promise." He could promise that, truly. Because if he was caught stealing, he'd never eat another lunch with his brother and sister in the mill. He'd be eating in the town jail, or worse.

Liam thumped Patrick on the arm. "You aren't eating your dinner." He leaned over and tickled Patrick in the ribs, hoping for a laugh. Patrick knew this, and forced himself to grin. "I'm all right, little brother," Patrick said. "Just hot and tired is all. The bundling has been especially furious these past weeks, what with the new looms upstairs and the river being so high and fast. I've got a third more to do in the same time, it seems."

Liam said, "They should hire another boy or girl for doffing and oiling. I've got two machines to attend. Two of those long, blasted things! It used to be easier, but now my head spins, just like the bobbins, so fast I can hardly see. I've been kicked twice today for not moving quickly enough."

"I'm sorry," said Patrick.

Then Abigail said, "Oh, there is Mr. Lance!"

Patrick swiped sweat from his eyes and watched the man as he strolled about, watching over his charges.

He was younger than most of the overseers and second hands at the mill, in his midtwenties at the most. He seemed energetic, with neatly combed blond hair and a trim mustache. His clothes, although coated with lint, were in good repair and of good quality. But it was clear he was none too happy to be in the noisy mill. He strode boldly as though he were only passing through.

"I don't know him," said Patrick. "Many second

hands move up from other jobs, but I've never seen him before, and I've worked all over this place. How long has he been here?"

"About six months," said Abigail.

"And where did he come from?" asked Patrick.

"I'm not sure," said Abigail. "Sarah says he must be the son of a stockholder, with those clothes. Isn't he fine?"

"Why would a stockholder's son work as a second hand? That's beneath his station."

"I don't know and I don't care," said Abigail. She touched her face and rose up on her knees a little. "He isn't married."

"What importance is that?"

Abigail turned a furious eye on her younger brother. "Don't be naive. And I won't say more in front of Liam."

"Abigail, you know nothing about this man. He kicked your little brother."

"I know, and I'm sorry for that. But Liam does tend to dawdle, if you haven't noticed. And Mr. Lance didn't really kick hard."

"He kicked hard," said Liam.

"Would you two just be quiet?" said Abigail. "You don't know anything!"

"Don't make a spectacle," said Patrick. "And don't do anything foolish."

Abigail pushed loose hairs back from her face. Her mouth was set with resolve. "I'll do what I have to do," she said.

Mr. Lance passed them, staring straight ahead. Abigail's gaze followed him for a moment. She said, "Eat your meal, Patrick. You've only got a few minutes before the break is over. I won't have you here any longer, trying to spoil my chances." Her eyes twitched and her mouth set in a straight line.

"He kicked our brother," Patrick said. But Abigail ignored him.

Patrick pretended to chew his food, but he couldn't swallow it, and when time came to go out, he spit most of it back into his pail.

19

STEPPING OFF THE bridge onto Burris Street, Patrick wiped rainwater from his eyes and said, "Go on home without me tonight. I've got something to do."

Liam's nose wrinkled. "Like what? It's raining. What have you got to do in the rain?"

"I know it's raining. Just go on."

"But why?" asked Abigail.

"It doesn't matter. Just do this for me, all right?"

"I don't understand," said Abigail.

Frustrated, Patrick drew his fists up in his pockets. "You don't have to understand everything I do, do you? Can't I ever have time to do anything by myself? I just need time by myself. Is that so odd?"

Abigail stared at Patrick a moment, then took Liam by the arm. "Fine, then," she said. "You go right ahead. Don't melt."

His brother and sister strode up Burris as Patrick moved over and waited under the lip of the supply store's roof. He watched workers come in and out of the store. The red-haired girl he thought was cute came out with her father, and he turned his head and dipped his chin into the collar of his coat, hoping she wouldn't recognize him tonight.

When his sister and brother were out of sight, he walked back out to the road. An old man, digging through a pile of rubbish beside a shop door, looked up at him, water coursing from the brim of his battered hat, and said, "You got something for me, boy?"

Patrick said, "Nothing, you worthless bum." The cruel words stung his lips, but he held on to the burn to punish himself. He walked up Burris, gaslights humming in the growing darkness, passing the closed shops and men who were coming out of shop doors, locking them and double-checking them because there were always thieves wanting to help themselves. He headed for Charlotte Road.

Mrs. Wilson had wanted him to visit again. "Why not tonight?" he mumbled to himself. "Maybe she can talk me out of going with James."

He quickly climbed her steps and tapped on her door. He tipped his head and listened. "Mrs. Wilson?" he called. A little girl, farther down the hall in near darkness, said, "Hey, mister, where you going?"

Patrick sneered and said, "Go home, little girl. There are dangerous men about!"

She squealed and ran into her flat, slamming the door.

Now I'm talking like this to children, Patrick thought. *What is wrong with me?* "Mrs. Wilson?"

The door opened, and he went inside.

She was wearing a pale pink dress, old but attractive. She smiled broadly and touched his arm in tentative yet friendly greeting. Motioning to the wooden chair for Patrick, she sat opposite. The room smelled good, like cooked apples. The cookstove was scrubbed, the wooden floor had been washed. Clean bowls and plates lined the shelf, and beside them, the silver tea set gleamed.

Mrs. Wilson handed a note to Patrick.

So glad you came back! I love visitors. How was your day at the mill?

Patrick looked up from the paper. He said, "The same. It's always the same." He wanted to tell her of his despair, but was hoping, instead, that she would read it in his tone, in his face. "Work is hard. I don't think the world will ever run out of cotton for cloth."

Mrs. Wilson leaned back her head as if to chuckle. She wrote:

You may be right. And people will always want more cloth, so work is steady. That's good.

Patrick felt like balling this note up. Instead, he put it on his leg. Rainwater dripped from his clothes to her floor, making small puddles. "It's not so good. Our wages are lower now than they were a year ago. So many people are needing jobs now. We Yankees. The immigrants, flooding in, wanting work. Competition is fierce for those jobs. The immigrants have been willing to work for less pay, so the mill owners have brought the wage levels down for us all. Everyone loses, Mrs. Wilson. Everyone, that is, except the stockholders." He paused and blew out an angry breath. "Everyone except people like the Clatterbucks."

Mrs. Wilson wasn't smiling now. She had folded her hands across her lap, and her head was tilted. She nodded, sighed, then lifted her pen again.

You not only look like my Andrew, but you sound like he used to sound. He saw how bad things could be when we worked back at Pemberton. He often said, "The rich men line their pockets with gold. But they should make it fairly, with fibers and not with our blood." Andrew had many listening to him. I loved to hear him as much as anyone. Then he led the turnout and found the company to be stronger than he was.

Patrick read the note. He said, "I may feel like that, but as I've said, I can't see myself going out on strike. I'm not that brave."

As I've said, there are different ways of fighting. Different kinds of bravery. You came up here to visit me, and you didn't even know me. You may well have thought me to be a crazy woman, but you came. You are brave. And as a writer, you can be a powerful fighter. Words have strength of their own.

Patrick looked away from the woman. Surely she must be able to see that he was nothing special.

I believe you have a good heart. You'll follow it.

Patrick looked at the floor. He hesitated, then said, "Mrs. Wilson . . ."

And then the door was shoved open, and a man came into the tiny room. He was tall and pale with a large, bent nose. When he swiped his hat from his head, his bald head reflected the lamplight.

"Mr. Steele!" said Patrick.

The man frowned and pushed the door closed with his foot, looking from the old woman to Patrick. He said, "Mother, what is this boy doing here?"

Mrs. Wilson began to write, but Patrick stood quickly, notes fluttering to the floor. He stammered, "I came to visit. She invited me."

Mr. Steele tossed his hat onto the small table. His face flushed red, more red than Patrick could ever remember, even on the hottest summer days in the storage room. "How's that? She can't speak! Are you checking on me, boy?"

"No!"

"Have the supervisors paid you to spy on me, to find a reason to let me go? Has my past so stained me that I'll not be wanted anywhere? There's nothing I've instigated in Leeland. I have never even encouraged men to turn out, you know that!"

"I know that, Mr. Steele," said Patrick. "Wait, please."

Mrs. Wilson stood from her chair and jammed a note into her son's hand. He read it, stammered, then shook his head. He walked to the window and, much as his mother often did, put his hands on the sill and gazed down into the street. Only there were very few hairs stirred by the breeze.

Patrick's heart was hammering. Mr. Steele was a

rabble-rouser? This bald, thin, coughing man didn't have a leader's bone in his body!

Mrs. Wilson scribbled a quick note and gave it to Patrick.

Will you stay for dinner?

Patrick shook his head. "No, thank you." He'd wanted to hear her words of wisdom, but there was no way he could talk candidly with Mr. Steele in the room. Maybe fate had played this hand for him. He waved at Mrs. Wilson, then left the flat.

At home, on the steps, he wrote,

People change. Mr. Steele changed. I've changed. I know the truth about myself now. I'm a mill rat. It's time I understood and accepted that.

He kicked a road stone and sent it flying.

I'm just a mill rat. So be it.

20

PATRICK, HOLD STILL. I can't pin this if you keep pacing round the kitchen!"

Abigail sat at the kitchen table, straight pins in her hand. Her face was pinched in a frustrated scowl. Patrick, sighing, wandered back from the window. "Sorry."

Abigail grabbed his sleeve once more and said, "This isn't going to take but a minute. You just have to make your feet stay put. I have to let the cuffs down in that shirt. You look like a scarecrow with such long arms."

"Scarecrow!" chuckled Liam, who was in the bedroom with the door open, an oil lantern on the floor at his feet. He was cleaning the family's shoes with a rag, trying to keep the leather from cracking any more than it already had.

Patrick tried to stand still with his arms out as Abigail adjusted the freed hems of the sleeves. He knew they wouldn't be long enough even if she let them out to the very ends, because it was a shirt he'd had for two years, and his arms had grown like vines.

"We'll have to use some of our family savings to buy cotton cloth for a new shirt for you soon," said Abigail in resignation. "It can't be helped."

"I suppose," said Patrick. "The mill should give us some as bonus, but that will never happen, will it?" In the flat next door, something slammed the wall. A rough voice yelled something, and a woman began to cry.

"So," called Liam. "You really talked to the witch? You really scolded her, and told her she best leave us be?"

For the tenth time since he'd come home, Patrick said, "Yes, Liam. She cowered at my words and slunk back into her flat. She'll never gawk at us again."

"That's wonderful!"

"I suppose it is," Patrick said. He had thought of telling his sister and brother the truth about Mrs. Wilson, but the idea of their seeing him as a hero was too strong. He was desperate for them to think highly of him tonight; their awestruck admiration was like a strong, if temporary, tonic. The truth of the old woman would have been an empty victory.

There was another thump on the wall, and another shout.

"I wish the Pattersons would quiet down at night," said Liam. "They yell so much. Maybe they would be nicer if they just got some rest."

"Hush and clean those shoes," said Abigail. "We haven't got time to worry about Pattersons. Patrick, hold still!"

Patrick again tried to plant his feet and make

them behave. But nervousness thrummed through his muscles like the waves on the river. Tonight Robbie and James were going to the Clatterbucks' house to rob them. What would Mother say if she knew?

A moment later, after some tugging and *tsk*ing, Abigail said, "There. Done. Take the shirt off and I'll stitch the hems up."

Patrick slipped out of his shirt and gave it to his sister. He said, "If we were as rich as the people Mother works for, you wouldn't have to take such care with such a poor excuse for a shirt, trying to make it into something it doesn't want to be."

"Wouldn't that be something!" said Liam. "Polly Bruce says her uncle, who lives in Baltimore, is so rich he has a tailor to make different shirts for each day of the week! Seven shirts, can you see that?"

"My," said Abigail. She threaded a needle, holding it close to the light of the kitchen's lamp, and slipped a knot into the thread's end. "To be so wealthy! Mother could have a fine house with a porch, and she could sit and knit all day if she wished. Or take a nap."

Liam came into the kitchen and put the shoes on the table. "I'll be an overseer one day, and will make enough money to buy Mother a nice house by the river."

Patrick looked at his brother's nine fingers but said nothing.

"I'll be out of the mill in a year, maybe less," said Abigail. She held one shirt cuff up close and ran the thread in and out, securing the raw end of the material. "Just you wait."

"How is that?" asked Liam.

Patrick went to the kitchen window and looked out at the wooden steps and the black, callous night. "Answer your little brother, Abigail," he said, looking around.

"Oh," his sister said. "I have my plans." She gave Patrick a furious look but said no more on the matter.

The wall between the O'Neills and the Pattersons was slammed again, and the man began yelling. His voice rambled on and on, rising in pitch and going down again.

"They have to be quiet," said Abigail, her voice pinched with irritation. "We need to get some sleep soon."

Patrick walked over to the wall and put his ear against it. "That's rude," said Abigail, but Patrick flicked his hand at her.

Patrick couldn't hear the words, but the emotion was instantly clear. This wasn't the usual Patterson argument; something was wrong. Both Mr. and Mrs. Patterson were crying, yelling, pleading.

"Patrick, get away from that wall this moment," said Abigail. "Have you no manners at all?"

Liam said, "Patrick, stop it."

"Shhh," he said. He pushed his ear harder against the wood, causing it to sting. He could hear footsteps, pacing. Then Mrs. Patterson was against the wall, and her agonized words were finally clear.

Patrick listened, swallowing hard, then moved away and dropped into a kitchen chair.

"What?" asked Abigail.

Patrick put his forehead down on his arms. He could smell his own skin, feel the light tickle of the hairs. Surprisingly, tears came to his eyes, and he rubbed them away.

"Patrick, what is it?" demanded Abigail.

"It will never stop. We're locked in, like forgotten ponies."

"What are you talking about?"

"Their son was crippled today. Richard Patterson. His legs were cut off," Patrick said, his head not lifting, his words buffeted against the skin on his arms. "Richard. The only one of the family to ever give us a smile. I liked him."

Abigail shook her head.

Patrick spat, "Are you surprised? Should any of us be surprised? What have we learned these years in the mills, Abigail? That hard work will make our lives better? I think not!"

"You're scaring me, Patrick," said Liam.

Abigail said, "We have to take something to them. Mother would be angry if we didn't take bread, something. We should be good neighbors in this terrible time!"

"You visit them, Abigail!" Patrick shouted, his head going up, his eyes locking with his sister's. "We have our own matters to attend to. We can't save the world!"

"What's wrong with you? What is making you talk like this?"

"Nothing," Patrick said. "Nothing. I'm just wonderful." He stormed out of the flat and sat on the steps to wait for midnight and for James. He would go tonight. It was decided. His arms itched as though someone were tickling them with feathers.

Lucy came home, climbing the flights of wooden

steps with slow, steady footsteps. She frowned when she saw Patrick on the landing, but he assured her he was fine and just wanted a little time alone. He didn't tell her about Richard Patterson. Abigail would do that. A half hour or so later, he heard no more sounds in the O'Neill flat, and knew they had all gone to bed.

Across the alley, in other brick tenements, other families were sleeping. Only rare and occasional lights could be seen from windows. The air was scented with another impending rain, and the sky was a pewter cloud, heavy and threatening thunder and lightning.

Storm's coming, Patrick thought. He crossed his arms and put his chin on them. *Storm is on the way.*

"Pssst!"

Patrick glanced down. James, in a dark, tattered overcoat, broad-brimmed black hat, and scarf, stood gazing upward. The overcoat and hat looked much like Union issue from the war. This startled Patrick for a moment. His father had worn a hat and coat just like that. Where would James have found old uniforms?

Besidc James was another form in dark clothes, head down. Both had burlap bags tucked over their arms.

"You coming?"

Patrick nodded.

"Good, then. Let's be off! We must have this done before the rain. I don't care to trade a chill for a dollar."

Patrick took a deep breath, then slipped down to the alley. He had no coat to wear. He suddenly wished he'd put on the wool shirt, or the jacket he wore in winter. Not because he was so cold, but because covering would give him more of a sense of secrecy. It would cover his exposed nerves and calm him.

"You're shivering," said James.

"No, I'm not," said Patrick.

"Nervous?"

"Should I be?"

James grinned, then put his hand on the shoulder of the person with him. He turned the person around so Patrick could see the face. "Here's me Robbie. Robbie, this is me best friend, Patrick Thomas O'Neill."

Patrick gasped audibly. Robbie, dressed in trousers and coat and cap, was a girl.

21

NOW, PADDY, I can't see why you're worried," said James, lighting a cigar as the three crept down side streets, moving toward the lane along the river. "Does it make a difference to you whether a thief be a boy or a girl?"

Patrick hadn't looked at Robbie—or Roberta, as James had explained—since they'd left Patrick's alley. He had his hands shoved into his trouser pockets, heavily. His suspenders cut into his shoulders, but he didn't care.

"Paddy," said James. "I asked you a question."

"It matters," said Patrick.

"Why?"

They reached an intersection, and James peeked around the corner first before waving them on. They hurried across the open space and into another narrow road. There was only another quarter mile until they reached their target.

"Patrick," hissed James, blowing out a thick puff of smoke. "I asked you why."

"I don't know," said Patrick. Robbie walked beside him quietly, with a soft tread.

"It's all right for a man to be crooked, then, and not a woman?"

"I suppose so."

"A woman should be virtuous, Paddy?"

"My mother and my sister work hard for their money."

"Robbie works hard for her money, too," said James. He drew on the cigar and grunted hoarsely. "Her mother worked hard, and she died for it. Came down with consumption because of that damned mill. Left Robbie alone, so where was she to go? She worked the mill for a while, then something happened and she was discharged. Either thievery or prostitution. Not much of a choice, eh?"

Suddenly a strong female voice said, "James, you needn't tell him anything. He doesn't care, and I don't waste breath on those that don't care."

"Aye, Robbie, don't worry. He's good stock, he is. Irish from a ways back, like us," said James. "He cares."

"Don't think so," said Robbie. She looked directly at Patrick then, and he at her. Her eyebrows drew a distrustful line across her shadowed face. Her eyes, which sparkled golden brown in the faint haze from a distant streetlight, narrowed and twitched. "He don't live in the Grove, does he, out in the shanties with the others? He don't have our way of talking. He sounds like a native-born to me."

"He is native-born," said James. "I told you that. But he's a fair shake."

Robbie took a deep, loud breath, then turned her attention forward. She shifted her burlap bag from one arm to the other.

James dropped his cigar to the road and pressed the smoldering tip out with his shoe. He said, "She was a worker at Leeland. Spent her time in a carding room, and you know how hard that work is. Those machines'll eat you up and spit you out."

Like Liam, thought Patrick. *Like Richard Patterson.*

Robbie swore and kicked at a rock on the road.

"But being such a pretty girl," James went on, "it was too much for a new second hand, and he took advantage."

Patrick stopped in his tracks. "What are you saying?"

"She's got a bairn on the way now," said James.

"A . . . ?"

"Bairn, Paddy. A child."

Patrick looked from James to Robbie. Both stared at him, looking so much alike in their clothes, only Robbie's face thinner and more drawn, and James's face covered with several days' unshaven growth.

"A second hand?" asked Patrick. "And now there's going to be a bastard child?"

Suddenly James was on Patrick, his fist in Patrick's stomach, his other hand wrapped tightly about Patrick's neck. Patrick gasped and tried to pull free.

"Don't you ever say that about me, Robbie!" James snarled. "There's no bastard!"

"James, stop it!" Patrick managed.

"There's no bastard! Robbie's me wife, Patrick!"

"What?" Patrick struggled, trying to get away.

James gave a shove, sending Patrick to the ground. "I said she's me wife!"

James stepped back, blowing angry breaths and slamming his fists one in the other, as though he was trying hard not to strike Patrick again. "Aye, you heard right. I found her one night a month ago, dismissed from Leeland Mill for un-Christian character. Un-Christian!" James spat the word out as if it was foul to his mouth. "The second hand violates her, makes her a mother before her time, before she is even fifteen, and they deem her a bad lot! She was curled up under some stairs, by rubbish piles, fighting not to cry."

"I didn't cry," said Robbie.

"I know you didn't cry, you fought hard," said James. Then to Patrick he said, "If I was a mill worker at that moment, I'd have called to my fellow operatives for a turnout. I'd have beat the man, then shouted and caused as much trouble for the mill as possible. But as it is, I'm only a street urchin. I had nothing to offer this girl."

"It's getting late," said Robbie. "We best get down to that house and get our job done." She walked off, leaving James and Patrick behind.

"And you've married this girl?" asked Patrick.

"Well, married in me mind and in hers," said James softly now. "We's as good as married. We stick together now." He sighed. Then he smiled a wan smile. "Never could see me as a husband, could you, Patrick?"

Patrick said, "No."

"Enough dallying," James said. "Gimcracks waiting. Ah, glimmering, gilt-edged gimcracks!"

"Yes."

The boys trotted quietly down the road and caught up with Robbie, who was quite a ways ahead.

22

THE CLATTERBUCK HOUSE, standing tall and foreboding in its fence-enclosed yard, was dark. No lights were visible. The family had retired for the night.

Robbie, Patrick, and James stood out on the lane, huddled at the base of an oak tree, watching for any signs that might indicate someone inside was still up and moving about. The other large houses along the lane were dark, too, and only a single dog, deep within the confines of one home, barked a string of muffled complaints. Overhead, thunder rumbled, but no rain fell.

The Clatterbuck house was silent. Still. And sleeping. James tapped Patrick on the arm. "We'll lead on in, Paddy. I ain't asking you to take anything this go-round. Just you remind us where you saw the best trinkets, and if there is anything we might stumble over in the dark."

"I don't remember that well," said Patrick.

"Sure you do. It'll be a lark, this trip out. And you be at the ready at the door when time comes to leave."

"How do we get inside?"

"We check doors, then windows," said James. "Bound to be something loose or ill shut. Have a knife to pry a loose latch if need be. We'll be in and out and have time to celebrate before the old sun even has an inkling to come up and shine."

"There's many a slip between a cup and a lip," said Patrick.

"But the nectar's sweet once it's in the mouth," answered James. "Here." He pulled the scarf from around his neck and handed it to Patrick. "Your face is as white as a fish belly. Wrap your head and stay low."

Patrick nodded. James pulled his collar up and then ran out from the tree, planting his hand on top of the waist-high fence and hurtling it with the skill of a deer. Robbie followed, hopping the fence just as easily. Patrick tied the scarf around his head as he would have tied a bandage for a toothache, then scurried after. His leaping of the fence wasn't as graceful as the other two, but he made it on the first bound, and felt quite proud.

But his heart thundered painfully.

The grass inside the yard was shorter than that outside it by the lane. Clearly Jed, the gardener and livestock man, had trimmed it in the last few days. The grass trimmed. And what of the ponies and their hooves?

"Psst, come on," James called in a whisper. He and Robbie were already up on the front porch. Patrick followed, stepping lightly, hoping there was no squeaking board or loose nail to trip them up and give them away.

"We'll try this window first," said James, moving behind a tall potted fern and touching the sill. "Best to go through a window if possible. They don't have to open as much, and let in less air and less sound. You stay low with Robbie there, and I'll give it a try. If it goes up, Robbie will go first, then me, then you. Now, what might I find below this window inside?"

Patrick shook his head. "I don't know."

"Shake your head," said Robbie. "You must remember. James said you knew this house."

Patrick tried to think. The room was a study, full of many bookshelves and vases and chairs. But what was where?

"Think, Paddy," said James. He pushed his palms against the window. The glass wouldn't budge. He tugged the knife from his pocket and picked at the seam. Still it wouldn't move.

"Locked," he said. "And no latch I can pick." He climbed out from behind the fern, his face set in new determination.

The window on the other side of the porch was locked as well, tight and secure with not a loose space to be jimmied.

"But look," said Robbie, who was standing at the front door. "The wood here is flaking. See by the knob? Carve it a bit, and I'll get a finger in to flick the latch over."

"Good," said James. Patrick stood back, feeling helpless and frightened, as James began to whittle away chunks of wood from the space by the knob.

Patrick flushed cold, then hot. This delay was making the whole escapade unbearable.

But then James whispered, "Aye, Robbie, those little fingers are better used here than in some blasted mill!"

The door was swinging open, and with blessed silence. Someone had oiled the hinges. Lucy O'Neill, possibly. "She does her job well," Patrick said softly to himself.

The three crept inside the dark, cluttered hallway. They stopped a few feet from the door, and James reached back for Patrick's hand. He leaned around Robbie and muttered, "Where are the best items?"

There were items all over, many of value, Patrick was certain, but which ones would bring the most cash on sale? He couldn't know. So he pointed to the left, into the parlor where the piano stood with the dragon lamp. "Be careful," he whispered, his voice sounding in his ears like trumpeting calls. "There are things everywhere that can be knocked over."

James and Robbie nodded. They moved slowly into the room on the left. Patrick stood by the door, ready to pull it open when it was time to get away.

There was silence, then a soft tapping and clinking sound as James and Robbie picked up trinkets and slipped them into pockets and into the burlap bags. Patrick stared ahead at the staircase. Up those steps his mother's employers slept, unaware of the intruders.

From the parlor came airy murmurs of appreciation. Patrick was struck with a bizarre sense of pride beneath his fear. Pride that he'd brought James to a house with things good enough to put his friend at awe.

And then there was a thumping upstairs.

Patrick's jaw dropped open, his blood stopped in his veins. *No!* He looked into the parlor, at the shadowy figures of James and Robbie, afraid to speak to tell them of the sound, terrified not to.

"Ah, beautiful," James said softly.

Patrick took several steps forward, his gaze locked on the grayness at the top of the stairs. Maybe it was only the creaking house, settling on its foundation. He skirted a hall table and put his hand on the bottom of the banister, tilted his head, and squinted to see farther. There were no lights up there, no visible movement.

"And this is for you," whispered James. "I have chosen something special for you, me friend!"

Robbie said, "That should hold us. Let's be out of here."

There was another creaking sound, this time accompanied by a flash of light. A lamp. Someone was awake upstairs!

"James!" hissed Patrick.

The light up the stairs seemed to explode into full brightness. There was a man's shout, a woman's gasp.

"James!" It was a cry now, because there were shadows in the light at the top of the stairs, shadows moving quickly, feet hitting the landing and then the steps.

There was a crash in the parlor as James and Robbie scrambled, trying to get around the chairs and trinket shelves and out to the hall.

"Hold the door!" James screamed.

Patrick stumbled backward, feeling frantically for the door, watching the couple descending the stairs.

"Halt!" shouted George Clatterbuck. "Halt or I'll shoot!"

"Run!" cried Patrick.

Then Robbie and James were beside him, around him, past him, racing out the door and into the night. Patrick slammed into the doorframe, still staring at the man and woman and the gun, which was now leveled in his direction.

"Halt!"

Patrick backed through the front door just as a bullet whizzed past his ear. Mrs. Clatterbuck screamed.

"Run, James!" Patrick shouted.

The man was faster than the woman. He leapt down the stairs two at a time, dressing coat flapping like a giant bird's wing. "Stop or I'll stop you dead!"

Spinning around, Patrick jumped off the porch onto the walkway. His ankle twisted beneath him as he hit, and he went down on his knees on the brick. That instant he was pushing himself upward, the palms of his hands ripped raw, shoving himself back to his feet. He teetered with the stabbing pain in his ankle, but the bullet that zipped over his head was enough incentive to ignore the pain. He ran down the walkway, into the shadows that were his only salvation.

Two more bullets, in quick succession, flew by.

He reached the fence and cleared it by a foot, but landed on the bad ankle with all his weight and cried out with the agony. Glancing back, he saw Mr. Clatterbuck on the porch, reloading his revolver, while his wife stood, silhouetted behind him, her hands wringing one inside the other. And then light from an upstairs window caught Patrick's gaze, and he looked up.

There was a girl there, his age, looking down into the yard, holding a candle to the glass.

It was Nancy, the oldest daughter. Nancy, who had taken Patrick's part at the cursed birthday party. Patrick swiped sweat from his eyes and stared. *Can she see me?* He could see Nancy in the candle glow, the mouth open slightly in surprise or fear, the hand against the closed window glass.

I'm sorry, Nancy, Patrick thought. *I didn't mean this against you.*

"Halt, thieves!" Mr. Clatterbuck aimed the revolver again, and Patrick ducked, missing a bullet. He scrambled up, wheezing, panting, his hands stupidly grabbing for air to pull him forward.

And then he had his balance.

He ran.

He had no idea where Robbie and James were at this moment, but it didn't matter. He raced along the lane, his ankle complaining with each step, away from the rich homes and the river, up toward the belly of the town where there would be buildings and street corners around which to hide. His lungs ached; his temples throbbed with the panic.

I want to go home!

He reached the end of the lane and darted into an alley behind a row of shops.

I'm safe! I'll make it home!

And then someone jumped out from behind an

empty wagon and tackled him, bringing him down hard, face in the stone and dirt.

"Ugh!" Patrick groaned as his jaw hit ground and sent a fire flash of pain up through his skull.

"You said my name!" It was James, screaming in his ear.

"Get off me!"

James turned Patrick over and straddled him, his hand clamped around Patrick's throat. Patrick twisted violently, trying to shake James off, but the boy clung tightly. "You said my name, you imbecile! You want me found? You want me hanged?"

Patrick slammed his fist into James's chest, and James grunted but didn't let go.

"James. . . . !" Patrick managed.

"Curse you!" James hit him in the head, the chest, the arms, each blow like a crack of steel against Patrick's body.

And then there was someone else beside James, taking his arm and yanking him sideways. His grip loosened on Patrick's throat. Patrick began to cough, clutching at his neck and rolling from beneath James, stopping with his face in the dirt of the road. There was Robbie's higher-pitched voice saying, "James, leave off him. He didn't do nothing wrong."

Patrick ached all over. His ankle, his lungs, and now his arms, chest, and throat. He knew he'd be bruised mightily by morning. And he wouldn't be surprised if something was broken.

"Patrick." It was Robbie, standing over him now. "Patrick, can you turn over?"

Patrick worked his elbows against the rough

ground. There was grit in his mouth and his eyes. He spit. Then he gingerly turned himself over and looked up at Robbie.

"James didn't mean to be so hard," she said. Her dark hat was off her head now. He could see she had fine, blond hair that was pulled back in a braid. "He didn't mean to hurt you."

It felt like he did, Patrick thought.

"But you shouldn't have said my name!" James stood by Robbie now, bending over slightly, staring at Patrick on the ground. "Paddy, you were so careless!"

Robbie looked at James. "There are hundreds of Jameses," she said. "I don't think you'll be found for a single name."

"Maybe," said James. "Maybe not."

Patrick forced himself to sit up. He touched his ankle, his arms. Nothing seemed broken, but they hurt dreadfully. He stood, sucking air through his teeth.

"No one seems to be after us," Patrick said. "We're safe."

James scowled, kicking at the alley dirt, swearing silently to himself. Then he said, "I'm sorry, Paddy. I just . . ." His voice trailed.

Patrick stood as straight as he could. "Yes, I know," he said to James.

Then James burst into uncontrollable laughter. He bent over, clutching his knees. "What a poor shot Mr. Clatterbuck turned out to be!" he said. "How many bullets were there? And not a one striking the target! He must have been on the rebel side during the war!"

Patrick was surprised to hear himself beginning to laugh, too. "I'll bet he was. I'll bet he killed himself a lot of trees and fences with that revolver of his!"

The boys laughed, long and hard, while Robbie stood by silently. And then, when the chuckling eased, she said, "I don't think he were such a poor aim, James."

James said, "What?"

Patrick's smile faded. He frowned at Robbie.

"He got me arm, James. I'm hit." She held up her left arm and tugged back the baggy sleeves of her coat and blouse. It was too dark in the alley to see red, but there was blood there on the skin, black and wet as tar.

"Gone clean through," she said. "In and out. I'm bleeding pretty bad."

James went to Robbie, catching her arm in his hands and pressing the wound. Robbie gasped, but didn't cry out. "Why didn't you say something before now?" asked James. His voice had changed; it was pinched with dread. "Robbie, why didn't you tell me right off?"

"We needed to get away," Robbie said.

"But you're hurt bad!"

"James, we needed to get away. Now we can tend to this." She sucked air with the pain. "I'll be all right."

"Give me the scarf!" James said. Patrick quickly unwound the scarf from his head and tossed it over. James wrapped it about the wound and drew it in tightly, tying the ends.

"You should see a doctor," Patrick said.

"No doctor works for free, Paddy," said James.

"And you think we can give trinkets for cash and not be traced to the crime?"

Patrick stood helplessly as James finished the makeshift bandage, then held Robbie in a clumsy, distraught embrace. After a moment, James collected the burlap bags they'd dropped in the alley, and fished around inside. He pulled out the dragon lamp that had been on the Clatterbucks' piano.

"This is for you, for your trouble," he said. "Take it and sell it. It'll make tonight worth your while."

Patrick didn't know what he was going to say until the words were tumbling out of his mouth. "I don't want it, James."

"Take the thing, Paddy."

"This is blood money, too. Like the mill's profit. Robbie's as wounded as a mill worker would be if she was struck by a flying shuttle on a loom. I won't have it."

James slammed the lamp back into the bag and collected both of them. He slipped his free hand gently around Robbie's waist, then said, "Suit yourself. I haven't time to argue. I've got to find a safe place for Robbie."

Patrick nodded numbly.

"When Robbie's resting tomorrow, what say we do the tobacco shop on Forsyth? I've not tried them, but tobacco is a dandy to many men, and I would think there are coins aplenty in such a shop."

"You want to keep on, after what's happened to Robbie?"

It was Robbie who answered, angrily. "You keep to your business, boy, and we'll keep to ours. I'm fine, and James is here for me."

"The Clatterbucks deserve to be robbed for the robbing they do of their workers," said James. "And the others, the shops and stores? Do you think any of them cares a whit for them that slaves away in the mills? "They do not! Why, it's the mills that owns the stores, and its the mill that sets the prices. So you tell me, Patrick, who's robbing who?" Then James turned, and he and Robbie limped down the alley and out of sight.

The Union cap had fallen to the road, and Patrick picked it up and held it in his hands. He put his face to the rough material and shut his eyes for a moment.

"James is wrong," he whispered.

The he opened his eyes again. "He's wrong!" he shouted to anyone, to no one. His voice echoed, and several distant dogs barked in response, kindred spirits of the night and the desolation.

23

September 18, 1870

Today at the mill there were rumblings about Richard Patterson's amputations. I heard men talking in whispers during the lunch break that enough was enough.

I pretended I didn't hear their talk, but I listened closely. The term "turnout" was on nearly all their lips. They want to strike tomorrow. I wonder what will happen if they do. There have been other strikes, but most of them small, and workers only ended up reprimanded or let go. But this seems to have the whole mill talking. Even Liam said there was quiet talk in the spinning room, and I heard the dock men chatter about it on our way home.

As I sit here on the steps, I am wearing the Union cap that James lost. It feels strange yet good on my head. What a silly comfort. Maybe I'm crazy like James, only I don't know it yet!

Maybe James is right. I wonder what the justice is

of men dying in a war to free the slaves, just so they can become slaves to the mills.

But it doesn't seem right what James is doing. Thieving isn't the answer. I know Polly Bruce told the truth about one thing. There is gold out west. There is money for the taking if someone could get there.

I'm tired.

I can hardly see the stars tonight at all. Everything seems so far away. The stars. Dreams. Everything.

24

THERE'S TALK OF a turnout on behalf of Richard Patterson," said Mr. Steele early Wednesday afternoon as he slammed a load of folded cloth into a crate. "Heard mutterings on my way to the mill this morning."

"I haven't heard a thing," said Patrick around a mouthful of nails.

"Well, now you have," said Mr. Steele. He pinched his nose and sniffed, then coughed out onto the floor. "Now you've heard from me. What're you going to do about it?"

Patrick hammered a nail into the corner of a crate lid, then moved to the next corner. He spit a nail into his hand and hammered this corner, too. Then he said, "Why should I do anything about it?"

"You know Richard. He was a bale breaker, and so were you before you moved here to packing. You must have worked with him for more than a year."

"Working together doesn't mean intimate acquaintance," said Patrick. He drove the final nail in and hoisted the crate onto a flat, wheeled dolly, then pulled an empty one from his stack and reached for more sheared cloth to fold.

"Didn't say intimate acquaintance," said Mr. Steele. He coughed onto the floor. It was hard to see in the dim, dusty light, but the phlegm seemed to have a red tint to it. "Just said you knew him. And a man crippled is a sorry thing."

Patrick sighed and scratched his forehead with the tip of his hammer. "I know him."

"Live near him, too, don't you?"

"All right, I live near him. Next door to him, in fact. What do you want me to say?"

Mr. Steele coughed, wiped his mouth, and glanced about the huge room, where packers were doing identical work: folding, packing, hammering. Other men pushed loaded handcarts out through the packing room door to the train tracks, where the crates were going into boxcars. Mr. Depper was talking with a packer not too far away, but well beyond hearing range considering the scraping of crates and the overhead pounding of the looms.

"I want you to say," said Mr. Steele, "that my mother hasn't tried to talk you into anything. She admired me once, but no longer. I want you to say you'll stay here with me and those who have sense about them."

"Your mother is a smart woman. She didn't try to talk me into anything. I'm not going out. Richard Patterson was a fool for stumbling in front of a train car."

"Good for you," said Mr. Steele. "That's sensible.

You strike and they'll look at me, too, working next to you and all. I can't have them thinking I'm not loyal."

The afternoon dragged on. The train took off with the fabric, heading for distant destinations.

But suddenly the sounds of the machines stopped. It was as if they had all died suddenly, without warning.

It was four o'clock. The set time.

"They're going out!" a packer shouted.

"Blast!" said Mr. Steele.

Patrick watched as some of the men crowded to the open door. He saw Mr. Depper, appearing from behind a stack of crates, his hands clenching.

"You men get back to your stations!" shouted Mr. Depper. "There is no need or concern outside for you!"

More men went to the door, some of them shouting now, pushing, angry and loud. They huddled together, heads whipping back and forth as if deciding to make a break for it. As if deciding whether Richard Patterson was incentive enough to go out the door, around the building, and join the others who protested mill conditions that could lead to such a crippling. The voices were those of old men, teenagers, middle-aged men. Some high, some low, some growling, some yelling. Through the stacks of crates and bundles of cloth Patrick could make out single words, echoing back.

"Death trap!"

"Inhuman!"

"Unify!"

The men glanced out at the sunlit train yard and

then back into the shadows, struggling with their decision. Mr. Depper was wringing his hands now, clearly taken aback. Mr. Spilman was out of the room, so it was Mr. Depper's task to go into the mob alone.

"Back to work, the whole of you!" he said. He hurried forward into the thickest pack of men, his chubby fists raised now, fleshy clubs that would have no impact, Patrick knew, if the men chose to go. "Don't do this! It will mean your jobs!"

"It might save our lives!" shouted someone in the mob.

Mr. Steele whispered, "Fools. The mill is stronger than we are. How does a rat stand up against a cat?"

Several men in the bunch broke and ran outside, calling back, "Let's all go! There's strength in numbers!" They were cheered on by the others, although some of those cheering were obviously not brave enough to follow.

Mr. Depper, wringing his hands, shouted, "You'll be sorry!"

"Strength in numbers," Patrick said softly. He'd never heard that saying before. "Strength in numbers," he repeated.

"They'll be sorry," said Mr. Steele.

"But if everyone goes, then who is sorry but the owners?" said Patrick. "They can't replace every operative, can they?"

Mr. Steele grabbed Patrick by the arm and drew him up close. Patrick had never seen the old man so furious. "Be quiet! We must save our jobs!"

Patrick looked at Mr. Steele, then back to the door, where only a third of the men had gone out to join the protest. Mr. Steele was right. Not everyone was going, and so those who did were fools.

"I'll be quiet," Patrick said. Mr. Steele let him go, and Patrick went back to fold cloth into yet another crate.

25

"THE TURNOUT WAS turned back so quickly," said Liam as the O'Neills walked home that night. "It was loud at first, with people leaving their frames and shouting, but only a few went out."

The night hung heavy; there were no stars, only the tainted yellow of heavy clouds, threatening rain. The Merrimack reflected the yellow, seeming to turn the world on its head.

"A lot of our men went out," said Patrick. "What happened after that, do you know?"

Abigail lifted her skirt slightly as they stepped from the bridge and down to the road. "The striking operatives didn't get far, I heard. They gathered in the front yard, yelling and demanding all mill machinery be turned off until there could be talk between operatives and owners. But the overseers got the clerks from the counting room and they all blocked the bridge. The workers would have rushed them, except the Leeland police showed up. They were threatened with arrest. They were told they would never work in another mill if they took this course. That cooled them down, and it was over."

"Our men were back in twenty minutes," said Patrick. "Was anyone hurt?"

"I don't think so," said Abigail.

"I wanted to go out with them," said Liam. "Only Abigail wouldn't let me."

"You, Liam? A striker?" asked Patrick.

"Richard Patterson was hurt. It could have been you, Patrick. Or me."

"Yes, but . . ." Patrick had nothing else to say. The matter was done and over. Not to bc thought of again. They walked another minute. Raindrops began to fall, at first slow, irregular plops, then heavier, rhythmic drips. Today they were going to the market before they went home; because of the operatives' late hours at the mill, farm folk would stay until dark with their wagons, waiting to make a few last sales. Patrick had in his pocket a little money with which to buy whatever vegetables were available, and to pick up a small bag of flour so Abigail could bake tonight.

"Strength in numbers," Patrick muttered, remembering the packer's shout.

"What?" asked Liam.

Patrick shook his head. "Nothing. It was nothing at all."

"Blast," said Abigail. She looked up, put her hands over her head, then lowered them. "If I should only be able to afford a parasol for rain. My hair will be a fright by the time I get home."

"At least it's not snow or sleet," said Liam. "It's not so cold."

Abigail smiled at her little brother and put her arm around him. "Optimist!" she laughed.

The market was one street over from Burris, at a wide intersection of laid brick. Much of the brick was ground down and shattered from wagon wheels and animal hooves, but it was still a busy gathering place for the poorer citizens of Leeland. As the rain continued its steady drone, Patrick bought cornmeal and wheat flour while Abigail and Liam chose beans, corn, and spinach. Patrick paid for each selection, then the family walked back to Burris and up to Charlotte. Then the downpour came.

Abigail shrieked and Liam laughed, and the three held their sacks over their heads as they raced to their tenement building. Patrick didn't even glance up as they passed Mrs. Wilson's window.

Lucy was home already, and was quite irritable. She was suffering with sniffles and a sore throat, and had reluctantly come home early when Mary Clatterbuck had complained of the maid's constant sneezing. Abigail was subsequently irritable, as well, used to being the only woman in the flat until at least eleven, having to defer all her housekeeping decisions to her mother.

"That coffee can be saved," Lucy said as Abigail prepared to take leftover, days-old brew out to dump from the steps. "We can't afford to waste, Abigail."

Abigail clenched her jaw and looked at Patrick for support, but Patrick was seated at the table, one hand caught up in his hair, the other under his chin, unable to care much about the women's disagreement.

"Mother, this is foul," Abigail said. "It's just a taste, and if I leave it in the pot, it will make the coffee tomorrow taste nasty."

"Bring it back," said Lucy. "We won't waste."

Abigail brought the coffee back in. A few minutes later, Lucy stood over Abigail as she mended her stockings. "That seam is crooked," she told her daughter. "You don't want to be seen with uneven seams."

"I don't really care, Mother," said Abigail. "No one sees beneath my skirts but me."

"If you don't take care of small things," said Lucy, sneezing and dabbing at her nose with a dingy handkerchief, "then how can you be trusted with larger things? Rip out that seam and start over."

Abigail snorted, driving her heel down on the floor hard enough to make the floor shake, but she ripped out the seam and began again.

The clock on the mantel read 9:45. It was a good night to go to bed early. Liam bid his family good night and playfully tossed a sock at Patrick, but when Patrick didn't toss it back, he went into the bedroom and dropped onto the bed.

"What is wrong with you?" said Lucy, tiring, finally, of correcting Abigail and ready to straighten out someone else. "You have barely said three words since you came in."

"Tired," said Patrick.

"So am I, but I have the common courtesy to be civil to my family."

"I'm civil. Just tired. Too tired to talk."

"You're upset," said Lucy. "You have no right to be upset, Patrick. Did you know the Clatterbucks were robbed last evening? So much of what they had in the parlor gone! If anyone has a right to be upset, it is they. Now, what's the matter?"

"Nothing," he said.

"I heard there was a turnout at Leeland Mills today," pressed Lucy. "Were you involved? Is that why you are upset?"

Patrick stood up, slamming his chair over, his fingers drawing up into claws. "I wouldn't waste my time on a turnout!" he said. "And I'm not upset! Leave me alone!" He stormed through the doorway and into the dark bedroom. He stripped off his trousers and suspenders and shoes, then climbed into bed beside his brother. His pulse raced, his temples pounded. He took the Union cap from under his pillow and pressed it to his cheek.

"Patrick," said Liam. "Tell me a funny story. Please." The boy's voice was gentle, expectant. If there was any betrayal at all in Patrick's new self, it was in failing Liam.

"I don't have a story to tell," said Patrick. "I'm sorry."

"That's all right," said Liam. "Good night." He patted Patrick on the back, then rolled over with a sigh.

And sometime later, over the quiet arguments of Abigail and their mother, Patrick surrendered to sleep.

26

A HAND CAME down on Patrick's mouth, and he awoke with a terror-filled start.

"Don't move, idiot," came a whispered voice. "You'll wake your brother."

Patrick sat up, pushing the hand from his mouth. The voice said, "Be quiet, Paddy!"

James?

Patrick squinted at the form in the darkness. He stopped fighting, and the hand came away. "James," he whispered, "how did you get in here?"

He watched as James left the bedroom for the kitchen. Patrick stood, shaking fogginess from his mind and lifting the cover back onto his sleeping brother, and went out with James. He glanced at the mantel clock. It was 2:35 in the morning.

"I don't believe this," he mumbled to himself.

James stood at the door. "To the landing," he said, whirling his hand for Patrick to come after.

The boys went out to the landing. They stood in

silence, James staring out across the alley, Patrick scratching his head and trying to guess what would make James break into a friend's house. The air smelled of the recent rain.

Finally James said, "So you think I can get into shops and stores but can't manage the door on a tenement flat? I'm disappointed in your lack of confidence."

Patrick stretched his shoulders. "What is this about?"

James said, "I'm going back, Patrick. You may go with me if you'd like."

"Back? Back where?"

"To the Clatterbucks'. I'm going again. Tonight. I didn't take enough from them to make up for what they took from me."

Patrick stared at his friend with his mouth open. "Clatterbucks'? Why, James? You can't. They have a gun and you know they sleep lightly!"

"I don't want them to sleep lightly. I'm going to take a few more things, then I'm going to announce meself. I'm going to tell them what they did. I'm going to shout it from their hallway before I leave. Hah! I hate them! They need to know what they did, Paddy."

Patrick pushed a strand of hair from his forehead. "I don't understand you."

"Robbie," said James. "She lost her baby."

"She what?"

James ripped at a fingernail with his teeth, then spit it out. "Lost it. All the running, the injury in her arm. Gone, Paddy. Early this morning, as we was sleeping in the shed behind the Unitarian church, she went into fits, and not an hour later, the child was out and dead. Me Robbie never screamed, she just held my hands and her breath. I know, though, that she was in bad pain. And so, what I thought was to be my family is gone. Half of me true family struck down and gone."

"The child wasn't yours," said Patrick.

"Its spirit was mine," said James. "Robbie told me so from the beginning. Since I cared about it, its spirit was mine."

"I'm sorry."

"Sorry doesn't change anything. Robbie's so weak now. I have to do something. Something! Someone has to pay, Patrick!" James paused, turned his head away from Patrick, and Patrick was sure the boy was crying. But James would never let Patrick see such a thing. After a few moments, he dragged his hand viciously across his cheeks and chin and looked back. "Going back, Patrick. You come with me?"

"I'm afraid."

"And I ain't?"

"James, the real culprit is the man who violated Robbie. Not the Clatterbucks for protecting their home."

James nodded. "Aye, and I'd kill this bloody Mr. Lance if I could, but I don't know who he is. Where he lives, what he look's like. Robbie refused to tell me. And I ain't about to go poking around the mill to find out. Not yet anyway. But I will. And then there will be hell to pay. You can be bloody well certain of that, me friend."

"James, are you speaking of Mr. Lance who is now second hand in Spinning Room Four?"

"I reckon that must be the one. Why do you ask? Are you saying you know him?"

He shook his head. "No," he lied.

"Come with me, Patrick?"

"No," said Patrick, trying to wave James off. "I have to get some sleep." He felt dazed.

"Didn't think you would," said James. "Is there anything, then, you'd like me to pick up for you?"

Patrick stood, rubbed his arms, and said, "Free the ponies."

"The what?"

The ponies, Patrick thought. But then he said, "Nothing, James. Just my sleepy mind rambling."

James tipped his head, confused. But he said nothing.

And then Patrick went back into the tenement.

27

LUCY WAS NO better the next morning, although she was up with the rest of her family before the mill bell rang, drinking her coffee, preparing to go to the Clatterbucks'.

"They'll only send you home," said Abigail.

"They'll think I've forgotten myself," said Lucy as she stood at the tiny kitchen window, gazing out at nothing. "I can't just not show up."

"They know you're not well; they sent you home last night. Mother, go back to bed and sleep a day. You'll be the better for it tomorrow."

"I know myself, Abigail," said Lucy. "I'm going."

And the four of them went out of the flat, passing the Pattersons in the hall and mumbling an awkward greeting, then down to the alley to head off in their own directions.

As they crossed the covered bridge and Liam found some friends with whom to walk, Patrick said, "Abigail, wait. I need to ask you something important. What do you know of Mr. Lance?"

Abigail blushed and said, "He has money. Shy around ladies, but that's not to be taken as a fault. I think he'll like me if he notices me, Patrick. He just has to notice."

"Keep away from him."

Abigail stopped and frowned. Several mill operatives, walking behind her, bumped into her and then moved around, grumbling. "What business is it of yours?"

"He's not so inexperienced as you might think. He's not a nice man."

Abigail threw back her head and giggled. Her pinned hair threatened to shake loose. "Patrick, I miss Father, too. But you don't need to take his place!"

Patrick caught his sister by both arms and drew his face in close to hers. "Abigail, I'm not trying to father you. I'm trying to protect you."

Abigail's laughter slowed, then vanished. "Let me go. I can't be late to spin and you can't be late to pack."

"We won't be late if you let me say what I have to say. It's only one request. Stay away from Mr. Lancc."

Abigail's face darkened, her eyes bright like taunting moons. "What do you want me to be, Patrick? What do you want me to do? Stay as I am now, a little mill girl at her frames, running back and forth day after day, on my feet year after year, with nothing more than that to entice me into my womanhood? I'll have more than you and Liam and Mother, and I'll do what I must to have it!"

"Abigail!" He grabbed for her then, as if holding

on to her would keep her safe and out of harm's way, as if it would protect her from all the dangers of the mill, of Leeland, of the world. But Abigail pulled back just as hard, and with a flip of the head, she spun around and vanished into the flow of operatives.

Patrick watched after her, then looked down at the river. To jump into it now, to wash away like a random stick or leaf, to ride on currents to places unknown. To be free. It would be the easiest way out. He sighed, and it hurt his chest. He jammed his hands into his pockets, finding the Union cap in the right one. It was warm like a glove.

Patrick thought, *Maybe James doesn't know who Mr. Lance is, but I do. I'm forewarned. I know about the man, who he is, what he looks like. I must protect Abigail!*

Work was fast and nonstop, although for a packer to complain to almost anyone else in the mill would be considered an insult. This work didn't take fingers off or crush bones or bring as many workers down with consumption. Beside him, Mr. Steele grumbled occasionally, but Patrick was a master at blocking out what he didn't want to hear. The morning hours lumbered on.

Right before noon, a packer came by Patrick and Mr. Steele and in a quick and subtle motion pulled a folded paper from his shirt and dropped it on the floor. "Read with care," he said as he moved by, looking straight ahead. Patrick watched as the man moved on down the line of packers, dropping papers as he went.

"What is that?" Mr. Steele asked, but Patrick was

faster than he in snatching it from the floor and opening it.

It was one typeset page, a tiny newspaper. *The Workers' Voice.*

Mr. Steele, looking over Patrick's shoulder, said, "Throw that away! We'll be in certain trouble for even looking at it!"

Patrick read the headline of the first article. 'TURNOUT TURNED BACK; WORKERS DECRY MUTILATION OF DOCKWORKERS!'

That the paper was out so quickly indicated it had been done locally. And it was sympathetic to the workers.

Mr. Steele grabbed at the paper. Just before he caught hold of it, Patrick was able to see at the bottom a request: "Writers needed."

"Writers needed," Patrick said to himself as Mr. Steele tore the paper into tiny bits and tossed them away.

It was Thursday, so Patrick was supposed to eat in the packing room. But he would go up to talk to Abigail no matter what. She needed to hear the truth about Mr. Lance. He went to the door, but it was locked as he'd thought it would be. Mr. Depper saw him and called, "Get to your lunch, boy!"

"I need to go upstairs," Patrick said.

Mr. Depper came up to Patrick. He waved his thick index finger and said, "You are going nowhere."

Patrick eyed the keys on Mr. Depper's belt loop. "I have to, sir," he said. "It's life or death."

A number of packers nearby heard this and stopped eating. They walked closer, listening, watching. Patrick recognized these men as some who had gone on yesterday's turnout.

Mr. Depper laughed out loud. "Life or death? Really?"

"Please unlock the door."

Mr. Depper said, "I won't repeat myself! Go back to your station."

Patrick hesitated. He looked at the packers, hoping they would follow his lead. He said, "All right, then." He took a step forward, then stumbled into Mr. Depper, pulling the fat man down to the floor with a grunt.

Suddenly the packers were all around them and over them, lifting Mr. Depper up and brushing him off, asking if he was all right. They moved their bodies to block Patrick, so he was able to take the keys he'd tugged from the man's waistband and quickly unlock the door. Then he brought the keys to Mr. Depper.

"Here," he said, handing them over. "These dropped to the floor."

Mr. Depper scowled, took the keys, and tied them back to his belt loop. "Now back to your station, boy. And the rest of you men, return to lunch!"

The men went back. Several gave Patrick a knowing wink. And as soon as Mr. Depper was on his way to the other side of the room, Patrick opened the door quietly and escaped.

He raced up the wooden stairs to the third floor. He waited by the door until a child came out with a cart of fluff, then slipped in. He found his sister and brother in their usual spots on the floor in the aisle.

"Hello!" said Liam. "What are you doing up here today?"

"Patrick?" said Abigail.

"I must talk to you, Abigail. We must talk now."

"Really?" she said. "I don't have time to talk to you. I'm busy."

"Busy eating?"

"Yes," she said, rolling her eyes. "And other things you don't care to hear about."

Patrick could see Mr. Lance now. He was coming their way, although he was not looking at them. On his face was a greasy smile. It made Patrick's stomach turn.

"Patrick, guess what," asked Liam. "Polly Bruce's grandmother was a queen in Europe; did you know that?"

"Be quiet a moment, Liam," said Patrick. Abigail ran her hands through her hair, causing it to ripple down around her shoulders.

"A queen!" said Liam. "I think it would be just fine to go visit her in Europe. Polly said when she's sixteen she'll pay for all of us to go with her and—"

Patrick had reached his limit. He turned on his brother. "Why do you believe that girl and all her lies? Are you so likely to be led around by the nose, taking for truth everything you hear? She's got no money. Her family is poor like we are."

Abigail tossed her head a little, then patted her temples as if she was straightening loose strands to pin them back.

"Patrick, that's mean," said Liam.

"It's not mean, it's real. Now, be quiet!"

Liam's cheeks puffed and his eyes grew tight.

"Be a man," Patrick said.

"I'm not a man," said Liam.

"You might as well be. You're in a man's world." Then he said, "Abigail, listen to me. I have news about your Mr. Lance, and it's not good. Hear me out. It's for your own good."

Abigail ignored Patrick. She called to her friend Sarah, who was a number of yards down the aisle, sitting in the dust, eating her lunch-pail meal with another girl. "Sarah, do you have an extra hairpin? I can't seem to get mine back up the way I should!"

Mr. Lance, who was standing not far behind Sarah, finally looked in Abigail's direction. He crossed his arms and licked his lips. One eyebrow went up.

Sarah called back, "No, I don't have an extra. You best make do with what you have. The frames will be going again in just a minute."

Patrick grabbed Abigail's hand. "Listen to me, Abigail! Mr. Lance is a bad man!"

Abigail twisted away and said, "You don't know anything! Leave me alone! You aren't Father!"

"I know I'm not! But you're my sister!"

Mr. Lance stepped around Sarah, coming toward them. Lunch was nearly over. Operatives all along the aisle stood up, brushing themselves off, stretching arms overhead, readying themselves for the next long hours of work.

"Get out of here, Patrick," Liam said. "Go back to your own work. We are mad at you."

Mr. Lance's eyes winked. He was staring directly at Abigail. It was all Patrick could do to keep from lunging around his sister and driving his fist into the man's face.

Abigail pretended not to see Mr. Lance noticing her.

"Mr. Lance," Patrick said, standing, clenching his fists so he wouldn't lose his nerve, "I must talk with you. Right away."

Mr. Lance looked from Abigail to Patrick and his expression changed. "Hey, there," he said, lifting a finger and shaking it. "Are you supposed to be here today?"

Abigail glanced at Patrick, her face full of horror. "Patrick!"

"This will be brief, Mr. Lance. It's quite important. Please, step back with me for a moment."

Mr. Lance put his hands on his hips. "I beg your pardon, boy?"

Patrick crushed his hands into fists. "Don't beg my pardon. Just listen to me!"

Mr. Lance brushed by Abigail and stopped directly in front of Patrick.

"Boy." The condescension in the voice drew angry sweat from Patrick's arms, but he held his ground. "How can you still stand there when you've been spoken to? You best do what you're told. Get on now!"

"I'm not a mill rat," said Patrick. "In spite of what Mary Clatterbuck says."

The man almost laughed. "What are you talking about?"

"We aren't mill rats!" said Patrick.

"Go, Patrick!" said Liam. The little brother was

trying to be the big brother now. "Go downstairs where you belong!"

"Listen to your brother," said Mr. Lance.

Abigail's face twitched with anger, disappointment.

But Patrick trained his stare on Mr. Lance and in a low, controlled voice said, "Stay clear of my sister!"

Mr. Lance's jaw dropped open. "What did you say?"

"I said I know about the girl you got pregnant. Have there been others, or do you even care? You stay away from my sister." Patrick's blood rushed in his veins. His breathing came in shallow, sharp bursts.

The man roared then, like a lion, and he slapped Patrick with his open hand. "Insubordinate fool!" he shouted. Patrick stumbled, but held his ground. Suddenly the gears along the ceiling kicked into motion, and with deafening thunder the leather belts began to whirl, and the machines began to spin.

Mr. Lance grabbed Patrick by the arm, meaning to throw him down the aisle. But Patrick ducked and shoved, slamming his fists into the second hand's stomach. Mr. Lance stumbled over Liam and into Abigail.

"No!" Patrick screamed.

Abigail's long hair billowed as Mr. Lance bumped her and she tumbled backward. She fell against the corner of a spinning frame, and her hair was caught in the whirling leather belt. Her head snapped and an airy whistle issued from her mouth. A huge hank of hair ripped from her head and went up toward the ceiling, tangled in the still-moving belt.

And then Abigail fell, limp, to the floor.

"God, no!" Patrick ran to his sister and dropped on his knees. There were others around him instantly, Liam, Sarah, Rebecca, and operatives he didn't know. But he couldn't see them. He could only feel them. Could feel their disbelief and their horror. He laced his arm around his sister and lifted her to his chest. She was warm. She was still.

He raised his head to the ceiling, his eyes closing.

"Oh my God, no!" And then his face fell and he buried it against Abigail's neck. He wanted to shake her, to shout at her, "Stay low! Watch out! Be careful and come home with us to our flat!"

But she didn't move.

Liam grabbed on to Abigail then, his shoulders convulsing. His hands clutched his sister as if to squeeze the life back into her.

Someone took Patrick's arms and lifted him up. He couldn't fight, he had no strength. There was screaming and crying around him now; he could hear it because the belts had been stopped and the machines silenced.

And then he heard Mr. Lance say, "Get her out of here. Careless idiots, her whole family! You all saw what happened. It wasn't my fault! Get her out of here! And that meddling brother, as well! We have an evening's work to do!"

Patrick felt himself release Abigail as Sarah and Rebecca and an old man, a machine mender, lifted her up to carry her out.

But then his mind shut down and he was running and he felt nothing, nothing at all. And even the demons screaming at his back couldn't keep up.

28

HE STOOD ON the Clatterbuck porch. He didn't remember getting there, but there he was, tears and sweat drying on his face, leaving salty tracks, his clothes filthy not only from mill dirt, but from times, he guessed, he'd fallen on his way. There was a hole in the right knee of his trousers, and a spot of blood within.

He pounded on the door.

An old woman in a cleaning apron answered. "May I help you?" But before Patrick could speak, Mrs. Clatterbuck was at the door, pushing the old woman aside. Her face, lit up with expectation, dropped when she saw Patrick.

"And what business do you have here in the middle of the day? You're Lucy's boy, aren't you?"

Patrick said, "I need to see my mother."

Mrs. Clatterbuck put one hand on her hip. A white-gloved hand touched her lips, then the bridge of her nose. She scowled. "Lucy's employed. She has her work. You'll have to wait until she is given her leave this evening."

Patrick's breathing quickened. He could see someone moving behind Mrs. Clatterbuck, peeking over her shoulder to see who was at the door. It was Nancy. Patrick said, "I need to see my mother. Now."

"Don't use that tone with me," said Mrs. Clatterbuck. "I'm the mistress here. I said you'll have to wait."

"Now."

"I'm closing the door, boy! Go away!"

"No! I want to see her now!"

Nancy brushed past her mother and stepped into the doorway. She said, "Patrick, isn't it?"

"Nancy!" said Mrs. Clatterbuck. "How dare you push me!"

"I didn't push, Mother, I merely mean to have conversation with Patrick. And, Molly," Nancy said to the old woman in the apron, "go get Mrs. O'Neill. She is in the backyard. Patrick needs to talk with her."

"Come inside and shut that door, Nancy!" Mrs. Clatterbuck demanded.

"Mother," said Nancy, "you've been worried all morning about the construction of your new pantry. Would you please go back to supervise?"

With a huff, Mrs. Clatterbuck gave Patrick one last look, then turned and disappeared down the shadowed hallway. Nancy came out to the porch, shaking her head. "Your mother will be here momentarily. I'm sorry about my own mother. She's in a tizzy. We had yet another robbery last night, but Father was much quicker this time. The thief was brought down with a bullet to the thigh. The police have him in custody."

James, oh, God, not you, too.

"Oh, don't worry, we're all fine," said Nancy. "No one hurt, nothing taken this time. But the thief was young. And to have ruined his life so soon. A shame, really, although Mother would throttle me for having pity on a burglar. We may be of the same blood, but often I find we aren't of the same heart. But you, Patrick?" She paused, as if she was seeing Patrick's condition clearly at last. "You're hurt there, on your knee."

Patrick knew he was bleeding, but he didn't feel it. The only ache was in the palms of his hands, and in his chest, his heart. He took a breath and said, "Yes."

And then Lucy was at the door, standing half in, half out, wiping her hands on the bottom of her apron, her forehead lined with a scowl. Nancy withdrew without another word.

"What is it, Patrick? You've left work? You haven't quit there, have you?"

"No," said Patrick.

"No? Then why are you here? We've both work to do!"

"Abigail's dead."

Lucy came out to the porch, her eyes never leaving Patrick's. The hem of her apron dropped. The corners of her mouth flinched, but there was no other sign she'd heard. She pulled the front door closed behind her. "What are you saying, son?"

"Neck broke, caught in a belt. I was there. There was a fight, and the second hand knocked her back.

I. . ." He swallowed. His throat was full of dry pebbles. "Mother, she's gone."

"Gone?"

"Yes." And Patrick stepped to his mother and folded into her, his arms wrapping her neck, his face against her shoulder. The sobs came, relentless, swollen and aching. He cried without relief, his soul twisting itself inside out, his body craving motherly caresses to help ease the agony.

But Lucy merely stood, and after a minute, she pushed Patrick away. Her eyes were closed, her mouth parted slightly. She shivered, as if shaking off a sudden chill, and then her eyes opened. But there were no tears.

"We can't change what's done," said Lucy. "I'll take a few days off and we'll see Abigail has a proper burial. But I will have no more crying. Longing does no good."

"We must go on, right, Mother?" said Patrick, hot, bitter sarcasm stinging his voice.

Lucy nodded, and touched her son's shoulder. This was the best she could do, Patrick knew. His heart was hollow. "I'll ask for leave," she said. "I'll be home soon. Wait for me there, and we'll make the arrangements. We will keep the apron Abigail wore when this happened, in her honor. It always bothered me that the army sent your father home in his civilian clothes."

What are you talking about? How on earth could this matter, Mother?

"My family always kept a piece of clothing that the deceased was wearing. It was our tradition. But the army kept his uniform. I didn't get it. Not his boots, nor his jacket. Not even a Union cap." She touched her lip, then went inside.

Patrick slowly walked down the porch steps to the walk. He could barely lift his head, it was so heavy.

Then a voice from the porch said, "I heard what you said, Patrick. I'm so very sorry! Is there anything I can do?"

Patrick looked back at Nancy. She was just outside the door.

"There's nothing anyone can do," said Patrick.

"Are you certain? Surely there must be—"

"No, there isn't," said Patrick. Then, because his mother would have expected politeness even now, he added, "But thank you just the same."

Nancy went back into the house without another word.

29

PATRICK STARED UP at the silver sliver of sky beyond the trees. There, occasional clouds drifted by, and the moon, a tiny white outsider in the daylight, held still and waited.

It waited for Patrick's decision.

And the decision came with a sigh, a drooping of the shoulders, and a painful core of resignation in Patrick's heart.

"I'll go away," he said to himself. He looked back down, across the lawn to the Clatterbucks' porch, speaking as though his mother were listening. "I'm going away, Mother. I'm going west. What is there here for me now? Abigail is dead. My best friend arrested, to be tried soon for robbery. Liam is angry at me, and you are strong enough to survive any loss. What would be another one?"

Patrick watched as sunlight winked through tree leaves, sparkling silver on the grass of the Clatterbucks' lawn. "If I'd kept the dragon lamp James had offered me, I could have sold it," he murmured. "It would have been enough to get on the train Polly Bruce has talked about so much and travel across the country."

The silver light winked at him as if it agreed.

"I should leave. It will be better for everyone. They will survive. If only I'd kept the lamp."

Then he thought of Mrs. Wilson's tea set. It was the answer. It was valuable.

"I'll miss Liam and Mother," he said. "I'll miss Mrs. Wilson and James. But I can't let that matter. I don't have any other choice."

There was one good thing he could do before he was gone. It wouldn't make up for the lies and the cowardice, but at least it was something. Moving away from the tree, Patrick sneaked around to the back of the Clatterbuck house, hiding in the shrubbery just outside their fence line. He skirted the corner, passed the compost pile, and walked quietly over the graveled pathway to the small, bare ground paddock. He knew he should be nervous, with the chance that Jed or John or even Mary would see him. But he couldn't feel anything except the need to do this, his one last good act before he sealed himself as a proven scoundrel.

Carefully opening the corral gate, Patrick stepped inside. Instantly the ponies stuck their heads out of their stalls and nickered. "Shh," he whispered.

At least there will be something Father could have been proud of, he thought. He crept to the first stall and unlatched it, then glanced down at the stall's floor. Jed had been right. The straw was old and beginning to mold. There was a dreadful smell, thick and foul.

The pony's legs were coated with manure.

"Run," Patrick said softly, waving his hand. "Run away and be free!"

The pony shivered, its eyes growing wide, then suddenly bolted from the stall, out into the corral, where it circled twice, then through the gate. It vanished between the trees that led to the river.

Quickly Patrick opened the other four stall doors. "Go," he ordered. "Run away while you have the chance!" Two others raced out, streaking through the gate, disappearing with tails held high.

Yes, Patrick thought as he watched them. *They're free. Someone will find them and care for them. But they're no longer at the mercy of people who have forgotten their conditions.*

He looked back. Two ponies, the chestnut and the dun, still stood in their stalls. They snorted and stomped, but were clearly too afraid to go outside. "Run," Patrick urged. "Here is your chance!" But they wouldn't go, even when he flapped his arms and clucked his tongue.

"Have you accepted this lot in life? Do you think there is no better?" he asked them.

The Clatterbucks' back door slammed shut. Patrick dropped to his knees and peered at the house through the fence slats. Emily was coming down the steps with a bucket of kitchen scraps. In a moment she'd be at the compost pile and would see him for certain.

Without looking back at the two ponies, he scuttled through the corral gate on hands and knees, over the gravel path, then stood and ran along the shrubs back to the front of the house and the tree-shaded lane.

As he straightened and glanced over his shoulder to assure himself that he hadn't been seen, he thought, *Father, this is all I can offer. You were a fighter, I am not. I'm sorry. I hope you won't know what I'm going to do now.*

Then he let his mind shut down, blocking out anything but the feel of his feet carrying him forward into town, up toward the tenements along Charlotte and the old woman's second-floor flat.

30

MRS. WILSON WASN'T home. It was a small miracle that he couldn't have hoped for. He knocked for a full minute, but received no answer. She was most likely at the market, or at the company store. Patrick could have gone in with Mrs. Wilson there, of course, and sneaked it beneath his shirt, but breaking into the flat would be easier because he wouldn't have to see her again.

Down on Charlotte Street, Patrick could hear the first of the operatives returning home from their long day at the mill. It was after seven o'clock. He would have to hurry. A swift kick against the doorknob and he knew the weak board would give way. On his head was the Union cap.

Then it would be a matter of a few seconds to go in, cram the silver tea set, a few doilies, some of the old teacups, and anything else he could grab beneath his shirt, and leave. Surely he'd get more than nineteen dollars for the whole of it from someone in a nearby town. And the train would be waiting; he would make his escape.

And what of the nineteen dollars in the wall of his own bedroom? Going back was out of the question. Mother and Liam were there. He did not want to see them. He would write Lucy soon and let her know where the money was hidden. She would find use for the money.

He lifted his foot to drive it against Mrs. Wilson's door.

There were voices and footfall at the bottom of the steps outside. Patrick plunged forward with all his strength. With a sudden, single crack, the latch shattered and the door crashed open.

He stepped into the doorway and stopped.

It was there still, as sure as the moon and the river and the bell in the tower. Mrs. Wilson's dignity, her honesty.

Patrick couldn't cross the threshold. His fingers caught themselves on the frame; his feet planted themselves beneath him.

He tried to push himself forward but couldn't move.

"It's too late!" Patrick cried to nobody. "Too late for me! I have to go in."

And then there were people in the hall with him. Men, women, children, pressing around him, talking with each other, coughing, shuffling. Someone caught him by the arm and he looked around. It was a girl a little younger than Liam; the girl he had screamed at one night not long ago.

"Mister," the girl said. Her face was streaked with

dirt and tiny pieces of lint. She must be a sweeper. "You visiting Mrs. Wilson?"

Patrick nodded. The cap felt very tight on his head.

The girl said, "Mrs. Wilson writes good, and I need her to do something for me. May I come in and talk with her?"

"She's not home."

"Then would you tell her something, please?" The girl paused, glanced down at her shoes, then looked back into Patrick's eyes. "Tell her would she write a letter to my mama for me? I want to go home and live with her. A girl was killed today, up in a spinning room. Broke her neck! They want to move me there to take her place." The girl shuddered. It was all she could do to finish her request. "They say I'm old enough to learn the frames. But I'm afraid! It won't change and I'll be killed, too! Please, tell Mrs. Wilson to write my mama. She's wrote her before. It's not too late if she will write it tonight. Will you ask her for me? I'm Anna Sewell."

"Yes."

"I wish I could write," the girl said solemnly. "There's so much can be done with words on paper."

"Yes."

The girl's eyes closed briefly as if in a thank-you. Then she said, "I'll come back after my chores and maybe she'll have the letter ready?"

"Maybe she will," said Patrick.

The girl followed the others down the hall. Patrick slowly pulled Mrs. Wilson's ruined door closed and went down to the street. He sat on the edge of a horse trough.

"A simple letter can save Anna Sewell's life," he said to himself. "Writing can be powerful indeed. I can write. I am stuck here in Leeland, where everything continues like it has been since the mill was built. But I can write."

He sat straight.

"*The Workers' Voice* said writers were needed. I could do that. I could share my thoughts with others besides myself and make a difference at the mill. Maybe I won't be making more money. Maybe I'll never get to college. But my writing can make a difference."

In the packing room he had heard a man say, "Strength in numbers!" This was true for a factory, true for a turnout. It was true for an army. It could be true for a band of renegade newspaper writers, as well.

Patrick dipped his hand into the trough and rubbed the water on his neck. It was cool and calming on his skin. He pulled the cap from his head and traced his finger on the inside band.

There was writing inside. It was pale and faded. Patrick squinted, holding it up and trying to see more clearly. The smudged ink looked as if it spelled "O'Neill."

Impossible.

Patrick's heart stood still. Was this his father's cap, taken from him before his body was sent home? Was this his father's way of letting him know he was still with him, still watching?

"Impossible," he said softly. "This is most likely

some other man's hat, some other man whose name begins with an *O*. But it doesn't matter. As it might be another man's, it might also be my father's. I can believe what I want."

Patrick grinned and hugged the cap. His father, a soldier of the army, was still with Patrick, who would soon be a soldier of the word.

And then someone tapped his arm and he spun about. Mrs. Wilson stood there, a bonnet shading her face, a smile on her lips.

Patrick said, "A little girl named Anna wants you to write a letter to her mother about her going home. Will you find her and take her letter down for her?"

Mrs. Wilson nodded.

Then Patrick said, "Mrs. Wilson, I have to tell you something terrible. You will probably never want me to visit again, but I must be truthful with you."

Mrs. Wilson smiled and tipped her head in a question.

Patrick said, "You've been so kind to me. Too kind. I wanted to take advantage of your kindness. I tried to rob you."

Mrs. Wilson waved her hand in the air. It said, "Be quiet and follow me." Still smiling, she climbed the steps to her apartment. Patrick followed, scrambling to find the words to explain. He would show her the door, tell her what he'd done, and ask her forgiveness. It was another beginning.

Mrs. Wilson paused briefly at the shattered door, then went inside and sat in her chair. She picked up pen and paper and began writing. Patrick sat in his chair. He said, "Mrs. Wilson, please listen to me. Stop writing and listen."

Mrs. Wilson held up her hand for him to be quiet, then returned to her scribbling.

"No." said Patrick. "I must explain, although no explanation can be an excuse. I broke your door. I was going to rob you." He paused, watching her, hoping for something. Not absolution but acknowledgment, something. But she didn't look up. She kept on writing.

He said, "I hate the mill; you know that. I wanted to go to college. My sister . . ." He felt his voice quivering, but he fought his way through it. "My sister was killed today. I came to rob you and run off. Mrs. Wilson, I don't ask forgiveness. I just wanted to tell you."

There was silence, and it stretched uncomfortably long. Patrick linked his fingers around his knees and waited. "I'll fix your door," he said.

She worked on the note, head nodding in rhythm with the pen strokes.

Patrick sat and watched. Mrs. Wilson was likely writing a tirade, and one he deserved. He would take it as he would take foul medicine if the ailment required it.

She finally put her pen down and held out the note. Patrick took it, blinked, and read.

Patrick, hush about trying to rob me. You didn't do it. Only that door is ruined, but it's so dry-rotted I've needed another for a long time. This will give my son the incentive to find a new door. The tea set is gone as you can see, but you didn't take it.

Patrick looked up. The tea set was indeed gone. Where was it? Had someone else stolen it? He continued reading.

I sold the tea set and some other silver this morning. I need my medicine, and Andrew's pay can't always keep up. Medicine is more important than silver when you're growing old and feeble.

Patrick looked up at her, then back at the note.

But I wanted to give you something, too. Andrew never married. I'll never have grandchildren, as he is my only son. After the Pemberton incident, we both became so cautious about so much in life. I love him, but any thoughts he may have had about improving his life's condition became stagnant. But ever since I first saw you out on the street, I've come to think of you as a son. First because you look like Andrew, and then because you were considerate of me. Many young people don't give old people attention. You were nice to me.

Patrick's pulse picked up its pace. The corners of his eyes began to blur, but he read on.

I received $40 for the silver tea set and several other family items I took to the jeweler's. I want to give you half. It's not much, but maybe you can put it to good use. Maybe it will help get you to college someday. Take it, with my love.

Patrick couldn't look up. He was crying and didn't want her to see. He said, "Thank you, Mrs. Wilson."

He heard her write. Then she stood on her old knotted legs and came over to Patrick. She put the note in his lap.

I am so very sorry about your sister. Is there anything I can do?

After a moment, he lifted his face. It was tear-streaked, but suddenly he didn't care. He said, "You already have. And I'll make you proud of me."

Mrs. Wilson patted his hand.

"I really will."

31

HE FOUND ROBBIE in the shed where James had left her. She gasped in shock and panic, but when he spoke, she slumped back on her wool blanket and turned away.

"Robbie, I'm so glad you're still here," Patrick said. "James told me where you were hiding, but I was afraid you would be gone when I got here. Or worse."

"Worse?" she said, her voice muffled in the darkness. The sun had set outside, and only pale street gaslight filtered through the small shed windows. "What, that I'd died? I'm too ornery for that."

Patrick eased the shed door shut, squinting, his eyes finally making sense of the shapes in the shed. He knelt down on the bare ground amid the tools and building implements. A cobweb crossed his face and he scratched it off. "I want to help you, Robbie. How is your arm?"

"Why do you want to help? You've got a family to

worry about, you have a job. I'm nothing to you."

"You're a friend."

Robbie rolled over and looked at him. "Friend? I don't have friends. James never came back and I think he's run off on me."

"No. He's arrested."

"Oh, God."

Patrick said, "Can you walk?"

"I don't know."

He put his arms under hers, glad she didn't fight him. He helped her, limping, to the door and out into the sunshine.

"Where are you taking me, Patrick? To the police to be with James?"

"To a doctor on Burris Street."

"I haven't any money! I can't trade the gimcracks in this shed or they'll know me as a thief, and James didn't have time to sell them properly." She was shaking fiercely.

Patrick said, "Don't worry. I have a little extra money. Just lean into me. I'll get you there safely."

Robbie hesitated, then put her head on Patrick's shoulder. "He will not be willing to see me. It's nighttime."

"We'll knock until he answers. We'll make him listen."

"And you'll pay for me?"

"Yes."

He felt her relax. And his heart soared.

32

September 23, 1870

The air is beginning to feel like autumn. I can smell something on the breeze, not the brisk, sharp scents of the country but a change, nonetheless. There is a crispness, an urgency, in this air. I welcome it.

My family is asleep at last, behind me in our flat. Mother was first to succumb; Liam followed not long after. It is nearing midnight. I'll try to sleep very soon.

Abigail rests in the public mortuary. We certainly cannot have a wake here; there is no room. Mother was agitated at having Abigail's body rest for a night where no one knows her, but tomorrow there will be a burial outside of town where the Irish and Canadians lay their own dead to rest. Tomorrow we'll bid her farewell and, as Mother says, go on. We are going to keep her apron as Mother requested; the rest we will give to the poor.

I'll miss her so.

Dear Abigail. She, too, had her dreams.

But for those of us who remain, there is work to do. There is a battle to fight. I will wage it with my written words. After this journal entry, there are two more things I must write before I go to bed. First, petitions to strike on behalf of Abigail. Liam and I will take them tomorrow and get them to as many as possible who can sign their names or mark their X. *Then I will write an article for* The Worker's Voice. *There are things to do now, things that feel good and strong and right.*

I wish James were here, to sit by me and chide me with his good humor. What will become of him, I don't know. I have never loved a friend as much.

But I believe Robbie will be all right. The doctor treated her arm wound with the incentive of a few dollars, even though he was in his nightshirt and cap and yawned several times during the treatment. When we were back on the street afterwards, I asked if she would come live with us. We've got an extra cot. But she said she didn't know, and vanished without another word.

My invitation remains open. I hope she will reconsider. If so, I hope Mother and Liam will accept her. I like to think they will.

Will anyone in the years that come read my journal, the letters I will write, the stories I plan to pen about our struggles here? Will they understand?

Patrick paused, looked up at the night sky, tilted his head, and nodded slowly.

The moon watches me still, as it has my whole life. But tonight it is not sneering. It is not taunting.

Tonight the moon is smiling.